SLAVERY AND REBELLION IN
SECOND-CENTURY BC SICILY

Edinburgh Studies in Ancient Slavery
Series editor: Ulrike Roth, University of Edinburgh

Original research in ancient slavery studies

The study of slavery is an essential element of the study of the ancient world. This series publishes the latest research on ancient slavery, including Greek, Roman and Near Eastern slavery, as well as Jewish and early Christian slavery, from c. 1000 BC to AD 500.

Written by experts in the field, from the rising star to the well-established scholar, the books offer cutting-edge research on key themes in ancient slavery studies, which will enhance as well as challenge current understanding of ancient slavery. The series presents new insights from a range of disciplines, including history, archaeology and philology.

Advisory board

Dr Bassir Amiri
Professor Jean-Jacques Aubert
Dr Lisa Fentress
Professor Jennifer A. Glancy
Professor Deborah Kamen
Professor Noel E. Lenski
Dr David Lewis
Professor Henrik Mouritsen
Professor Walter Scheidel
Dr Jane Webster
Dr Cornelia Wunsch
Professor Rachel Zelnick-Abramovitz

Books available

Kostas Vlassopoulos, *Historicising Ancient Slavery*
Pedro López Barja, Carla Masi Doria and Ulrike Roth, *Junian Latinity in the Roman Empire Volume 1: History, Law, Literature*
Peter Morton, *Slavery and Rebellion in Second-Century BC Sicily: From* Bellum Servile *to* Sicilia Capta

Visit the series webpage: edinburghuniversitypress.com/series-edinburgh-studies-in-ancient-slavery

SLAVERY AND REBELLION IN SECOND-CENTURY BC SICILY

From *Bellum Servile* to *Sicilia Capta*

PETER MORTON

EDINBURGH
University Press

Edinburgh University Press is one of the leading university presses in the UK. We publish academic books and journals in our selected subject areas across the humanities and social sciences, combining cutting-edge scholarship with high editorial and production values to produce academic works of lasting importance. For more information visit our website: edinburghuniversitypress.com

© Peter Morton, 2024, 2025

Grateful acknowledgement is made to the sources listed in the List of Illustrations for permission to reproduce material previously published elsewhere. Every effort has been made to trace the copyright holders, but if any have been inadvertently overlooked, the publisher will be pleased to make the necessary arrangements at the first opportunity.

Edinburgh University Press Ltd
13 Infirmary Street,
Edinburgh, EH1 1LT

First published in hardback by Edinburgh University Press 2024

Typeset in 10 / 12 Bembo by
IDSUK (DataConnection) Ltd

A CIP record for this book is available from the British Library

ISBN 978 1 3995 1573 3 (hardback)
ISBN 978 1 3995 1574 0 (paperback)
ISBN 978 1 3995 1575 7 (webready PDF)
ISBN 978 1 3995 1576 4 (epub)

The right of Peter Morton to be identified as the author of this work has been asserted in accordance with the Copyright, Designs and Patents Act 1988, and the Copyright and Related Rights Regulations 2003 (SI No. 2498).

Contents

Series Editor's Preface	viii
List of Illustrations	x
Acknowledgements	xii
Abbreviations	xvi
Introduction: The Problem with the 'Sicilian Slave Wars'	1

Part I: The Wars in Sicily Reassessed

1. The Coinage of King Antiochus: The War in Sicily of 136–132 BC through Rebel Eyes — 19
2. The Slave-Owner Narratives of the 'First Sicilian Slave War': Eunus and His Rebels — 68
3. The Creation of an Alternative State: Reassessing the Rebels in the War of 104–100 BC — 96

Part II: Slave Revolts in Ancient Historiography and the Wider Historical Context

4. The Slave Revolt *topos*: Thinking with Servile Unrest in Ancient Historiography — 129
5. How to Define Revolt? Ancient Slave Rebellions in the Global Context — 153

Conclusion: The Romano-Sicilian Wars in Context — 188

Appendix 1: The ΦΙΛΙΠΗΙΟΝ Gold Coinage	195
Bibliography	197
Index	216

For Chuck

Series Editor's Preface

Edinburgh Studies in Ancient Slavery provides a forum for the latest research on all aspects of slavery and related forms of unfreedom around the Mediterranean basin and in its hinterland in antiquity. The exploration of slavery has been critical to research on this ancient world from the beginning of concentrated study in the nineteenth century. This is in many ways unsurprising given that there exists plenty of evidence for slavery and other forms of unfree labour and enforced subordination in antiquity, from the British Isles in the northwest, to the Persian Gulf in the southeast, from the Sumerian to the Visigothic kingdoms. Slavery in the ancient Mediterranean and beyond has manifested itself in myriad ways. The surviving evidence stretches the full panorama of our sources, material and textual, documenting cogently the pervasive nature of slavery in ancient society, across uncountable contexts and disparate settings. The diversity of the source material forcefully underpins the need for multi- and interdisciplinary approaches, including collaborative and comparative efforts; the intricate nature of the evidence calls moreover for a preparedness to combine traditional with innovative methods, empiricist work with theoretical perspectives. Notwithstanding these evidential, contextual and methodological challenges that the study of slavery brings with it, in the light of the influence that the history of the region has had on the evolution and development of numerous modern societies and the world at large, the study of ancient Mediterranean slavery is imperative for a full understanding of the contemporary world.

The present series is not the first to give ancient slavery centre stage. The study of especially classical slavery has been an academic battle-ground at prominent modern historical crossroads, framed by its exploration under the abolitionist banner in the nineteenth century at one end – combatting the apologist uses to which the study of the classical past had been put by pro-slavery advocates, and its mobilisation on both sides of the Iron Curtain during the Cold War in the twentieth century at the other. Research agendas on ancient slavery have thus at times been powerfully influenced by modern, socio-political concerns. But even when the large political stage was not a key driver, work on ancient slavery has more often than not been inspired by, and reflective of, contemporary developments. Pioneering work on enslaved women, for example, was carried out in the 1970s, when the feminist movement was at its first peak in Western society; a decade or so later, an interest in the labour roles of enslaved individuals, and the ways in which they mobilised the world of work in creating their own identities, changed the modern appreciation of enslaved life at a time when labour force participation in Europe and the US – the hubs of research on ancient Greek and Roman slavery – was broader than ever before. It is fair to say that each generation of scholars brings its own preoccupations to the drawing-board of slavery studies, thereby ensuring the regular adjustment of our analytical gaze, and enabling the steady discovery of new facets of an institution that is not only as old as our historical records, but that has profoundly shaped social relations at the critical intersections of age, class, gender and race for generations to come. The rapid changes and momentous transformations that characterise contemporary society, often directly related to the many deeply troublesome legacies of slavery across human history, beget an opportune moment, and indeed constitute an urgent call, for a fresh, concentrated effort to reflect on the world we live in through the lens of an institution that was not less peculiar in antiquity than it is, sadly, still today, drawing on as wide a set of questions, approaches and perspectives as possible, thus also to reflect on and challenge the scholarly implication in the maintenance of the noted legacies.

Ulrike Roth

Illustrations

Maps

1.1	Sites taken or attacked during the first war	21
1.2	Coin circulation in Morgantina	36
1.3	Coin circulation in Ietas	39
1.4	Correspondences with King Antiochus' coinage	52
3.1	Sites involved in the second war	114

Figures

1.1	Coin of Centuripae, *c.* 231–150 BC; Zeus on obverse with winged thunderbolt on reverse	25
1.2	Coin of Syracuse, *c.* 230–216 BC; Gelon on obverse with winged thunderbolt on reverse	25
1.3	Coin of Syracuse, 215–214 BC; Hieronymus on obverse with winged thunderbolt on reverse	25
1.4	Coin of Demetrius I Soter, *c.* 162–150 BC; Demetrius on obverse with quiver on reverse	25
1.5	Coin of Halaesa, after 241 BC; Artemis on obverse with quiver on reverse	27
1.6	Coin of Syracuse, after 212 BC; Artemis on obverse with Apollo standing on reverse	27
1.7	Coin of Agyrium, *c.* 345–300 BC; helmeted head on obverse with club on reverse	28
1.8	Coin of Aluntium, *c.* 212–150 BC; Herakles on obverse with club and quiver on reverse	28
1.9	Coin of Centuripae, *c.* 212–150 BC; Herakles on obverse with club on reverse	29
1.10	Coin of Cephaloedium, *c.* 241–210 BC; Herakles on obverse with club on reverse	29
1.11	Coin of Menaenum, after 210 BC; Herakles on obverse with club on reverse	30

1.12	Coin of King Antiochus/Eunus, *c.* 136–132 BC; veiled head of Demeter on obverse with an ear of barley on reverse	30
1.13	Coin of Centuripae, *c.* 212–150 BC; Demeter on obverse with plough on reverse	31
1.14	Coin of Leontini, after 210 BC; Demeter on obverse with bushel of corn on reverse	31
1.15	Coin of Catana, third–second century BC; Apollo on obverse with Isis on reverse	31
1.16	Coin of Mamertines, third–second century BC; Zeus on obverse with advancing warrior on reverse	31
1.17	Coin of Mamertines, third–second century BC; Apollo on obverse with standing Nike on reverse	47
1.18	Coin of Mamertines, third–second century BC; Ares on obverse with horseman on reverse	47
1.19	Roman as, 169–58 BC; Janus laureate on obverse with prow on reverse	47
1.20	Coin of Syracuse, after 210 BC; Poseidon on obverse with trident on reverse	48
1.21	Coin of Syracuse, after 210 BC; Apollo on obverse with trident on reverse	49
1.22	Coin of Syracuse, after 210 BC; Zeus on obverse with *biga* on reverse	49
1.23	Coin of Syracuse, *c.* 247–216 BC; Hieron II on obverse with horseman on reverse	49
1.24	Coin of Morgantina, *c.* 215–212 BC; Kore-Persephone on obverse with *biga* on reverse and ΣΙΚΕΛΙΩΤΑΝ legend	49

Tables

1.1	Provenance of the coinage of the First Romano-Sicilian War	23
1.2	Morgantina coin finds	34
1.3	Percentages of main mints in Morgantina	35
1.4	Ietas coin finds	37
1.5	Percentages of main mints in Ietas	38
1.6	Suggested values for King Antiochus' coinage	41
1.7	Weight bands for King Antiochus' coinage	42
1.8	Weight bands for Catanian and Syracusan coinage post-210 BC	42
1.9	Types of Syracusan coins, Hieronic and post-210 BC	48

Acknowledgements

This book started in the autumn of 2006 in my first efforts to answer an essay question about the causes of slave revolts in the Roman world. The question was set for a course on Roman Slavery taught by Ulrike Roth at the University of Edinburgh. I have been trying to answer this same question for the past seventeen years over the course of an MA, PhD and the years thereafter. I hope that this book goes some way toward an answer, if not *the* answer. Most of all, I hope that arguments put forward here stimulate others to think critically about how we study events called revolts by those opposed to them and how we write the histories of those who do not speak directly to us from antiquity.

A project this long can be only ever be completed with the help of many others, and this book is no different. In the first instance, I owe many institutional debts. I would like to thank all the various funding bodies and institutions that have made this study possible. The School of History, Classics and Archaeology funded my MSc, and the College of Humanities and Social Sciences at the University of Edinburgh awarded me a full studentship for my PhD; without either of these awards this book would never have been written. The Baldwin Brown Travelling Scholarship twice funded research trips to Sicily during my PhD, both of which provided valuable stimulus for my research. The Wiedemann Trust Fund, as well as the CA (twice), the international conference on Diodorus Siculus in Glasgow, and the Triennial Conference in Cambridge all offered me bursaries to help attend conferences and pursue research in the libraries of London; these opportunities have aided my academic development immensely. Benet Salway and Simon Corcoran at Projet Volterra offered me work at the project that helped to fund an extended stay in London, during which time a large portion of the book was written; for this I thank them both very much. While at William Penn Charter School, I have been ably assisted by Doug Uhlmann and Bhelly Bagbonon in tracking down resources. Carol MacDonald, Rachel Bridgewater, Grace Balfour-Harle and Jane Burkowski at EUP displayed their considerable expertise in smoothly guiding this book to publication. Finally, the universities of Edinburgh and Manchester generously employed me for my first three academic jobs across 2013 to 2019, without which I could not have continued my research.

I owe many personal debts as well. Sabine Lefebvre kindly invited me to present at '*Qui sum? Provincialis?* Manifestations identitaires dans le cadre supra-civique. Les identités provinciales et régionales' in Dijon in 2013, and the Royal Historical Society funded the trip. Anna Field, Bronach Kane and Beth Jenkins invited me to present at a Royal Historical Society Symposium in Cardiff on 'Conflict in Historical Perspectives', and James Thorne invited me to the 'Liverpool–Manchester Workshop on the Western Provinces under the Republic and Early Empire' in Manchester in 2012. Lisa Eberle and Michael Taylor included me in their panel on 'Power and Politics: Approaching Roman Imperialism in the Republic' at the SCS in Toronto in 2017, and Lisa Eberle and Myles Lavan invited me to their conference on 'Unrest in the Roman Empire: Discursive History' in Tübingen in 2019. Laura Pfuntner invited me to Belfast to present at the workshop on 'War and Peace-Making in the Roman Provinces in the First Century BC' in 2018, which was a lovely way to finally visit Belfast and exchange ideas about war and peace. I must also thank audiences across the UK and North America for their questions on and responses to the papers I have presented over the past ten years as I have tried to put my thoughts in order (always a slow process): thank you to those in Edinburgh (STAGE, CCC 2014, CA), Manchester, Seattle (APA), Exeter (CA), Toronto (SCS) and Liverpool (CA). Finally, Lisa Hau and Piotr Wozniczka deserve special thanks for inviting me to two meetings of the Diodorus Siculus Research Network, one in Glasgow and one in Trier in 2016 and 2018 respectively, which were enormously enjoyable events – I hope one day to return the favour here in the USA.

Many teachers and colleagues have generously taken time to sit and talk to me about my research, and I beg forgiveness from those whose names I cannot recall for this list. Thank you to Catherine Steel, John Marincola, John Richardson, Christian Stein, James Thorne, Stephen Todd, David Langslow, Peter Liddel, Polly Low, Jenny Bryan, Tim Parkin, Roz Bell, Tim Cornell, Piotr Wozniczka, Lisa Hau, Alexander Meeus, Harriet Flower, Suzanne Frey-Kupper, Roberta Mazza and Andrew Morrison. Jonathan Prag went out of his way to support my research during the tricky transition between my PhD and my first postdoctoral post, for which I am extremely grateful; he also provided detailed comments on a previous, quite different version of this book, the benefits of which I hope can be found in this version. Michael Crawford kindly opened his home to me and discussed and improved my ideas over grappa and dark chocolate, which was a privilege and a pleasure. I am grateful to Keith Rutter for kindly allowing me to see a copy of a draft of *Historia Numorum: Sicily*. To my colleagues at Edinburgh and then Manchester, thank you for making those five years so much fun, despite the interesting times we experienced (especially at Manchester): I was lucky to work in these two exceptional departments and cut my teeth teaching Roman history alongside kind and welcoming colleagues and friends. I must also thank Nick Fields and Sandra Bingham for inspiring me to drop geography and geology in my first year of undergraduate and to focus instead on the ancient world; I hope that I am evidence that the best teachers inspire their students for a lifetime. In both institutions I am also grateful to my students, who made the whole experience so fulfilling. I am especially grateful to Ben Salisbury, Luke Wilkinson, Bram Bentham, Grace Thornhill, Femi Karjalainen and William Kerrs-Farmer, for being the kinds of students who inspire me to teach and made the work more like fun: I owe you much more than you owe me, if indeed that is anything. Mahnoor Javed constantly forced me to confront theory and my own inadequacies in this area and generously offered thoughts on chapters from this book. My examiners, John North and Andrew Erskine, made the viva itself an enjoyable experience and provided exceptional critique and comments on the thesis and wise advice on how to improve it. Finally, my supervisors, Ulrike Roth and Keith Rutter, took my unpolished ideas and helped me to shape them, smooth the rough edges and write proper English: I cannot thank them enough for their guidance, their support and their belief that the thesis made sense. I am especially proud to have gone from their student to their colleague and finally to their friend. Ulrike has unfailingly supported my career in every detail since my viva in 2012, and I know I would not have had any career without her encouragement and friendship.

Finally, I owe many debts to my friends and family. My fellow postgraduates at Edinburgh and London made sure that the PhD was relatively stress-free and put up with me talking slaves at them for years. Thank you in particular to Belinda, Brie, Amy, Abby, Gavin, Francesco, Ryan, Fiona, Lily and Alex M. My friend Niels went from PhD colleague to flatmate during an eventful period in the PhD – I miss the chats, the *very* hot curries, and the smoky whisky! I am grateful to have completed the PhD and had my first three jobs alongside Uncle Juan, whose generosity with knowledge and wine over the years was very much appreciated and enjoyed. Raphaëla became a close friend who reminded me that academia is not everything and that the world outside it is wide and exciting and full of literature, films and music that is worth exploring and enjoying, a huge debt to owe. Fred read the whole book and helped to refine the arguments with her insightful questions. Most of all, her enthusiasm for any and all publications kept reminding me that some people do want to read odd thoughts about long-dead and sub-standard historians. Alex and Rachael welcomed me into their home in Edinburgh to help with the homesickness and supported me in keeping in touch with friends back home: thank you both for your kindness and generosity. Niven, Caitlin, Amy, Hank, Mike, Tom, Jamie, Adrian, Russel, Tony, Lindsey, Derrek, Tamsin and Oliver all made the PhD and the years before and after fun and rewarding in different ways, all important. Eddie and Mary deserve special thanks for being the kind of friends everyone deserves; we must game soon! My family, Tom, Sabrina, Rosie, Andrzej, little Franek, Helena and Louie, Fran, and my mother, Anne, kept me going through the thesis and the early steps of my career, despite the growing physical distance between us all. All the following helped me to stay sane, even as I struggled to get the book in shape and manage moving home seven times over the past ten years, and I owe them each an enormous debt: Chu, B. T. S., G. T. S., R. T. S., H. S., Randolph, Harold, Fritz, Hans, Olivine, G. H., Strawberry, Puffin, Puppy, Galena, Galenus, Opal, Harriet, Leopold, Thespia, Pauly, Humphrey, Sven, Howard, Howardina, Jugurtha, Gertrude, Bertrude, Hamilcar, Columba, Podrick, GiGi, Nutty, Hibby, Petunia, Dolly, Pierre, Cleopatra, Pom Pom, Gretel, Goldy, Peanut, Geraldo, Penelope, Quackers, Carlos, Bernard, Alphonso, Periwinkle, Jean-Luc, Dou Dou, Siobhan, Engelbert, Freddie, Frieda, Hermes, Jacques, Lucy, Gerard, Ulrike, Francesca, Howardino, Shopska, Banitsa, Truffles, Roscoe, Izzie, Jürgen, Bing, Reggie, Phoebe, Pippa, Pika, Lucky, Cat, Jerry, Barrels, Mina, Toots and Clem. Spodumena, Palinka, Clodius and Milo all willingly accepted tummy rubs and cuddles, and their furry hugs and twitching whiskers drove away even Manchester winter blues. If this list of thanks is long it is only because I know what it took to finish this book and who I owe for getting this far. I only hope I can repay these debts, but it would be remiss not to record them.

Last, but by no means least, Nicole, who read and improved every page, who never minded when I had to write down a thought in the middle of the night about a tiny detail, who picked me up when academic life and research got me down, who kept me going when an earlier version of this book was rejected, and who has made every second of the past thirteen years more fun and more fulfilling. You are the hip to my po. This book is dedicated to you, as it should be. Without you there is no book and my horizons would be forever limited.

The cover image depicts a twentieth-century AD statue of Eunus in Enna, Sicily, with the inscription: 'Ad Euno. Lo schiavo ribelle. Araldo di libertà.' In 1960, the city erected a plaque next to the statue recording Eunus' achievements in relation to those of Abraham Lincoln:

> Duemila anni prima che Abramo Lincoln liberasse l'infelice turba dei negri, l'umile schiavo Euno da questa sicana fortezza arditamente lanciava il grido di libertà per i compagni di sventura suoi, il diritto affermando di ogni uomo a nascere libero ed anche a liberamente morire.

One wonders what King Antiochus would have made of this commemoration, with its emphasis on nudity, chains, anguish and above all slavery, a question worth carrying throughout this book.

Abbreviations

Abbreviations of ancient sources follow the conventions of the *Oxford Classical Dictionary*, 4th edition. The following abbreviations of modern works are used:

BNJ	Worthington, I. ed. 2006–. *Brill's New Jacoby*, accessed at https://scholarlyeditions.brill.com/bnjo.
BTCGI	Nenci, G. and Vallet, G. eds. *Bibliografia topografica della colonizzazione greca in Italia e nelle isole tirreniche*.
CAH^2 *IX*	Crook, J. A., Lintott, A. and Rawson, E. eds. 1992. *The Cambridge Ancient History*, vol. 9, 2nd edition (Cambridge).
Calciati I–III	Calciati, R. 1987. *Corpus Nummorum Siculorum: La Monetazione di Bronzo*, 3 vols (Milan).
Campana	Campana, A. 1997. 'Corpus nummorum antiquae Italiae (zecche minori): Sicilia: Enna (440–36 a.C.)', *Pan. Num.* 112–13, 145–67.
CNG	Journal 1987–. Classical Numismatics Group.
FGrHist	Jacoby, F. 1923–. *Die Fragmente der griechischen Historiker* (Berlin).
FRHist	Cornell, T. J. 2014. *Fragments of the Roman Historians*, 3 vols (Oxford).
IG I^3	Lewis, D. M., Jeffery, L. H., Erxleben, E. and Hallof, K. eds. *Inscriptiones Graecae, I. Inscriptiones Atticae Euclidis anno anteriores*, 3rd edition (Berlin).
IG XIV	Kaibel, G. 1890. *Inscriptiones Graecae, XIV. Inscriptiones Siciliae et Italiae, additis Galliae, Hispaniae, Britanniae, Germaniae inscriptionibus* (Berlin).
RE	Pauly, A., Wissowa, G., and Kroll, W. 1893–. *Realencyclopädie der classischen Altertumswissenschaft* (Stuttgart).
RRC	Crawford, M. H. 1974. *Roman Republican Coinage* (Cambridge).

SEG	Journal 1923–. *Supplementum epigraphicum Graecum.*
SNG ANS 3	Troxell, H. A. 1975. *Sylloge Nummorum Graecorum: The Collection of the American Numismatic Society Part 3* (New York).
SNG ANS 4	Jaunzems, E. 1977. *Sylloge Nummorum Graecorum: The Collection of the American Numismatic Society Part 4* (New York).
SNG ANS 5	Bérend, D. 1988. *Sylloge Nummorum Graecorum: The Collection of the American Numismatic Society Part 5* (New York).
SNG Cop.	Breitenstein, N. 1942. *Sylloge Nummorum Graecorum: The Royal Collection of Coins and Medals. Danish National Museum. Sicily* (Copenhagen).
SNG Morcom	Morcom, J. 1995. *Sylloge Nummorum Graecorum X: The John Morcom Collection of Western Greek Bronze Coins* (Oxford).

Introduction: The Problem with the 'Sicilian Slave Wars'

In 136 BC, and again in 104 BC, two of the largest slave revolts of antiquity broke out in Sicily – so we are accustomed to think. On each occasion thousands of individuals seized the opportunity to claim their freedom and violently resisted the Roman authority's attempts to stop them. The rebels, in seemingly perverse imitation of the society they struggled against, chose men from among their numbers to be kings, who affected the look and ideology of Hellenistic kings. Indignant ancient writers seethed over the defeated Roman commanders and grudgingly admitted that the slaves succeeded in taking several important Sicilian cities. In each event Rome regained control of the province only through the application of large-scale military force. From these revolts ancient writers drew, moreover, clear warnings of the dangers of excessive arrogance, luxury and greed, and developed them into carefully composed moral tales (Diod. Sic. 34/5.2 and 36.1–10; Val. Max. 2.7.3, 2.7.9, 4.3.10, 6.9.8, 9.12.1). For some the collapse of Sicilian society into slave revolts was an intrinsic part of the gathering speed with which the Roman Republic hurtled headlong into autocracy (Flor. 2.7; App. *B Civ.*1.9). The dramatic nature of these events as recounted by various ancient authors is matched by the near uniqueness of these rebellions. Thus, with the addition of the revolt widely known as the Spartacus War in 73 BC and a revolt in Sarmatia in AD 334, these four events constitute an oddity in the history of antiquity: only on these four occasions in the ancient world have slaves been recorded to have risen in such numbers, or resisted their masters for such lengths of time.

Despite the apparent importance of these two wars to the history of ancient slavery, we have only an imprecise understanding of their chronologies as they are preserved by the ancient historiographical tradition. That said, in the case of the first of the two wars that befell Sicily, we have far greater knowledge about the conflict's opening years. The narrative of the event as the tradition records it can be reconstructed briefly as follows. The revolt started in the household of a violent slave owner named Damophilus. His mistreatment of his slaves, we are told, drove them to plot against his life (Diod. Sic. 34/5.2.10, 34–7). After encouragement from a wonder-working slave named Eunus, these slaves attacked and seized the town of Enna at night and killed their hated masters (34/5.2.11–14, 24b). The Greek-writing Diodorus Siculus indicates that during the years preceding this outbreak, the landowners in Sicily had been importing and abusing vast numbers of slaves, which had resulted in a rise in lawlessness in the Sicilian countryside caused by desperate slaves (34/5.2.2, 26–9). In the aftermath of their victory at Enna the rebels proclaimed Eunus king, were joined by another rebellion that had started near Agrigentum under the leadership of a herdsman named Kleon, and defeated a Roman army under the command of a praetor called L. Hypsaeus (34/5.2.14–18, 41). After this point our information becomes even more incomplete. The rebel army grew from 10,000 to 200,000 men, according to the more outlandish figures reported in the ancient sources, and forced Rome to send a consul to Sicily each year from 134 to 132 BC.[1] Over the course of the revolt the rebels seized several important Sicilian towns, including Enna, Morgantina, Tauromenium, Agrigentum and Catana, with the likelihood that they also attacked Syracuse (Diod. Sic. 34/5.2.20–2, 43; Strabo 6.2.6; Oros. 5.9.5), and they apparently won a number of battles against Roman commanders (Diod. Sic. 34/5.2.18–20; Flor. 2.7.7–8).[2] In the final year of the war the Roman consul, P. Rupilius, besieged the rebels in Enna and Tauromenium and took both citadels through their betrayal (Diod. Sic. 34/5.2.21). The rebel leader, Eunus, was captured as he fled Enna and thrown into jail, where he died, perhaps from scabies (Diod. Sic. 34/5.2.23).[3]

The later of the wars followed a pattern similar to that of the earlier one, at least as our ancient literary tradition presented it.[4] This tradition suggests that it started in the vicinity of the town of Heraclea Minoa, with a group of slaves murdering their owner, P. Clonius (36.4.1–2).[5] This murder occurred shortly after a failed outbreak near Halicyae, which had been put down by the Roman governor, P. Licinius Nerva (36.3.4–6). The revolt near Heraclea grew rapidly following the governor's initial failure to destroy it with a garrison drawn from Enna (36.4.2–3), and so the rebels elected a slave called Salvius, later to be called Tryphon, to become their leader. The new king marched his force of 20,000 men to attack the eastern city of Morgantina. In the process of the unsuccessful siege Salvius/Tryphon and his men defeated a force of 10,000 Sicilians and Italian Greeks led by Nerva (36.4.5–8). Meanwhile, a second revolt started in the area around Segesta and Lilybaeum, led from the beginning by a Cilician named Athenion. These rebels besieged Lilybaeum, but following a failure there were forced to withdraw (36.5). By this time, Salvius/Tryphon's forces had broken off the siege at Morgantina, sacrificed a toga at the shrine of the Paliki in the east of the island, and proceeded to seize the town of Triokala in the west in order to build a palace there (36.7). Salvius/Tryphon summoned Athenion, and the two groups united. In response Rome assigned L. Licinius Lucullus to the command against them. He attacked the 40,000-strong rebel army in open battle with only 16,000 troops. Although his side won comfortably, Lucullus failed to press his advantage, thus allowing the rebels to regroup at Triokala (36.8). In a desire to discredit his successor and prevent prosecution for his actions, Lucullus burned his camp and disbanded his army; this caused the next praetor, C. Servilius, to achieve nothing of note in his praetorship, during which time the rebels gained the upper hand (36.9). Finally, M'. Aquilius was assigned as consul to the command and in

---

[1] For 10,000 men, see Diod. Sic. 34/5.2.16; for 200,000, see Diod. Sic. 34/5.2.18. There is a variety of reports of the total rebel strength, including 70,000 (Livy, *Per.* 56) and 60,000 (Flor. 2.7.6), although it is freely admitted here that these figures (especially the 200,000) seem inflated.

[2] For a discussion of the attack on Syracuse, see Morton 2014, 25 n. 20.

[3] On this, see Keaveney and Madden 1982, 87–99, and Morton 2013, 242.

[4] See Morton 2014 for a consideration of the differences between the Roman responses to each war.

[5] Every reference in this paragraph is to a passage in the narrative provided by Diodorus Siculus.

a single engagement crushed the rebels and killed Athenion, who was by this time king (36.10). Subsequently, Aquilius cleared the province of pockets of resistance and celebrated an ovation on his return to Rome.[6]

The basic narrative regarding these events in Sicily in the 130s BC and again some thirty years later, here sketched primarily along the account of Diodorus Siculus, is found in all the standard modern reference works for the ancient world. A key example readily illustrates this point: the discussion offered in Volume 9 of *The Cambridge Ancient History*. In this volume, the events of the two wars are, in essence, a rewording of the ancient narrative given in Diodorus, Florus and various other authors from antiquity.[7] Furthermore, in the brief account given in the *CAH*, we find all of the features that are prevalent in other modern accounts. There is a stress on the chain-gangs supposedly working in Sicily in this period (26), the moralising tone of the main ancient narrative is noted (26), and the importance of the actions of the free poor in Sicily during the conflicts is suppressed (26–7), often quite dismissively (27): 'Although poor Sicilians became involved, their activities were marginal . . .' Throughout the rest of the volume the two wars are then given as evidence of the availability of slaves in the second century BC and the growth of their numbers in Italy (55, 605); of the escalation of violence and corruption in Roman politics (60–1); of the 'land problem' in Italy in the mid-second century BC brought on by excessive use of slave labour, and combated by the Gracchi (73); of the gradual worsening of slave treatment in the second century BC in Italy (605); and finally, of the rise in the importance of the villa economy in Italy (620). In short, the two wars, understood as slave rebellions, are considered, throughout the *CAH*'s treatment of the second century BC, to be a key aspect used to interpret the development of Italy's agriculture and society, although only a very short section considers the relevance of the wars to Sicily itself (25–7). With only one exception – the traditional narrative's neglect of the island's Greek landowners in its explanation – the information given is offered with certainty, which is derived from the authority of the principal ancient literary account – the account of Diodorus Siculus.

Despite the attention given in various sources to both conflicts and the certainty of the interpretation expressed in the authoritative *CAH*, there is little hard evidence for either of the two wars. The narrative that we can reconstruct is piecemeal in many places. In terms of literary evidence, to reiterate, we rely for the most part on the fragmentary narrative of books 34–6 of Diodorus Siculus' *Bibliotheke*, composed in the first century BC, besides a short account in Florus, written over a century later. Other authors record a few details, typically in anecdotes or short impressionistic narratives: in this category we find the *Periochae* of Livy, Valerius Maximus' tales, Strabo's geographical narrative, Orosius' history and Cicero's *Verrine Orations*. It is an indication of the paucity of the surviving literary evidence that our main account of the conflicts preserved in Diodorus survives only in an epitome written by Photius in the ninth century AD (in a work known also as *Bibliotheke*) and in the excerpts ordered by the Byzantine emperor Constantine Porphyrogenitus in the tenth century AD. To this collection of literary evidence we can add the important material evidence of a

---

[6] Ath. 5.213b; Cic. *De or.* 2.195.
[7] A. Lintott, 'The Roman empire and its problems in the late second century', in *CAH IX*², 16–39.

handful of coins from the first of the two conflicts and a collection of slingshots from each event. In fact, the evidential basis for understanding the events in question is so poor that it is unclear not only when and with what forces Roman commanders were assigned to the *provincia*, but also when the first war began.[8]

In spite of the problematic evidence for both events, there has been considerable scholarly interest in them in the past. That interest has been particularly focused on two distinct spheres: slavery[9] and Sicily. In the first of these spheres the main emphasis has been on explicating the literary evidence, and on reconstructing – as far as possible – the historical context of these outbursts of – and as – servile insurrections. Notably, the main authority of the past thirty-five years on these events, Keith Bradley, in the preface to his monograph on the topic, noted that he considered there to be 'a need . . . for a straightforward narrative of the slave rebellions, set within their immediate context, that at the same time is related to the wider background of modern slavery studies'; Bradley went on to comment on his hope that his monograph would contribute to the history of 'Roman social relations in particular and to the history of slavery in broader compass'.[10]

Bradley's intention to find the 'immediate context' for the conflict is evident in the majority of scholarship on the subject, including scholarship less focused on the servile dimensions than Bradley himself. To this end, a number of contexts have been drawn on to explain peculiarities in the literary evidence or to contextualise the rebels' actions. These contexts include Syrian nationalism amongst the enslaved,[11] the opportunities for and settings of marronage,[12] as well as numerous efforts to understand the particular social requisites necessary for widespread servile discontent, often with a focus on the religious characteristics of the leaders of each revolt.[13] The search for explanatory and contextual foundations has often led scholars further afield than the location of the events in Sicily itself; indeed, for many of the analyses cited above the most 'immediate context', that of the island itself, has been missed. A striking exception to this is Finley's study of the wars set into the context of a work on Sicily's history, albeit neatly separated from the non-servile history by the placement of the wars into their own chapter, rather than integrated into the chapter on 'The First Roman Province'.[14] In addition, all of these approaches have emphasised the primacy of the literary evidence for the conflicts and display a general reluctance to

---

[8] For discussion of the dating of the outbreak of this conflict, see Bradley 1989, 152–7 and 170–83; Brennan 1993, 153–84; Keaveney 1998, 73–82.

[9] I exclude from this category any work which is not directly interested in engaging with the evidence for the two Sicilian 'Slave Wars': a great many articles and books refer to the two conflicts, but only to comment on the topic that is more immediately relevant to the work; see the account given in *CAH2* XI, 25–7, and discussed above.

[10] Bradley 1989, ix.

[11] Vogt 1965, 41–3.

[12] Bradley 1989, xiv–xv, 123–6; 2011, 365.

[13] This category encompasses the majority of the works on the two events: see Pareti 1927; Westermann 1945; Westermann 1955, 63–9; Green 1961; Toynbee 1965, 316–27, 405–7; Canfora 1985; Dumont 1987, 197–268; Sacks 1990, 144–9; Callahan and Horsley 1998; Mileta 1998; Shaw 2001; Wirth 2004 and 2006, 125–8; Urbainczyk 2008a and 2008b; Strauss 2010.

[14] Finley 1979, 137–47.

analyse the other, non-literary evidence preserved, such as the valuable but limited amounts of numismatic and epigraphic material. Additionally, in spite of the emphasis given to the literary evidence, scholars have been hesitant to subject it to detailed study, not least because of its fragmentary nature. Bradley summed up much of the widespread scholarly hesitation to subject the literary evidence to greater scrutiny when positing that 'it requires too great an act of faith to believe that the excerpts now extant [of Diodorus] preserve evidence of literary ingenuity . . .'[15] This view has led to interpretations that have accepted the assertions made by the principal literary source because of an assumed lack of historiographic creativity on the part of the author, Diodorus Siculus. In short, whatever the shortcomings of this evidence, it is, at base, seen as reliable in its portrayal of the two events in question, and in particular of its portrayal of these events as slave wars.

In the second sphere of interest, Sicily, scholars have additionally adopted two further approaches. The first is to use the evidence of the two events to define a watershed moment in Sicilian history. For instance, Verbrugghe and Manganaro have argued that the earlier of the two wars can be reinterpreted as a provincial revolt against Rome.[16] Verbrugghe argued that Diodorus' opinion that the herdsmen acted as the chief culprits of this war was inaccurate because Sicily's main agricultural produce was grain, as emphasised by Livy and Cicero in passages unrelated to the conflicts, rather than pastoralism. Moreover, it is assumed that there could not possibly have been 200,000 rebels involved had they all been slaves (Diod. Sic. 34/5.2.18). Yet, even for Verbrugghe, the Sicilian context is only used to disprove that the event in question was a slave revolt; he suggests no reason for a Sicilian revolt beyond a history of rebelliousness, and does not suggest why, in the mid- to late second century BC, a revolt would have taken place.[17] Furthermore, Verbrugghe, despite his attacks on certain details in Diodorus' narrative, accepts without question Diodorus' stereotypical assertions regarding the character of the first war's leader as that of an eastern wonder-worker.[18]

The other approach focuses on the maintenance of Sicily's strong Hellenistic civic culture and its identifying structures. Thus, scholars note that the two wars contrast with the view of Hellenistic Sicily that is now emerging from detailed study of the island's archaeology, epigraphy and numismatics. Two examples will demonstrate this. First, Wilson's study of the Sicily of Cicero's *Verrine Orations* from an archaeologist's perspective.[19] Wilson argued that the substantial material remains of Sicily showed an island with a powerful economy capable of supporting a provincial elite that was politically active and financially prospering from Rome's stewardship.[20] However,

---

[15] Bradley 1989, 136.
[16] Verbrugghe 1972 and 1974; Manganaro 1982; 1983; 1990b; 2000.
[17] Verbrugghe 1972, 53–8.
[18] Verbrugghe 1974 is not alone in accepting without question Diodorus' account of Eunus: for a reassessment of Diodorus' depiction of Eunus, see Morton 2013.
[19] Wilson 2000, 134–60.
[20] Wilson concluded with similar comments again in his contribution to *The Hellenistic West*, for which see Wilson 2013a, 100. Similar conclusions can be found in Prag 2003; Campagna 2006, 15–34; Bell 2007, 118; and in many papers in Ampolo 2012

when moving on to the archaeological evidence for the development of Sicily's agriculture, Wilson noted that

> One thing which is strikingly clear from Cicero's accusations is the apparent prevalence of farmers with small- to medium-sized estates, and this provides a striking contrast to the picture provided by Diodorus and others of the Sicilian countryside being dominated by vast estates (*latifundia*) with huge slave run ranches. There must have been plenty of examples of the latter in Sicily – otherwise the island would never have experienced two slave wars at the end of the second century BC – but that they coexisted with small- and medium-sized estates at the time of Verres' governorship (and no doubt before) seems certain.[21]

Wilson earlier commented that while the archaeological field survey evidence is far from complete for Sicily, it is nonetheless the case that in areas that have been surveyed, the pattern of land use is complex, even if 'the limited amount of field survey evidence . . . suggests the presence in the countryside of plentiful smallholdings in the first half of the first century BC'.[22]

A similar concern for this disconnection between the evidence for the two wars and the growing body of evidence for the vitality of Hellenistic Sicily can be seen in a recent contribution by Prag. In this, Prag noted that the traditional narrative of Sicilian history was one in which

> the island drops out of mainstream (i.e. Roman) history following the establishment of Roman provincial government in the third century BC, and the island's cities suffer a comprehensive loss of autonomy, worn down by the demands of Roman taxation and the effects of Roman rule; this process culminates towards the end of the Republican period with the depredations of Verres and the impact of the civil wars; and the island becomes a quiet backwater of veteran *coloniae* and the extensive *latifundia* of absentee landlords, a peaceful *suburbana* of Imperial Italy. This narrative follows easily from the literary sources, dominated as they are by Cicero on Verres and Diodorus on the Slave Wars.[23]

Prag contrasted the narrative of Sicily that arises from the literary evidence with the recent advances in our understanding of the chronology of the impressive monumentalisation of Sicilian towns, which is drawn from examining the archaeology, epigraphy and numismatics separately from the literary narrative. In particular, Prag

---

[21] Wilson 2000, 159.
[22] Wilson 2000, 149. Further notable work on field surveys in Sicily include the following: Wilson and Leonard Jr. 1980; Wilson 1981; Thompson 1999, 444–57; Albanese Procelli et al. 2007; Bell 2007, 121; Kolb 2007; Leone et al. 2007; Perkins 2007, 38–41; Bergemann 2012; Belvedere and Burgio 2012; De Graaf 2012, 91–2; Puglisi 2014.
[23] Prag 2015, 165.

observed that the transformation of Sicilian urban centres is now recognised as having taken place in the

> two or three generations before Verres, in the period directly contemporary with the Slave Wars. Such transformation would appear directly to contradict the traditional picture outlined above, which focuses instead on the negative impact of Roman rule and Roman taxation.[24]

In short, the interpretation of Sicilian civic and cultural development is derived from the archaeological, epigraphic and numismatic evidence and does not include the evidence for either war in the reconstruction – understood, as the quotation from Prag emphasises, as slave wars. Oddly, this interpretation appears to contradict directly the evidence for these wars. On this reading of Hellenistic Sicily, it is evident that some aspects of the traditional war narratives do not sit well with the picture of an island that was home to such successful city states and that a degree of integration between the two narratives of Hellenistic Sicily would be helpful. Nonetheless, before we attempt to integrate both wars into a more holistic narrative, it is necessary to reassess key aspects of what the evidence for these can tell us. This is especially the case in light of two important points regarding the scale of the two military conflicts under scrutiny and the ancient literary sources for them.

First, as observed at the outset, the two wars are unusually long in comparison to other events considered to be servile revolts, in antiquity and world history more generally.[25] Each conflict took a minimum of three years to suppress and required the dedication of the highest level of Roman magistrate and military strength to defeat. The rebel forces in both conflicts came to number tens of thousands. In the first war they besieged and captured several strategically important Sicilian towns, in some cases while Roman armies led by consuls were in the field against them. In the second war the rebels were less successful in siege warfare, but nonetheless kept Rome at bay for several years. Few other revolts in the global history of slavery match the scale and longevity of the two Sicilian revolts, and the wars that arose from these, here analysed. Those that do include that of Spartacus in Italy from 73–71 BC and the Sarmatian slave revolt of AD 334 – also already mentioned – the Zanj revolt in ninth-century AD Iraq, and the revolution in Haiti from AD 1791 to 1804, famously led by Toussaint Louverture and Jean-Jacques Dessalines.[26] Revolts of this scale are not normal in the history of slavery and require explanation on their own terms, an important reason for the exclusion of extensive discussion of Spartacus from this book: the focus here is on Sicily, and Spartacus' uprising deserves its own, extended analysis on its own terms; it must not, *a priori*, be subsumed under the same or similar narrative frame without due scrutiny.

---

[24] Prag 2015, 166.
[25] For further discussion of other slave revolts, especially in world history more generally, and how we might come to define what we mean by the term 'slave revolt', see Chapter 5.
[26] On the Zanj, see Popović 1999; Furlonge 1999; Kennedy 2016, 153–5. On Haiti, see James 1963; Geggus 1982; Fick 1990; Trouillot 1995; Geggus 2002; Dubois 2004; Dubois and Garrigus 2006; Fiering and Geggus 2008; Jenson 2011; Girard 2016.

Second, as we noted above, previous studies of the two Sicilian wars have placed great emphasis on the narratives preserved in the literary sources for the conflicts.[27] These texts have been accepted as broadly authoritative but lacking in the ability or inclination to present more than a basic narrative of the events.[28] This emphasis has come at the expense of a detailed analysis of the (admittedly) limited but nonetheless important non-literary evidence for the wars. Yet it has been demonstrated in a series of articles by two scholars that it is precisely the scrutiny of the literary sources, combined with the integration of the non-literary sources studied in their geographical context, that can develop our understanding of the conflicts. With regard to the first war, Manganaro argued that it is only by incorporating the numismatic evidence into our study of the conflict that we can begin to understand the rebel movement on its own terms. He showed that these coin issues can be best understood in the context of Sicilian numismatics in the second century BC, and that the coins strongly implied that the rebels, whoever they were, attempted to appeal to the people of Sicily in their struggle.[29] This is not clear from the literary evidence alone. Intriguingly, Rubinsohn later argued, through a close reading of Diodorus' text and a consideration of the broader historical context of the Mediterranean, that the explanation of the second war as a slave war 'does not do justice to the rather complex phenomena involved in it'.[30] He noted that Diodorus' narrative preserves telling evidence of internal disorder among the free of Sicily, and in particular 'between the influential bourgeoisie and the poor'.[31] Most importantly, both Manganaro and Rubinsohn acknowledged the importance of understanding the evidence for both conflicts in their immediate chronological, geographical and political contexts, suggesting, as seen, new ways of looking at the events as a result.

A New Approach

I propose to take a different approach in this monograph to those that have dominated the discussion, outlined above. In this work I intend to show that the two wars commonly known as the Sicilian Slave Wars can be profitably understood not as slave uprisings, but foremost as wider and hugely complex events that require their own analysis, separate from any possible servile involvement. A closer analysis of the rebel actions and the perspectives of the rebels will show that we hinder our understanding of these events if we insist on studying them as slave revolts. Instead, these two revolts can be fruitfully studied as evidence for the socio-economic difficulties and political struggles that Sicily faced in this period on the larger societal plane in the face of an

---

[27] What an anonymous reviewer of a previous version of this monograph called the 'most reliable evidence'.
[28] See the quotation above on p. 5 from Bradley 1989, 136, and also Verbrugghe 1974, and Rathmann 2016, 301–2, and the anonymous reviewer above. Angius 2020 has provided a recent reconsideration of Diodorus' narrative, intended to provide (10) 'una guida agli eventi che parta innanzitutto dal testo' of Diodorus, which while acknowledging the existence of non-literary sources is nonetheless structured around the interpretative framework of the ancient literary evidence.
[29] Managanaro 1982; 1983; 1990a and 1990b.
[30] Rubinsohn 1982, 436.
[31] Rubinsohn 1982, 450.

ever more influential Rome. When viewed in this light, they offer a unique opportunity to study how the Roman empire – of which Sicily was a small part – was formed and challenged. This thesis will be demonstrated in two distinct parts.

Part I: The Wars in Sicily Reassessed

In the first part I will offer a reassessment of the two wars by going back to the extant evidence, however fragmentary, and assessing it in its 'immediate context', as Bradley put it, that of Sicily in the second century BC.[32] I will initially turn to the first of the two wars and to the only extant evidence for the revolt that comes directly from the rebels themselves: a handful of coins produced during the first war bearing the name of their king, Antiochus, more commonly known as Eunus in the literary sources, which are often read as evidence of the rebels' attempts to harness the power of Seleucid monarchical symbols. We will see that when viewed in the context of Sicilian numismatics of the second century BC, the coins produced by the rebels can be profitably understood as an attempt to emphasise a connection with the peoples of south-eastern Sicily via a monarch, who is presented as a Hellenistic king with close cultural ties to south-eastern Sicily. This body of evidence offers the possibility to open up an alternative perspective on this event to that foregrounded in both ancient and modern accounts: in short, one in which the rebels fought not as the enslaved or formely enslaved, focused on their individual liberty from slavery under the law, but as members of the population at large, that is commonly appreciated as the free population of Sicily. This is not to say that many of the rebels were not enslaved: the surviving literary evidence, for what is is worth, insists that many if not most involved in the revolt had been subjected to slavery. Yet, as will be seen, any possible externally imposed servility was not the focus of the rebels' own self-identification, nor was it a part of their self-presentation to the peoples of south-eastern Sicily. More crucially still, this chapter will contend that this coinage can be interpreted as an attempt by the rebels to rouse the people of Sicily in a united insurgency against the Roman-backed status quo on the island. This can also be seen in the rebels' actions at certain points in the war, and it will be argued that it is entirely plausible that notable swaths of the Sicilian population in the island's south-east were sympathetic to the rebel cause, irrespective of the role of slavery in their lives: in other words, that this event was not centred on individual freedom for the rebels, but was a vastly complex conflict that reflected and was contingent on the support of certain parts of the Sicilian populace at large.

In the second chapter, I will examine the literary evidence for the first war and present a new interpretation of Diodorus' text from a narratological point of view, thus to unpack the distorting interpretative layers of this key account. The argument will be presented from three angles. First, I will demonstrate that the portrayal of the character of the slave Eunus, the leader of this war, is a construct based on Hellenistic stereotypes of femininity, cowardliness and magic designed to weaken this figure. Second, I will show that the character of Kleon, Eunus' subordinate, is likewise described using stereotyped character traits of a violent bandit in order to complement the figure

---

[32] Bradley 1989, ix.

of Eunus as a cowardly king. Third, I will argue that if we consider key moments in the narrative that is preserved by Diodorus from a rhetorical and narratological viewpoint, we can see that parts of the narrative are carefully focalised to present a 'correct' reading of the rebel actions that is focused on their mistreatment by their masters, to the exclusion of all other concerns. This focalisation, combined with Diodorus' deliberate portrayal of Eunus through the noted stereotyped character traits, profoundly questions how much we can rely on Diodorus' depiction of the motivations and intentions of the rebels throughout his narrative: in a sense, it diminishes the value of this text for the purpose of historical reconstruction. Finally, the discussion will show furthermore that the same themes drive the representation of the rebels in the other literary texts for this war. In the chapter's conclusion, the conflicting images of the revolt that can be found in literary and numismatic sources for the war will be reconciled. These conflicting images will be shown to be the result of competing perspectives on the conflict: in the literary sources the war is a narrative about the correct treatment of subordinates and the dangers of transgressing acceptable behavioural norms, which is intricately bound up in the system of slavery; in the numismatic evidence (difficult to reconstruct though it is) the war is revealed as an assertion of a new political authority that has nothing to do with gaining liberty from servility, but one that expressed itself in an entirely appropriate form of contemporary government – Hellenistic kingship.

Chapter 3 turns to the second war. This war, like the first, offers us an opportunity to contrast the literary sources with another body of evidence: inscribed slingshots bearing the names of the rebel leaders. However, in this case the material evidence is less extensive than that of the first war. Chapter 3, therefore, will deal with both the relevant literary evidence and the inscribed slingshots side by side. In the first part of the chapter, I will argue that the two leaders of the war, Salvius/Tryphon and Athenion, were described in the literary tradition using the same matrix of ideas that was present for Eunus and Kleon, albeit in new combinations. In this case, Salvius/Tryphon is implied to be an effeminate leader lacking military skill, while Athenion is described as a charlatan prophet and a brave soldier. These character depictions, I argue, set up the narrative so that the subsequent interactions between the two men, and the events of the war in general, are read in the manner desired by the texts' authors. This is the case in particular for Salvius/Tryphon's foundation of a politically active society at Triokala, which demonstrates an important contrast between Salvius/Tryphon and Athenion, whose actions appear in consequence to have lacked any coherent social purpose. In the second part of the chapter, I will argue that if we study specific moments in Diodorus Siculus' narrative of the war – especially Salvius/Tryphon's dedication of a toga at the shrine of the Paliki, and the creation of a city at Triokala – and read them alongside the inscribed slingshots bearing Salvius/Tryphon's and Athenion's names, we can instead begin to see the events in a new light. In particular, the dedication at Paliki strongly suggests that Salvius/Tryphon's forces included free combatants. More than that, each leader of the revolt appears to have attempted the creation of an ordered state. To this end, these men used a variety of ideologies and symbolisms to bind together the disparate groups of people under their banner, whatever their (former) legal status. What stands out throughout, however, is the effective representation of the rebels as rebels on the larger societal plane, rather than as rebels concerned with the rejection of individual enslavement. These issues make this event, like the first war, not easily categorised as a slave revolt, despite the narrative presented in the ancient literary tradition.

These three chapters will mark a distinct departure from previous analyses of these two wars. An analysis of these two wars that seeks to understand how these events were perceived by and what they meant to those rebelling against the established authority is long overdue. Admittedly, doing so will entail several methodological approaches to the ancient evidence that may be uncomfortable for some. The ancient literary texts on which our narratives of these events are based – those of Diodorus Siculus, Livy, Florus, Orosius, Cicero and Valerius Maximus – are slave-owner narratives without exception. By this I mean that these are texts derived from a historiographical tradition that was written by and for elite slave owners. The tradition sought to explain these events to those whose livelihood and social status depended upon the maintenance of slavery and especially an economy fuelled by slavery. The perspective offered by the literary texts, while valuable, should not be taken as authoritative statements about the intent, nature or meaning of these events. These perspectives are primarily indicative only of how slave owners perceived the events in relation to themselves, or rather how they were able to appreciate these events within a matrix defined by slavery. These texts are by definition poor guides to the rebel perspective. Moreover, if we base our understanding of these events solely on these texts, we risk writing (yet another) slave-owner narrative that diminishes the perspective of those who rebelled, whatever their individual fates; in turn, we diminish our own understanding of the ancient world. None of what will be argued seeks to suggest that the rebels envisaged a society without slavery. But given the methodological conundrum faced by the modern scholar caused by the nature of the surviving evidence, analytical clarity alone demands a rigorous identification of the literary evidence as set within a dominant culture of slave-owning. In sum, these texts cannot be read as straightforward historical narratives; they are complex literary constructions, regularly employing the themes of slavery in general and slave rebellions in particular to comment on the nature of leadership or social interactions, including beyond the historical contexts at their core.[33]

We can escape the interpretative confines of these slave-owner narratives and access a different view of these events by turning to the evidence that originates directly from the rebels themselves, as will be argued in Chapters 1 and 3. It is my conviction that allowing the servile identity ascribed to the rebels by slave owners to overwrite the rebels' self-expression of identity – that is, to assume that the literary sources have greater merit in our reconstruction than any other sources – is to repeat the slave-owner narrative. In doing this, we lose a valuable alternative to the traditional elite view of the ancient world. It is better, as the first three chapters of this book will demonstrate, to examine these two views of the conflicts alongside one another, and to appreciate in consequence the much greater complexity of the events. This approach will demonstrate that these events are characterised by features other than the discontent of

---

[33] This has been demonstrated primarily for Diodorus Siculus' narrative in terms of Hellenistic leadership and social commentary, for which see Morton 2013 and 2018 respectively.

enslaved people or a challenge to the system of slavery, and that they stand apart from other slave revolts. As we have seen, then, the first part of this monograph, which is comprised of Chapters 1, 2 and 3, aims to show that the actions and intentions of the rebels demonstrate that we should not discuss these wars as slave revolts. The second part of my study, then, will assess how these conclusions affect the ways in which these two Sicilian conflicts fit into the bigger contexts of late Republican historiography and slave revolts in world history. It is to this part that we now turn.

Part II: Slave Revolts in Ancient Historiography and the Wider Historical Context

The second part of this book and its argument will be developed in two chapters. Chapter 4 will consider how the literary sources for the two wars fit into their historiographical contexts. We will see that our ancient sources describe many conflicts as slave revolts, in addition to those in Sicily. The accusation of inciting slaves to insurrection to support political ends is a commonplace of ancient historiographical and political texts, but there has never been a detailed study of what this approach sought to achieve in ancient literature. In some cases, as we will see, the events described as slave revolts were not actually instigated by enslaved people but were political or military events driven and inspired by the actions of free people. This chapter will illustrate that fact and how labelling an event as a slave revolt was applied by ancient historical and political writers throughout antiquity to achieve several different objectives, including political attacks, commentary on free society, and explanations of the existence of social and cultural features of the ancient world. Using the slave-revolt label could extend to attempts to denigrate and deny legitimacy to political, cultural and military opponents whose actions threatened the acceptable status quo, but could equally be used to describe the origins of religious cults or even cities. Far from a scientific label intended to delineate the actions of those subject to slavery from those of the free, referring to an event as a slave revolt was rather a historiographical *topos* with a variety of functions. When read in light of this literary and historiographical tradition, we will see that the use of specific terminology referring to slave revolts in Diodorus Siculus, Florus, Livy, Cicero and Valerius Maximus cannot be used as an authoritative guide about these events that furthers our understanding of the complex nature of the two wars at the centre of this book. The conclusions will further challenge the unproblematised labelling of the two events under scrutiny in this book as slave rebellions, slave revolts or slave wars.

The final chapter will reassess what we mean in modern discussion when we talk of slave revolts. As noted above, the terminology used to describe events in modern scholarship can have an effect on how we study these events. We implicitly link the two wars in the manner that we name them – the two Sicilian Slave Wars. The slave label implies a similarity between these events as well as with other slave rebellions, whether in antiquity or more modern times; slave label apart, calling them the 'First' and 'Second' of the Sicilian Slave Wars cements a degree of similarity, or rather relationship, between these two ancient events themselves – merely on the basis of the supposed centrality of slavery to these wars, without further explanation of why or how *two* such massive slave rebellions should have arisen in Sicily in the period.[34] However, these two wars are unusual in the history of slavery, ancient and modern, on several scores, including their length and scale. As will be argued in Chapter 5, when we compare these two events with servile uprisings from antiquity and the modern world, we will see that they do not fit the pattern of revolts that are clearly documented as slave revolts, that is typically regular, short revolts that lasted less than a week, with participants numbering in the hundreds at most. Based on this comparison the two wars will be shown to be atypical, requiring more than the flimsy literary narrative to securely identify these wars as slave wars; the interpretative tension caused by interpreting these wars as slave wars becomes even clearer if the two wars are recognised, as argued in this book, as intricately connected to the broader Sicilian context.

It might be objected at this point that it is mere semantics to insist that these events are not slave revolts on the basis that the insights emerging from the evidence left behind by the rebels themselves do not fit well with this perspective; after all, the literary sources are consistent in portraying those involved as rebellious slaves, and any alternative nomenclature can be less satisfyingly clear.[35] Yet, as argued above, calling these events slave revolts because our elite, slave-owning sources called them such presupposes a specific viewpoint about the wars and their participants that, in my opinion, sits uncomfortably in a modern, critical narrative. Perhaps most problematically, it implies that the principal unifying feature of the rebel forces was that they had been enslaved, despite the fact that the evidence that derives directly from the rebels may suggest otherwise. It also implies that individual slavery was the decisive point of departure for their actions. Instead, this book looks beyond the servile dimensions that are attributed to these rebellions in the ancient literary record and much modern scholarship to date. To look beyond the servile dimensions is not to suggest that individuals can only have agency when thought of as free people. Nor does the argument presented in this book seek to simplify the complexity of servile rebellion, or to minimise the impact of servile uprisings on the larger historical plane. What I suggest, rather, regarding the particular historical context under scrutiny is that we can understand more sensitively the agency of the rebels if we listen to them directly, for lack of a better word: what did the revolts mean to them and how did they identify themselves?

Aspects of this concern with the voice of the rebels have been outlined above for Chapters 4 and 5, and they will surface throughout this monograph. It is opportune to note at this junction that the issue of taking full account of the perspectives of enslaved people who take up arms against slave owners is a debated one in modern slavery studies. A good example is Barcia's study of uprisings by enslaved persons in Bahia and Cuba during the eighteenth and nineteenth centuries AD. Barcia noted that modern analyses of these respective instances have followed the terminology of the

---

[34] The problem with assuming similarities between the two events is explored with respect to how they were fought in Morton 2014.

[35] See, e.g., Rubinsohn's 1982, 443, suggestion of 'Events (or Disturbances, or Disorders) in Sicily, 104–100 B.C.' as an alternative title for the second of the wars. Alternative titles for the two events will be suggested in Chapters 2 and 3, but it must be emphasised that the nomenclature is less important than the methodology with which we study the wars.

'dominators' point of view' in using the terms 'slave revolt' or 'slave insurrection' to describe them.[36] For those enslaved Africans fighting against the plantation owners, these events, as Barcia has shown, were considered to be instances of war, with no connotations of specifically servile revolt or uprisings.[37] For this reason, Barcia proposed that when scholars approached these conflicts from the perspective of those enslaved Africans involved in the events, it would be better to use terms such as 'slave military revolt' or 'African military uprising'. Barcia argued that these terms would 'allow for a more critical assessment and understanding of what [these events] meant to those who organized them and carried them into practice'.[38] Similar approaches can be found in recent work on revolts in other parts of the modern world, notably the Caribbean, where the importance of finding the experience and voice of rebels and enslaved peoples and emphasising their agency has been critically explored not least by scholars such as Ferrer, Brown and Hanserd.[39] In agreement with the concerns outlined above, and with a similar intention to Barcia, Ferrer, Brown and Hanserd to understand these revolts on the terms of the rebels, I avoid referring to the rebellious forces as slaves throughout this study. Indeed, whatever the role played by individual slavery in the two Sicilian wars at the heart of this study – a role that we are likely never to appreciate fully – I hope to show that there is power and utility in understanding these events from the perspective of those in revolt, that is as expressions of Hellenistic Greek culture, albeit by a group marginalised in the surviving ancient literature, and history. I trust nonetheless that this study also makes a contribution to the study of slavery more broadly, despite its essentially agnostic take on the role of slavery in these two Sicilian revolts, for reasons that will become apparent as the argument progresses.

But I must also acknowledge some clear differences to the cited modern work in the present undertaking. These differences are necessicated by the quite different nature of the available evidence and the resulting images of the conflicts under scrutiny. Thus, as may be obvious by now, I am not concerned with choosing one particular term for the conflicts under discussion, such as war, revolt, rebellion or uprising. In effect, I use these and similar terms nearly interchangeably in what follows. That said, I refer specifically to the events primarily as wars when I discuss features that pertain to the wars themselves, that is the military exchanges between the rebels and Rome that followed the initial actions. Similarly, when talking about the bigger contexts, I primarily speak of revolts (rather than wars), given that the wars that ensued were but one part, if a seminal one, of the revolts themselves. These are distinctions, however, that are not critical for the thesis presented in this book. What *does* matter in the present undertaking, as stated, is a serious reconsideration concerning the application of the term 'slave' to the events under scrutiny. Logically, the term 'rebels'

---

[36] Barcia 2014, 103.
[37] Barcia 2014, esp. 100–5.
[38] Barcia 2014, 103–4, quotation at 104.
[39] Ferrer 2014; Hanserd 2019; Brown 2020. This book, written in large part long before the author read Barcia, Ferrer, Hanserd and Brown, is nonetheless intended to offer a contribution that responds to and speaks to their approaches: not to repeat their conclusions, but to build on the kind of work they have started and to thus (re)discover the world our ancient rebels sought to build.

is preferred with regard to those in revolt, in place of 'slave rebels'. This is a term that fits well with the historical context – the rejection of Roman power on the part of the revolts' protagonists – hence rebels vis-à-vis (and against) Rome. To underscore this wider dimension of the rebel actions, while taking account of the rebels' defeat, I draw in the title to this book on a term and imagery that moves the consequences of the two events on to the grand scheme of Roman history – where, as I explore further in the Conclusion to this book, the two events must be registered too: *Sicilia capta*. Moreover, to remove the slave label from the titles used to refer to these revolts, I will also introduce new terms by which these events are to be known – or at least their martial dimensions: the Romano-Sicilian Wars. As will be argued in the ensuing chapters, this is perhaps the most neutral manner by which to call the events, putting Rome and the Sicilian rebels on a par, at least by title.

What the following analysis thereby also brings to the table of slavery studies is the knotty question of the role played by a person's subjection to slavery in the interpretation of their actions. Crudely put, if an enemy of Rome were to be subjected to capture and enslavement, and then rebelled, are we to understand their actions solely within the confines of slavery, or on the broader plane that turned them against Rome in the first instance, prior to their enslavement? This is the kind of issue that Barcia dealt with in his work on Bahia and Cuba when arguing for the necessity to move beyond the interpretative labels used by those in power and to avoid repetition of the perspectives championed by slave-owner narratives.

In the case under scrutiny in the present work, and in keeping with the desire to move away, then, from the confines of the literary slave-owner narratives, the ensuing analysis begins with the best-preserved evidence from the rebels in either conflict: the coinage produced by the rebel kingdom in the revolt that began in 136 BC. The following chapter will argue that when these coins are viewed in the context of Sicilian numismatics of the second century BC, they are best understood as emphasising the Sicilian dimension of the uprising, rather than any servile connotations. Indeed, these coins express no servile ideology at all, but rather proclaim a state led by a cornerstone of Hellenistic politics: a monarch. Finally, we will see that the carefully chosen imagery on the coins implies that the rebels, whatever their undoubtedly diverse legal statuses before their revolt, aimed to rouse the people of Sicily in a united political venture as much as they sought to create solidarity among individuals of diverse backgrounds. This suggests, in turn, that this event was not, from the rebel perspective, a slave war, but something quintessentially different that reflected and was contingent on the support of certain parts of the Sicilian populace at large: it is in this broader context that the event must be appreciated first and foremost.

Part I:

The Wars in Sicily Reassessed

1

THE COINAGE OF KING ANTIOCHUS: THE WAR IN SICILY OF 136–132 BC THROUGH REBEL EYES

THE BEGINNING OF THE CONFLICT that broke out in Sicily in 136 BC is well known.[1] As noted on the foregoing pages, in Diodorus Siculus' narrative of the events, the fullest literary account that has survived to us from antiquity, the explosion of violence and resistance had its roots in the mistreatment of slaves near Enna by a pair of slave owners, Damophilus and Megallis. The ferocity of the response to how these two individuals treated those enslaved people under their control is recorded in a striking passage (34/5.2.14): in the midst of a show trial in the theatre of Enna, and midway through Damophilus' pleas for mercy, two rebels, Hermeias and Zeuxis, beheaded him. These two slave owners, Damophilus and Megallis, we are told, flogged their slaves without cause, arrogantly beat and dismissed those who came to them for clothing, and made their servile shepherds work without sufficient food or clothing (34/5.2.36–7). In this behaviour they mimicked the Italian landowners on Sicily, and the treatment of slaves more generally in the area (34/5.2.34–5). In contrast, their daughter, who had cared for the beaten slaves after her parents had finished with them, was spared from any violence and was escorted to relatives in Catana, away from the revolt (34/5.2.39). In other passages, the rebels' extreme violence against their masters is clearly attributed to anger at their masters' arrogance and mistreatment (34/5.2.24b and 40). The chief developments are striking too. In particular, led by their wonder-working leader, a fire-breathing slave from Syria named Eunus, the rebels seized first Enna, and then several other towns across the Sicilian east. In the midst of the revolt, in the heady moment that followed their victory at Enna, the rebels acclaimed their leader king (34/5.2.14). While one Diodoran passage suggests that the revolt took place unexpectedly (34/5.2.25), the overall effect of the narrative is to suggest that the arrogance and insolence of slave owners across Sicily received the reaction one should expect: violence and resistance.[2]

Diodorus' narrative, and the shorter versions of the story preserved in Florus, the *Periochae* of Livy and other texts, underpin the majority of analyses of this war. These

---

[1] For a comprehensive overview of Diodorus Siculus' narrative in the context of ancient slavery studies, see Bradley 1989, 46–65, which is the fullest in recent scholarship; see also the relevant comments on Bradley's contribution in the Introduction. See further Green 1961; Vogt 1965, 29–30 and 41–3; Urbainczyk 2008a; Angius 2020.
[2] I have argued elsewhere that Diodorus' account of this Sicilian war is best read as a piece of social commentary, with a particular focus on the role of arrogance (ὑπερηφανία), kindness (φιλανθρωπία) and fairness (ἐπιείκεια) in the social interactions. For this, see Morton 2018.

narratives, as the Introduction has laid out, present numerous problems if we want to understand from more than a single point of view what this conflict was about. First, these texts are focused on the moment of revolt, and offer almost no information for the years of conflict that followed the initial decision to revolt. We are well informed about the violence that precedes these wars, as the ancient literary sources understood it, but are comparatively poorly informed about the years that the rebels spent defining their movement after they had first revolted. Moreover, Photius and the excerpters working under Constantine Porphyrogenitus, the writers who preserved Diodorus' text for books 34 and 35 of his *Bibliotheke*, show great interest in the leader of the revolt, Eunus.[3] This larger-than-life figure dominates the extant portions of Diodorus' text, as well as the narrative preserved by Florus. Finally, Diodorus Siculus, Livy, Florus, Orosius and Valerius Maximus were all writing within their own historiographical traditions. The historiographical complexities of these texts, in particular the role of Eunus in the literary narratives for this war, will be the focus of Chapter 2, but it is important to reemphasise here that these texts must be read with their rhetorical and historiographical contexts in mind.

Second, as I argued in the Introduction, these literary texts are all slave-owner narratives written after the event. While they provide important factual information about certain aspects of the war, they describe and understand the war from the perspective of the slave owners after the conflict was settled: that is, at a safe distance. In this respect they are useful, but limited. If we want to go beyond retelling these stories as the slave owners understood them and try instead to appreciate these events outside this particular lens, and especially in a contemporary perspective, we must look for other evidence; where such other evidence is missing, we must accept that our own narratives will be incomplete and distorted.

Yet, with this war we have an almost unparalleled opportunity to assess what the rebels sought to do once they had survived the initial revolt at Enna. As will be explored in greater detail in Chapter 5, slave revolts rarely last more than a few days, and almost never several years. The rebels in this war fought actively across south-eastern Sicily and sought to control access routes into this area (Map 1.1).[4] This fact alone suggests that the revolt was atypical of slave revolts. More crucially, it is in this period of active campaigning across the south-east that we are able to study the rebels through extant evidence that derives directly from their kingdom: their coinage. The opportunity afforded by these coins to assess an event of this kind from the perspective of the rebels is almost unique: this evidence will allow us to contextualise the rebel actions on the basis of evidence produced by *them*.[5]

In this chapter, therefore, we will focus our attention on these coins. The aim is to investigate how these rebels presented themselves outwardly and on their own terms

---

[3] On the Byzantine preservation of Diodorus Siculus' text in these books, see Dumont 1987, 202; Goukowsky 2014, 43–5; Pfuntner 2015, 266–7.

[4] For a full discussion of the geographical extent of this war, and the strategic concerns connected to this, see Morton 2014, 25–9.

[5] The only comparable examples of which I am aware are the texts and literature produced by the leaders of the Aponte conspiracy and the Haitian Revolution: Ferrer 2014, 271–328; Jenson 2011; and Chapter 5 below.

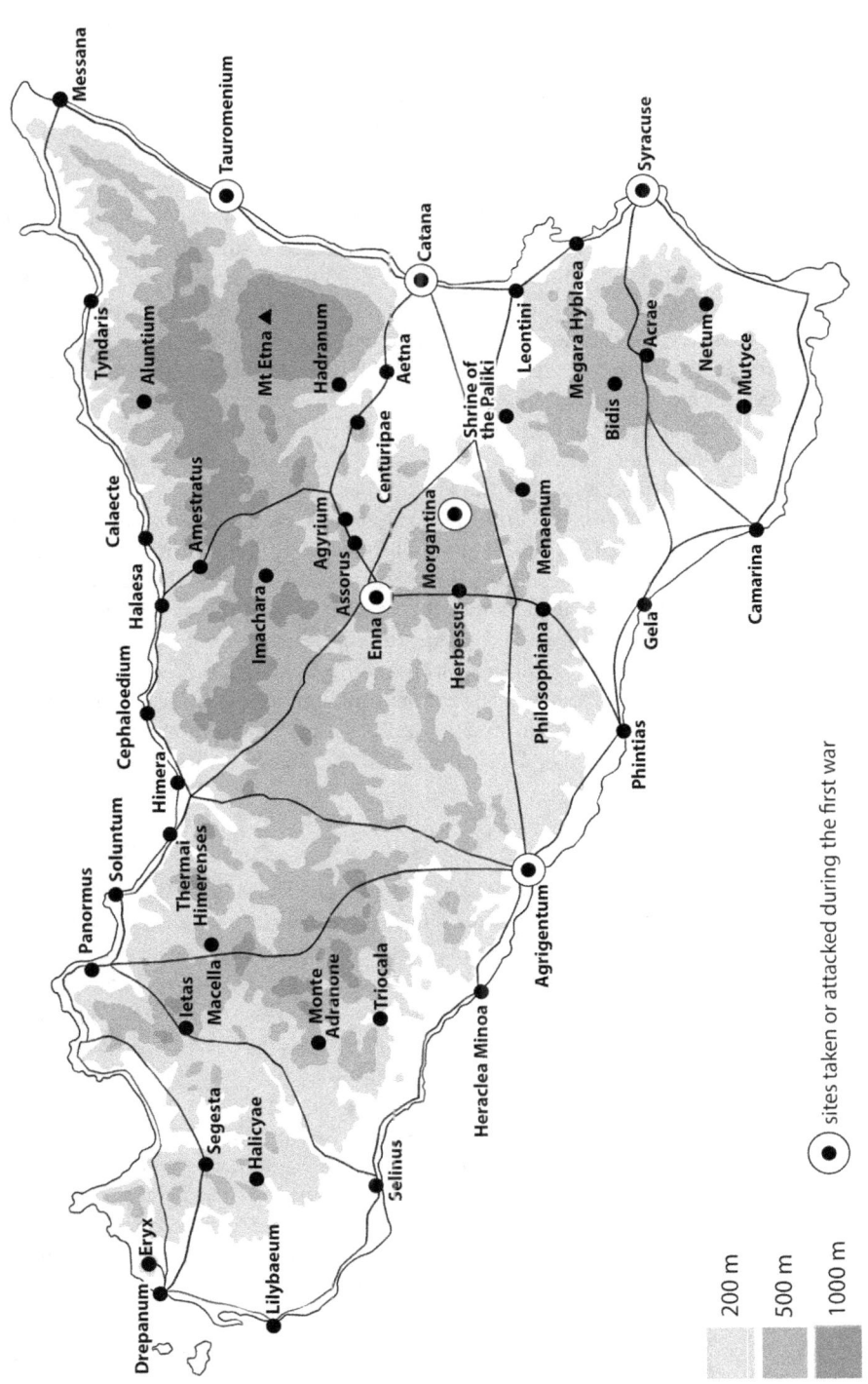

Map 1.1 Sites taken or attacked during the first war. © Frances Morton.

through this medium. This evidence will allow us to understand not only who the rebels claimed to be, but also how they sought to integrate themselves into Sicily's political, social and cultural landscape. In order to avoid repeating the slave-owner narratives of the rebel movement offered in ancient historiography, the following analysis of this coinage will avoid drawing on the literary sources for the conflict as far as possible. Instead, the coinage will be read in its most immediate context: the numismatic culture of Hellenistic Sicily. The analysis will be broken down into three sections. In the first section, I will first present the four surviving issues of coins produced by the rebels, totalling nineteen coins. This presentation will cover the provenance, history and iconography of the coinage as systematically as possible, in order to contextualise fully the discussion that will follow. While the influence of Seleucid monarchical practice will be acknowledged for the coins, given the Syrian origin of the monarch and his choice of royal name, contextualising the coins in especially Sicilian numismatics will show that the coins drew on iconography typical of south-eastern Sicily and presented the rebels not as slaves, but as free members of a Hellenistic state that had close cultural ties to south-eastern Sicily. The second section will assess how we should understand the purpose of the coinage in relation to the population of south-eastern Sicily. Here it will be argued that the limited evidence we have for the rebels' behaviour towards the free population of Sicily that fell under their control during the war suggests that the rebels appealed to the free population of Sicily not only via their coinage and a (purported) shared cultural heritage, but also through their actions. Finally, I will suggest that some aspects of Rome's actions after the conflict show that the rebel claims had made some impact on the island. From the rebel perspective, as we will see, this was not a slave revolt, but a movement that was contingent on free support and concerned with Sicilian society more broadly.

The Coins

The coins in question are underwhelming on first sight. As already stated, there are only nineteen coins in total, all in bronze, and they are badly worn in every case.[6] The small number and poor quality of the coins, it must be admitted, makes them a limited basis from which to judge a group. Nonetheless, these nineteen pieces of bronze are the sole surviving evidence for the identity and culture that was claimed by the rebels after their success at Enna. They remain understudied in comparison to the comparatively fuller literary evidence for the revolt, and they are relegated in many cases to the footnotes of the monographs and articles whose stated purpose is to understand and explain the very group from which these coins arose. Despite this, some aspects of the rebel movement can be discerned from the coinage, albeit without precision in every case. The most telling feature of the coins is that each one bears a legend proclaiming the name of a monarch, the man who was the leader of the revolt: King Antiochus (see also Diod. Sic. 34/5.2.24). This feature and their shared provenance from Sicily itself connect these coins to the conflict in question.

[6] Two gold coins have been attributed to the rebels in this conflict, but the attribution is uncertain, and the coins are probably forgeries. For a full discussion see Appendix 1: The ΦΙΛΙΠΗΙΟΝ Gold Coinage.

The Coins: Provenance

A useful starting place for our discussion of these coins concerns their provenance. Absolute precision is impossible owing to the fact that only two of the nineteen coins under consideration here are held in public collections, while the majority are kept in private collections in Sicily. Table 1.1 gives an outline of the origins recorded for each collection mentioned here.[7]

Table 1.1 Provenance of the coinage of the First Romano-Sicilian War.

Collection	No. of coins	Origin of collection	Citation
British Museum	1	Sicily and islands	Robinson 1920, 175
Cammarata	12	Piazza Armerina, Sicily	Manganaro 1982, 239
Bruno	2	Enna, Sicily	Manganaro 1990, 418
Pennisi	1	Acireale, Sicily	De Agostino 1939, 85–6
Vagliasindi	1	Randazzo, Sicily	Manganaro 1990, 418
Vetri	1	Enna, Sicily	De Agostino 1939, 85–6

In sum, eighteen of the coins are from collections that have their origins in Sicily. The sole coin without any origin is example one of Issue 2, which was advertised in a Classical Numismatics Group auction catalogue. Following the reports of the private collections' origins, the seventeen coins (89 per cent of the total) from those collections were found in the east of Sicily, in the area from around Enna and Piazza Armerina up to Acireale. If the Cammarata collection was formed from finds in the area around Piazza Armerina, as Manganaro suggests, this accounts for twelve of the nineteen coins (63 per cent of the total). We can tentatively suggest, therefore, that these coins represent the output of a group located in Sicily, with a focus that

[7] I have undertaken direct autopsy of the coin held in the British Museum and examined a cast of the coin held in the Museo archeologico regionale Paolo Orsi di Siracusa. These two coins are both examples of Issue 4. I am reliant in many cases on the opinions of and information reported by a small number of scholars for the claimed provenance of the coins, esp. Robinson 1920, 175; De Agostino 1939, 85–6; Manganaro 1982 and 1990a. Robinson 1920, 175, notes that the coin held in the British Museum (example two of Issue 4) was most likely Sicilian for reasons of its 'style . . . the epigraphy with its round sigma, and the fabric, which lacks the characteristic bevelled edge of Syria'. He argued that as the coin was bought in a collection that was entirely from Lipari or Sicily, it was 'humanly speaking, certain that this coin also was found in the Western Mediterranean'. Twelve coins are held in the collection of Vincenzo Cammarata, a resident of Piazza Armerina in Sicily. This collection includes at least one example of each coin type. Manganaro 1982, 239, has claimed that this collection was formed and composed 'supera l'area locale'. Two coins are held in the collection of Bruno, which Manganaro 1990a, 418, described as 'una vecchia collezione formata dallo zio Restivo Navarra a Enna'. The single coin from the collection of Pennisi was recorded by De Agostino 1939, 85–6, as 'nella Collezione Pennisi di Floristella ad Acireale'. Manganaro 1990a, 418, commented that he measured the example from the collection of Vagliasindi 'molti anni fa a Randazzo', a town just north of Mt Etna in Sicily. Finally, the coin held in the Museo archeologico regionale Paolo Orsi di Siracusa came, according to De Agostino 1939, 85–6, 'dalle Collezione del farmacista Vetri di Enna'.

appears to be in the south-east of the island. We should look to this area for precedence with regard to imagery. To this end, we can now turn to the coins themselves. The brief catalogue below follows the outline given by Campana, who offers the closest correspondence to the private collection of Enzo Cammarata, which holds the majority of the examples under discussion.[8]

Before turning to the catalogue, an important admission on the practicalities of studying the four issues under discussion is necessary. As I noted above, only two coins from Issue 4 are held in public collections and accessible for study. The catalogue that follows is, regrettably, offered without illustration with the exception of Issue 4 (Figure 1.12).[9] Given the lack of access to the coins held in private collections, most publications on the conflict under scrutiny are able to include an image only for Issue 4, and – at best – to visualise the imagery through comparison with other coinages, as will also be done here.[10] The description of the four issues is based upon the testimony of Manganaro and Campana, both of whom were able to gain access to Cammarata's collection, alongside my own autopsy of the copy of Issue 4 in the British Museum and the images provided by Vincenzo Cammarata on CD.[11]

Issue 1 – One example (Campana, Enna 11)
Obv: Male head right, bearded and diademed: Zeus(?) or Antiochus(?).
Rev: Winged thunderbolt(?); BACIΛEΩC upwards at left, ANTIO downwards at right.
1)   10.50 g[12] = Cammarata 1 = Calciati 9 = Manganaro 1990a, pl. 85 fig. 5

This issue exists in only a single example from the collection of Cammarata, weighing 10.50 g.[13] The legend on the reverse reads BACIΛEΩC ANTIO, indicating a regal coinage. The obverse features a bearded and diademed male head, facing right. The reverse is very hard to read from the images available but is agreed by those who have conducted a physical autopsy to feature a winged thunderbolt.[14] This would indicate that the obverse head is Zeus, exactly as on coins from Centuripae (Figure 1.1). Yet, the presence of the legend suggests that the head can instead be read as that of the

---

[8] Campana 1997, 155–7. The catalogue given here also draws in a limited amount of supplementary material from Manganaro 1990a, 418, who records additional examples of Issue 2 and Issue 3 held in the private collections of Bruno and Vagliasindi. In places, Manganaro's record of the coinage held by Cammarata does not correspond with the records of either Campana or Cammarata. The catalogue below attempts to match Manganaro's examples from Cammarata's collection to those recorded by Campana for the same collection, marking uncertain matches with a question mark.

[9] I have corresponded with Vincenzo Cammarata, whose collection is the only one to feature examples for all four issues, and have received a CD of high-quality images of each coin in his collection, for study. I have not received permission to publish these images. The other published images of these coins, in Cammarata, Campana and Manganaro, are of poor quality. See Cammarata 1987; Campana 1997; Manganaro 1982; 1983; 1990a.

[10] See, e.g., Finley 1979, pl. 8b.

[11] Manganaro 1982; 1983; 1990a; and Campana 1997, with the comments in n. 8 above.

[12] Both Cammarata 1987, 33, and Manganaro 1990a, 418, record the weight for this coin as 10.50 g. Campana 1997, 155, gives the weight as 10.05 g.

[13] Another example was published by Minì 1977, 186 n. 481, with a weight of 5.25 g. However, both Manganaro 1990a, 418, and Campana 1997, 155, have argued that the coin is too corroded to allow the identification to be certain.

[14] See, e.g., Calciati 1987, 237; Manganaro 1990a, 418; Campana 1997, 155.

Figure 1.1 Coin of Centuripae, c. 241–150 BC; Zeus on obverse with winged thunderbolt on reverse. Courtesy of the American Numismatic Society.

Figure 1.2 Coin of Syracuse, c. 230–216 BC; Gelon on obverse with winged thunderbolt on reverse. Courtesy of the American Numismatic Society.

Figure 1.3 Coin of Syracuse, 215–214 BC; Hieronymus on obverse with winged thunderbolt on reverse. Courtesy of the American Numismatic Society.

Figure 1.4 Coin of Demetrius I Soter, c. 162–150 BC; Demetrius on obverse with quiver on reverse. Courtesy of the American Numismatic Society.

monarch named on the coins, Antiochus, as Lorber has proposed.[15] It was a particular affectation among Hellenistic kings to place their own head on the obverse of Zeus/Thunderbolt coins, as we find also in Sicily.[16]

Issue 2 – Eleven examples (Campana, Enna 12)
Obv: Male head right, bearded and diademed: Herakles(?) or Antiochus(?).
Rev: a) Quiver(?); ΒΑCΙΛΕΩC upwards at left, ΑΝΤΙΟΧΟΥ downwards at right.
      b) Quiver(?); ΒΑΣΙΛΕΩ upwards at left, ΑΝΤΙ downwards at right.
Var. a) 1) 10.00 g = CNG 37/1996, 98
        2) 7.40 g = Cammarata 2 = Manganaro 1990a, pl. 87 fig. 2(?)
        3) 7.60 g = Cammarata 2a = Manganaro 1990a, pl. 87 fig. 4(?)
        4) 7.35 g = Cammarata 2b = Calciati 10
        5) 4.80 g = Cammarata 2c = Manganaro 1990a, pl. 87 fig. 5
        6) No recorded weight = Collection Bruno = Manganaro 1990a, pl. 88 fig. 1
        7) No recorded weight = Collection Bruno = Manganaro 1990a, pl. 88 fig. 2
Var. b) 8) 5.40 g = Cammarata 4 = Manganaro 1990a, pl. 87 fig. 3(?)
        9) 4.70 g = Cammarata 4a
       10) 5.00 g = Cammarata 4b = Manganaro 1990a, pl. 87 fig. 8(?)
       11) 3.75 g = Cammarata 4c

The second issue survives in two different varieties. The first variety, of which seven survive, has the legend ΒΑCΙΛΕΩC ΑΝΤΙΟΧΟΥ, and ranges in weight from 4.80–10.00 g. The second variety, of which four survive, has the same legend, but with a non-lunate sigma: ΒΑΣΙΛΕΩ ΑΝΤΙ. This variety has a tighter weight range, from 3.75–5.40 g. The coins are principally from two collections (Cammarata and Bruno). Cammarata thought that there were two different types, one featuring a lit torch on the reverse, the other a quiver, but Campana argued that there is a single type in different styles.[17] Manganaro has variously identified the image as a club, as a bunch of grapes, and most recently as a quiver with a cap and swollen base.[18] The latter is the most probable, as Manganaro's comparison with other quivers on coins of Demetrius I Soter and a coin from Halaesa dateable to after 211 BC has shown (Figures 1.4 and 1.5 respectively). The latter coin features Artemis on the obverse. Artemis is not a rare type in Sicilian numismatics. Coins from Halaesa, Syracuse and Morgantina (Hispanorum) all feature Artemis on coins dating from after 210 BC (Figures 1.5 and 1.6 respectively).[19] This leaves a puzzling obverse. The absence of a club alongside the quiver would appear to

---

[15] Lorber 1994, 2.
[16] Fleischer 1996, 38, described this phenomenon among Hellenistic kings as one of a number of aspects of their repertoire of imagery on coinage, and he called this aspect 'affinity to gods'. Divine patrons were a well-established motif of justifying claims to kingship; see Lund 1992, 162. For this practice in Sicily, see coinage from Hieron II featuring the head of his son Gelon on the obverse of similar coins, and the coinage of Hieronymus (Figures 1.2 and 1.3 respectively).
[17] Cammarata 1987, 33; Campana 1997, 156.
[18] See respectively Manganaro 1982, 237; 1983, 405; and 1990a, 418.
[19] Halaesa after 211 BC: SNG ANS 3 1191; Syracuse after 212 BC: SNG ANS 5 1104; Morgantina (Hispanorum) c. 150–50 BC: SNG ANS 4 481.

Figure 1.5 Coin of Halaesa, after 241 BC; Artemis on obverse with quiver on reverse. Courtesy of the American Numismatic Society.

Figure 1.6 Coin of Syracuse, after 212 BC; Artemis on obverse with Apollo standing on reverse. Courtesy of the American Numismatic Society.

indicate that the quiver is to be linked to Artemis, not Herakles (see Figures 1.7–1.10), yet the obverse design features a male head. Manganaro's solution was that the types on these coins were paired with those of Issue 3.[20] This would make the obverse on these coins Herakles, paired with a club on Issue 3, and Ares on the obverse of Issue 3 with the reverse quiver on Issue 2. There is no precedent in Sicilian numismatics for Ares combined with a quiver. Moreover, this interpretation requires, I think, too complex an interrelationship between the two issues, and can therefore be dismissed. In terms of Sicilian numismatics, the quiver is an intelligible design clearly linked to Artemis, and we do not need to link the type to the obverse of another issue of coins. The problem of the obverse head remains. While the head could be that of Herakles, he is almost always shown wearing a lion's skin on Sicilian coins.[21] Campana has noted that the head is similar to that on the obverse of Issue 1, even allowing for the poor quality of the coins.[22] It is possible that this coin also features its monarch on the obverse. This

---

[20] Manganaro 1990a, 418–19.
[21] A minority show him wearing a *tainia*, which looks very much like a diadem. For Herakles wearing a lion's skin: Aluntium (*SNG ANS 3* 1193), Cephaloedium (*SNG ANS 3* 1332), Thermae (*SNG ANS 4* 190), Menaenum (*SNG ANS 4* 288), Messana (*SNG ANS 4* 396), Mamertini (*SNG ANS 4* 417), Panormus (*SNG ANS 4* 605), Selinus (*SNG ANS 4* 716), Solus (*SNG ANS 4* 735). For Herakles wearing a *tainia*: Agyrium (*SNG ANS 3* 1167), Centuripae (*SNG ANS 3* 1327), Syracuse (*SNG ANS 5* 732), Tauromenium (*SNG ANS 5* 1133).
[22] Campana 1997, 155–6.

Figure 1.7 Coin of Agyrium, c. 345–300 BC; helmeted head on obverse with club on reverse. Courtesy of the American Numismatic Society.

Figure 1.8 Coin of Aluntium, c. 212–150 BC; Herakles on obverse with club and quiver on reverse. Courtesy of the American Numismatic Society.

affectation would fit with Hellenistic monarchical coinage, as discussed above, but cannot be proven.

Issue 3 – Four examples (Campana, Enna 13)
Obv: Head right, helmeted: Athena(?).
Rev: Club(?); BACIΛEƱC ANTI upwards at left and curling round the coin.
1)   5.70 g = Cammarata 3[23]
2)   2.60 g = Cammarata 3a = Manganaro 1990a, pl. 88 fig. 3
3)   No weight recorded = Collection Pennisi = Campana 1997, 157
4)   No weight recorded = Collection Vagliasindi = Manganaro 1990a, pl. 88 fig. 4

Four examples survive of this coin type, from three different private collections in Sicily: Cammarata, Pennisi and Vagliasindi. Only two are recorded with weights: 5.70 and 2.60 g. The coins feature the legend BACIΛEƱC ANTI curving around the top of the reverse side, with an upside down Ω in the word BACIΛEƱC. Campana suggests that the obverse head is Ares because of the helmeted design, while he suggests that the club invokes Herakles; but coupling Herakles with Ares on a Sicilian

---

[23] Campana 1997, 157, notes that this coin, which is held in the Museo Alessi di Enna, was re-struck over a bronze of Tauromenium, with the head of Apollo on the obverse and a tripod on the reverse, dated to the second century BC. For this type, see Calciati III, 219–21, nos 21 or 25. If this is the case, this gives a *terminus ante quem* for the production of at least some Tauromenitan coinage in the second century BC.

coin would be unprecedented.[24] The club is almost certainly a reference to Herakles, with a strong precedence from several examples of coinage from Aluntium, Caleacte, Centuripae, Cephaloedium and Menaenum (Figures 1.8–1.11).[25] The obverse remains a difficult image to identify. The head may be that of Athena rather than Ares, given the goddess' links in mythology to Herakles. Herakles' importance to Sicily, especially to eastern Sicily, is an intelligible reason for the choice of the imagery. Florenzano has argued that Athena represented part of the nucleus of deities typical of Hellenistic monarchy.[26] The use of Athena fits the mould of Hellenistic monarchical coinage, alongside the legend on the coin, but this identification remains tentative at best.

<u>Issue 4 – Three examples (Campana, Enna 14 – Figure 1.12)</u>
Obv: Head of Demeter right, veiled.
Rev: Ear of barley; BACI upwards at left, ANTI downwards at right.
1) 3.65 g = Cammarata 5 = Calciati 11 = Manganaro 1990a, pl. 86 fig. 5(?)
2) 3.43 g = London, *BM* = Manganaro 1990a, pl. 86 fig. 3
3) 2.70 g = Syracuse, *Museo archeologico regionale* = Manganaro 1990a, pl. 86 fig. 4

Figure 1.9 Coin of Centuripae, *c.* 212–150 BC; Herakles on obverse with club on reverse. Courtesy of the American Numismatic Society.

Figure 1.10 Coin of Cephaloedium, *c.* 241–210 BC; Herakles on obverse with club on reverse. Courtesy of the American Numismatic Society.

---

[24] Campana 1997, 156–7. Agyrium may offer a much earlier precedent (Figure 1.7: 345–300 BC), but the coin is so worn that the head could be Athena.
[25] Aluntium *c.* 212–150 BC: Calciati I, 68–9, nos. 9–10, *SNG ANS 3* 1193; Caleacte *c.* 241–150 BC: Calciati I, 130, no. 5, *SNG Cop.* 157; Centuripae *c.* 212–150 BC: Calciati III, 176, no. 9; Cephaloedium *c.* 241–210 BC: Calciati I, 373–4, no 10; Menaenum after 211 BC: *SNG ANS 4* 288–9.
[26] Florenzano 2005, 27.

Figure 1.11 Coin of Menaenum, after 210 BC; Herakles on obverse with club on reverse. Courtesy of the American Numismatic Society.

Figure 1.12 Coin of King Antiochus/Eunus, c. 136–132 BC; veiled head of Demeter on obverse with an ear of barley on reverse. Courtesy of the British Museum.

The final type has three surviving specimens, with a weight range of 2.70–3.65 g. Once again, the legend reads BACI ANTI. In contrast to the other coins of this *Basileus Antiochus*, there has never been any debate about the imagery of these coins. The image of Demeter associated with grain is present on coins of Centuripae, Hybla Magna and Leontini into the second century BC (Figures 1.13 and 1.14),[27] and so the reverse image of this coin would suggest very strongly that the identification of Demeter on the obverse is safe.[28]

Despite the many uncertainties, taken altogether these coins possess a number of elements that make clear the monarchical aspect of the coinage under discussion here. First, the uniting feature of these issues is the legend, which represents a claim to a kingdom under the leadership of a *Basileus Antiochus*. Second, the collective imagery supports this reading of the coins. Regardless of the identity of the obverse heads on Issue 1 and Issue 2, which I have argued could both depict the monarch of the legend, the coins combine iconography representative of Zeus, either Apollo or Artemis,

---

[27] Centuripae c. 212–150 BC: Calciati III, 175–6, nos 7–8, *SNG Morcom* 569–71; Hybla Magna after 210 BC: Calciati III, 41, no. 2; Leontini after 210 BC: Calciati III, 81, no. 9.

[28] A similar coin type from Enna was minted at some point after 340 BC, which also has a head of Demeter on the obverse and an ear of barley on the reverse: see Robinson 1920, 175–6; Verbrugghe 1974, 53.

Figure 1.13 Coin of Centuripae, c. 212–150 BC; Demeter on obverse with plough on reverse. Courtesy of the American Numismatic Society.

Figure 1.14 Coin of Leontini, after 210 BC; Demeter on obverse with bushel of corn on reverse. Courtesy of the American Numismatic Society.

Figure 1.15 Coin of Catana, third–second century BC; Apollo on obverse with Isis on reverse. Courtesy of the American Numismatic Society.

Figure 1.16 Coin of Mamertines, third–second century BC; Zeus on obverse with advancing warrior on reverse. Courtesy of the American Numismatic Society.

Herakles, Ares or Athena, and Demeter, the nucleus of deities associated with Hellenistic monarchs. Whatever else the iconography and legend indicate, therefore, the best framework to assess the manner of presentation and function of these coins is that of Hellenistic kingship.

The catalogue given in this section offers a starting point for questioning the purpose of these coins and what they can tell us about how the rebels producing these coins viewed what they were doing. A first step in this investigation is to outline the numismatic context in which these coins would have circulated. This can be best expressed as a simple question: what other coins would the four issues presented above have circulated alongside?

Coin Circulation in Sicily

The study of coin circulation in Sicily in the second century BC is fraught with problems. The island experienced in the period after 210 BC a flourishing of localised bronze coinage featuring city ethnics. Until recently, the chief problem with the study of these civic coinages was that it was not clear when they were produced except that they arose after Rome's defeat of Syracuse in the Second Punic War. For this reason, in many catalogues they are dated 'after 210 BC'. The situation regarding the dating of these civic coinages is now much clearer for the west of the island at least. Frey-Kupper has shown that they date to the period after 130 BC.[29] Frey-Kupper's detailed analysis of coin finds at the site of Ietas in the west of the island has allowed her to clarify the relative and absolute chronologies for the coinage in Sicily after the Second Punic War. Nonetheless, her study focused for the most part on the west of the island due to the lack of detailed information on stratigraphic evidence from the east.[30] It is reasonable to suppose that the eastern coinages are also to be dated to after 130 BC in many cases. This has been suggested by Frey-Kupper based on her analysis of coin finds in Ietas and has been argued separately for the HISPANORUM coinage from Morgantina.[31] Nonetheless, this cannot be proven absolutely for the rest of eastern Sicilian coinage as the evidence stands. It is hard to give greater precision to the chronology of these coinages, and refining the chronology is in any case beyond the scope of this monograph.

The following section, therefore, offers a tentative reconstruction of the circulation of bronze coinage in Sicily that is focused on the period from the Roman takeover of the Kingdom of Syracuse, roughly 211 BC, until the beginning of Sextus Pompeius' dominion over Sicily, in order to provide a context for the analysis of the coinage under discussion here. The reconstruction of circulation offered below is

---

[29] Frey-Kupper 2013, 16–25, 184–271, 294–5, and 350–1.
[30] The circulation of coinage in Archaic, Classical and early Hellenistic Sicily has been studied in considerable detail, not least in Puglisi 2009 and Frey-Kupper 2013. For further bibliography, see the extensive list of works in the bibliographies provided by Puglisi and Frey-Kupper. On the period following the Second Punic War see now Frey-Kupper 2013; Holloway 1960 and 1965; Frey-Kupper 1992 and 1993; Puglisi 2009; Manganaro 2012.
[31] See Frey-Kupper 2013, 294–6; Buttrey et al. 1989, 38–9.

based on two sets of data: the coin deposits for Morgantina in the east of the island and Ietas in the west, derived from Buttrey, Erim, Groves and Holloway and Frey-Kupper respectively.[32] In addition, supplementary data has been drawn from the Ietas excavation reports.[33] These two sites have been chosen for two reasons. First, they are the most fully reported excavations in terms of numismatic material on the island and therefore offer statistically significant bodies of evidence to study. Second, the two sites are from geographically distinct areas of Sicily, sitting opposite one another in the south-east and north-west of the island (Map 1.1). The analysis of these two sites is not intended to offer an exhaustive picture of coin circulation within Sicily, but to show that its cities had their own localised circulation of coinage that nonetheless matched wider patterns across the island as a whole. If similar analyses were conducted of other sites, similar results would be produced, and indeed have been produced.[34]

The discussion is accompanied by tables that offer a breakdown of the coin finds of both sites. Each table includes: the general geographic region of the entry; the specific town or people to which the coins belong; the total number found; the metal used for the coins; and the catalogue number for the coins recorded in Buttrey, Erim, Groves and Holloway and Frey-Kupper for Morgantina and Ietas respectively. The catalogue numbers are given in **bold**. The number of coins corresponding to each catalogue number or series of catalogue numbers is given in brackets afterwards in any case where the catalogue number is not recording a single coin or inclusive of every coin in the entry.

Coin Circulation: Morgantina

Morgantina was situated on the Serra Orlando ridge, north-east of modern Aidone. During the excavations of the city from the 1950s over four thousand individual coins have been found that date from the period after the Second Punic War, outlined in Table 1.2. These finds provide an excellent opportunity to gain an insight into the circulation of coinage in a specific, regional context – eastern Sicily, Morgantina specifically. When they are analysed as a collection, it is remarkable that out of the 3,999 recorded bronze coins, 3,301 (83 per cent) come from just five mints, as we can see in Table 1.3.

Four of the five mints are in the east of Sicily, and Messana is far from the open plains of south-eastern Sicily that the other sites cluster around. We can study this collection of coinage in greater detail in two ways. First, we can consider the coinage as a whole. When viewed in this way, the eastern coinages from the area around the plains south of Mt Etna make up the majority of the finds there. Only 1,112 coins come from other sites, or 28 per cent. Overwhelmingly, as it appears from this data,

---

[32] Buttrey et al. 1989; Frey-Kupper 2013.
[33] Reusser et al. 2010; Reusser et al. 2011; Reusser et al. 2012; Reusser et al. 2013.
[34] Frey-Kupper 2013, 320–7, analysed the coin finds from Ietas, Soluntum, Entella, Segesta, Halaesa, Morgantina and Camarina, that cover the dates 220/210 BC–AD 40/50. She found that these sites all show a similar pattern of coin ratios between their own coins, the major regional coinages and supraregional coinages such as those from Rome. See also below at p. 40 for further discussion.

Table 1.2 Morgantina coin finds.

Country	Town	No.	Metal	Catalogue Nos (no. of each)
Outside Sicily/Italy	N/A	12	11 AE + 1 AR	2, 3(3), 5, 464, 465, 475, 477, 481, 484, 485
Italy	Bruttium – Rhegium	123	AE	57–64
Italy	Other	2	AE	26, 32
Italy	Rome	324	AE	527–8(10), 531, 533–41(11), 543(2), 545–60(31), 562(2), 564, 566–70(6), 572(2), 574(2), 576(3), 578–81(7), 584(2), 586–90(220), 594, 599–600(2), 625–6(20), 628
Italy	Rome	150	AR + AU	529–30(3), 532, 542, 544, 561, 563, 565, 571, 573, 575, 577, 582–3(2), 585, 591–3(5), 595–8(5), 601–24(35), 627, 629–90(88)
Sicily	Aetna	233	AE	68–9
Sicily	Agrigentum	19	AE	87–90
Sicily	Agyrium	1	AE	95
Sicily	Aluntium	11	AE	107–11
Sicily	Amestratus	2	AE	112
Sicily	Caleacte	9	AE	113–16
Sicily	Catana	1,212	AE	130–45
Sicily	Centuripae	57	AE	146–50
Sicily	Cephaloedium	1	AE	153
Sicily	Cossura	3	AE	453–5
Sicily	Enna	11	AE	159–61
Sicily	Gaulos	3	AE	456
Sicily	Gela	5	AE	179–81
Sicily	Halaesa	19	AE	99–105
Sicily	Hispanorum	706	AE	249–57
Sicily	Ietas	1	AE	191
Sicily	Leontini	29	AE	197–205
Sicily	Lilybaeum	7	AE	206–7
Sicily	Menaenum	36	AE	209–14

Country	Town	No.	Metal	Catalogue Nos (no. of each)
Sicily	Messana	548	AE	**225–42**
Sicily	Panormus (including Romano-Sicilian)	12	AE	**264–72**
Sicily	Soluntum	1	AE	**290**
Sicily	Syracuse	511	AE	**376–99**
Sicily	Tauromenium	86	AE	**414–26**
Sicily	Thermai	2	AE	**189–90**
Uncertain	N/A	14	AE	
	Total bronze	3,999		
	Total	4,150		

Table 1.3 Percentages of main mints in Morgantina.

Catana	1,212 coins	30%
Hispanorum	706 coins	18%
Mamertini	548 coins	14%
Syracuse	511 coins	13%
Rome	324 coins	8%

western Sicilian coinages did not circulate in any significant numbers into the area around Morgantina; nor did northern coinages – Messana apart.[35] Catana and Syracuse alone account for 1,723 (43 per cent) of all the bronze coins found in Morgantina. Morgantina appears to have a largely south-eastern circulation, with only a quarter of the coins found there coming from places beyond the plains of the south-east. Map 1.2 visualises this information: the arrows in black indicate sites contributing more than 5 per cent of the coinage to Morgantina, and the arrows in grey indicate sites contributing more than 1 per cent of the coinage.

The second approach is to look in greater detail at the south-eastern coinages. Of the 2,887 coins found in Morgantina from the south-east, 2,662 (92 per cent of the 2887) come from just Catana, Syracuse, Morgantina itself and Aetna. We can conclude from this that despite the proliferation of small-scale bronze issues in Sicily throughout the period following the Second Punic War, they did not significantly challenge the dominance of the major mints in the south-east of the island. Moreover, the high number of Morgantina's Hispanorum coins found there should not over-inflate their importance to the south-eastern context as a whole, as the vast

---

[35] Even the northern and western coinages are dominated by four sites: of the 638 coins from these regions, 598 come from just Panormus, Agrigentum, Halaesa and Messana.

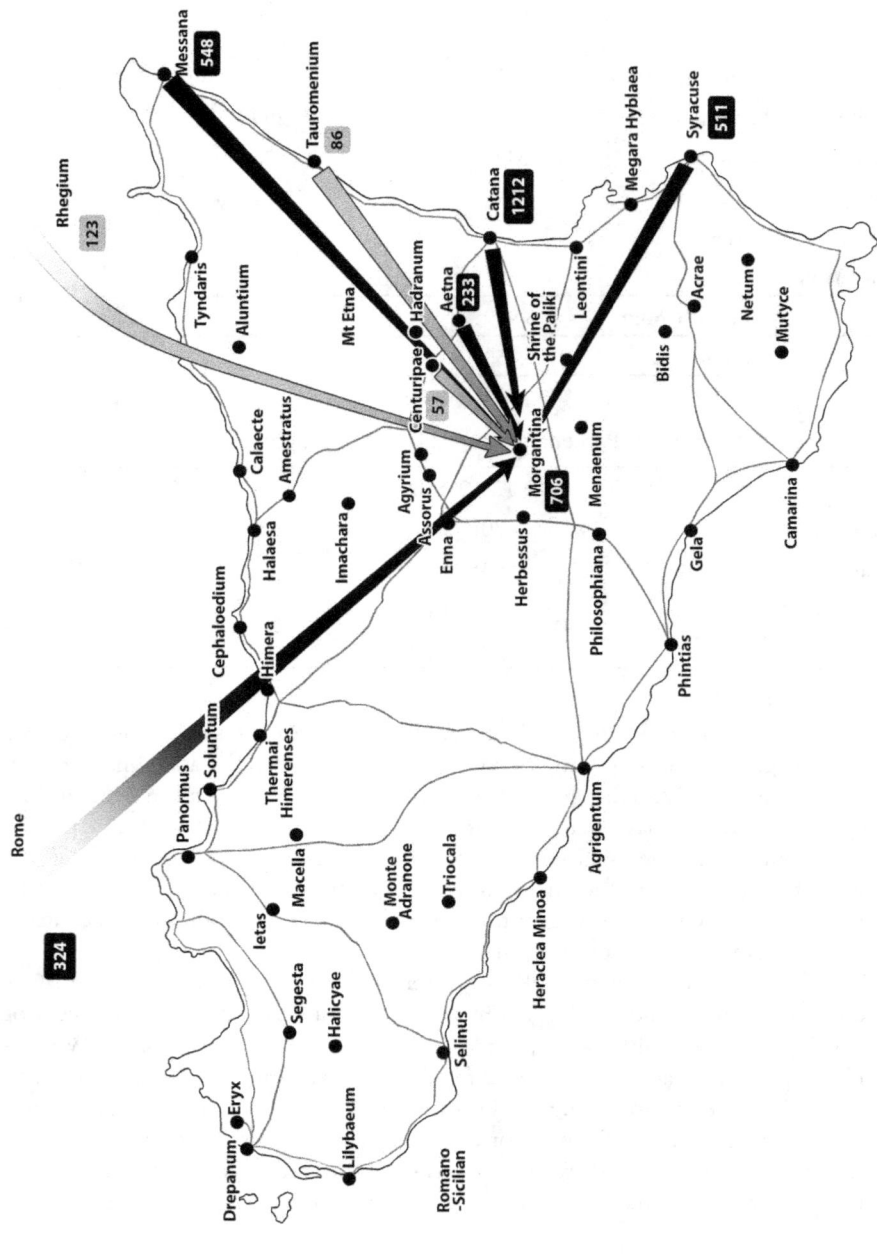

Map 1.2 Coin circulation in Morgantina. © Frances Morton.

majority of these coins found in Sicily have been found in Morgantina itself.[36] Taken together with the scarcity of other south-eastern local bronzes in the overall finds of Morgantina, the Hispanorum coins emphasise the limited circulation of localised bronze coinages, even within the context of south-eastern Sicilian numismatics. Overall, we may conclude that Morgantina's coin circulation was largely dominated by a few very productive mints – Catana, Messana and Syracuse representing the majority – with only a slight intrusion from other areas, and only very little from the north and west of Sicily.

Coin Circulation: Ietas

Ietas is the best-excavated site in western Sicily, but in comparison with Morgantina the coin finds are much fewer, as we can see in Table 1.4.[37] In contrast to the 4,150 coins found in Morgantina, the excavations at Ietas have produced 538 coin finds for this period. Out of the 519 bronze coins, we again find a noteworthy concentration of coins from a small number of locations, as seen in Table 1.5 five mints account for 79 per cent, or 404 coins.

Table 1.4 Ietas coin finds

Country	Town	No.	Metal	Catalogue nos (no. of each)
Italy	Other	3	AE	19, 25–6(2)
Italy	Rome	34	AE	1221–46(2), **Ietas 2009**(1), **2010**(3), **2011**(1), **2012**(2)
Italy	Rome	19	AR	1247–64(18), **Ietas 2010**(1), (1295 – uncertain date)
Sicily	Aetna	1	AE	27
Sicily	Agrigentum	1	AE	36
Sicily	Aluntium	1	AE	38
Sicily	Catana	1	AE	161
Sicily	Centuripae	3	AE	162–4
Sicily	Halaesa	1	AE	37
Sicily	Himera – Thermai	2	AE	54–5
Sicily	Ietas	93	AE	68–148(81), **Ietas 2009**(1), **2010**(7), **2011**(2). **2012**(2)

(continued)

---

[36] After the sack of Morgantina in 211 BC during the Second Punic War, the Romans repopulated the town with Spanish mercenaries, who subsequently produced a coinage bearing the legend HISPANORUM; see Livy 26.21 concerning the sack of Morgantina.

[37] Coins found in later excavations at Ietas are recorded in bold in Table 1.4, noting the date of the excavation report. For coins found three times in the 2009 excavations, and four times in the 2010 excavations, this would take the following form: **Ietas 2009**(3), **2010**(4).

Table 1.4 *(continued)*

Country	Town	No.	Metal	Catalogue nos (no. of each)
Sicily	Leontini	1	AE	165
Sicily	Lilybaeum	4	AE	198–201
Sicily	Lilybaeum – Romano/Sicilian	32	AE	166–97
Sicily – Island	Melitus	4	AE	1174–7
Sicily	Menaenum	1	AE	205
Sicily	Messana	61	AE	207–63(57), **Ietas** 2009(1), 2011(2), 2012(1)
Sicily/Italy	Messana/Rhegium	10	AE	264–73
Sicily	Panormus	57	AE	389–432(43), 450–5(6), **Ietas** 2009(1), 2010(3), 2011(2), 2012(1)
Sicily	Panormus – Romano-Sicilian	104	AE	291–388(98), **Ietas** 2010(4), 2011(1), 2012(1)
Sicily	Romano-Sicilian	23	AE	680–701(22), **Ietas** 2012(1)
Sicily	Segesta	2	AE	538–9
Sicily	Soluntum	4	AE	542–5
Sicily	Syracuse	10	AE	671–6(6), **Ietas** 2009(1), 2010(3)
Sicily	Tauromenium	1	AE	678
Spain	Ebusus	1	AE	1
Uncertain	Uncertain	64	AE	1349–412
	Total bronze	519		
	Total	538		

Table 1.5 Percentages of main mints in Ietas

Romano-Sicilian	159 coins	31%
Ietas	93 coins	18%
Mamertini	61 coins	12%
Panormus	57 coins	11%
Rome	34 coins	7%

These findings can again be summarised in the form of a map (Map 1.3): as before, the arrows in black indicate sites contributing more than 5 per cent of the coinage to Ietas, and the arrows in grey indicate sites contributing more than 1 per cent of the coinage. If we compare the map for Ietas with the map for Morgantina, we can see that Ietas provides us with a striking similarity to the situation in Morgantina, even allowing for the relative paucity of evidence. We find the divide between the east and

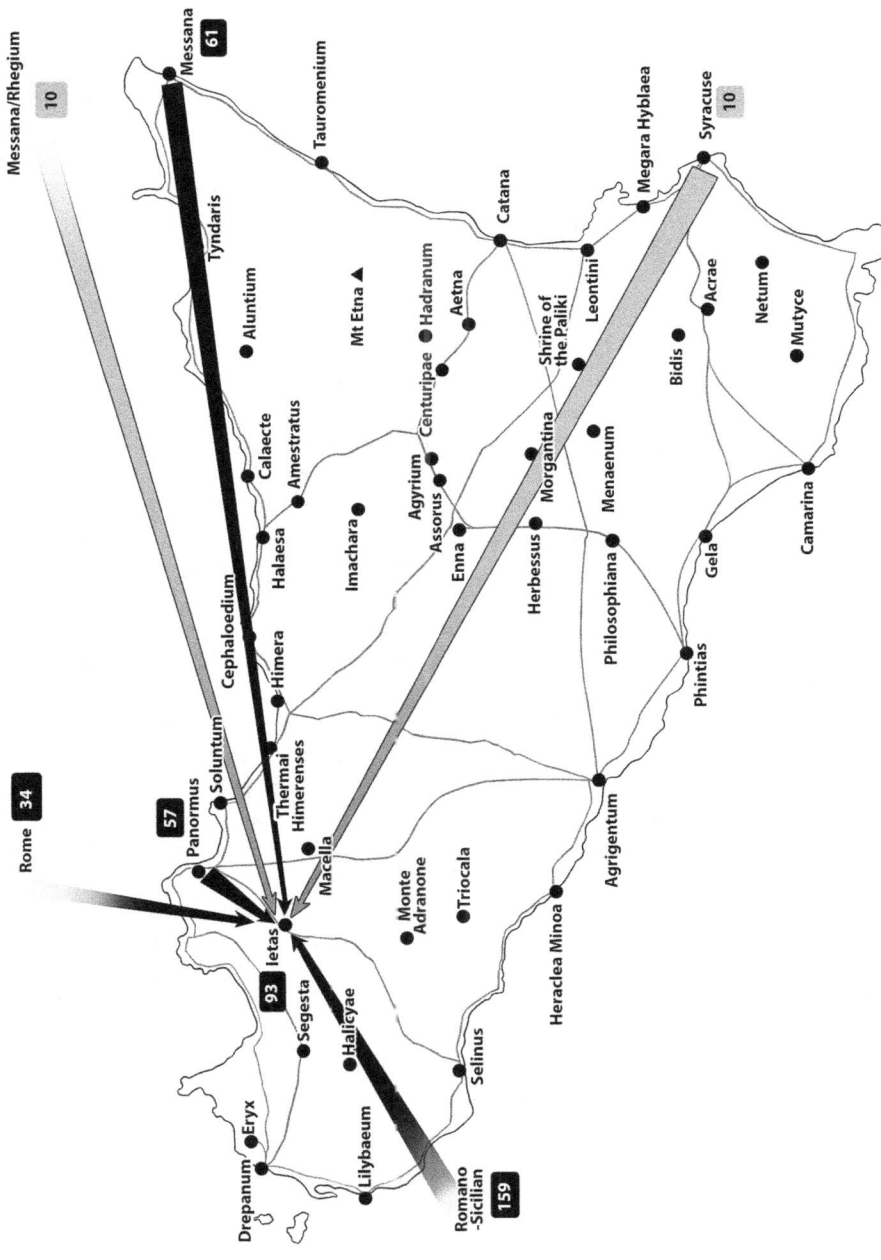

Map 1.3 Coin circulation in Ietas. © Frances Morton.

west of Sicily, which we already saw above with the coinage of Morgantina, with only eighty of the bronze coins (15 per cent) found in Ietas coming from the east of the island. In contrast to this, 62 per cent come from the west of the island. In addition, the local context is dominated by major mints – in this case Panormus, Ietas and the Romano-Sicilian coinage – in a similar ratio to that for Morgantina: these three mints account for 60 per cent of the coins, compared to 43 per cent of coins from Catana and Syracuse in Morgantina. Likewise, Ietas itself accounts for 18 per cent, compared to the Hispanorum coinage in Morgantina accounting for 18 per cent, and Rome accounts for 7–8 per cent in both contexts.[38] Frey-Kupper has noted that the numismatic correspondence between these two sites continues even when including finds dateable down to the end of Sextus Pompeius' reign on the island.[39]

Coin Circulation: Interim Conclusions

We can draw some interim conclusions from the above analysis. Overall, the two sites demonstrate that circulation of bronze coinage in Sicily was primarily localised, albeit with different regional or supraregional mints dominating. Frey-Kupper has conducted similar analyses for a range of other sites across Sicily and has found that the pattern is repeated from site to site.[40] It is probable that if we were to take any given site in Sicily the same pattern would repeat. This pattern can be summarised as follows: the local mint accounts for $c.$ 11–25 per cent of coinage; major supraregional mints such as Rome and Messana make up $c.$ 20–35 per cent combined; of the remainder, the majority, $c.$ 40–5 per cent, will come from one or two of a few regionally dominant mints, for example Syracuse or Panormus, depending upon each site's geographical location: Sicily, therefore, had no single circulation region. Nonetheless, the analysis above does suggest that among the diverse local mints a select few major regional mints dominated circulation in their own regional context.

In addition, there are no internally produced precious metal coinages circulating in this period. After the Second Punic War, Roman silver came to dominate Sicily's economy. This is evident from the finds in Morgantina and Ietas, with both sites showing an almost total dominance of Roman precious coinage (150 examples in Morgantina; 19 in Ietas), and is supported by the hoard evidence in Sicily. All 7,417 precious metal coins found in coin hoards dateable to the period following the Second Punic War were Roman in origin.[41] The last significant issues of silver coinage from Sicily were connected with Syracuse's governments during the Second Punic War. The lack of Sicilian precious metal coinage after the Second Punic War is not surprising. For example, the close economic ties between Macedonia and Thessaly in the fourth and third centuries BC led to a cessation in the production of Thessalian

---

[38] The correspondence between the make-ups of coin finds in Morgantina and Ietas has already been noted: Frey-Kupper 1992; 2013, 326–7.
[39] Frey-Kupper 1992; 2013, 326–7.
[40] See above, n. 34, and Frey-Kupper 2013, 320–7.
[41] The data for this was drawn from Puglisi 2009, and includes the hoards numbered 33, 35, 65–8, 70, 101, 112–15, 174–82, 234–5, 255–7, 274, 287–9, 312, 314, 316–22 and 378–85 recorded in her monograph.

silver coinage as the Macedonian silver became the dominant currency.[42] The use in Thessaly of a well-known and convenient silver coinage from outside the region is a situation that bears striking similarities to that in Sicily in the centuries following the Second Punic War. It is clear that Sicilian coinage in this period had become isolated, and the legends on the coins will, in the vast majority of cases, have proclaimed the authority of small municipal authorities or of the state of Rome.

We can now return to the coinage introduced in the catalogue presented above. There is no precise information regarding the circulation of this coinage, but certain points can be made. First, the rebels fought for control of the island's south-east, focusing their efforts on the wide grain fields between Syracuse, Catana and Enna (Map 1.1). Second, the majority of the nineteen coins reside in private collections that are claimed to have been created from finds in south-eastern Sicily. This area's coinages and the broad patterns of coin circulation there offer the best context in which to discuss the purpose and iconographical meaning of these coins; the coinages of northern and western Sicily are correspondingly less significant, as by any reckoning they made up only a small proportion of the circulating coinage in the south-east. In the first instance, therefore, the discussion of the rebel coinage will focus on how this coinage relates to the numismatic system of south-eastern Sicily.

The Coins: Weight, Value and Authority

When taken altogether, the coins in the catalogue range in weight from 2.60 g up to 10.50 g. No coin features a value mark, and this has led to uncertainty regarding their valuation. Cammarata, Manganaro and Campana offer the suggestion laid out in Table 1.6.[43]

Table 1.6 Suggested values for King Antiochus' coinage

	Campana	Manganaro	Cammarata
Issue 1	Dekonkion/ten chalkoi	Six chalkoi	Dekonkion
Issue 2	Hemilitron/six chalkoi	Three chalkoi	Four unciae/pentonkion
Issue 3	Pentonkion/four chalkoi	One chalkous	Two unciae
Issue 4	Hexas/two chalkoi	Two chalkoi	Three unciae

The coins are universally worn, making their original weights difficult to determine. Even so, the coins do seem to fall into four broad categories of weight shown in Table 1.7.[44]

It is difficult to establish weight standards with bronze coinage that does not have value marks, and judging value by weight is complicated by the fact that bronze

---

[42] On this, see Martin 1985, 46, 153–6 and 164–5.
[43] Cammarata 1987, 33; Manganaro 1990a, 418–19; Campana 1997, 155–7.
[44] The low weight recorded here in the list of half/*tetras*, 2.60 g, is reflected only on no. 2 of Issue 3. It is possible that this very low weight is the result of wear to the coin.

Table 1.7 Weight bands for King Antiochus' coinage

	Weights (g)	Avg. (g)	Med.(g)	Examples
Full/*litra*(?)	10.50	10.50	10.50	Issue 1
Two thirds/*hemilitron*(?)	7.35–10.00	8.09	7.50	Issue 2 nos 1, 2, 3, 4
Half/*tetras*(?)	2.60–5.70	4.56	4.80	Issue 2 nos 5, 8, 9, 10, 11; Issue 3 nos 1 and 2
Quarter/*hexas*(?)	2.70–3.65	3.26	3.43	Issue 4 nos 1, 2, 3

Table 1.8 Weight bands for Catanian and Syracusan coinage post-210 BC

	Catana Cat. Refs	Avgs (g)	Syracuse Cat. Refs	Avgs (g)
Full/*litra*(?)	**131, 134**	8.90–9.49	**380, 384**	9.38–11.50
Two thirds/*hemilitron* (?)	**130, 132**	7.69–7.79	**381–3, 386, 395, 399**	6.94–7.60
Half/*tetras*(?)	**133, 135, 139**	4.11–5.79	**376, 385, 397**	5.67–5.76
Quarter/*hexas*(?)	**136–8, 140–2**	1.53–3.17	**377–8, 387–91**	1.41–2.79

coinage is often badly worn, as these coins are.[45] As should be clear from the disagreement amongst Campana, Manganaro and Cammarata cited above regarding how to relate the rebel coinage to specific values of coinage, the matter is complex. Importantly though, Bussi has argued that this group of coins fits the weight system used across Sicily and that they were therefore carefully integrated into the context of Sicilian numismatics in order that they would circulate easily and be usable in commercial transactions.[46]

Comparison with other well-preserved Sicilian coinages that also lack value marks shows that Bussi's suggestion regarding the weight is probably right. As we saw above, in the south-east of Sicily, the most common coinages came from Catana and Syracuse. These two cities both produced coinage in this period that falls into four bands of weight, shown in Table 1.8.

The figures in the table are the range of average weights for the coins recorded in the catalogue of coin finds from Morgantina. The specific catalogue numbers are also given. There is a good overlap between the bands of weight for the coinages of Catana and Syracuse and those of the rebel coinage – comparison with coinage of Aetna, Catana and Centuripae that have value marks suggests that these weights could be referred to as *litra*, *hemilitron*, *tetras* and *hexas*.[47] Catana and Syracuse represent 40 per cent of all the bronze

---

[45] E.g., Buttrey et al. 1989, 39, chose to weigh only the best-preserved examples of the HISPANORUM coinage excavated from Morgantina.
[46] Bussi 1998, 24–5.
[47] See catalogue nos **68, 69, 141–3** and **147–8** in Buttrey et al. 1989.

coins found in Morgantina and were arguably the major regional mints for south-eastern Sicily. The correspondence between their coinage and that of the rebels with regard to weight reinforces the impression that the rebel coins were designed to seamlessly blend into their prevailing numismatic context in the south-east of Sicily.[48]

This rebel coinage, therefore, was intended to fit its context and to become part of a wider bronze circulation zone. At the very least the rebels appear to understand some crucial practical concerns. On this basis, Bussi has argued that this demonstrates the purely pragmatic nature of the coins – that is the facilitation of the rebels' commercial activities:[49]

> se le monete emesse da Euno si integrano, a loro volta, nel sistema monetario in corso, ciò significa che egli le coniò con l'interno che esse avessero una reale circolazione e che servissero agli schiavi per le transizioni commerciali loro necessarie durante i lunghi anni della loro 'egemonia' sulla Sicilia.

This must go some way to explaining the function of these coins. Bussi pushed this argument further and concluded that the intention for the coins to circulate freely in Sicily also explained their choices of imagery, since 'questi bronzi dovevano circolare in Sicilia ... ed è pertanto logico che alle monete correnti della Sicilia essi si rifacciano'. Nonetheless, an explanation of this coinage solely based on its financial function risks minimising a chief purpose of coinage, besides missing the subtleties of this particular coinage's imagery. It also runs the risk of assuming that because the coins were financially compatible with the circulating coinage of the period, they were also designed to blend into the background in terms of iconography and legend also. Indeed, the legend, which unites these individual coins as a group, complicates the assumption that these coins were designed to fit seamlessly into Sicily's numismatic context in every particular: this must now be explored in detail.

As we have seen, all the coins discussed above include a variation of the same legend, BACIΛEΩC ANTIOXOY. This legend declares the power that claimed both the right to produce the coins and the authority through which they were guaranteed. It has been well noted in the past that the production of coinage in King Antiochus' name will have directly established a regal aura;[50] but we can go further than this in understanding the significance of this coinage. As we saw above, after the Second Punic War the only silver coinage on the island proclaimed the authority of Rome. Moreover, in the west of the island the principal bronze coinage pre-130 BC had

---

[48] The low value of these rebel coins, resulting from their production in bronze, means that they are unlikely to have been produced in order to fund a war. If the rebels produced a silver coinage, it has not survived. Two gold coins are ascribed to the rebel movement, but this attribution seems unlikely. For a full discussion see Appendix 1: The ΦΙΛΙΠΗΙΟΝ Gold Coinage.

[49] Bussi 1998, 25.

[50] E.g. Bradley 1989, 120: 'the fact that Eunus minted coins could be urged as evidence of an aspiration on his part toward a highly formalized monarchy'. Note the suppression in Bradley's text of the monarch's chosen name in favour of the name he is given in the slave-owner narratives. Further examples of this approach: Green 1961, 16; Finley 1979, 141; Shaw 2001, 84; Urbainczyk 2008a, 42; Angius 2020.

a Latin legend publishing Roman magistrates.[51] In the east of the island, the major regional bronze coinages were of Messana, Catana and Syracuse, all civic coinages emphasising the authority of individual towns. When compared to these coinages, the declaration of King Antiochus' royal status, and therefore his authority to produce coinage, would stand in direct contrast to the growing Roman economic dominance of the island and the status quo that had gradually been established there. It had been sixty years since Sicily had seen a Greek king, Hieron of Syracuse, also based in the south-east of the island. The legend ΒΑCΙΛΕΩC ΑΝΤΙΟΧΟΥ, by its very nature, represented a reversion to older patterns in the political make-up of that region that ran back to the late fourth century BC. The proclamation of a new king, and therefore a new kingdom in the south-east, would upset the system put in place in Sicily by the Romans, and the coinage is evidence for (and medium of) one part of this disturbance. On this view, the importance of the financial compatibility of these coins must not be overstated: the legend they bore constitutes an important differentiation of these coins from their numismatic context. Even so, the legend of a coin only represents a part of its meaning and message, and it is only one step towards understanding these coins to argue that they established an aura of kingship around their identifying monarch. It remains to be seen what type of monarch is being proclaimed on the coins. To assess this, we need to look again at the images on the coins, corroded and difficult to read though they may be.

The Imagery

What kind of a monarch can we infer from these coins? As noted above, a focus in the past has been on explaining the coins as statements of monarchical authority. In this context, the coins' imagery has been read as servile in nature or connected to Seleucid practices in light of the literary sources for the conflict that emphasise the servile and Syrian aspects of the conflict's narrative. Bradley has argued that the coinage represents the rebel efforts to maintain their revolt, through solidarity among the 'slave participants', but also with a focus on the importance of food to the rebel efforts; Vogt, followed recently by Kunz and Engels, has argued that the rebel coinage is a mimicry of Seleucid monarchical practices, also demonstrated by the choice of regal name, Antiochus.[52] Vogt, Kunz and Engels all looked towards the eastern Mediterranean, with its dominant Seleucid monarch, and the widespread movement of Syrian slaves east to west to contextualise the supposed Seleucid nature of Antiochus' court. The principal source for the Syrian focus is Diodorus Siculus' account of the revolt. On two occasions the Diodoran text makes direct use of the term Σύρος to describe the rebels. On the first occasion, in a disconnected sentence that follows the end of Photius' summary of Diodorus' text (34/5.2.24), we read that Eunus called himself Antiochus, and named his rebels Syrians. On the second occasion (34/5.8), which is

---

[51] For the most up-to-date discussion of the Romano-Sicilian coinage of western Sicily, see Frey-Kupper 2013, 204–71.

[52] Bradley 1989, 116–20; Vogt 1965, 40–3; Kunz 2006, 329–48; Engels 2011, 235–51; Angius 2020, 78–81.

separated from the rest of the narrative of the war, Diodorus notes that οἱ Σύροι οἱ δραπέται τῶν αἰχμαλώτων amputated their captives' whole arms.

The effort to unite formerly enslaved Syrians under a form of monarchical authority that they recognised offers us one possible reading of these coins, and a reading that connects closely to the regal name chosen by the king.[53] This is a valuable approach to the revolt. Nonetheless, we should not assume that these coins were intended to be understood at only one level, and so we should consider the immediate context of these images and how they might have been read or been intended to be read by those living in the area in which they circulated: that is, we should consider what kind of monarch they present when read against their most immediate context, the coinage of south-eastern Sicily. As I argued in the Introduction, these coins offer us the unique opportunity to read a variant narrative of the events in question, representing as they do the only remaining source of evidence that allows us to view a form of self-identification and self-presentation within the rebel cause.

For this question, as I have argued above, south-eastern Sicily presents us with the most immediate context, which has been observed by both Verbrugghe and Manganaro.[54] Verbrugghe argued that the references to Demeter on Issue 4 demonstrated an appeal to prior Sicilian history. In this regard he connected the rebel coinage to White's demonstration in 1964 of the exploitation of Demeter's cult for political gain throughout Sicily's Archaic, Classical and Hellenistic history. This line of analysis was continued by Manganaro in 1982. He argued – when first publishing an example of Issue 2 – that the coins known to him seemed to relate to Sicilian types and culture. He suggested that the types chosen reflected an interest in the culture and lives of the people of Sicily, and were designed as part of an effort to garner support for the rebellion from the people of Sicily, not the slaves – an appeal he considered successful.[55] In a later article, he argued that '(q)ueste emissioni costituiscono un'affermazione di potere e la risposta a una esigenza "economica" dell'area territoriale controllata dal re Antioco (Euno), il quale appare l'ultimo difensore della independenza dei Sicelioti (o almeno di alcune città come Enna, Morgantina, Katane e Tauromenium) contro Roma'.[56] Others have since developed this idea in varying ways, albeit agreeing with the core of Manganaro's thesis.[57] Manganaro's argument that Antiochus appealed to Sicily as 'l'ultimo difensore della independenza dei Sicelioti'[58] is an intriguing way to view the coinage that can be developed further. This is the case not least because Sicily itself cannot be considered a monolithic entity, as we have seen above in the presentation of coin finds in Morgantina and Ietas.

---

[53] For the Syrian origin of King Antiochus, see Diod. Sic. 34/5.2.5; Flor 2.7.4; Livy, Per. 56. For consideration of the names of the rebels given in the text as 'Syrian', see for example Green 1961, 20–1; Aberson 2016, 11.

[54] Verbrugghe 1974, 53–4; Manganaro 1982, 1983; 1990a.

[55] Manganaro 1982, 240–3; 1983, 405–7. He concluded this from the coin evidence and from passages in Diodorus which detailed the actions of certain free people during the war (Diod. Sic. 34/5.2.48). See also Yarrow 2006, 222.

[56] Manganaro 1990a, 419.

[57] Guzzetta 2007, 190–1, followed Manganaro closely, even quoting Manganaro 1983, 406, directly. See also Sánchez León 2004.

[58] Manganaro 1990a, 419.

The Imagery: South-Eastern Precedents

The manner in which the rebel coinage fits into the numismatic culture of south-eastern Sicily is connected directly to the kind of monarch the coinage sought to display. Had the intention been for these coins to blend in with the circulating coinage of south-eastern Sicily, then mimicking already prominent coinages would have offered one avenue for this. If we return to the site of Morgantina, then we can see that four mints represent the principal coinages of the area: Catana, the Mamertini, Rome and Syracuse.[59] These four were the dominant regional and supraregional mints of the Sicilian south-east; in this analysis, Morgantina is merely representative of typical coin circulation in south-eastern Sicilian towns. The most prominent among these four dominant mints are the coins of Catana, with 1,212 examples. Of these 1,212 coins, 1,057 were variations of a single type, which had on the obverse a head of Apollo, and on the reverse Isis (Figure 1.15). The other types of Catana that make up the remaining 155 coins include as their images the Catanean brothers, Serapis, and Zeus. On this analysis, the rebel coinage was not imitating one of the most prevalent bronzes of the south-east, and this reticence to imitate important coinages extends also to the coinage of the Mamertini of Messana. This coinage – which, as we saw above, is consistently one of the dominant supraregional mints across Sicily – also has a variety of images (Figures 1.16, 1.17 and 1.18). A study of the issues minted after 210 BC shows that the Mamertini coins have several important similarities across all their types: of the twenty-three issues minted after 210 BC,[60] nine have a reverse with either a warrior or horseman standing or charging, ten have a standing figure of a god or goddess (Apollo, Artemis or Nike), while the remaining four types have on the reverse a variety of designs that do not relate to one another. This leaves nineteen of the twenty-three with a design featuring a standing figure. All twenty-three types feature an obverse design showing the head of either a god or goddess. Only three of the obverses, however, show gods other than Zeus, Apollo, Ares and Herakles, and Apollo accounts for nine of the twenty coin obverses with these four gods on them; the three remaining coins feature Aphrodite and Artemis (Särström Series XIV Group D, Särström Series XV Groups D and F respectively). If we compare the images typical to Mamertine coinage to those of the rebel coinage, once again we can see that the types are quite different. No piece of rebel coinage features standing figures on the reverse, and there is certainly no martial element to the designs. There is some overlap of obverse designs, including repetition of references to Zeus and Herakles on the rebel coinage, but these overlaps should not surprise us: there is no subsequent overlap in the combination of types from obverse to reverse. It is worth noting that

---

[59] This excludes the Hispanorum coinage, which is representative for Morgantina of the 'local' coinage, that makes up c. 18 per cent of coinage in any given site. As we saw above, a similar make-up of circulating coinage can be found across a number of Sicilian sites. See also Frey-Kupper 2013, 320–7.

[60] The issues are given in Särström 1940 as follows in the Särström Series: Särström Series XI Group A, Särström Series XII Groups A–C, Särström Series XIV Groups A–D, Särström Series XV Groups A–E, Särström Series XVI Group A, Särström Series XVII Group A, Särström Series XIX Group A, Särström Series XX Group A, Särström Series XXI Group A, Särström Series XXII Groups A–B, Särström Series XXIII Groups A–C.

Figure 1.17 Coin of Mamertines, third–second century BC; Apollo on obverse with standing Nike on reverse. Courtesy of the American Numismatic Society.

Figure 1.18 Coin of Mamertines, third–second century BC; Ares on obverse with horseman on reverse. Courtesy of the American Numismatic Society.

Figure 1.19 Roman as, 169–58 BC; Janus laureate on obverse with prow on reverse. Courtesy of the American Numismatic Society.

King Antiochus' coins show no overlap in terms of imagery with the principal bronze coinages of Rome in this period. The vast majority of the Roman bronze coins found in Sicily in this period are *asses*, and as such feature the Janus-head on the obverse, and a ship's prow on the reverse (Figure 1.19), and indeed the other bronze coins feature the designs one might expect of their different values.[61]

Out of the four principal mints of south-eastern Sicily, this leaves Syracuse still to be discussed. This city's coinage is of special interest in comparison with the rebel

---

[61] See Sutherland 1974, 60 and 60 n. 74.

Figure 1.20 Coin of Syracuse, after 210 BC; Poseidon on obverse with trident on reverse. Courtesy of the American Numismatic Society.

Table 1.9 Types of Syracusan coins, Hieronic and post-210 BC

Metal	Period	Obverse	Reverse
AE	Post-210 BC	Poseidon	Trident
AE	Post-210 BC	Apollo	Torch/tripod
AE	Post-210 BC	Zeus	*Biga/quadriga*
AE	Hieronic	Hieron II	Horseman
AR/AV	Hieronic	Arethusa/Kore/Hieron II/Philistis	*Biga/quadriga*
AR/AV	Hieronic	Athena	Pegasus
AR	Hieronic	Gelon	Winged thunderbolt

coinage because the city was home to the last Greek kings in Sicily. The most common types of bronze and silver coinage from the Hieronic period and post-210 BC are summarised in Table 1.9.

The bronze coins that Syracuse produced after 210 BC had three main types: the first is a classic Syracusan Poseidon obverse and trident reverse that continued a tradition of bronze coins in this style that started with Hieron II;[62] the second features Apollo on the obverse and either a torch or a tripod on the reverse; and the third has Zeus on the obverse coupled with either a *biga* or *quadriga* on the reverse (Figures 1.20, 1.21 and 1.22 respectively).[63] A final common bronze coin from Syracuse that was produced during the reign of Hieron II showed Hieron's head on the obverse and a horseman on the reverse (Figure 1.23). It appears that the rebel coinage was not imitating the most common

---

[62] The Poseidon bronze was minted in enormous quantities under Hieron II, in two different forms – a wide flan series and a small flan series – and accounted for a large part of Hieron II's coinage (see Rutter 1997, 178). The coins of this style minted after 210 BC lacked the characteristic double-letter control system of the Hieronic coins of this style: see Buttrey et al. 1989, 149.

[63] The *biga/quadriga* type was minted in silver with Arethusa on the obverse until the end of the Syracusan monarchy in 212 BC: see Kraay 1976, 293; Rutter 1997, 177–9. The type was copied across Sicily, and the head of Arethusa, on later issues, was replaced with the head of Kore, especially under the reign of Hieron II, and dates back to Agathocles: see Rutter 1997, 175 and 178; de Lisle 2021, 120–2.

Figure 1.21 Coin of Syracuse, after 210 BC; Apollo on obverse with trident on reverse. Courtesy of the American Numismatic Society.

Figure 1.22 Coin of Syracuse, after 210 BC; Zeus on obverse with *biga* on reverse. Courtesy of the American Numismatic Society.

Figure 1.23 Coin of Syracuse, c. 247–216 BC; Hieron II on obverse with horseman on reverse. Courtesy of the American Numismatic Society.

Figure 1.24 Coin of Morgantina, c. 215–212 BC; Kore-Persephone on obverse with biga on reverse and ΣΙΚΕΛΙΩΤΑΝ legend. Courtesy of the British Museum.

coinages of the Syracusan monarchy, at least when compared to the coinages that were iconic monarchic coinages such as those featuring Poseidon/trident or Apollo/torch or tripod. Although the monarch presented on the rebel coinage is depicted as a Greek king, it does not appear that he was being presented as a continuation of the Syracusan monarchic tradition.

The less common Syracusan bronzes do have some overlaps with the rebel coinage. The imagery of Issue 1, strongly connected to Zeus, is found on Syracusan coinage, as is the quiver of Artemis on Issue 2 and ears of wheat related to Demeter as on Issue 4. The first of these types, however, should be understood as a key part of any Hellenistic monarch's self-presentation, as argued above. The second type, which is connected to Artemis, was not specific to Syracuse. The final type is of more interest. On this coin, produced by Hieron II for his wife Philistis, her image is combined with ears of wheat on the reverse. This image appears to have been used by Hieron II to lay claim to legitimacy and demonstrates the importance of Demeter to the south-east; this will be discussed in greater detail below, pp. 55–7. There are, therefore, some overlaps with Syracusan imagery, but they are importantly not amongst those coinages that were produced in largest quantity by Syracuse. If we take this conclusion with the one reached above regarding the coinages of Catana, Messana and Rome, then it seems that the rebel coinage under discussion here does not mimic the majority of 65 per cent of the bronze coinage found in the south-eastern numismatic context, as represented by the site of Morgantina. If Antiochus' coinage was designed to blend into its context, as Bussi has suggested based on its weight, then in iconographic terms it does not appear to have achieved this objective, at least when compared to the major coinages of south-eastern Sicily produced by four notable mints, despite the overlap with some minor coinages from one of these four, Syracuse.

The Imagery: Individual Precedents

This is not to say that the coinage under discussion here does not fit into the area of its probable circulation. There are a number of correspondences between this coinage and the less prominent civic issues of cities around the plains of south-eastern Sicily in the last two centuries BC. When first describing the coins, I noted that the types relate to certain other coins from a Sicilian context, and it is this that needs to be examined further. As we saw above, Issues 1 and 2, which feature imagery connected to Zeus and Artemis, correspond to certain Syracusan issues. Issue 2 has on the obverse a head that is perhaps identifiable with that of King Antiochus, and on the reverse a quiver, which most probably invoked Artemis. This goddess was typical of other south-eastern coinages: Centuripae and Morgantina (Hispanorum) both used imagery similar to that on this coin.[64] Issue 3, which has on its reverse the image of a club, also has links to the south-east, with its type strongly connected to Herakles: Centuripae and Menaenum

---

[64] Other sites across Sicily use the image of Artemis – e.g. Amestratus – but the use of a quiver to signify the goddess is peculiar to the south-east of Sicily.

minted coins bearing similar types.[65] Finally, the type of Issue 4, which connects it to Demeter, shows links to a very narrow area of Sicily, with Enna, Leontini, Gela and Hybla Magna as towns that also utilised these types. It can also be connected to coinages featuring Kore, produced by Syracuse and Menaenum.

If we look beyond the south-east of the island, there are a few more connections, but they remain in the Sicilian east, specifically the north-east: the western mints offer no correspondences. Caleacte issued coins featuring Zeus in this period, Halaesa produced coinage featuring Artemis and a quiver, and Aluntium, Caleacte and Cephaloedium all produced coinage connected to Herakles including the image of a club. If we consider all four issues of the rebel coinage together, then something important becomes apparent. While none of the types used on the issues could be called specific to any one town in Sicily, the iconographic motifs used to allude to the deity in each case arose only in contexts specific to eastern Sicily. In the majority of cases they were specific to south-eastern Sicily in particular (Map 1.4). Apart from a spread of Heraklean imagery across the north-east of the island, almost all the towns that use the same kind of iconographic types as the rebel coinage are clustered around the plains of south-eastern Sicily. While the iconography of the coins does not mimic the financially dominant coinages of the area, it was composed of images, especially those related to Demeter, that connected to the area's other coinage.

The Imagery: Conclusion

From the analysis given above of the rebel coinage in terms of its weight, value and iconography, we can begin to reconstruct, tentatively of course, what the rebels sought to achieve by this coinage, and what it can tell us about how they fashioned their cause. First, servile imagery is striking by its absence. This should not surprise us, but it is important to emphasise. Second, the images chosen, the only means by which we can assess the rebels' self-presentation, emphasise not freedom from servility, but subscription to a typical Greek political model, what we call Hellenistic kingship. Half of the coin types chosen can be understood as part of the construction of the aura of kingship around the rebels' leader, King Antiochus, in precisely this mould. This much is apparent from the use of the Zeus and Herakles imagery on Issues 1 and 3. On this reading, the rebels did not view their movement in terms of its relationship to slavery but as an episode of state-building. I freely admit that nineteen grubby coins offer a slim base on which to build this interpretation of the rebel cause, but it remains the fact that this evidence is all we have that was not written by rich, elite, Greek or Roman slave owners years later.

We can compare this interpretation of the rebel state with the limited evidence we have for their actions on practical grounds that are preserved in the literary tradition about the war. The fragmentary nature of much of Diodorus' narrative precludes a more detailed analysis, and the other sources do not help in this endeavour owing to

---

[65] Once again, the use of Herakles is not peculiar to south-eastern Sicily – see, e.g., Thermai Himerenses; Ietas; Soluntum – but the depiction of a club as a signifying image of Herakles is specific to only Aluntium, Caleacte, Centuripae, Cephaloedium and Menaenum.

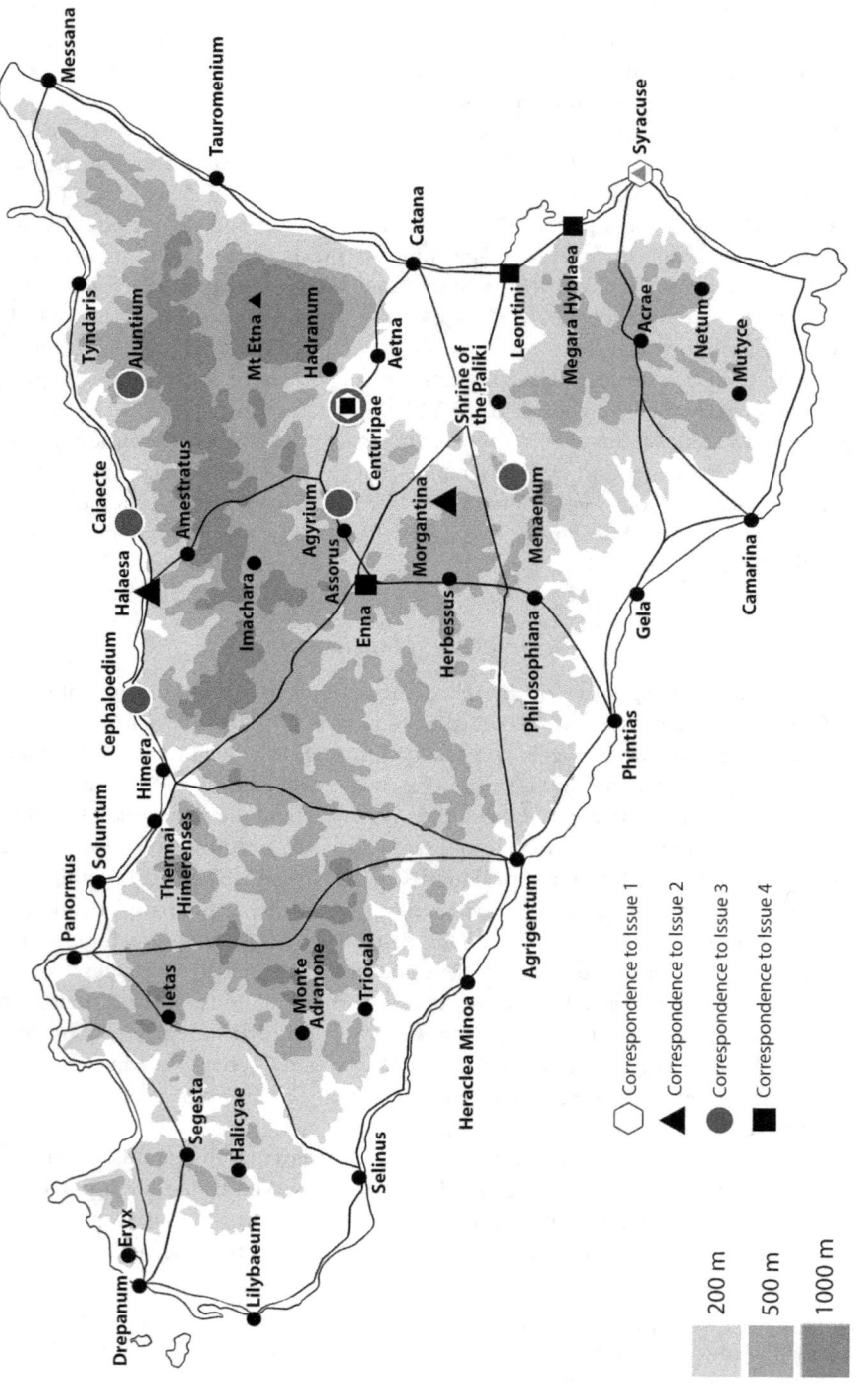

Map 1.4 Correspondences with King Antiochus' coinage. © Frances Morton.

their interest in the character of Eunus – for which see Chapter 2 – but some points can be made. At 34/5.2.16 and 34/5.2.42, Diodorus records that after the initial victory at Enna, the rebel leader, by this point acclaimed king, chose counsellors and appointed a particular man, Achaeus, on account of his perceived wisdom. From another passage a little later in Diodorus' narrative we learn that a leader of a second revolt, Kleon, followed the rebel kings' commands like a general (34/5.2.17 στρατηγός). We learn elsewhere (34/5.2.14–15 and 48) that the rebels formed an assembly, kept alive those in Enna who could manufacture weapons and later attempted to preserve those who worked the land in areas that they controlled.[66] The implications of this latter action with respect to the free people of Sicily will be explored further later in this chapter, but for now it is enough to note that we have evidence in the historical narratives for this war of actions undertaken by the rebels that are consistent with the self-presentation offered by their coinage. This point should not be pressed too far at this juncture, but I would argue that this demonstrates that the rebel cause certainly progressed beyond any potential initial escape from servitude that might have inspired its origins and became something altogether different, even if this new aim was not the revolt's key driver to start with. Judging by the stories of King Antiochus selecting counsellors after the victory at Enna, this development happened rapidly. In other words, even the main ancient narrative thread at the very least accepts that this revolt was only briefly concerned with the end of individual servitude.[67]

Finally, while Issues 1 and 3 fit the mould of Hellenistic kingship in general, Issues 2 and 4, with their types linked to Artemis and Demeter, do not fit so easily into this pattern. These two issues feature imagery that draws distinctly upon south-eastern Sicilian coin types. As we saw above, Manganaro concluded that the rebel coinage was designed to elicit a response from the people of Sicily in support of the revolt; but we can see that the aim was not to appeal to all of Sicily: the correspondences between the numismatic types on Issues 2 and 4 of the rebel coinage and those Sicilian coinages are all with coinages of cities and towns in the south-east of Sicily. Issues 1 and 3 suggest self-presentation based on Hellenistic kingship, perhaps Syrian, given the monarch's name, but Issues 2 and 4 appear to present the rebel efforts at state-building under a Hellenistic monarch connected to the culture of south-eastern Sicily: the coinage as a whole can be read in different ways by different audiences, and we must not lose sight of that potential. Nonetheless, they outwardly presented their state, however short-lived it may have been, to the general population of Sicily as a part of south-eastern Sicily.

At this point, it will be helpful to leave behind the Syrian interpretation of the coins and focus closely on the south-eastern Sicilian context in order to consider how this appeal to a shared cultural identity may have been received by the residents

---

[66] Both La Rocca 2004, 154–5, and Angius 2020, 72–6, consider the role of the people of Enna in the assemblies described in Diod. Sic. 34/5.2.14–15, with Angius positing that some free people in Enna (indicated by the term δῆμος at 34/5.2.14) may have taken part in the initial rebel assemblies. This is a tempting way to read the passage, albeit one that relies heavily on Photius' excerpt of Diodorus preserving at this point technical vocabulary that reflects both Diodorus' point of view and the reality of what took place in the earliest moments of a revolt that is presented in a highly stylised manner: see Chapter 2.

[67] See also Stewart 2012, 160–1, who notes the 'coherent action' of the rebels.

of the island's south-east. For this, we need to turn to the cultural meaning of the deity depicted on Issue 4, Demeter. Unlike the other iconographical choices on the rebel coinage, which are found largely in the south-east but also across Sicily, images of Demeter are found on coinage only from the south-east of the island. Moreover, her cult had a particular connection to the region, famed as it was for its capacity to produce grain. In the following section, first this cult's connection to south-eastern Sicily will be traced back to Sicilian history long before the Second Punic War. After the importance of the cult to these events is demonstrated, we will then consider the conflict's contemporary situation in order to show that the cult of Demeter remained a potent cultural touchstone that must be taken account of in our own explanatory efforts.

South-Eastern Sicily

Let us begin by outlining the picture sketched by the literary sources before drawing comparisons with other evidence. At the height of the Second Punic War, and as Rome struggled against Hannibal's Carthaginian armies up and down the Italian peninsula, Rome's long-serving and loyal ally, King Hieron II of Syracuse, died. On his death in 215 BC Hieron's grandson Hieronymus took the throne of Syracuse. His initial advances to Carthage in the wake of the battle at Cannae were cut short by his assassination, but owing to Rome's brutal sack of the town of Leontini the pro-Carthaginian party in Syracuse won out, and a siege ensued in 214 BC (Livy 24.4–7, 29–32; Polyb. 7.2–8). After the initial revolt at Syracuse, several other towns are recorded as having gone over to the Carthaginian side: Helorus, Herbessus and Megara Hyblaea. Megara Hyblaea was then sacked and devastated by the Romans (Livy 24.35). Not long after this the town of Morgantina sided with the Carthaginians against the Romans. This event triggered, so Livy tells us, a wave of betrayals of Roman garrisons across Sicily (24.37). In an effort to stem this problem, and in particular to prevent a betrayal by Enna, the Roman commander L. Pinarius pre-emptively massacred the men of Enna by tricking them into gathering in the theatre of the town in order to discuss their grievances and then turning on them and the city more generally. Marcellus, the Roman commander on the island, hoped that this would deter other towns from rebelling (24.37–9).[68] The effect was the opposite. Livy records that the Sicilians felt that the town of Enna was sacred to Demeter and this act was sacrilegious; it therefore resulted in a widespread outburst of disaffection (24.39).[69] In the series of revolts that followed, Livy informs us that Morgantina, once recovered, revolted again (26.21), as did Heraclea Minoa (26.41), Ergetium, Hybla and Macellum (26.21) in addition to the towns already mentioned. Furthermore, Livy mentions sixty-six other unnamed

---

[68] The episode is not commented upon by Plutarch in his *Life of Marcellus*: see Teodorsson 2008, 343.
[69] For Livy's complex interplay with Cicero's account of Enna in the *Verrine Orations*, see Hinds 1982, 477; Levene 1993, 55–6, and 2010, 212–13 and 341–3. Levene also argues that L. Pinarius' speech at 24.38, in which he appealed for help to Ceres and Proserpina, sets up an expectation of divine vengeance for Pinarius' actions in a city sacred to Demeter, and creates an expectation of Sicilian anger towards Rome's actions. See also Finley 1979, 118–19.

towns that also had to be recovered by the Romans. We must keep in mind that Syracuse also opposed Rome, and these sixty-six towns, plus the others also mentioned by Livy, indicate a widespread and profound rejection of Roman domination amongst the Sicilians.[70] In other words, Sicily in this period was a sea of potential and actual rebellion against Rome.

South-Eastern Sicily: The Cult of Demeter

The Roman reaction to the revolts was severe. Enna, pre-emptively punished, had suffered a ruthless loss of citizenry. Agrigentum and Morgantina, once recovered, were repopulated: most of Agrigentum's population was sold into slavery (Livy 26.40), while Morgantina, as noted before, was retaken and then handed over to Spanish mercenaries (Livy 26.21). The other towns, probably out of self-preservation following the collapse of the Carthaginian and Syracusan cause in Sicily, quietly surrendered (Livy 26.40). However, we should focus on the Sicilian reaction to Rome's sacrilege at Enna and how important the cult of Demeter was to the events. Rome's inopportune insult to the sacred ground of Demeter was critical to the continued massive spread of disaffection with Roman control of Sicily. This cult had a long and important history in south-eastern Sicily and had been regularly exploited for its potential to influence the peoples of the area as far back as the Deinomids of Syracuse, as White has noted.[71]

In the first instance, Telines manipulated the cult to heal a political discord in Gela (Hdt. 7.153). His descendent Gelon followed his own victory over the Carthaginians by introducing the goddesses Demeter and Kore into Syracuse (Diod. Sic. 11.26.7; Cic. *Verr.* 2.4.119). Dionysius I even attempted to use the cult to create a pan-Sicilian myth and identity.[72] The advent of the Corinthian Timoleon in Sicily resulted in the fullest utilisation of the cult to that date. Timoleon famously sailed to Sicily on a ship named *Demeter and Kore* (Diod. Sic. 16.66.4–5; Plut. *Tim.* 8). In the same period, although of slightly uncertain date, Aetna, Agyrium, Aluntium and Halaesa struck coinage showing a flaming torch between two ears of wheat with the legend SYMMAXIKON on the reverse.[73] A coin of uncertain mint, probably from Halaesa, combined this reverse design with an unprecedented obverse showing the head of a nymph named ΣIKEΛIA.[74] These coinages remained concentrated in their production in the eastern half of Sicily. The cult's importance remained after Timoleon and was drawn on by the rulers of Syracuse throughout the fourth and third centuries BC: Agathocles sacrificed to the two goddesses before his expedition to Africa (Diod. Sic. 20.7; Justin 22.6); and Hieron II made use of symbols related

---

[70] Finley 1979, 117–20.
[71] White 1964, 262–9.
[72] For this, see now Schipporeit 2008, 41–6.
[73] For these coins, see Rutter 1997, 167–8; Castrizio 2000, 51–72. See Caltabiano 2008, 123–34, for a full discussion of the role of Demeter and Kore on Sicilian coinage throughout the Archaic, Classical and Hellenistic periods.
[74] On this coin, see Holloway 1991; Wilson 1994, n. 1; Castrizio 2000, 103–4; Prag 2013, 37–8.

to Demeter in his coinage for his wife Philistis, including flaming torches and ears of wheat, thereby attempting to give his claim to the throne of Syracuse legitimacy.[75]

Whatever the embellishments on the part of the cited authors, if we return to the Second Punic War, we will see that there is evidence to suggest that this cult was still a cultural component of south-eastern Sicilian unity during the war, as documented once more through numismatic evidence. A number of coins have been found in Sicily with the legend ΣΙΚΕΛΙΩΤΑΝ on their reverses (Figure 1.24).[76] These same coins feature reverses showing Nike driving a *quadriga* or *biga*, and in one case a galloping horseman instead. The obverse type is uniformly a wreathed head of Persephone, with the exception of one type that features Zeus. The issue has been dated from hoard finds and stylistically to 212 BC.[77] They borrow in stylistic and iconographic terms from the coinage of Hieron II and the Syracusan democracy, especially on their obverse images.[78] Sjöqvist first linked these coins to the resistance to Roman rule displayed by Sicilian cities during the Second Punic War. He argued that no coin bearing this legend had been found with a provenance other than Morgantina or Enna.[79] He further argued that this indicated that these coins were linked to this resistance, although he accepted that many of the examples had no recorded provenance.[80] The connection to the cult of Demeter via the image of Persephone on the ΣΙΚΕΛΙΩΤΑΝ coinage was appropriate, not least in light of the cult's importance to south-eastern Sicilian unity throughout previous history, which has been outlined above. The imagery chosen for the coinage drew on the same connection to Demeter and her cult as the previous monarchs and rulers of the same area had done in the past. What is more, this coinage was minted in south-eastern Sicily by a group that was facing Roman aggression, and the coinage represents a manifestation of the efforts to unite this group.

The cult of Demeter, as we have seen, played a key role in the politics and culture of south-eastern Sicily, and was an essential part of the movement that produced the

---

[75] For the argument that the cult of Demeter/Kore was one that appealed to all the Greek inhabitants of Sicily and could therefore be termed a 'popular' cult, see also Ciaceri 1911, 187; Florenzano 2005, 6. On Agathocles and Kore, see de Lisle 2021, 174–6.

[76] On the legend, and on the use of ΣΙΚΕΛΙΩΤΑΝ as a mark of identity, see Prag 2013, 37–53.

[77] Buttrey et al. 1989, 31–4.

[78] Sjöqvist 1960b, 55–7, identified them as stylistically similar to Hieronic or Syracusan democracy coinage, while Buttrey et al. 1989, 33, noted that hoard finds in Morgantina in addition to stylistic similarities placed the date of the coins to *c*. 212 BC.

[79] Sjöqvist 1960b, 61–3. He made this connection on the strength of personal comments from two different sources. One source was a landowner in the area around Aidone, who reported that his estate had, at some prior date, unearthed a coin with the ΣΙΚΕΛΙΩΤΑΝ legend in an area that is now known to be the area of Morgantina's *agora*. The second source was that of the collection of Dr Joseph V. Caltagirone of New York, who owned a private collection of antiquities, all of which had been discovered on the Serra Orlando ridge (the site of ancient Morgantina), in which collection there was a coin with the ΣΙΚΕΛΙΩΤΑΝ legend. See Sjöqvist 1960b, 62–3.

[80] Sjöqvist 1960b, 59, followed by Bell 2000, 246, also argued that the unusual symbol on the coins, which appears to be a T atop an M, but both turned on their side, represented a symbol for Morgantina. Buttrey et al. 1989, 33, did not consider the argument to be strong enough to account for the unusual symbol. See Burnett 2000, 102–13, who notes that a metallurgical analysis of these coins cannot identify their origin, except to rule out Syracuse as the mint, in contrast to his earlier reading, 1995, 395, of the coins' provenance on stylistic grounds.

ΣΙΚΕΛΙΩΤΑΝ coinage. White has suggested that the cult's involvement in unrest against Rome can be linked to its subsequent treatment by the Romans.[81] He noted that in the period of the revolt's suppression, or immediately after, there is archaeological evidence that the cult centres of Demeter were affected directly. He focused in particular on the archaeological evidence for the destruction in 211 BC of Demeter's shrine at Morgantina that occurred during the wider destruction visited upon the city. Thereafter it ceased to function as a sanctuary, which White considered to indicate the strength of the Roman response against the cult.[82] Tempting though this argument may well be, especially in light of the importance of Demeter's cult to the unrest against Rome, it is assuming too much to see direct Roman involvement in the cult's decline. Hinz argued that the decline in the cult's activities is more easily understood as part of a general shift in the nature of the cult. This shift marked the end of certain archaeologically visible forms of votive offerings, rendering Demeter's cult less distinct from other cults.[83] It is unlikely that Rome's intervention caused the general collapse of the cult – and indeed beyond the destruction of the sanctuary in Morgantina there is very little evidence for violent suppression of the cult. Rather, the sanctuary's destruction may be connected more generally to the city's punishment by Rome following its repeated revolts in the Second Punic War.

Even so, what is clear is that the cult had a highly charged political role in addition to its religious role, particularly in the area of south-eastern Sicily. This can go some way to explaining the use of Demeter iconography on the rebel coinage. Prag has argued that the ΣΙΚΕΛΙΩΤΑΝ coinage of the Second Punic War represents the last and final attempt to utilise the cult of Demeter as part of an effort to unite Sicily against an external threat.[84] We could, rather, see the rebel coinage presented earlier in this chapter as the remaining evidence of the last invocation of this idea, centred on the figure of their monarch, King Antiochus himself, as Manganaro has argued. In essence, the rebels presented their state through these coins as representative of an idea of south-eastern Sicily unified in purpose against external aggressors. King Antiochus was depicted as a man entirely at home in the area and rooted in its history and traditions. As such, Antiochus became another in a line of Sicilian monarchs and rulers going back to the Deinomids of Syracuse to utilise the cult of Demeter for these purposes. This is one reading of the coinage that sits alongside the emphasis placed on the Syrian aspects of the coinage discussed by other scholars. However, as we will see in the next section, good contemporary reasons for the rebel appeal to Demeter's cult can also be found in the evidence for the event itself, thereby corroborating the ideas presented so far.

---

[81] White 1964, 271–3.

[82] Stillwell 1959, 169, 171; Sjöqvist 1960a, 133; Stillwell 1963, 169–70; White 1964, 276; Verbrugghe 1974, 54–5. White also connected the cessation of activity at the shrine in Agrigentum to the same suppression; on this see further Marconi 1933, 108–9; White 1964, 273; Verbrugghe 1974, 54–5.

[83] Hinz 1998, 230–2. This argument was followed by Kunz 2006, 67. Florenzano 2005, 11, 27, argued that this reduction in votive offerings should be linked to the Roman domination of Sicily in the period.

[84] See Prag 2009b, 88; and further Manganaro 1981–2, 49; Bell 2000, 249; Antonaccio 2001, 139; Péré-Noguès 2006, 67.

South-Eastern Sicily in the Second Century BC

As we saw above, pp. 51–3, the rebel forces appear to have given some consideration to practical matters in the early stages of the war and thereafter. These extended to the acclamation of a king, the formation of an advisory council, the production of regal coinage, and the sensible treatment of those people under their control who could contribute in material ways to the rebel cause: metalworkers and farmers. The passage recording the rebel treatment of the farmers offers us evidence not only that the rebels were conscious of practical concerns regarding provision of food, but also that some Sicilian cities experienced a period of disorder during the revolt. It will be helpful to consider the passage in full (Diod. Sic. 34/5.2.48):

Ὅτι πολλῶν καὶ μεγάλων κακῶν ἐπισυμβάντων τοῖς Σικελιώταις, τούτοις ἅπασιν ὁ δημοτικὸς ὄχλος οὐχ οἷον συνέπασχεν, ἀλλὰ τοὐναντίον ἐπέχαιρε προσεπιφθονῶν ἀνίσου τύχης καὶ ἀνωμάλου ζωῆς. ὁ γὰρ φθόνος ἐκ τῆς προγεγενημένης λύπης μετέβαλεν εἰς χαράν, ὁρῶν τὸ λαμπρὸν τῆς τύχης μεταπεπτωκὸς εἰς τὸ πρότερον ὑπ' αὐτῆς ὑπερορώμενον σχῆμα, καὶ τὸ πάντων δεινότατον, οἱ μὲν ἀποστάται προνοηθέντες ἐμφρόνως περὶ τοῦ μέλλοντος οὔτε τὰς ἐπαύλεις ἐνεπύριζον οὔτε τὰς ἐν αὐταῖς κτήσεις καὶ καρπῶν ἀποθέσεις ἐλυμαίνοντο, τῶν τε πρὸς τὴν γεωργίαν ὡρμηκότων ἀπείχοντο, οἱ δὲ δημοτικοὶ διὰ τὸν φθόνον ἐπὶ τῇ προφάσει τῶν δραπετῶν ἐξιόντες ἐπὶ τὴν χώραν οὐ μόνον τὰς κτήσεις διήρπαζον, ἀλλὰ καὶ τὰς ἐπαύλεις ἐνεπύριζον.

When many great evils fell upon the Σικελιῶται, the δημοτικὸς ὄχλος was not only unsympathetic to them, but on the contrary rejoiced, since they grudged the former their unequal fate and irregular way of life. For envy arising from earlier suffering turned into joy when the mob saw that the success deriving from chance had changed into a form previously overlooked by it. Most terrible of all, the rebels, exercising rational forethought concerning the future, neither set fire to farmhouses nor damaged the stock in them and the harvest lying in store, and held off from those who had turned to farming. The δημοτικοί, however, because of their envy, and behind the pretext of the runaways, went out into the countryside and not only plundered the estates, but even set fire to the farmhouses.

The date for these events is uncertain. The passage is preserved in the *Excerpta de Sententiis* of the Constantinian excerpts, and comes before two other observations, one that describes the actions of some recently captured barbarians and one that describes Ti. Gracchus' efforts to depose his rival tribune, Octavius, from the tribunate in 133 BC.[85] A precise date is impossible, even if 134 or 133 BC is plausible; in any case,

---

[85] Dowden *BNJ* 87 F108s–v has argued that the former passage concerns captives from Numantia, and that this means the passage quoted above must date from the first year of the Sicilian conflict, roughly 134 BC; Dowden therefore connected the passage to the capture of either Tauromenium or Morgantina, but this is not certain. If Diodorus followed a strictly annalistic pattern for this narrative (on which, see Stylianou 1998, 135–7), then Dowden's argument is convincing, and this extract can be dated to 134 or 133 BC, but Diodorus did not always maintain an annalistic style. This argument rests on Diod. Sic. 34/5.9 (*BNJ* 87

the date is not directly relevant here.⁸⁶ The passage is also vague about the location of this disorder. The contrast between the actions of the δημοτικὸς ὄχλος and the rebels suggests that these events took place among the cities in or near the area of rebel activity, which as we have seen places these events in the south-east of the island (Map 1.1).

The passage attributes the unthinking actions of the δημοτικὸς ὄχλος to their envy of a group called the Σικελιῶται. The antithesis set up between these two groups, and in particular the fact that this antithesis is based on the good fortune of those called Σικελιῶται, suggests that this latter group is to be understood as members of the elite within their communities, but this is inferred from context, and we cannot be more precise.⁸⁷ The δημοτικὸς ὄχλος appears to be a form of Diodorus' shorthand for non-elite members of polities. The term ὄχλος in particular, when not referring to an army's baggage train, is used consistently in Diodorus to describe a group in opposition to leader(s) within a state.³⁸ The few uses of the full phrase δημοτικὸς ὄχλος are explicitly negative, as in the case here, not least because they act more thoughtlessly than the rebels in the countryside and destroy farms and are driven by their envy (φθόνος) for the life enjoyed by the Σικελιῶται. There are limits to how far we can push the interpretation of this text in terms of those involved and the causes of their actions. Even so, the passage gives reason to think that some Sicilian towns, probably those in the south-east, experienced internal divisions.⁸⁹ It seems that unacceptable

F108w), which describes the punishments meted out to unnamed people who ate sacred fish, referring to actions undertaken by the rebels in this conflict. If correct, then this reinforces the annalistic structure of his text, since this passage is also preserved in the *Excerpta de Sententiis*, but after the two passages concerning Ti. Gracchus and Numantia(?); but this reading is not certain. In any case, there is no longer ground to support a definitively late date in the war for 34/5.2.48, as I suggested in the past: see Morton 2014, 28–9.

For further comments on the preservation of Diodorus Siculus' text in the Constantinian excerpts, see Chapter 2.

⁸⁶ I hope to return to this passage and another passage from the second of the wars discussed in this book (Diod. Sic. 36.6, 11), in the context of Sicilian social disorder, in the future.

⁸⁷ In addition, the term Σικελιῶται only occurs in the first line of the passage and may be part of a contextualising sentence added by the excerpter; we cannot place too much weight on the use of Σικελιῶται for this reason. See, e.g., Diod. Sic. 34/5.2.42, where the excerpter adds a gloss concerning Achaeus as advisor to the rebel king before he has been appointed to the role a little later in the passage.

⁸⁸ The term appears 106 times in Diodorus. On the definition in relation to the ruler or elite, see, e.g., 11.66.3 (Micythus departs with goodwill of the 'common people'), 14.18.4 (Dionysius recruiting the 'common people' to build a wall) and 32.6.4 (the Carthaginian populace meets their returning ambassadors). For the latter meaning, often including their negative effect upon the army, see, e.g., 17.32.4, 18.15.1 and 20.29.6. Context could create a negative meaning, closer to 'rabble' or 'mob', especially in those cases where the ὄχλος acted impulsively or were fooled by powerful leaders. For impulsive 'common people': 15.58.4 (Persian mob spurred by women); fr. 15 (Italian crowd kills *equites* in Rome); 33.4.1 ('common people' taken in by flattery). For leaders fooling the 'common people', see, e.g., 4.51.1 (Medea), 9.20.1 (Peisistratus), 13.95.5 (Dionysius), 20.34.5 (Agathocles) and 31.40a.1 (Andriscus). Overwhelmingly, however, the term is descriptive, and it is context that provides the reading.

⁸⁹ We cannot say for certain if this divide encompassed everyone in the town or towns in which this disorder took place – there is no reason to think that all the 'common people' engaged in these activities, or that they acted and thought as a monolithic whole, even if the passage tries to suggest as much – but it does appear that those involved in this disorder came from different socio-economic backgrounds: this was, in part, a conflict between classes. On this passage, see also Angius 2020, 86–9, although we might note that taking Diodorus' word on the motivations of the δημοτικὸς ὄχλος is risky when trying to understand the cause of this disorder.

levels of inequality between the two groups played a role – whatever an unacceptable level of inequality may have been – if that is what the text means by the Σικελιῶται enjoying an 'irregular way of life' (ἀνωμάλου ζωῆς). Moreover, this lack of unity offered space for a new political group to offer an alternative: Hellenistic monarchy. I have argued elsewhere that the rebels protected the farmers as though these workers were part of their 'home ground'. I noted that the locations taken or attacked by the rebels – Enna, Morgantina, Agrigentum, Catana, Tauromenium and Syracuse – are all places that would have enabled the rebels to control access to and exploitation of Sicily's fertile grain fields in the island's south east. By inserting themselves into the political landscape under a Hellenistic monarch and acting to protect farmers in this area, the rebels acted as though the farmers were part of their state.[90] This interpretation of the rebel actions, I think, offers us some ways to tentatively suggest why the rebels appealed to Demeter, and how this appeal may relate to the contemporary disorder in some towns in the area. The two matters, the rebel appeal to the Demeter cult and the disorder in the south-eastern Sicilian cities, may well relate to the product of the island for which it was best known, and to which Demeter was most intimately connected: grain.

I argued above (pp. 50–4) that the rebel coinage should be read in part as an outward presentation of the rebel state as part of south-eastern Sicily in addition to a statement of self-identification by the rebels. The choice of iconography on the coins that fit the immediate numismatic context and that, in the case of Demeter especially, connected to important cultural markers for the area reinforces this interpretation; this does not mean that these rebels necessarily were Sicilian, but rather that they understood how to present themselves in this Sicilian context. Yet this self-presentation can be found in the limited evidence for the rebels' actions as well. This is most clearly the case with the protection of farmers under their control seen above. The manner in which the rebels sought to shield the south-eastern Sicilian farmers from harm during a lengthy conflict fits well with their self-presentation.[91] Indeed, any attempt to appeal to the free people of south-eastern Sicily through a shared cultural heritage would be empty rhetoric without the concrete actions described in Diodorus' text.[92] The connection between the rebels' expressed ideology and their actions is confirmed, albeit

---

[90] For an expanded version of this argument, see Morton 2014, 25–9.

[91] In some respects, this bears similarities to the manner of self-presentation found on the Polla Stone. This stone from southern Italy, the date and meaning of which are hotly debated, has recently been argued in Adamo 2016 to date to the 150s or 140s BC, rather than to the period of the war led by King Antiochus as often supposed. The inscription boasts the achievements of a Roman magistrate in supporting agrarian farmers against pastoral farmers, among other things. The precise context of this support, including where these farmers were, is uncertain, although Adamo 2016, 86–90, argues that this took place in Sicily itself. The important point here is the political capital in presenting oneself as supportive of farmers in the mid-second century BC, regardless of the precise context of the stone. For further consideration of this stone and for a full account of the bibliography relating to it, see Bernard et al. 2014; Adamo 2016.

[92] For the suggestion that some rebel appeals to free peoples in Sicily may well have been complicated by the violence inflicted on some poor people by herdsmen before the war (for which see Diod. Sic. 34/5.2.28), see La Rocca 2004; Angius 2020, 87–9.

indirectly, by an exclamation in Cicero's *Verrine Orations*. In the fourth oration of the second *Actio*, Cicero described the attempt of Verres, the corrupt governor of Sicily in the late 70s BC, to plunder Demeter's sanctuary at Enna. Cicero took this opportunity to compare Verres' impious actions with the manner in which the 'barbarous' rebels treated the shrine (2.4.112):

> *Henna tu simulacrum Cereris tollere audebas, Henna tu de manu Cereris Victoriam eripere et deam deae detrahere conatus es? quorum nihil violare, nihil attingere ausi sunt in quibus erant omnia quae sceleri propiora sunt quam religioni. Tenuerunt enim P. Popilio P. Rupilio consulibus illum locum servi, fugitivi, barbari, hostes, sed neque tam servi illi dominorum quam tu libidinum, neque tam fugitivi illi ab dominis quam tu ab iure et ab legibus, neque tam barbari lingua et natione illi quam tu natura et moribus, neque tam illi hostes hominibus quam tu dis immortalibus. Quae deprecatio est igitur ei reliqua qui indignitate servos, temeritate fugitivos, scelere barbaros, crudelitate hostes vicerit?*

> It was from Enna that you [Verres] dared to remove the image of Ceres, from Enna that you attempted to snatch a victory from her hand, and to withdraw one goddess from another? Of these things they dared to violate and touch nothing, those in whom there was everything closer to wickedness than piety. Indeed, in the consulship of P. Popilius and P. Rupilius, this place was held by slaves, runaways, barbarians, enemies; but they were less slaves of their masters than you of your desires, less runaways from their masters than you from justice and laws, less barbarians in speech and nation than you in nature and customs, less enemies of man than you of the immortal gods. What plea, therefore, is left to him who overcomes a slave in unworthiness, a runaway in foolhardiness, a barbarian in wickedness and an enemy in cruelty?

Cicero's castigation of the rebels' character aside, which is as much a part of his attack on Verres as an attack on the rebels, this passage is evidence that the rebels respected Demeter's shrine at Enna. We do not need to share Cicero's surprise about how these 'wicked' rebels acted, I think, if we consider their actions in relation to how they presented themselves outwardly. Preservation of Demeter's shrine fits with their expressed ideology, and it makes a great deal of sense to respect a cult they directly invoked on their coinage. When viewed in this way, the appeal to Demeter combines both the historical meaning of the cult that we saw in the previous subsection with a contemporary concern for those working the land of south-eastern Sicily.

The appeal to Demeter, therefore, is evidence that those involved in the revolt conceived of it as a movement or state that was interested and involved in more than just collectively challenging individual servitude: it can be understood as part of an attempt to draw support from the general population of south-eastern Sicily, and, perhaps, to rouse them in opposition to an external aggressor, Rome. The Roman response to the war offers two more reasons to think that those fighting against the revolt at the time thought that it had become about issues bigger than individual servitude. First, in 133 or 132 BC a commission of *xviri* was sent to the shrine of Demeter at Enna and the shrines of Zeus Aetnaeus across the island.[93] Cicero records the commission in the most detail in the *Verrine Orations* (2.4.108):

> *Itaque apud patres nostros atroci ac difficili rei publicae tempore, cum Tiberio Graccho occiso magnorum periculorum metus ex ostentis portenderetur, P. Mucio L. Calpurnio consulibus aditum est ad libros Sibyllinos; ex quibus inventum est Cererem antiquissimam placari oportere. Tum ex amplissimo collegio decemvirali sacerdotes populi Romani, cum esset in urbe nostra Cereris pulcherrimum et magnificentissimum templum, tamen usque Hennam profecti sunt. Tanta enim erat auctoritas et vetustas illius religionis ut, cum illuc irent, non ad aedem Cereris sed ad ipsam Cererem proficisci viderentur.*

> In this way, in the time of our fathers, a dreadful and dark state, when Tiberius Gracchus had been killed, a fear of great dangers was indicated by the prodigies. In the consulship of P. Mucius and L. Calpurnius [133 BC] the Sibylline Books were consulted; from them it was discovered that it was necessary to placate most ancient Ceres. Then priests of Rome, from the renowned college of Decemvirs, although there was in our city a most beautiful and magnificent temple of Ceres, nevertheless travelled all the way to Enna. So ancient and mighty was that cult that, since they went there, it seemed they travelled not to her dwelling, but to Ceres herself.

The exact reason for this commission is unclear, but it is most likely to have taken place towards the end of the war that gave rise to the coinage at the heart of this chapter. Cicero dates the commission to 133 BC and connects it to the murder of Ti. Gracchus in 133, but Dillon has recently argued that the commission would only have reached Sicily by 132 BC.[94] Dillon argued, moreover, that the commission's purpose was 'to reconcile the gods of Sicily to its Roman rulers', and was not a sign of solidarity with the Sicilians or atonement for the murder of a tribune, as it has been interpreted in the past.[95] It was instead a piece of religious self-interest designed to win back divine favour to Rome that had been so conspicuously lost during the preceding conflict.[96] As Dillon noted, this interpretation is strengthened by Diodorus' claim that this same delegation of *xviri* visited and limited access to shrines of Zeus Aetnaeus seemingly across Sicily, but especially at Mt Etna (34/5.10.1):[97]

> ὅτι ἡ σύγκλητος δεισιδαιμονοῦσα ἐξαπέστειλεν εἰς Σικελίαν κατὰ Σιβυλλιακὸν λόγιον. οἱ δὲ ἐπελθόντες καθ' ὅλην τὴν Σικελίαν τοὺς τῷ Αἰτναίῳ Διὶ καθιδρυμένους βωμούς, θυσιάσαντες καὶ περιφράγματα ποιήσαντες ἀβάτους

---

[93] See Cic. *Verr.* 2.4.108, Val. Max. 1.1.1, Obsequens 27a, Oros. 5.6.2 and Lactant. *Div. inst.* 2.4.29 for the *xviri* sent to Demeter, and Diod. Sic. 34/5.2.10.1 for the *xviri* at the shrines of Zeus.
[94] Dillon 2013, 101–2.
[95] White 1964, 278, argued that the embassy was also inspired by a desire to expiate the goddess because of the war. See also Le Bonniec 1958, 367–8; Vogt 1965, 40; Manganaro 1967, 216; MacBain 1982, 38 with n. 84. See Dillon 2013, 93–5, for an overview of the differing readings of this delegation of *xviri*.
[96] Dillon 2013, 101–3; and generally Dillon 2013 for further bibliography and discussion of these episodes.
[97] See Dillon 2013, 98, for discussion of this passage.

ἀπεδείκνυον τοὺς τόπους πλὴν τοῖς ἔχουσι καθ' ἕκαστον πολίτευμα πατρίους θύειν θυσίας.

That the Senate superstitiously sent a delegation to Sicily according to the Sibylline oracle. Those sent travelled to altars established to Zeus Aetnaeus throughout all Sicily, sacrificed and erected barriers, declaring the sites off limits except to those in each community who had to perform ancestral sacrifices.

We can add to this interpretation of the delegation of *xviri* by considering these priestly visits in relation to the rebel actions and self-presentation outlined above. The Roman attempts to engage in 'pious self-interest' can be temptingly read as a counter-claim to the rebel assertion of divine support; read in this way, it lends support to the argument made above that the cult of Demeter was an important part of the rebel self-presentation and self-identification. The conflict was being fought not only over control of south-eastern Sicily, but also the favour of its gods. It is worth adding here that there is no reason that we must view the delegation's purpose in terms of either/or. Cicero evidently connected the delegation to the murder of Ti. Gracchus, and it is entirely possible that contemporary Romans saw a connection between events in Rome and events in Sicily during the 130s BC.[98] In this way the Romans could placate Demeter for the murder of Ti. Gracchus while simultaneously challenging the rebel assertions of divine support through Rome's own act of 'pious self-interest'.

Second, there is the peculiar evidence preserved in Cicero's *Verrine Orations* (2.2.32) for the reforms instituted by P. Rupilius with a commission of ten senators following the conclusion of the war. These reforms laid down guidelines for the correct assignation of judges for legal cases in Sicily, dependent upon the origin of the parties in the case.[99] One particular aspect of relevance here is that these reforms increased the role played by the *boulai* of Sicily in legal cases. Cicero makes it clear in this passage that in legal cases between an individual and a community, a *boulē* from another city was appointed to preside over the case. Overall, the stipulations of Rupilius' reforms served not only to clarify legal procedure, but also to reinforce a social framework for the Sicilian cities that placed the aristocracies of these towns on top. This increased the importance of elite civic institutions in relation to one another after the war. Fournier has argued that utilising Sicily's *boulai* in this manner was unusual in the Hellenistic period, and suggested that this fits well Rome's general tendency 'de favoriser l'importance du Conseil au sein de l'appareil politique et judiciaire des cités'.[100] It is also probable that the qualifications to be eligible to act as a judge

---

[98] My thanks to Harriet Flower for suggesting this.
[99] On the *lex Rupilia*, see now Maganzani 2007 and Fournier 2010, and earlier Crawford 1990, 119–21. See Capozza 1956–7, 91–2, for a more imaginative recreation of the actions of Rupilius that ran along the lines of the Gracchan attempts at reform in Italy in the same period. There is no evidence to support this supposition. See also Pinzone 1999, 393, for a sceptical view of any imaginative recreation of Rupilius' reforms. For the suggestion that reforms can be linked to the flourishing of local coinages across Sicily in the second half of the second century BC and that this was in turn linked to Rupilius' reforms, see Crawford 1985, 115; 1987, 48; 1990, 119–21.
[100] Fournier 2010, 169.

were aligned with financial and social criteria.[101] This legislation appears to coincide with the material development of some Sicilian urban centres, which included the construction of new *bouleutēria*, and seems to be part of a general trend towards oligarchic government in many Sicilian towns, the south-east included.[102] Even so, these reforms sit peculiarly as a response to an event that is usually understood to be a slave revolt. Yarrow has recently argued that commissions of senators had no specific action that they were required to undertake, but were free to do what was deemed necessary in the situation.[103] It is remarkable in this context that the reforms undertaken by Rupilius and his commission regard the legal systems of Sicily. It is possible and likely that legal reform was not the only matter the commission attended to, but it is the only detail recorded, and it is striking that it was undertaken at all. One way to understand these reforms, however, is to connect them to the period that immediately preceded them, and to the manner in which the rebels sought to appeal to south-eastern Sicily: in other words, to issues of grain provision and taxation.

Unusually among Roman taxation of provinces, the tax of Sicilian produce was administered locally in Syracuse, was sold by district, and could be bid for by Romans and Sicilians.[104] It is evident that bidding for and collecting the tithes was a method of making money.[105] One possible method by which profit could be achieved was slightly under-bidding for the tithe, with the expectation that the tax farmer was only obliged to part with grain equal to the winning bid, not the actual tithe.[106] Prag and Rathbone have both suggested that tax collectors were most likely to be members of the local elite, who were in a position to bid for the contracts but also to profit from the taxation of their district.[107] Prag explains that, where localised purchase of the taxes is concerned, it is 'dans l'intérêt de chacun, à l'exception des autorités romaines, que les demandes restent les plus basses possibles ... La sous-évaluation augmentait à la fois le profit potentiel du *decumanus* et réduisait l'éventualité que ce dernier tente de tirer avantage qu'une dîme du fermier'.[108] If, as has been suggested, Rome allowed

---

[101] See Fournier 2010, 179–81, for a consideration of these criteria through comparison with the legal systems of the Greek East and Rome, as well as hints that survive in Cicero's *Verrine Orations*.

[102] On this, see Prag 2015, 175–81.

[103] Yarrow 2012, 180–1.

[104] For the sale in Syracuse: Cic. *Verr.* 2.3.149; the sale of tithes by district: see, e.g., Cic. *Verr.* 2.3.61, 67, 72–8, 83–4, 99–101; the bidding undertaken by varying groups: Cic. *Verr.* 2.3.77, 86, 148. On the peculiar nature of this tax, see Prag 2003, 127.

[105] By the time of Verres' governorship there were companies dedicated to the practice, at least in some sectors: e.g. Cic. *Verr.* 2.2.167–91 and 2.3.167–9 for the company of *publicani* contracted for the *portaria* and *scriptura*, for which see also Aubert 1994, 342–7. Nonetheless, we must be wary of assuming this was also the case in the second century BC. Even so, the presence of corporations working for profit in this sector in the first century BC indicates the likelihood of the taxation being profitable to tax farmers in the previous century also.

[106] See, e.g., Scramuzza 1937, 256–9; Nicolet 1994, 217.

[107] See Prag 2003, 127–9, where he discusses an unpublished paper by Rathbone in 2001: 'Sicily: from Hellenistic to Roman taxation', presented at 'Sicily and Italy in the Age of the Roman Republic: a One Day Colloquium on Cultural Change and Directions of Study', London, 9 November 2001. Jones 1974a, 120 n. 35, argued that profits for tax farmers under Verres could reach 120 per cent. See also Brunt's note at 181 of Jones 1974b, where he comments that even during the Empire local tax collectors were more likely.

[108] Prag 2003, 128.

and encouraged Sicilian elites to operate and profit from the agricultural taxes on the island, the solidification of their authority and primacy through Rupilius' reforms with regard to legal matters becomes part of a wider effort by Rome to incorporate the members of Sicilian *boulai* into their machinery of imperial management. Rupilius' reforms were not the only cause of a move towards stronger elites in Sicily, but they can be understood as an important part of a general trend in that direction that can be seen in the epigraphy and archaeology of many Sicilian towns.[109] Even if localised collection of taxation was not employed, the use of external Sicilian *boulai* to preside over cases within other cities encouraged solidarity among all members of Sicilian *boulai*, in effect among Sicilian elites, elites that were, as a result, positively predisposed towards Rome.

This change, therefore, makes sense if we connect it to the way in which the rebels in this war sought to connect to local farmers in the south-east of the island. The rebels, on this reading, offered an alternative to the Roman-backed status quo on Sicily, with their offer of a south-eastern Sicilian monarchy that held the favour of an important local cult, in many ways an implicit challenge to the oligarchies of Sicilian towns. Rome's response to this was to bolster their own connection to the cults of Demeter and Zeus on the island and to reinforce the centrality and importance of the Sicilian *boulai* in contrast to the short-lived monarchy that had challenged its power. This argument is admittedly and self-consciously hypothetical, as we do not have the evidence to speak with greater certainty about interactions between the rebels and those who lived alongside them during the years of the conflict, or about the connection between the rebels' actions and the Roman response after the war.[110] The rebel coinage is, sadly, our best evidence for one part of what must have been a continual and (no doubt) heated communication between the putative rebel state and those people in the cities around it and encompassed by it.[111] Nonetheless, as seen above, the argument is supported by evidence from the conflict itself and by the south-eastern Sicilian context more broadly, and makes best sense of how to interpret the rebel actions towards the population of south-eastern Sicily at large and the Roman counter-actions.

---

[109] See, e.g., Wilson 1990, 20–8; 2000, 140–50; 2013a, 101–14; 2013b, 488–92; Campagna 2003, 23–7; 2006, 31–3; 2007; 2011, 162–7; Prag 2009a, 2015.

[110] Unless the reference to the δῆμος in Diod. Sic. 34/5.2.14 does indeed refer to free inhabitants of Enna taking part in rebel assemblies, although I have my doubts: see n. 66.

[111] As an example of an interaction that doubtless took place, but for which we have no evidence in this conflict, there must have been negotiations during the sieges that punctuated the warfare, not to mention negotiations for supplies and perhaps even support from cities and towns that were not directly involved in the fighting. Evidence for this does not exist but, to reduce the point to absurdity, unless the rebels slaughtered everyone they met (and the little evidence we do have suggests that this is unlikely), they had to talk to some people, even (perhaps especially) those opposed to them. See Levithan 2013, 54–6, on the pre-engagement contact that took place between armies and cities in anticipation of siege warfare, and also 56–60 for consideration of the communication that took place between besieging armies and those besieged during the initial stages of a siege. What is clear from Levithan's study is that the early stages of siege warfare would have included intense communication as a matter of course. See also Gilliver 1999, 155.

Conclusion

We started this chapter with the expressed aim to investigate how the rebels behind the war that rocked Sicily from 136 to 132 BC presented their cause and their own identity via the only evidence we have that comes directly from them: their coinage. The intention has been to look at and interpret these coins within the context in which they would have been seen and used: in this case, the numismatic culture of south-eastern Sicily. On one, somewhat limited level, these coins have previously been understood as a means to unite formerly enslaved Syrians under the authority of a monarch who drew on Seleucid nomenclature to reinforce his authority. On another, much broader level, the present analysis has shown that the coins resonate with the numismatic context of south-eastern Sicily powerfully in terms of their weight, style and iconography. Most of all, we have seen that servility and slave identity do not feature in the rebels' self-presentation, and that their monarch was no 'slave king', at least in the rebels' own, numismatic articulation.[112] Their coinage expresses instead a Hellenistic state under the leadership of a Hellenistic king that derives its identity and meaning from both the Seleucid east and its immediate geographical and political context in south-eastern Sicily. Their monarch, in turn, is presented outwardly as a monarch specifically of that region, while nonetheless emphasising his Syrian origin, no doubt in part for reasons of native pride, while surely also appealing to the regions' Syrian residents, whatever their legal statuses, and especially those under Antiochus' command.[113]

This same monarch acted as any Hellenistic monarch would: he appointed counsellors, spared those who could work metal and farmed his land, and fought to control his kingdom.[114] This king's coinage, to conclude, did its bit to communicate to the multiple audiences that made up south-eastern Sicily – free people explicitly included. The rebels, in sum, presented themselves as any group governed by a Hellenistic monarch would, and their cause as one interested in the concerns of the wider population of south-eastern Sicily. In addition, the rebels chose to fit their actions to their rhetoric: they protected the farmers of the area under their control, and they respected an important shrine in their kingdom. What is more, there is some evidence, slight though it is, that the contemporary Roman response to this revolt reflected this view to some extent: on the war's conclusion, the Romans propitiated the chief deities of south-eastern Sicily and sought to reaffirm the power of the ruling elites in Sicily.

Leaving aside the tentative connections between Demeter, grain and the shape of south-eastern Sicilian society considered above (pp. 55–65), what should be clear from this chapter is that discussing this event as a slave revolt, however defined, does little justice to the complexity of what took place and runs the risk of burying the rebel viewpoint of what this conflict was about. It was not, on their evidence, about individual freedom from slavery, even if there can be little doubt that slavery and its forceful rejection at the individual level played a role in the conflict – as it did in so

---

[112] Contra Bradley 1989, 116–23.
[113] Diod. Sic. 34/5.2.5; Flor 2.7.4; Livy, *Per.* 56; Strabo 6.2.6; Amm. Marc. 14.11.33.
[114] See Morton 2014, for a discussion of the rebels' strategy in the war.

many others in antiquity. To what extent issues to do with breaking the chains of slavery at the individual level constituted the initial spark that created the momentum for the ensuing war cannot be known from the rebels' coinage. But, at least, the coinage demonstrates that the rebels attempted to access the power of popular Hellenstic deities in order to communicate the meaning of their movement to those around them. The worn and hard to read coinage discussed in this chapter offers us the opportunity to see just a small part of a complex dialogue between an incipient rebel state and the established social structures of south-eastern Sicily, dominated in turn by another, external power – Rome. Despite the fact that these coins cannot provide a full narrative of events, replete with the colourful characters and plucky servile resistance that we find in the ancient historiographical narratives of these events, they are an important part of our understanding of what took place in Sicily in the 130s BC. Crucially, these coins open a window on to a different view to that propagated by the winners of the conflict – the almighty power of Rome, and the slave owners that fashioned the events as the occurrence of misplaced servile insurrection. Most of all, these coins demonstrate that the rebels under the banner of King Antiochus presented their state in part as representative of south-eastern Sicily, whatever those opposed to them thought of their origin, state or movement – either then or later. We lose a great deal of our understanding about Sicily in this period if we choose to ignore this aspect of the conflict and insist, on the slave owners' words, that the event was a slave revolt, an occurrence that by its supposedly highly specific nature stood apart from the broader power game that Rome was so proficient at playing. It is merely stating the obvious in conclusion to this chapter that had the relevant literary evidence not survived, no one would ever think of associating the numismatic evidence and its historical context with an episode of slave rebellion. This is not to suggest that slavery and freedom played no role in this war. The group behind the coinage were rebels, seen from the perspective of Rome, here in many ways adopted. They fought for freedom from Rome: the rebels' state and the war they fought stood in opposition to the powers that were (and remained). No doubt many of these rebels fell into slavery following their defeat, as was standard practice in the period, whether or not they had experienced slavery before the war. There can also be little doubt that slavery would have been part and parcel of the state set up by King Antiochus: the exploitation of other human beings under the banner of slavery was a standard feature of ancient states, Hellenistic kingdoms fully included. But whatever the social realities of Antiochus' kingdom, it will not do to continue silencing the rebels' voices by given centre stage to the winners' accounts. And that voice speaks of notable political opposition to Roman domination in Sicily that ignited a war in 136 BC. We should not let Rome win again by marginalising the insights gained from the rebels' coinage in favour of a narrative packed with tropes of slave ownership.

2

THE SLAVE-OWNER NARRATIVES OF THE 'FIRST SICILIAN SLAVE WAR': EUNUS AND HIS REBELS

THE MAIN NARRATIVE SOURCES for the war of 136–132 BC are the remains of books 34 and 35 of Diodorus Siculus' *Bibliotheke* and Florus' *Epitome* of Livy. Of these two, Diodorus' text is the fundamental source; yet it is a reflection of the dearth of evidence for these events that even this text is not complete, as we saw in the Introduction. Diodorus' narrative for this war is preserved only in fragmentary form, in an epitome recorded by Photius and in the Constantinian excerpts. Neither text preserves Diodorus perfectly. While the Constantinian excerpts are often verbatim quotation, they do also include changes for a variety of reasons.[1] Photius' epitome, on the other hand, typically preserves a more coherent summary, with a particular focus on and verbatim quotation of parts that were of special interest to Photius, but even so a great deal is compressed and lost.[2] Nonetheless, this text is important for any analysis or overview of the events of this war that goes beyond a basic statement that the war took place: however fragmentary and manipulated, Diodorus' narrative has assumed primary importance in modern reconstructions of what is commonly known as the First Sicilian Slave War.

Despite the text's importance, the low regard in which Diodorus is held amongst many modern scholars has meant that relatively little attention has been paid to his historiographic setting or to the narrative's construction by those interested in these texts for his war account. One reason for this is that Diodorus is widely held to be a derivative historian, one whose text is to be read primarily in order to access the source that he relied upon.[3] In the case of his account of the war that broke out in

---

[1] See, e.g., Matsubara 1998, 11–17, who argued that the Constantinian excerpts are normally verbatim, with changes made for explanation; to omit information that the excerpter was not interested in; through misreading or a different manuscript tradition; and through abbreviations, for a similar reason to omissions.

[2] See again Matsubara 1998, 17–29, who noted in particular the description provided for Eunus as being especially full (Diod. Sic. 34/5.2.5–9). On Photius' preservation of Diodorus, see now Wozniczka 2018.

[3] Hau 2016, 72, felt the need to justify including a chapter on Diodorus in her study of Greek moral history, and started her chapter: 'Diodorus may seem an odd choice of focus for an entire chapter.' Although there have been studies dedicated to understanding Diodorus' *Bibliotheke* on its own terms, these remain in the minority when compared to those who view Diodorus as either a mindless or unskilled copier of other sources, although this situation is changing rapidly. For studies dedicated to Diodorus, see, e.g., Sacks 1990; Yarrow 2006; Goukowsky 2014; Hau 2016; Muntz 2017; Stronk 2017; Angius 2020. For the more common view, see, e.g., Murray 1975; Hornblower 1981; Stylianou 1998. In each category these are only representative examples.

136 BC, the underlying source for Diodorus' text is thought to be that of Posidonius of Apamea, a Stoic philosopher. Confirmation of this dependence is thought to be found in a fragment of Posidonius preserved in Athenaeus that describes the character of Damophilus in strikingly similar vocabulary to Diodorus' version.[4] This has led Bradley to comment that 'if Diodorus followed his usual methodological procedures when using [Posidonius' history], [Diodorus'] account of the slave wars could be assumed to be reasonably accurate, reliable, and comprehensive'.[5] Yet, as noted above, the extant text of Diodorus has not been transmitted to us from antiquity without complication, and his text is filtered through a Byzantine layer of interpretation.[6] The desire to read past Diodorus in order to reach a more reliable source text has meant that the narrative itself remains understudied, not least within the context of the *Bibliotheke* itself.[7] Finally, as I argued in the Introduction, the literary texts for the war in focus in this chapter are, without exception, slave-owner narratives, and must be read and understood as such before we can use them in a critical manner as a basis for our own reconstructions of the ancient world.

The aim of this chapter, therefore, is to revisit the principal literary sources and study them as literary texts produced by slave owners rather than as historical sources or as cover texts for Posidonius. It will be more profitable for our own understanding of the events in Sicily in the 130s BC to reassess our literary tradition in this light before basing our reconstructions of events on it. This study will focus, mainly, on Diodorus Siculus, but other sources will be discussed where necessary. By doing so I will show the careful literary construction of the rebel leaders' characters, the purpose of this construction in the narrative, and how Diodorus' narrative in particular sought to be understood by its ancient readers.[8] This, in turn, will reveal that many of the descriptions offered by Diodorus (and used by modern scholars) to write the history

---

[4] Ath. 12.59.21–9. This passage is verbally similar to Diod. Sic. 34/5.2.34. For discussion of this passage 'confirming' the Posidonian origin of Diodorus' narrative see Malitz 1983, 37; Theiler 1982; Momigliano 1975, 33–4; Laffranque 1964, 119 n. 43, and 147–8; Brunt 1980, 486; Ambaglio 2008, 27. For a more sceptical view, see Stronk 2017, 76–7.
[5] Bradley 1989, 134.
[6] See Dumont 1987, 201–3; Goukowsky 2014, 51–3; Pfuntner 2015, 256–72, for important reminders of the key role played by the transmission of these narratives in Photius' *Myriobiblos* and the Constantinian *Excerpta historica*.
[7] See, e.g., Vogt 1965, 21; Verbrugghe 1975, 189–91; Bradley 1989, 133–4; Ambaglio 2008, 27, 68. For a new reading of the slave-war narratives as part of the *Bibliotheke* as a whole, see Morton 2018. For a full reading of the text more in the form of a commentary, see now Angius 2020.
[8] Diodorus had his own expectations of who his audience would be. The following discussion follows Pelling 2000, 15–16, in arguing that ancient authors, like Diodorus, would have constructed the meaning in their narratives from how this imagined audience thought. This is based on a reader-response form of audience reconstruction (Slater 1990, 5–7) in which the reader imagined has the (6) 'minimum knowledge of linguistic, cultural, and literary background to elicit meaning from the (text)'. Diodorus imagined that his history would inspire the leadership of the ancient world to undertake noble deeds (1.1.5) and also be relevant to those men who were inspired by history to found cities, revise law and push the boundaries of science (1.2.1). He also suggested that his work had benefited from being written in Rome (1.4.2). Moreover, regardless of the authorship, the text, written in Greek, and in particular the narrative under discussion, relied on an implicit understanding of Hellenistic culture and literary *topoi*: this would suggest at the very least literate Greeks but perhaps also Hellenised Romans.

of the events that unfolded in the 130s BC are unsuitable for historical reconstruction. In consequence, if we base our understanding of the happenings solely upon the literary sources, or give them primacy in our interpretative framework, we run the risk of distorting our lens on the past, not least by missing important perspectives on these events. This argument will be demonstrated across three sections.

In the first section, I will analyse the depiction of the rebel king. This figure, as I noted in Chapter 1, is the principal figure of the extant narratives for the war, and deserves study in his own right. My analysis will focus on three areas. First, we will study how Eunus is stereotyped as unsuitable for kingship owing to his cowardice, military inexperience and desire for luxury. Second, we will examine the narrative ring-composition that connects Eunus' vices to those of his master, Antigenes. Finally, the analysis will focus on Diodorus' use of terms relating to wonder-working (τερατεία; τερατευόμενος; μάγος) in order to castigate Eunus further as a leader. The chapter's second section will concentrate on Eunus' subordinate, Kleon. We will see that this man is described in the text in formulaic terms as a bandit, whose violent character offered a counterpoint, also negative, to Eunus' effeminate cowardice. Finally, the third section will show that key passages of Diodorus' narrative were fashioned using rhetorical techniques and narratological devices in order to offer a 'correct' reading of the rebels' motivation that emphasised the importance of smooth master–slave relations from the slave owner's point of view. These same passages downplayed the rebels' agency in their own revolt. Overall, we will see that the principal literary source for the war cannot be used as straightforward evidence for the nature of its causes, or for excavating the motivations of the rebels. Moreover, the rhetorical embellishments of the text make interpretation of many details concerning the rebel leadership fraught with difficulty. The ancient historiography for this war must be understood and read for what it is: the retrospective depiction of events from a slave-owning perspective. So what do slave owners make of the rebels and their king when they reflect on the events nearly a century later? We start our investigation with the figure that dominates the extant literary narratives for these events: the slave king Eunus.

King of the Slaves

The Coronation

Eunus is introduced into Diodorus' narrative as (34/5.2.5) τις οἰκέτης Ἀντιγένους Ἐνναίου, Σύρος τὸ γένος ἐκ τῆς Ἀπαμείας,[9] ἄνθρωπος μάγος καὶ τερατουργὸς τὸν τρόπον, '. . . a certain slave of Antigenes of Enna, a Syrian from Apamea, a magician and wonder-worker in manner'.[10] He is described as having cultivated a reputation in Sicily as a prophet (one who, we shall see, was a charlatan), which led to the slaves of Damophilus turning to him to receive consent from the gods for their rebellion (34/5.2.10–11, 24b). Eunus succeeded in exhorting the slaves to seize the town of

---

[9] The formulation of the phrase Σύρος τὸ γένος ἐκ τῆς Ἀπαμείας is similar to those found on manumission inscriptions for slaves at Hellenistic Delphi: see Lewis 2011, 93–8.

[10] I here summarise and develop an argument I have put forward at length elsewhere: Morton 2013.

Enna, and in the aftermath they proclaimed him king. His coronation defines not only Eunus' character, but also the unlikelihood of his continuing success, and even defines his relationship to his subjects. After the sack of Enna and the execution of various notable slave owners, Diodorus continues (34/5.2.14):

ἐκεῖθεν αἱρεῖται βασιλεὺς ὁ Εὔνους οὔτε δι' ἀνδρείαν οὔτε διὰ στρατηγίαν, διὰ δὲ μόνην τερατείαν καὶ τὸ τῆς ἀποστάσεως ἄρξαι, ἅμα δὲ καὶ τῆς προσηγορίας οἱονεί τινα καλὸν οἰωνὸν ἐχούσης πρὸς τὴν τῶν ὑποταττομένων εὔνοιαν.

Then, Eunus was chosen king, and not because of his courage, nor his generalship, but only because of his knowledge of wonders and his setting of the revolt in motion, but also at the same time because his name seemed to hold some favourable omen with regard to the goodwill of his subjects.

In the first case, we should note the negative assessment this passage suggests of Eunus' suitability for kingship. The passage implies that he has neither ἀνδρεία, 'bravery', nor στρατηγία, 'generalship'. It seems that Diodorus did not have a high opinion of Eunus' worth, and that he also judged the critical faculties of the men selecting Eunus to be poor: he was elected for superficial reasons based on his name,[11] his wonders – I shall return to both later – and the fact that he had incited the revolt. There is reason to think that these two terms – ἀνδρεία and στρατηγία – originate from Diodorus himself. The qualities of ἀνδρεία and στρατηγία feature regularly together in the extant Diodoran text to denote 'good' leaders.[12] The wide chronological spread of the uses suggests that this was a favoured expression of Diodorus himself, and not one lifted from his sources. Yet, the use of this phrase for Eunus is the only occasion, out of a total of twenty-eight, in which the expression is given in the negative. Notwithstanding the fragmentary nature of Diodorus, it appears that Eunus is rhetorically set up as the antithesis of all the previous leaders described with this phrase.

Diodorus' concept of what made a good leader also connects to aspects of wider, Hellenistic ideals of kingship.[13] Hellenistic kings were ideally courageous and warlike,

---

[11] If it was a slave name then it is possible that it was one of the many defining features over which enslaved persons were usually powerless: perhaps the name came from the master.

[12] Diodorus consistently used expressions based on the phrase ἀνδρεία τε καὶ στρατηγία, sometimes varying with ἀρετή, 'valour', for ἀνδρεία and στρατηγικός, 'general-like', for στρατηγία, to denote the qualities of generals and kings whom he considered to be exceptional leaders. This expression, in all combinations of ἀνδρεία and ἀρετή with στρατηγία or στρατηγικός, features twenty-eight times throughout the *Bibliotheke*: Descendants of Scythes (2.43 4); Herakles (4.53.7); the Dioscuri (6.6.1); Leonidas (11.4.2); the citizens of Athens (11.62.2, 85.2); Gelon (11.67.2); Pericles (12.39.3); King Agesilaus (15.31.3); Timotheus (15.36.6); Epameinondas (15.39.2, 88.3); Chabrias (15.69.4); Pelopidas (15.80.1); Philip II of Macedon (16.1.6); Dion (16.6.3); Nypsius (16.18.1); Diophantes and Lamius (16.48.2); Timoleon (16.65.2); Memnon of Rhodes (17.7.2); Charidemus (17.30.2); Antiphilos (18.13.6); Fabius Cunctator (26.3.1); Scipio Africanus (29.20.1); Viriathus (33.21a.1); Cleptius (36.8 1); Sulla (37.25.1).

[13] The key virtues for a Hellenistic king, according to Hellenistic kingship ideology, included justice (δικαιοσύνη), self-control (σωφροσύνη), wisdom (σοφία), and courage (ἀνδρεία). For further discussion of this ideology see Walbank 1984, 66, 82–3; Cairns 1989, 18–21; Bertelli 2002; Murray 2007, 24–5. See Muntz 2017, 193–7, for the application of this philosophy to Roman governors in Diodorus' *Bibliotheke*.

although not excessively so, and their acclamation was often linked to these ideals.[14] Xenophon and Polybius both thought good leaders were unremitting in their effort, and that military success was essential both to the foundation of their rule, and the maintenance of their reign.[15] Indeed, failure as a military leader was enough to castigate a king as unmanly and feminine. The account of King Prusias preserved in Polybius gives a clear example of this form of denigration (32.15.9):

ἀνδρὸς μὲν γὰρ (ἔργον) οὐδὲν ἐπιτελεσάμενος κατὰ τὰς προσβολάς, ἀγεννῶς δὲ καὶ γυναικοθύμως χειρίσας καὶ τὰ πρὸς θεοὺς καὶ τὰ πρὸς ἀνθρώπους μετήγαγε τὸ στράτευμα πρὸς Ἐλαίαν.

After doing nothing worthy of a man in his attacks on the town, but behaving in a cowardly and womanish manner both to the gods and men, he marched his army back to Elaia.

The military sphere was a distinctly masculine one in antiquity; thus, a complete failure in the military sphere was connected to effeminate tendencies.[16] Leaders in the Hellenistic world were also supposed to focus on matters of administration and the military at the expense of all other considerations.[17] Diodorus' use of the phrase ἀνδρεία τε καὶ στρατηγία as a 'catch-all' definition of a good leader is in accord with the described Hellenistic attitudes about kingship: for Diodorus the best leaders were brave in battle and understood strategy.[18] It hardly needs to be added that a brave leader was not effeminate or luxurious.

Returning to Eunus, the slave king, we see that Diodorus has described Eunus' acclamation as taking place for the wrong reasons and Eunus himself as the inverse of

---

[14] On the courageous king, see Murray 1965, 169, and Phld. *On the Good King According to Homer* col. 9.13–14. With regard to acclamation, 'spear-won territory' was often considered the strongest right to rule: for example, according to Polybius (11.34.15–16) this was the method by which Antiochus III became considered worthy of his throne; Theocritus (*Id.* 17.90–4, 98–103) expresses a similar ideology concerning Ptolemy II Philadelphus, on which see Murray 2008.

[15] Unremitting in effort: see, e.g., in Xen. *Mem.* 2.1.212–34; *Cyr.* 1.3.20–3; 2.1.1–9, 4.13; 3.3.13–20, 46–7; 5.1.24–6; and Polyb. 5.40.1–2. See also Beston 2000, 317. On acclamation, see Austin 1986, 457; Plut. *Alex.* 34; *Dem.* 18; Polyb. 18.41. On continued success, and the potential for military and financial failure to ruin a monarch, see Austin 1986, 458–9; Bosworth 2002, 258; Plut. *Demetr.* 42.1–6; 44.8. Bradley 1989, 117, noted that the acclamation of Eunus was typically Hellenistic; see also Vogt 1965, 29–30.

[16] See, e.g., Polybius (28.21.3) and also Beston 2000, 316–17.

[17] See, e.g., Philopoemen in Polybius (11.8–9), who is considered by Champion 2004, 150, to be characterised by 'self-restraint in his private life and dress and self-control in money matters'; Pyrrhus in Plutarch (*Pyrrh.* 8.3); and the comments of Aristeas to Philocrates on good kings (*Ad Phil.* 245, 283). For a discussion of Aristeas' letter, see Murray 1967 and Cairns 1989, 15 and 20. Similar concerns are reflected in Diodorus' account of Viriathus, who eschewed expensive gifts, preferring to win eminence through ἀνδρεία, 'bravery' (33.7.1–4).

[18] At least in the context of Hellenistic monarchs. In book 1 of his *Bibliotheke* (1.69–76), Diodorus Siculus describes at great length the nature of Egyptian kingship, an alternative monarchical system in which the king is restrained by law, and therefore not kept in check, necessarily, by his own virtue. On this, see Murray 1970 and Muntz 2017, 197–206.

some aspects of what a Hellenistic king should be.[19] By describing Eunus' crowning achievement as he does, Diodorus is directly diminishing Eunus' success: it appears that the description of Eunus' acclamation was composed with the objective of characterising Eunus negatively. Furthermore, Diodorus achieved this denigration through an appeal to Hellenistic ideals of kingship, and so connected Eunus to a wider contemporary ideology, with all the salient links involved in this, albeit negatively loaded. Moreover, throughout his narrative, Diodorus continues to undercut Eunus' actions and abilities, and negate his successes, thus turning a Hellenistic reader against him. It is to Eunus' various undermined achievements that we now turn. This will allow us to consider in greater detail Diodorus' intentions and the literary means by which he weakens Eunus' character.

A Coward's End

From his apex, we turn first to Eunus' downfall. The narrative of it is compressed, with the final two or three years of the war preserved in only a few paragraphs of Photius' epitome (34/5.2.20–3). Nonetheless, it is clear that Eunus' demise came at the very end of the revolt and completed Diodorus' narrative of the war. After the town of Enna is retaken by the Romans, Diodorus gives an account of Eunus' flight and capture with a company of a thousand bodyguards (34/5.2.22–3). We are told that the bodyguards killed themselves to avoid capture, thereby taking the initiative, in a sense, from the Romans. Eunus himself fled to a cave and was captured there with four companions (34/5.2.22). After his capture Eunus died in Morgantina's jail from a disease which dissolved his flesh into lice. There are several aspects of this account that warrant attention.

Diodorus describes Eunus as fleeing ἀνάνδρως, 'in an unmanly fashion', and relates that he fled to the caves διὰ δειλίαν, 'through cowardice'. This is in keeping with the way Diodorus portrays Eunus' acclamation as king. Moreover, here Eunus' behaviour is explicitly contrasted with that of his followers: while he fled through cowardice, they bravely took their own lives. This is a damning indictment of Eunus: not only did he take the coward's way out, but his men also refused to fight for him.[20] Their actions mirror those of other soldiers of Hellenistic monarchs, who abandoned their leader because of flaws in their leader's character. Furthermore, for a king the manner of death was significant. Diodorus characterises Eunus' death as οἰκείως τῆς περὶ αὐτὸν ῥᾳδιουργίας, 'worthy of his knavery'.[21] He died, it has been argued, from scabies.[22] This particular form of decay, either by lice or by worms, was attributed to people

---

[19] For Dumont 1987, 207, Eunus was 'la parodie d'un vrai roi'.

[20] The portrayal of a leader as a coward was exploited for propagandistic purposes by other ancient authors as well. Polybius (29.18) presented Perseus as cowardly withdrawing from the battle of Pydna before it began (Polyb. 29.18). Both Chaniotis 2005, 219–20, and Walbank 1979, 390, thought that this was done to strengthen Polybius' pro-Roman bias.

[21] Not death at the head of any army, as was preferable for a Hellenistic monarch: see, e.g., Polyb. 18.41; Chaniotis 2005, 60–1; Landucci Gattinoni 1990. Dumont 1987, 206, described Eunus' death as 'la mort ignominieuse'.

[22] Keaveney and Madden 1982, 94.

who were the object of hostile narrative treatment, such as Antiochus IV Epiphanes, Sulla, Pheretime and Herod Antipater, thus fitting the wider, negative characterisation of Eunus.[23]

The Companions

Eunus' companions on his capture add to the negative characterisation in this passage. We learn that he had only four attendants left when he was dragged out of his cave: a cook (μάγειρος); a baker (ἀρτοποιός); a masseuse (τρίβων); and a drinking-party entertainer (τοῦ παρὰ τοὺς πότους εἰωθότος ψυχαγωγεῖν αὐτόν). Eunus was thus depicted as a degenerate monarch and therefore is contrasted directly with his former guards:[24] no military figure was left with him, only companions who could attend to his luxurious, physical desires. Eunus' companions intensify the accusations of cowardice in his flight with further suggestions of his excessively luxurious lifestyle, and they contrast Eunus with the prevalent model in Greek thought that a 'good' leader refused luxuries and excess.[25] The focus on luxury in his demise is designed to complement Eunus' characterisation as a cowardly and unworthy Hellenistic king. Moreover, Diodorus' language when describing the fourth attendant, the entertainer, relates directly to how he introduced Eunus himself into the narrative. This, we will see, suggests that the construction of Eunus' death narrative was serving a specific purpose in the overall story of the revolt.

The fourth attendant is described as one (34/5.2.22) τοῦ παρὰ τοὺς πότους εἰωθότος ψυχαγωγεῖν αὐτόν, 'who had been accustomed, throughout the drinking bouts, to beguiling (Eunus)'. The verb used, ψυχαγωγέω, meaning 'to beguile' in this context, echoes Eunus' introduction into the narrative, where Diodorus gave a lengthy aside on Eunus' history prior to his involvement in the rebellion. In particular, Diodorus describes Eunus' relationship with his master (34/5.2.7–8), telling us that Eunus' master, Antigenes, was rather taken with his slave's outspoken claims and made him into a dinner entertainer. However, the verb describing Antigenes' relationship to Eunus (ψυχαγωγέω) is used in exactly the same way as in the previous passage: Antigenes was beguiled by Eunus. The relationship between the passage describing Eunus' beguilement of his master and his own death is clear and suggests an effort at ring-composition in the construction of Eunus' character. For example, Eunus' beguilement of his own master took place in the context of dinner parties, while his servant (34/5.2.22) **παρὰ τοὺς πότους** εἰωθότος ψυχαγωγεῖν αὐτόν, 'had been accustomed, **throughout the drinking bouts**, to beguiling (Eunus)'

---

[23] Antiochus IV: 2 Maccabees 9:5, 8–10; Sulla: Plut. *Sull.* 36; Pheretime: Hdt. 4.205; Herod Antipater: *Acts* 12.23.
[24] Grünewald 2004, 61.
[25] Some Hellenistic authors singled out leisure, dining companions and the exercise of self-control as essential subjects for a king to attend to: see Aristeas, *Ad Phil.* 284 and 286; Ath. 166f–167c and 260d–261a; Xen. *Mem.* 1.5.1–5, *Oec.* 12.9–14; Pl. *Grg.* 527D; Isoc. *To Nicocles* 29 and *Nicocles* 39. For modern discussions see also Goodenough 1928, 69–70, 87–9 and 95; Schubart 1937, 6; Murray 1967, 356; Cairns 1989, 19–20; Flower 1994, 104–11; Bertelli 2002, 34–8; Murray 2007.

(my emphasis). While the context is not identical, the implication of luxury is there in both passages. The inference is that Diodorus is linking Eunus to his own master in order to create a neat circle in Eunus' personal narrative: he has gone from the beguiler of a foolish master to the beguiled himself (and by logical association, foolish as well). It also suggests that Diodorus' intention was to portray Eunus, in spite of his role as the leader of a revolt against the actions and mistreatments of harsh masters, as no better than the same men he had risen up against: in a sense, Eunus became the master he had put to death during the uprising (Diod. Sic. 34/5.2.15). The fragmentary state of Diodorus' narrative means that we can only hint at the full interrelationship between Eunus and Antigenes, but this allusion demonstrates the effort to create a convincing story about Eunus' character: through certain careful applications of vocabulary and a circular narrative, the text turns the reader against Eunus.[26]

We have seen that Eunus' character in the narrative of Diodorus is that of a luxuriant, militarily inexperienced coward described in terms that were consistent with Diodorus' own concept of (bad) Hellenistic leadership as well as wider, derogatory ideas about Hellenistic kingship. Furthermore, we have seen that Diodorus made explicit links between Eunus and his master Antigenes, creating a comparison between the two that ended with Eunus' assumption of the role that his master had filled in the narrative. It is also important to note that this portrayal of Eunus – in spite of the fragmentary and compressed nature of the source that does not give the full picture of his development – is consistent throughout his rise to power and his subsequent demise. There is a final aspect directly related to Eunus' character to consider, and that is Diodorus' insistent references to wonder-working when introducing Eunus, and, subsequently, when commenting on his rise to kingship.

Τερατεία and *τερατευόμενος*: 'Wonders' and a 'Wonder-Working'

In his introduction of Eunus, Diodorus included a lengthy aside on Eunus' actions prior to the start of the revolt that creates a context for the reader's interpretation of his actions throughout the narrative (Diod. Sic. 34/5.2.5–8). This episode, discussed in part above, demonstrates Eunus' pretensions to wonder-working. This aside outlined how Eunus gained fame for his apparent abilities at prophecy through his special relationship with Atargatis and his consequent position as Antigenes' dinner entertainer. In this capacity, Eunus had close access to Antigenes' dinner guests, who engaged with his alleged prophecy. This passage is highly important for the construction of Eunus' character in the narrative.

Eunus is described consistently. He is first introduced as a (34/5.2.5) μάγος καὶ τερατουργὸς, 'magician and wonder-worker'. Immediately afterwards, Diodorus clarifies that Eunus προσεποιεῖτο . . . προλέγειν τὰ μέλλοντα, 'claimed . . . to foretell

---

[26] Angius 2020, 108, notes that Diodorus' proem shows that Diodorus conceived of history as having a cyclical nature, guided by Providence (1.1.3), an idea that supports this reading of Eunus' characterisation.

the future' and that Eunus pretended (ὑποκρίνετο)[27] that he saw gods. In spite of his claims to the contrary, Eunus' actions are always described strictly in terms of creative impulse, not divine inspiration. This characterisation of Eunus is followed in the only Latin text to record anything significant about him. Florus (2.7.4) describes him as *(s)yrus quidam nomine Eunus . . . fanatico furore simulato, dum Syriae deae comas iactat . . .*, 'a certain Syrian named Eunus . . . counterfeiting an inspired frenzy and waving his hair for the Syrian goddess . . .' Florus is explicit that Eunus' frenzy is fake. However, these fraudulent claims gained Eunus considerable fame (Diod. Sic. 34/5.2.6). This reputation led to his position as entertainer at his master's dinner parties (34/5.2.8) and, ultimately, to his election as king. When Eunus was elected king, Diodorus remarked that it was principally because of his wonder-working (τερατεία). Throughout the passage quoted above (34/5.2.5–8), Diodorus consistently uses vocabulary based on this concept of 'wonders' (τέρατα: for example, see 34/5.2.5 for τερατουργός; or 34/5.2.8 for τερατεία and τερατεύομαι). The description of Eunus' reputation as a wonder-worker remains uniform, much like the insistence that Eunus lacked both ἀνδρεία and στρατηγία, and so Diodorus is again linking his portrayal of Eunus to general stereotypes. However, for Diodorus they seem to have a deeper pejorative sense than appears on the surface.

The negative connotations of the words τερατεία and τερατευόμενος can be found earlier than Diodorus in Polybius and his descriptions of other authors' techniques. The word is consistently used to describe 'tragic' history that focused more on sensationalism than historical 'fact'.[28] For Polybius, in the historiographical context, τερατεία and τερατευόμενος were both linked to ψεῦδος, 'falsehood' in history (for example 2.58.12), and Diodorus makes it quite clear that Eunus' τερατεῖαι were false; he seems to be working from the same concept of τερατεία as does Polybius.[29] Polybius, then, provides a framework for the proposed interpretation of Diodorus: Eunus' description is linked to a mode of behaviour stereotyped as deceptive and false. This can be explored further by investigating Greek ideas of 'magic' and 'magic-workers' to see how the connotations inherent in these concepts inform our interpretation of Eunus' character as they would have Diodorus' contemporary readers.

Diodorus labours to characterise Eunus' actions as illegitimate and fraudulent. Additionally, he describes Eunus as a μάγος: magician. There were several terms in the ancient world that came to be used synonymously and to carry the generic meaning of 'magician', normally as a pejorative: μάγος, 'magician'; γόης, 'sorcerer'; and φαρμακεύς, 'poisoner/sorcerer'.[30] Holy men and 'magicians' from the east of the

---

[27] The choice of ὑποκρίνετο to describe Eunus' actions is important. The verb's strong connections to acting on stage and exaggeration stress that Eunus' pretence was intentional.

[28] Polybius uses vocabulary connected to τερατεία in a number of places to describe the style of other historians: see, e.g., 2.56.10 and 2.58.12 for Phylarchus; and 7.7.1 for other historians (not named).

[29] For a discussion of the meaning of τερατεία in Polybius in relation to sensationalism and critique of other historians, see Marincola 2001, 135, and 2010, 453–4.

[30] Μάγος: this originally meant a Median priest, but during the Archaic period it came to mean a fraudulent magician; Nock 1972, 323–4; Gordon 1999, 99, 104; Dickie 2001, 14–15; Janowitz 2001, 9. Γόης: according to the *Suda* s.v. Γοητεία, a γόης designated a magician who summoned up corpses. Modern scholars trace the term γόης to one who used lamentations in summoning the dead:

Mediterranean were typically understood, in both the Greek and the Roman worlds, to be skilled in prophecy, provided their prophetic abilities were not used to enhance their own authority: in this case they were considered lowly magicians.[31] It is not surprising that in Eunus' case the word chosen was μάγος, in line with the Syrian connotations regarding his origin (Diod. Sic 34/5.2.5). The Romans believed, at least in the first century BC, that the religious observances of the μάγοι in Persia were suspect;[32] in Roman literature there were also clear distinctions between Roman 'state' religious practices, which were acceptable, and magical rites of a foreign and dangerous nature.[33] This led to the use of the terms μάγος and γόης for stigmatising 'socially deviant, and therefore undesirable, views and behaviour'.[34] Whatever the successes accomplished (and recorded) for such men, the terminology used to describe them was consistently negatively charged.

Furthermore, the centrality of this 'wonder-working' to Eunus' character returns, as we have seen, in his election to kingship: the apex of his success. After commenting on the qualities for which Eunus was not elected, ἀνδρεία τε καὶ στρατηγία, Diodorus informs us of the reasons for his election (34/5.2.14): διὰ δὲ μόνην τερατείαν καὶ τὸ τῆς ἀποστάσεως ἄρξαι, 'only because of his knowledge of wonders and his setting of the revolt in motion'. We can now understand Diodorus' tone in this exclamation, given his clear prejudices against the use of τερατεία. It is hardly positive that the rebels were duped by Eunus, and his false wonder-working could not be considered flattering. It is therefore apparent that part of Eunus' deplorable character infects his crowning achievement, further undermining his success, on top of his cowardice and military ineptitude. Moreover, there is an additional element of Diodorus' scorn for Eunus at his crowning moment that we have not yet examined.

---

see Johnston 1999, 103. Φαρμακεύς: this is related to the use of drugs or poisons, although it quickly lost this association; Dickie 2001, 14. See Nock 1972, 323–4, and Dickie 2001, 13–16, for the pejorative sense. They also carried an expectation of trickery: Dickie 2001, 75–6, noted that Herodotus called the Neuroi γόητες for their claims to change into wolves because he thought their claims to be false, and not because he believed they did magic.

[31] Dickie 2001, 112.
[32] See Catull. 90 and Graf 1985, 37–8.
[33] See Dench 1995, 167.
[34] Flintermann 1995, 67. See also Dickie 2001, 137–41. While we must not deny that Roman religion was, in some respects, open to other religious practices (e.g. North 1975, 8–11; Beard 1985; North 2000, 54–7), Roman religion was still closed to a variety of outside influences, especially after the third century BC, and could be vehemently opposed to certain cultic practices and groups, such as the Bacchanalia or the Chaldaeans: see Gallini 1970; North 1979, 85–9; Pailler 1988; North 1992, 181; North 2000, 63–8.

Despite these clear prejudices, some magical practitioners were remarkably successful: for example, Simon Magus from the *Acts of Peter*, or Alexander the False Prophet from Lucian's *Alexander*. We might even include Jesus of Nazareth: in Mark 3:22, Luke 11:15–20, and Matt. 10:24–5, 12:27–8, the scribes and Pharisees called Jesus a magician, who cast out demons in the name of Beelzebul. Smith 1978, 32 and 174, notes that this demon is (32) 'unmistakably Palestinian'. Moreover, Jesus was called (John 8:48) a Samaritan, a connection to Simon Magus, the Samaritan magician. Justin, *Dial.* 69.7, 108.2, preserves evidence of Jewish claims that Jesus was a magician (69.7: μάγος) and Origen, *C. Cels.* 1.68, notes that Jesus was compared to a γόης.

Setting the Revolt in Motion

We have seen above that Diodorus gave yet another reason for Eunus' election (34/5.2.14): τὸ τῆς ἀποστάσεως ἄρξαι, 'his setting of the revolt in motion'. To understand the event to which Diodorus refers, we must turn to a passage from earlier in the narrative preserved in the Constantinian excerpts. After describing the treatment of Damophilus' slaves, Diodorus relates that they went to Eunus to ascertain if they had the approval of the gods for their rebellion (34/5.2.24b):[35]

Ὅτι συνετίθεντο πρὸς ἀλλήλους οἱ δοῦλοι περὶ ἀποστάσεως καὶ φόνου τῶν κυρίων. παρελθόντες δὲ πρὸς τὸν Εὔνουν οὐκ ἄπωθεν διατρίβοντα ἠρώτων εἰ συγχωρεῖται παρὰ τῶν θεῶν αὐτοῖς τὸ βεβουλευμένον. ὁ δὲ τερατευόμενος μετ' ἐνθουσιασμοῦ καὶ περὶ τίνων ἥκουσι ἀκούσας διεσάφησεν ὅτι διδόασιν αὐτοῖς οἱ θεοὶ τὴν ἀπόστασιν, ἐὰν μηδεμίαν ὑπερβολὴν ποιησάμενοι παραχρῆμα μὲν ἐγχειρήσωσι ταῖς ἐπιβολαῖς· ὑπὸ γὰρ τῆς πεπρωμένης αὐτοῖς κεκυρῶσθαι πατρίδα τὴν Ἔνναν, οὖσαν ἀκρόπολιν ὅλης τῆς νήσου.

The slaves agreed with one another about revolt and the murder of their masters. They came to Eunus, who was spending time not far away, and they asked if their decision was approved by the gods. He began working wonders in a frenzy, and when he heard why they had come he made clear that the gods gave them permission to revolt, so long as they did not delay but immediately undertook their enterprise: for it was fated that Enna, the citadel of the whole island, was fixed as their homeland.

It is worth noting that Diodorus is consistent in the language he uses to describe Eunus' actions, which includes vocabulary based on τέρατα and its derivations. Moreover, Eunus' response to the rebels betrays a detail of his character. We learn that when asked the gods' opinions of rebels' proposal, Eunus began working wonders (ὁ δὲ τερατευόμενος), but waited until περὶ τίνων ἥκουσι ἀκούσας, 'he heard why they had come', to grant them permission, and encourage them to act quickly. The slaves only asked initially if their decision was approved (εἰ συγχωρεῖται παρὰ τῶν θεῶν αὐτοῖς τὸ βεβουλευμένον), but had provided no details, and it appears from the narrative that Eunus delayed his prophecy in order to hear the full details.[36] Eunus' prophetic powers are faked, as Diodorus has already made clear by this stage: he was not actually divinely inspired, and so preferred, as this passage implies, to know as much as possible before 'divining'.

Throughout the narrative, Eunus is described in strikingly different terms from those of the rebels he later led. Concerning the slaves, Diodorus tells us that the slave owners in Sicily were abusing their slaves through a combination of depriving them of adequate clothing, malnutrition, and continuing estrangement that provoked what

---

[35] There is a parallel passage preserved by Photius (34/5.2.10), which records the event in less detail.
[36] In contrast, the Photian version (34/5.2.10) has the slaves ask Eunus for advice, and immediately on working his wonders (μετὰ τερατείας) Eunus confirms that the gods approve: he acts without knowing what the slaves' resolve was.

they then called banditry (34/5.2.2 and 26). When describing Damophilus' treatment of slaves, Diodorus notes his lack of provisioning for his herdsmen (34/5.2.36) and his poor relationship towards suppliant slaves (34/5.2.38).[37] When this is compared with Eunus' experience, the contrast is apparent. Although we lack comment on any possible paucity in his own provisions, any potential association with such food paucity is offset in the narrative by his close access to his master at dinner parties and the added bonus that (34/5.2.8) τινες αὐτῶν ἀπὸ τῆς τραπέζης ἀξιολόγους μερίδας αἴροντες ἐδωροῦντο, 'some of (the dinner guests), lifting substantial portions from the table, gave them to him as gifts'.[38] Furthermore, Eunus' position as the dinner entertainer gave him a close relationship with his master; it appears from these aspects of the narrative that he was a favoured slave who enjoyed close access to his master, in contrast to the other slaves described in Diodorus' narrative. Up to the moment when the estranged and mistreated slaves came to Eunus, his lifestyle had been completely separated from theirs, as he had not experienced or shared in their collective plight. This suggests that his subsequent leadership of the revolt was vitiated in the mind of an ancient reader: Eunus was actually benefiting from his position as a slave and his opportunistic pretence of prophecy; his leadership of the revolt was a mark of further opportunism on his part. He shared no experience of bad treatment, creating a separation between Eunus and his subjects in the mind of the reader.

By singling out Eunus in this way, Diodorus set up the platform for his subsequent negative portrayal of Eunus, the cowardly king. Diodorus was not crediting Eunus with any positive characteristics. The connotations inherent in the language, shown above, and the clear indications given by Diodorus that Eunus was not actually a divinely inspired seer serve to denigrate his character in preparation for the portrayal of his subsequent important role. Indeed, the strength of this characterisation led one scholar – interested in magic and magicians, not slavery – to comment that the 'account we have of Eunus' career will be in some measure an imaginative recreation . . . based on patterns of behaviour with which [the author] was familiar'.[39] This description left little doubt about the author's opinion of the man.

The depiction of Eunus in Diodorus is unremittingly hostile. At no point in the narrative is Eunus praised unless the praise is tempered with a corresponding caveat or explanatory denigration of either him or his followers. The associations crafted throughout Diodorus' narrative with Hellenistic kingship and wonder-working are consistent from Eunus' introduction to his pathetic death in a Morgantina jail. It is striking that the strongest scorn is reserved for the most significant moment of Eunus' career, his acclamation to kingship. At this moment Diodorus ties together all the threads of abuse employed throughout the narrative against Eunus, negating

---

[37] See Roth 2005, 291–2, for the suggestion that the text's view of the provisioning of herdsmen may in fact be a deliberate misrepresentation or unintentional misunderstanding of a system whereby the enslaved provided for themselves via what has been termed personal production.

[38] Although it might be objected that this is a positive reading of a paternalistic relationship between the dinner guests and Eunus, despite the potential benefits to Eunus.

[39] Dickie 2001, 113.

the importance of Eunus' achievements and destroying any credibility of Eunus, once king. Furthermore, his depiction in Diodorus is composed to create certain narrative effects that are unlikely to correspond to reality, but are driven by different authorial interests. The symbolic connection between Eunus and his master, Antigenes, also indicates that, because of literary finesse that placed Eunus in the position of his own degenerate master by the end of his life, we cannot trust the impression of Eunus, the rebel leader, given by the text for historical purposes. Awash with stereotypes and literary plays, Eunus' character is a caricature designed to turn the reader against him. This observation can be strengthened by considering how Diodorus contrasted Eunus with his στρατηγός, Kleon.

A Military Man

As I argued above, one of Eunus' defining negative features at the moment of his acclamation as king was his lack of bravery and generalship (ἀνδρεία τε καὶ στρατηγία). Kleon's character, and to a certain extent that of his brother Komanus, contrasts with this aspect of Eunus' character as he fulfilled the role of general for his king, as Diodorus describes it (34/5.2.17), and thus completed the rebel leadership. There is considerably less comment on Kleon compared with Eunus, but the existing text suggests that his character, like Eunus', was generally portrayed negatively. Unlike Eunus, Kleon has only two defining moments in Diodorus' extant narrative, and although he is mentioned in other authors he does not feature prominently. Kleon's introduction into the narrative comes after the description of the initial uprising in two parallel passages in Photius and the Constantinian excerpts (34/5.2.17 and 34/5.2.43 respectively), the latter of which runs as follows:

> Ὅτι καὶ ἄλλη τις ἐγένετο ἀπόστασις δραπετῶν καὶ σύστημα ἀξιόλογον. Κλέων γάρ τις Κίλιξ ἐκ τῶν περὶ τὸν Ταῦρον τόπων, συνήθης ὢν ἐκ παίδων τῷ ληστρικῷ βίῳ καὶ κατὰ τὴν Σικελίαν νομεὺς γεγονὼς ἱπποφορβίων, οὐ διέλιπεν ὁδοιδοκῶν καὶ παντοδαποὺς φόνους ἐπιτελούμενος. ὃς πυθόμενος τὴν κατὰ τὸν Εὔνουν προκοπὴν καὶ τὰς τῶν μετ' αὐτοῦ δραπετῶν εὐημερίας ἀποστάτης ἐγένετο, καί τινας τῶν πλησίον οἰκετῶν πείσας συναπονοήσασθαι κατέτρεχε τὴν πόλιν τῶν Ἀκραγαντίνων καὶ τὴν πλησιόχωρον πᾶσαν.

> There was another revolt of runaways and a band worthy of mention. For a certain Kleon, a Cilician from a region about the Taurus, who was accustomed from childhood to a life of banditry and in Sicily became a herder of horses, constantly waylaid people and committed murders of every kind. When he learned of the progress of Eunus, and the successes of the runaways with him, he became a rebel and persuading some of the slaves nearby to share in folly with him he overran the city of Acragas and all the surrounding countryside.

From Valerius Maximus we gain the only mention of Kleon in Latin. In a short passage about the death of Kleon's brother, Komanus, Valerius records the following (9.12.Ext. 1):

Sunt et externae mortes dignae adnotatu. Qualis in primis Comae, quem ferunt maximi latronum ducis Cleonis fratrem fuisse.

There are external deaths too worth noting, such as that of Coma [Komanus in Diodorus], who is said to have been brother to Cleon, the great leader of brigands.

Descriptions of Kleon's character use two terms: *latro* and ληστής, 'bandit' or 'robber'.[40] It is with these core terms that we should begin to analyse the depiction of Kleon's character.

Bandits in the Ancient World

In the ancient world, as Shaw has shown, banditry was considered endemic.[41] Indeed, the terms *latro* and ληστής both carry with them a commonly understood knowledge that they spoke of someone engaged in violent robbery. However, the terms are more complicated. Legally *latro* meant a robber,[42] but it was also used to label people who fought against the Roman state by unconventional means, meaning that they could not be called *hostes* and were instead termed *latrones* (or *praedones*).[43] Beyond their legal meaning, the terms had strong connotations in literature. Often an ancient author writing about a conflict in which he had particular disdain for one party would use terms such as *latrocinium* and ληστήρια, 'banditry', in order to slander the scorned party.[44] Furthermore, these terms could be used to describe a great range of individual people whom an author particularly disliked, and in fact this became something of a political *topos* in the late Republic and thereafter.[45] In each case the actual events

---

[40] In this case used to describe the men that Kleon led: 'maximi latronum ducis', 'a great leader of brigands'. In the case of the passage above, it is a variant in the adjectival form: συνήθης ὢν ἐκ παίδων τῷ ληστρικῷ βίῳ, 'who was accustomed from childhood to a life of **banditry**'. It should be noted that the terms *latro* and ληστής have a far greater variety and complexity of meaning than the English translations 'robber' or 'bandit'. On banditry in the ancient world, see Briant 1976; Burian 1984; Shaw 1984.

[41] Shaw 1984, 9. See also Grünewald 2004, 18–25.

[42] The specific requirement to classify as a *latro* was the resort to violence (Call. *Dig.* 48.19.28.10), although another aspect of a *latro* was the gathering of a band (*factio*) around them (Marc. *Dig.* 48.19.11.2); see also Grünewald 2004, 15.

[43] Pompon. *Dig.* 50.16.118 pr.; Mommsen 1899, 629 n. 4; Grünewald 2004, 15–16.

[44] For example, Appian uses the term to describe the war with Viriathus (App. *Hisp.* 71.301; 73.310); in Tacitus' *Annals* Tacfarinas is described using this term (Tac. *Ann.* 2.52; 3.20, 32, 73; 4.23–6; Aur. Vict. *Caes.* 2.3); and Josephus used the term λῃσταί to refer to the Jewish rebels in the constant wars and battles in Judaea from 64 BC to the Jewish War. On the latter war see Rhoads 1976, 159–62, and Rajak 1983, 84–5, 123, 132, 161.

[45] See Watson 2002, 215–16. Cicero branded his political opponents such as L. Sergius Catilina (Cic. *Cat.* 1.9.23; 1.10.27; 1.13.31, 33) and M. Antonius *latrones*. In the latter case Cicero refers to Antony himself as a *latro* twenty-five times (*Phil.* 2.5.6, 5.9, 6.2, 9.10, 62.14; 3.29.11; 4.5.13, 15.3, 15.8; 5.23.6, 30.6; 6.12.10; 11.36.9; 12.12.15, 17.2, 20.4, 27.18; 13.10.5, 16.5, 19.2, 21.2; 14.8.2, 10.4, 27.15, 31.9), his band of followers as *latrones* eleven times (*Phil.* 2.87.6; 4.9.9; 5.6.10, 18.9; 6.3.14, 4.12; 8.9.2; 11.14.10; 12.15.7; 13.26.21; 14.21.3), and his associates and followers as *latrones* five times (*Phil.* 11.4.10, 7.5, 10.0, 32.5; 13.26.21). Cicero even compares Antony with Spartacus; see Cic. *Phil.* 4.15.3 and 13.22.16. On the use of *latro* in Cicero's speeches against Catiline, see Habinek 1998, 69–87. Leaders of guerrilla movements against Roman authority such as Viriathus or Bulla Felix were also described this way (Livy, *Per.* 52; Flor. 1.33.15; Cass. Dio 76.10).

taking place could hardly be realistically termed ληστήρια or *latrocinium*, 'banditry', and yet, nonetheless, the ancient writers used these terms as derogatory expressions to slander their enemies.

It should now be clear that by using the terms *latro* and ληστής to describe Kleon in the context of a conflict between an armed rebellious group and an established state (in this case Rome), the ancient authors were associating him with a well-known system of abuse that an ancient reader of their works would have understood. Furthermore, the actual narrative itself leaves no doubt concerning Kleon's character. Diodorus relates that Kleon (34/5.2.43) οὐ διέλιπεν ὁδοιδοκῶν καὶ παντοδαποὺς φόνους ἐπιτελούμενος, 'constantly waylaid people and committed murders of every kind'. In Hellenistic ideologies regarding kingship, an insatiable desire for warring was not a positive characteristic, as we have seen.[46] It is also clear from the description of Kleon's actions once in Sicily that he was not forced into his brutal behaviour; rather he was συνήθης ὢν ἐκ παίδων, 'accustomed from childhood', to this type of behaviour. Another aspect of his background further intensifies this fact: he is a Cilician. By the 70s BC, this area of the Mediterranean around Southern Anatolia had become infamous as a breeding ground and homeland of pirates in a narrative that was connected to Rome's claims about its role in keeping the Mediterranean peace.[47] Because of Rome's efforts to depict the Cilicians as pirates, an association built up in Roman (and Greek) minds that connected Cilicians with brigandage on principle: De Souza has shown that Strabo (14.3.2), Appian (*Mith.* 92), Dio (36.20–3) and Plutarch (*Pomp.* 24) presented a picture of Cilicians and Pamphylians as 'dyed-in-the-wool pirates'.[48] Diodorus' depiction of Kleon fits this particular prejudice: Kleon, a Cilician, was a brigand from childhood; indeed, calling him a Cilician underscored that point craftily.

A Natural Savage

Above we saw that Diodorus carefully segregated Eunus from his followers in terms of the treatment received by him from his master. We can see this pattern emerging again with Kleon. Kleon was not forced into brigandage, but having been accustomed to it from childhood then engaged in violent brigandage once in Sicily. In comparison, Diodorus makes it clear in his narrative that the acts of brigandage committed by the slave herdsmen of Sicily were the result of desperation caused by a lack of provisions from their masters (34/5.2.2, 27–8).[49] In fact, this detail is a key part of the background

---

[46] Following the reconstruction of Philodemus in Murray 1965, Philodemus argued that (col. IX 14–16) '(t)he good ruler must therefore be warlike, but not a lover of war or of battle'. Aristeas likewise argues that military exploits for their own sake are a negative characteristic of leaders (*Ad Phil.* 223): see Murray 1967, 354–5, and Schubart 1937, 5.

[47] On the role of Roman self-presentation and Rome's representation of the Cilicians, see Avidov 1997, De Souza 1999, 97–148, and De Souza 2008.

[48] De Souza 1999, 97. See also Grünewald 2004, 60 and 76–9. The association was long-lasting, even into the Byzantine period, when the area also produced the finest soldiers of the Byzantine army. See Ormerod 1924, 192.

[49] In 34/5.2.28 Diodorus explains that the herdsmen were compelled to turn to banditry διὰ δὲ τὴν τῆς τροφῆς ἔνδειαν, 'because of their lack of food'.

to the war given in both Diodorus and Strabo (6.2.6). Kleon stands in contrast to the other herdsmen described by Diodorus in his narrative because Kleon chose, once in Sicily, to continue his actions with unremitting violence. In another passage Diodorus clarifies that the slaves were not violent naturally but because of how they had been treated in Sicily (34/5.2.40). By contrast, Kleon is described as accustomed to violence throughout his life rather than through circumstances, which separates him further from his subsequent followers.[50]

The final facet of this characterisation lies in the origin of Kleon's decision to go to war. He was, at this stage, already a brigand, and his decision to revolt was predicated not on the fact that he was forced into brigandage, but merely because Eunus had been successful (34/5.2.43):

ὃς πυθόμενος τὴν κατὰ τὸν Εὔνουν προκοπὴν καὶ τὰς τῶν μετ' αὐτοῦ δραπετῶν εὐημερίας ἀποστάτης ἐγένετο . . .

When he learned of the progress of Eunus, and the successes of the runaways with him, he became a rebel . . .

Much like Eunus, who is presented as having joined the rebellion in what could be interpreted as an act of opportunism, Kleon also opportunistically seizes the moment. In spite of these negative pronouncements about Kleon's character, it is undeniable that he was a successful general for Eunus at first: under his command, the rebels captured, as we have seen, Enna, Morgantina, Tauromenium, Agrigentum and Catana (Diod. Sic. 34/5.2.20–2, 43; Strabo 6.2.6; Oros. 5.9.5), and won a number of battles against Roman commanders (Diod. Sic. 34/5.2.18–20; Flor. 2.7.7–8). Diodorus' record of this success does not outweigh the extensively negative account Kleon receives elsewhere in the narrative. It was not impossible in ancient narratives for wicked characters to be a successful generals: L. Sergius Catilina and Q. Servilius Caepio were both severely censured for the manner in which they gained their successes and victories.[51] Furthermore, it could be argued that the success attributed to Kleon, which had to be acknowledged given the length of the war and the extensive area that was controlled by the rebel forces, was undercut by the way in which the overall narrative of the war was presented in the ancient sources.

Death and Redemption

As we have seen, Kleon is presented as a bloodthirsty bandit. However, in one context he is described positively, as is his brother Komanus, and that is on the occasion of his

---

[50] See also Dowden (*BNJ* 87 F108o), where he notes that Kleon 'does not even take a breath between murderous robbery in Cilicia and the same in Sicily'.

[51] L. Sergius Catilina: despite being presented as 'malo pravoque' ('evil and depraved'), and as a person that 'bella intestina, caedes, rapinae, discordia civilis grata fuere . . .' ('revelled in civil wars, murders, pillage and political dissension', Sall. *Cat.* 5.1–2), he is later credited with considerable skills as a general (Sall. *Cat.* 59; 60.4–5) and bravery in death (Sall. *Cat.* 60.7). Q. Servilius Caepio: he was heavily criticised for the murder of Viriatus. See Val. Max. 9.6.4; App. *Hisp.* 69.295–300.

death. For Kleon, the passage is preserved by Photius' epitome of Diodorus in a very compressed form, but shows a brave ending to his life (34/5.2.21):

καὶ Κλέωνα τὸν στρατηγὸν ἐξελθόντα τῆς πόλεως καὶ ἡρωικῶς ἀγωνισάμενον μετ' ὀλίγων ὑπὸ τῶν τραυμάτων δείξας νεκρόν . . .

After the general Kleon had come out of the city, and had exerted himself heroically with a few men, Rupilius displayed him dead from his wounds . . .

There are some features here we will come back to, but for the moment it is necessary to note that Kleon is described as struggling ἡρωικῶς, 'heroically'. For Komanus, as already briefly discussed above, our evidence comes from Valerius Maximus, who recorded his capture and death at Tauromenium before the Roman commander P. Rupilius (noted in Diod. Sic. 34/5.2.20). In this passage, from a series *de mortibus non vulgaribus*, 'on deaths out of the ordinary', Komanus, called Coma by Valerius Maximus, is praised for his willingness to kill himself rather than holding out through torture so as not to give away any details of the rebels' efforts (Val. Max. 9.12.Ext. 1).[52] The regard that these two rebel leaders gained for their final actions is marked, but we must be careful to consider them in their context. In the narrative the deaths of the two brothers come immediately before Eunus' cowardly and unmanly flight discussed above. These heroic deaths – Kleon died while fighting μετ' ὀλίγων, 'with a few men', further augmenting his heroism – served to contrast with the failure of Eunus to end his life well: the narrative implies that even Kleon and his brother, brigands of the worst kind, could die in a brave manner.[53] By this narrative flourish, Diodorus adds yet another layer to the character assassination of Eunus. While their brave deaths do not make up for their otherwise wicked lives, Kleon and Komanus regain some recognition from Diodorus, designed, however, to contrast with Eunus, and thereby deride him further.

Discussion of Kleon and Komanus cannot go further; there are no further lines with which to pursue their characterisation. Nonetheless, from the little text that does survive it is evident that both Kleon and Komanus were negatively characterised in a similar manner to Eunus. For Kleon this was achieved through reference to preconceptions about behaviour and character linked to a geographical origin in Cilicia and political invective based on concepts of banditry (*latro*; λῃστής). These references suggested that he possessed a natural bloodlust at odds with his compatriot slaves: much like Eunus, he was distanced from his subordinates. Furthermore, his only redeeming feature, his brave death, can be read as part of a narrative structure that offered a counterpoint to Eunus' lack of bravery in his own death. In short, Kleon's character complements that of Eunus, configuring a match made in hell. The latter, a coward without military experience, is assisted by his στρατηγός, a bloodthirsty bandit. It is

---

[52] Grünewald 2004, 60, comments that Komanus' death fits the image of bandits in ancient literature that emphasised their 'invincibility' and their defiance towards their conquerors. Grünewald sees Komanus' death, therefore, as an instance of 'a basic characteristic of the ancient bandit'.
[53] My thanks to John Marincola for suggesting this interpretation.

clear that with Kleon, as with Eunus, Diodorus and the wider literary tradition used a vocabulary resonant with contemporary ideology and stereotypes. Taken together, these two men are presented in the ancient literary tradition as poor choices for leadership, and they dominate the narratives that survive. The intense interest of the extant literary narratives in the leadership is mirrored, as we will see, by a fixation on the role of (bad) master–slave relationships as the cause and driving aspect of the conflict. The following section will show that this interest in the master–slave relationship had an effect on Diodorus' narrative that altered the text's rhetoric in ways that make its presentation of the rebels' motivations and intentions problematic for the purpose of historical reconstruction.

Rhetoric and History

The ancient historiographical tradition of the war was also interested in what motivated the revolt itself in addition its interest in the characterisation of the revolt's leaders. In the developed narratives of this tradition there was one principal cause for the war: the arrogance of the slave owners living in Sicily, most clearly demonstrated in Diodorus' text but present in other narratives of the war, which led to the violent mistreatment of slaves.[54] This underpins all of Diodorus' narrative of the events in question. He comments throughout the text on the arrogance (ὑπερηφανία) of landowners on Sicily (34/5.2.26), Damophilus and his wife (34/5.2.10, 34, 35, 37, 38), and the rebellious slaves' masters generally (34/5.2.24b, 40, 46). This arrogance and the mistreatment that it caused drove the rebels to action (34/5.2.26):

> διὰ γὰρ τὴν ὑπερβολὴν τῆς εὐπορίας τῶν τὴν κρατίστην νῆσον ἐκκαρπουμένων ἅπαντες σχεδὸν οἱ τοῖς πλούτοις προκεκοφότες ἐζήλωσαν τὸ μὲν πρῶτον τρυφήν, εἶθ' ὑπερηφανίαν καὶ ὕβριν. ἐξ ὧν ἁπάντων αὐξανομένης ἐπ' ἴσης τῆς τε κατὰ τῶν οἰκετῶν κακουχίας καὶ τῆς κατὰ τῶν δεσποτῶν ἀλλοτριότητος, ἐρράγη ποτὲ σὺν καιρῷ τὸ μῖσος. ἐξ οὗ χωρὶς παραγγέλματος πολλαὶ μυριάδες συνέδραμον οἰκετῶν ἐπὶ τὴν τῶν δεσποτῶν ἀπώλειαν.

> Because of the excessive wealth of those enjoying the fruits of the most excellent island, nearly all of those who had become wealthy strove after first luxury, then arrogance and insolence. Because of this, and since the mistreatment of the slaves and their estrangement from their masters increased equally, there was, when opportune, a general outburst of hatred. From this, without formal command, tens of thousands of slaves joined forces for the destruction of their masters.

---

[54] Athenaeus preserves a fragment of Posidonius' history in which Damophilus is cited as the cause of the war (Ath. 12.542b). This passage is often taken to indicate that Posidonius' history is the source text for Diodorus' narrative of the war discussed here, for which see n. 4 above. In Orosius' brief account of the war, mistreatment of slaves is implied to be the cause of the revolt. He notes that the slaves of Messana did not revolt, because they had been treated fairly (5.6.4). Other briefer accounts give no indication of the cause or ascribe it to Eunus' inspiration: see Livy, *Per.* 56 and Flor. 2.7.4. Rathmann 2016, 301–2, argues that Diodorus ascribes the cause of the war to the actions of Italians and equestrians and their malpractice in Sicily, but underpinning this in the narrative is a clear interest in how slave owners more generally were acting. On this latter point, see Morton 2018.

In short, the revolt took place because of a failure of the master–slave relationship: this is in clear focus in the extant narratives for the rebel motivation, to the exclusion of all other concerns.[55] The rebel motivation is tied further in Diodorus' narrative to Eunus' capture of the rebels' loyalty and his use of their discontent to achieve his own rise to kingship. Eunus' role in the outbreak is evident in Florus' version of the events, in which he is given the sole responsibility for inciting the revolt (2.7.4), but it can be found also in Diodorus' depiction of Eunus encouraging Damophilus' discontented slaves to revolt (34/5.2.24b). The two aspects of the narrative are interlinked and deserve consideration alongside one another, not least because we have seen above that the way in which Eunus and Kleon were presented in the ancient literary sources is built upon ideology and stereotypes that created a specific narrative frame for these men. As we will see, similar concerns are at play in the description of the rebels' motivation.

In this section, therefore, I will offer a new reading of some important passages analysed above by studying the use of rhetorical and narratological strategies. The principal tools in this analysis include the rhetorical theory of 'identification' between rhetorician and audience and the narratological concepts of a covert narrator and embedded focalisation.[56] This section will focus on two aspects of Diodorus' narrative from a narratological perspective. First, we will analyse in brief how Diodorus deployed these rhetorical and narrative techniques in order to manipulate his readers into agreeing with his assessment of Eunus' character, and the implications that this has for our judgement of the rebels who chose him as their leader. Second, we will consider the rhetorical and narratological strategies employed in the depiction of the rebels' motivations in the text more generally, which throughout focuses on the importance of the master–slave relationship to the exclusion of all other considerations. We will start with a reconsideration of two passages in which Diodorus presents the relationship between Eunus and his followers.

Diodorus and his Reader

Diodorus attacked Eunus in his text through a consistent character assassination; demonstrating this was the focus of the first section of this chapter. We can understand the choices of vocabulary and ideology if we consider the narrative as a piece of rhetorical persuasion, in which the reader was intended to accept the descriptions

---

[55] Bradley 1989, 50–7, offers a discussion of this depiction of the master–slave relationship in the context of Roman slavery more generally.

[56] Aristotle considered the concept of identification in his *Rhetorica* (3.14.7–8) when he discussed the ways in which an ancient orator would strive, by appealing to respectability, to bring the audience on to their side: see also the discussion in Burke 1950, 55–6, which, although dated, is nonetheless a lucid analysis of 'identification' as a rhetorical technique. The ancient methodology of appealing to respectability, or any other trait thought acceptable to the audience (see also Cic. *De or.* 2.178; 182; 3.211–12) is also reflected as early as Booth 1961, 119–47, in his discussion of the role of shared beliefs and interests between the author and the audience in literature in general. The definition of embedded focalisation adopted here is that given in De Jong 2014, 50, where she describes this as a situation in which 'a primary narrator-focalizer can *embed* the focalization of a character in his narrator-text, recounting what that character is seeing, feeling, or thinking, without turning him into a secondary narrator-focalizer' (De Jong's emphasis). See also Bal 1985, 100–15, for a definition of focalisation.

given and draw the desired conclusions from them. To take this argument further, we should look again at two examples from Diodorus' narrative for which it seems more likely that he wrote inventively, rather than from a position of knowledge: Eunus' acclamation and the rebels' approach to Eunus before the attack on Enna.[57]

Thus, Eunus was acclaimed following the rebel capture of Enna and the execution of Damophilus and Megallis. Diodorus' description of this event defines Eunus as a coward with no military aptitude, but the manner in which he defines the positive and negative reasons for Eunus' acclamation deserves closer inspection. Diodorus tells us the following (34/5.2.14):

αἱρεῖται βασιλεὺς ὁ Εὔνους οὔτε δι' ἀνδρείαν οὔτε διὰ στρατηγίαν, διὰ δὲ μόνην τερατείαν καὶ τὸ τῆς ἀποστάσεως ἄρξαι, ἅμα δὲ καὶ τῆς προσηγορίας οἱονεί τινα καλὸν οἰωνὸν ἐχούσης πρὸς τὴν τῶν ὑποταττομένων εὔνοιαν.

Eunus was chosen king, and not because of his courage, nor his generalship, but only because of his knowledge of wonders and his setting of the revolt in motion, but also at the same time because his name seemed to hold some favourable omen in respect to the goodwill of his subjects.

In this passage, Diodorus is acting as a covert external narrator.[58] By this I mean that he does not overtly intrude into the narrative to give us his opinion of Eunus' election, and he was not taking an active part in the events described. Nonetheless, Diodorus' opinion of Eunus is focalised by the rebels in this passage in which we learn the thoughts of the rebels about why Eunus was acclaimed. In effect, our narrator has masked his opinion of Eunus' acclamation through an embedded focalisation, that is, through the eyes of the rebels. The rebels are not the primary narrator-focalisers of this text, but they are the point of view from which this passage is *presented*. Diodorus acts, therefore, as omniscient narrator, speaking what the rebels see and think. As Cohn has argued, for modern historiographical or even biographical texts, the narrator is expected to signpost moments of inference or conjecture, and there is a general admission that 'the minds of imaginary figures can be known in ways that those of real persons cannot'.[59] An omniscient narrator is quite at odds with what we might

---

[57] Finley 1985, 13–14, reminded us of the important consideration that on 'innumerable occasions Thucydides reported as a simple matter of fact that a political figure, a military commander, even a group of people adopted a particular course of action as the consequence of a particular idea, opinion or judgement when that was *at best* the historian's own assessment of the reason for the action, an inference back from the act to the thought' (my emphasis). The same, as we will see, can be said of Diodorus.

[58] The distinction between an 'overt' and 'covert' narrator follows the distinction put forward by Lubbock 1921, 62, 67, although the terminology of 'overt' and 'covert' does not stem from his work. For 'external' and 'internal' narrators, see De Jong 2014, 19; they can also be termed heterodiegetic and homodiegetic respectively.

[59] On the importance of 'conjectural and inferential syntax' in biographical and historiographical texts, see Cohn 1989, 9–10. For the quoted text see Cohn 1990, 785. These ideas were developed further in Cohn 1999, 18–37 and 109–31. Where the thoughts of past persons are reconstructed in modern works, Cohn argued, 1989, 10, this can only take place where there exist 'autobiographical documents', and even then, the pronouncements on what historical figures thought or felt can only be 'inductions'. On this, see also Collingwood 1946, 214.

expect to find in a modern historiographical account, where admissions of ignorance are accepted; the presence of such a narrator in this text, therefore, ought to make us concentrate much more closely not only on the veracity of what we are reading, but also its purpose.

For example, unless the acclamation was most irregular it is improbable that the rebels chose to acclaim Eunus for the reasons given. The context of this event is very important. Eunus had just won a significant military victory, secured the first stronghold of the rebellion, and to this point shown himself, to the rebels, to be nothing but a good leader. These features all fit with the Hellenistic ideology of kingship and acclamation. These are far better and far more 'Hellenistic' reasons to acclaim Eunus. What is being presented through this embedded focalisation at this point contradicts what we have been shown of Eunus.[60] Yet Diodorus as narrator describes this event using language that reflects a strong strand of Hellenistic ideology about kingship, albeit in a negative sense (ἀνδρεία; στρατηγία). Moreover, he chooses to emphasise at this point Eunus' connection to wonder-working, which he had been careful to assure the reader was fake. In keeping with Aristotle's pronouncement (*Rh.* 3.14.7–8) that a speaker causes an audience to favour a figure through carefully chosen agreeable traits, Diodorus attempts to turn his readers against Eunus by telling his audience that Eunus was the opposite of what the narrative showed him to be.

In the narrative context this can be argued as follows. At this stage in the narrative Eunus has not yet been 'shown' to be a coward. We have only Diodorus' word for it, and the rebels had no reason to think of him as such.[61] In order for this pronouncement to be agreeable to his audience, Diodorus had to link his depiction to the beliefs and attitudes with which his readers would identify. This desire for the narrative to be agreeable, or 'identifiable', in turn led to language that connected to Hellenistic ideals about kingship and stereotypes of religious behaviour. Moreover, Diodorus' use of the expression ἀνδρεία τε καὶ στρατηγία, seen already in his *Bibliotheke* so often, sets up anticipation in the reader of what is to follow: the moment Eunus is described as elected οὔτε δι' ἀνδρίαν, 'not because of his courage', the reader, by this point familiar with Diodorus' narrative style, can predict the completion of the phrase (οὔτε διὰ στρατηγίαν, 'nor his generalship'). As Burke put it: 'you will find yourself swinging along with the succession of antitheses'.[62] The predictable flow of Diodorus' prose is itself a rhetorical device. Eunus' unsuitability for kingship, therefore, is derived from Diodorus' plausible depiction of Eunus' wonder-working and the implication that Eunus was a coward: on Diodorus' terms Eunus is a poor choice for leader, and the rebels' reasons for choosing him are equally poor. Yet this says more about his and his expected audience's views on the critical faculties of the rebels for selecting their

[60] See Booth 1961, 3–9, for a discussion of this concept, and an explication of 'telling' as opposed to 'showing'.
[61] Even later in the narrative, while Eunus is in some respects 'shown' to be a coward, his actions in fleeing to a cave are judged by the narrator for his reader, thus leaving, as I have argued above, no room for interpretation (Diod. Sic. 34/5.2.22). One might reflect on the fact that breaking out of a Roman siege with a small band of followers has all the hallmarks (potentially) of a good action scene in a film, albeit one with a tragic end, if one were inclined to present the narrative differently, perhaps focalised through the rebels and their intrepid leader, as he may appear in that situation.
[62] Burke 1959, 58.

leader and the merits of that leader than it does about the rebels themselves or about their leader. At this stage of the narrative, the only reason that the reader knows that Eunus' wonders are fake is because the reader has been told so by the narrator: without this information the rebels' decision is far less absurd.[63]

Rhetoric and Rebel Motivations

Similar rhetorical and narratological techniques can be found in another passage that describes the rebel motivation. When the rebels approach Eunus to gain approval for their plans, Diodorus provides a narrative of events (34/5.2.24b; see also 34/5.2.10):

Ὅτι συνετίθεντο πρὸς ἀλλήλους οἱ δοῦλοι περὶ ἀποστάσεως καὶ φόνου τῶν κυρίων. παρελθόντες δὲ πρὸς τὸν Εὔνουν οὐκ ἄπωθεν διατρίβοντα ἠρώτων εἰ συγχωρεῖται παρὰ τῶν θεῶν αὐτοῖς τὸ βεβουλευμένον. ὁ δὲ τερατευόμενος μετ' ἐνθουσιασμοῦ καὶ περὶ τίνων ἥκουσι ἀκούσας διεσάφησεν ὅτι διδόασιν αὐτοῖς οἱ θεοὶ τὴν ἀπόστασιν, ἐὰν μηδεμίαν ὑπερβολὴν ποιησάμενοι παραχρῆμα μὲν ἐγχειρήσωσι ταῖς ἐπιβολαῖς· ὑπὸ γὰρ τῆς πεπρωμένης αὐτοῖς κεκυρῶσθαι πατρίδα τὴν Ἔνναν, οὖσαν ἀκρόπολιν ὅλης τῆς νήσου. τοιούτων λόγων ἀκούσαντες καὶ διαλαβόντες ὅτι τὸ δαιμόνιον αὐτοῖς συνεπιλαμβάνεται τῆς προαιρέσεως, οὕτως παρέστησαν ταῖς ψυχαῖς πρὸς τὴν ἀπόστασιν ὥστε μηδεμίαν ἀναβολὴν τῶν δεδογμένων ποιεῖσθαι. εὐθὺς οὖν τοὺς μὲν δεδεμένους ἔλυον … συνθέμενοι δὲ πρὸς ἀλλήλους καὶ πίστεις ἐπὶ σφαγίων ἐνόρκους νυκτὸς ποιησάμενοι καθωπλίσθησαν, ὥς ποτ' οὖν ὁ καιρὸς συνεχώρει· πάντες δὲ τὸ κράτιστον τῶν ὅπλων τὸν θυμὸν ἀνελάμβανον κατὰ τῆς ἀπωλείας τῶν ὑπερηφάνων κυρίων· καὶ τούτων ἀφηγεῖτο Εὔνους.

The slaves agreed with one another about revolt and the murder of their masters. They came to Eunus, who was spending time not far away, and they asked if their decision was approved by the gods. He began working wonders in a frenzy, and when he heard why they had come he made clear that the gods gave them permission to revolt, so long as they did not delay but immediately undertook their enterprise: for it was fated that Enna, the citadel of the whole island, was fixed as their homeland. Since they had heard these words and believed that the divine power was assisting them in their plan, they were so disposed in their minds for revolt that they made no delay in what they had decided … After making a covenant among one another and taking oaths of trust by night over sacrifices, they armed themselves as opportunity allowed at that time: all of them took up the strongest weapon of all, a desire for the destruction of their arrogant masters: and Eunus was their leader.

The entire passage is focalised through the rebels, indicated by the opening phrase συνετίθεντο πρὸς ἀλλήλους οἱ δοῦλοι, 'The slaves agreed with one another'.

---

[63] There has been a strong desire to read against the narrative with regard to Eunus' wonder-working and to demonstrate the historical context for Eunus' magic. See, e.g., Vogt 1965, 40–3; Bradley 1989, 55–7; Wirth 2004, 282, and 2006, 126. On this tradition, see also Morton 2013, 237–8.

Moreover, two parts of this passage suggest the action of an involved, but covert omniscient narrator, as with the passage that described Eunus' acclamation. There are two instances of embedded focalisation. In the first, we gain an insight into the minds of the rebels on hearing Eunus' proclamation about their plans, and learn that τοιούτων λόγων ἀκούσαντες καὶ διαλαβόντες ὅτι τὸ δαιμόνιον αὐτοῖς συνεπιλαμβάνεται τῆς προαιρέσεως, '(s)ince they had heard these words and believed that the divine power was assisting them in their plan, they were so disposed in their minds for revolt that they made no delay in what they had decided'. In the second, we learn that the rebels made a covenant amongst themselves and then used their desire for revenge against their masters to arm themselves metaphorically: πάντες δὲ τὸ κράτιστον τῶν ὅπλων τὸν θυμὸν ἀνελάμβανον κατὰ τῆς ἀπωλείας τῶν ὑπερηφάνων κυρίων, 'all of them took up the strongest weapon of all, a desire for the destruction of their arrogant masters'. In each case Diodorus as narrator is providing the reader with information that he could not have been party to. What is offered is a plausible suggestion of how the rebels felt, which is presented to us via focalisation of this section of the narrative. Each embedded focalisation serves an important function in the narrative at this point.

The first embedded focalisation is tied to Eunus' acclamation, where we learn that he was made king in part because of his wonders, and that this fulfilled one of his own predictions made at his master's dinner parties. As reader, we know at this stage that Eunus is a charlatan, and this knowledge colours, I think, how we read the relationship between the slaves and Eunus: in essence, the slaves are tricked into rebelling in order to fulfil Eunus' ambition, and therefore lose their agency.[64] Eunus is the driving force of the rebel insurgency throughout the extant narrative after his rise to the leadership. In the Photian epitome of Diodorus (34/5.2.1–24), after Eunus is introduced at 34/5.2.5, he features in every section of the narrative apart from 34/5.2.19–20. These sections of the narrative do not give any detail of the events: at 34/5.2.19 the text discusses slave revolts outside Sicily that were inspired (we are told) by the events on the island, and at 34/5.2.20 we are given a compressed overview of the entire conflict between the initial rebel successes and their defeat at Tauromenium in 132 BC, in the last year of the war. Eunus is the active agent at each critical juncture throughout Photius' text, with the exception of 34/5.2.18, which refers to the rebels as a whole in battle. It is also notable that Eunus is the very last rebel captured, and with his capture the narrative is wrapped up quite perfunctorily. In the Constantinian excerpts (34/5.2.24b–48) Eunus first appears at 34/5.2.24b when Damophilus' slaves approach him. From here he does not feature as prominently as in the Photian epitome, but this is because the Constantinian excerpts include several moralising passages (34/5.2.33; 39; 40; 47). Otherwise, in the passages detailing actions taken by the rebels, Eunus appears as the active agent in five out of six passages.[65] From the moment that the rebellious slaves

---

[64] We saw earlier that Diodorus made it clear in his introduction of Eunus that his prophetic abilities were not genuine: see 34/5.2.5–7.

[65] Eunus appears actively in Diod. Sic. 34/5.2.24b, 41, 42, 43 and 46. The only other passage is Diod. Sic. 34/5.2.40.

approach Eunus they lose agency in the narrative, and the wonder-working Syrian charlatan takes centre stage.[66]

Moreover, the second instance of embedded focalisation, in which we learn that the rebels armed themselves metaphorically with their anger against their masters, demonstrates an interest in master–slave relations that underpins nearly every passage that discusses the servile motivation for revolt. This theme is spread throughout the narrative and defines the manner in which the rebels are presented beyond their relationship with their leader. As we have seen above, the importance of servile anger against their masters is presented in the preliminary remarks concerning the conflict at 34/5.2.26. The theme consistently resurfaces across the text. For example, we hear that Damophilus and Megallis drove their slaves to savagery with their mistreatment of them (34/5.2.10: ἀποθηριωθέντες; 37: ἀπεθηριώθησαν), and that Damophilus' and Megallis' sudden murder in the midst of Damophilus' show trial at Enna was the result of two slaves' particular anger towards them (34/5.2.14: πικρῶς πρὸς αὐτὸν διακείμενοι). In a fragment from the Constantinian excerpts that appears to belong to early in the narrative, perhaps during the attack on Enna, we are told (as noted in passing above) that the slaves had become savage because of their mistreatment, and not because they were naturally so (34/5.2.40: ἀπηγριωμένων). Later we hear of a display during a siege in which the rebels, spurred by Eunus, mimed their revolts against their masters in order to demonstrate the result of the masters' arrogance and violence (34/5.2.46). Finally, in a passage that either comes before the tale of Damophilus' outrages or as part of book 34's proem, a direct connection is made between mistreatment of slaves (or, indeed, free people) and outbursts of savagery and lawlessness (34/5.2.33: ἀποθηριοῦται).[67]

In each of the cases just listed, the cause of the savagery and anger, and by connection the cause of the revolt itself and what drives the rebel actions thereafter, is the quality of master–slave relations. The interest of Diodorus' text when concerned with what drove the rebels is entirely upon how they related to their leaders, whom he works hard to vilify, and their masters: any other drive is absent. Diodorus' version of the events is the fullest account of the war that we have. As seen above, other accounts, such as those preserved in Orosius, Florus and the *Periochae* of Livy, all follow one or another of these interests. Nonetheless, we can pursue this line of

---

[66] Stewart 2012, 159–62, esp. 161, argues that the entire literary discourse on this revolt aimed to shift responsibility for the revolt squarely on to the shoulders of the masters for their failure to adhere to correct moral standards. This downplays, I think, the importance of Eunus to the narrative's construction. On Eunus taking centre stage, see also Dowden (*BNJ* 87 F198l) for the argument that Eunus' rise to kingship and the kindness he showed to those who rewarded him for his performances at his masters' dinner parties are part of the text's efforts to create a form of theatrical narrative around Eunus.

[67] Wozniczka 2021 has recently suggested that this passage may in fact come from the proem to book 34 of the *Bibliotheke* (originally presented in 'A new preface from Diodoros' *Universal History* (Book 34)?', at 'The First Meeting of the Diodorus Network', Glasgow, 9 December 2016). It does not affect the argument presented here, but for further consideration of this suggestion see Morton 2018. See also Stewart 2012, 159, on the ways in which the narratives of the war sought to 'belittle the slaves individually and collectively'. On the whole I agree with Stewart's analysis, although it is not the case that Diodorus' text describes the slaves 'as bestial in their very nature', not least because 34/5.2.40 notes quite pointedly that the slaves' brutality was caused by their masters' actions, not a natural savagery. See Yarrow 2006, 337.

argument only so far. Owing to the preservation of Diodorus' text in the Photian epitome and the Constantinian excerpts, we have an incomplete impression of the full text. Photius was evidently more interested in the first year of the war, and his narrative becomes hopelessly compressed after the capture of Enna; the Constantinian excerpts are little better, perhaps offering a longer chronological scope, but many of the fragments seem to relate to the early period of the war as well.[68] Moreover, both Photius and the Constantinian excerpts are interested most of all in Eunus and Damophilus, two characters that dominate what remains of the text. In any attempt to understand events later in the war, after the rebels had begun to successfully establish themselves as a force to be reckoned with, our literary sources are a poor guide. It is safest to conclude, therefore, that in what remains of the text servile motivation is bound up in two relationships: that with their masters, and that with their leaders. Both relationships deny agency to the rebels as a group and make the focus their superiors. What mattered was not why the enslaved population rebelled or how they thought except insofar as it connected to their relationships with their masters or rebel leaders: two sides of the same, deconstructive coin, so to speak. This presentation of the war is what we should expect, given the literary narratives were all written by slave owners attempting to come to terms with and, perhaps, downplay the nature of these events, notably in their consistent attempts to denigrate the rebel leadership, underpinned, as seen, by making the mass of enslaved persons involved play second fiddle.

A question remains from the preceding three sections of this chapter about how far we can rely on the impression given by the ancient literary traditions about this war for our own reconstructions. The question has no simple answer. With regard to the leaders, we encounter serious problems. Critical aspects of Eunus' and Kleon's characters belong to the ideology Diodorus, Florus and others attempted to share with their audience.[69] In some respects, for example Eunus' relationship with his own master and the narrative arc that connected them, it appears that elements belong to Diodorus' authorial artifice. It is hard to say whether the behaviour ascribed to Eunus and Kleon throughout the rest of the narrative has any foundation in reality or is wholly the product of the ancient authors' attempts to create a convincing depiction that persuaded their audience to side against the rebel movement. For the rebel motivation it seems that reducing servile agency and understanding the role of the masters in the initial outbreak was more important to the ancient authors than analysing the rebels on their own terms, although this conclusion has a significant caveat in the fragmentary nature of the extant narrative. What is clearer is that the portrayal of the rebels' motivations and relationships relied upon rhetorical and narrative embellishments in the form of focalised sections that guided the reader's response. But

---

[68] E.g., in the analysis above, 34/5.2.40, which is one of the later fragments of the narrative, appears to be best placed during or after the attack on Enna, i.e. at the start of the war.

[69] Even if the ideas present in Diodorus' narrative came from Posidonius it still remains that the language is Diodoran in many places and that he chose to keep these ideas in his narrative; this then reflects Diodorus' own identification with the narrative of Posidonius. This suggests that the ideas expressed had resonated in the ancient world for at least fifty years prior to Diodorus' own composition. On this relationship, see Hau 2016, 119–21 and 163–5.

without an alternative historical tradition it is not always possible to know which finer details are rhetorical and which are based on *some* hard core of historical data.[70] To return briefly to a detail noted in Chapter 1, when Eunus appointed Achaeus to be his counsellor on account of his wisdom (Diod. Sic. 34/5.2.16 and 42): was this wisdom something real, or was it portrayed as wisdom by the slave-owner narratives because he censured the rebels for their actions and warned of swift retribution? Was he real, or merely a wise counterpoint for the bombastic Eunus in the narrative? Firm answers are impossible to reach on this, among other details. Yet, we can say beyond doubt that the ancient authors who fashioned their various narratives have much to answer for.

This is not to say that the ancient literary tradition is not important or valuable for the purpose of historical reconstruction. There are some details that are not obviously created for narrative effect: there was a revolt in Sicily that started around Enna; this was led by a man known as Eunus, said to come from Syria, who was acclaimed king; this event started as a small-scale revolt, but escalated quickly; another rebellious group rose near Agrigentum under the leadership of a man known as Kleon, potentially a Cilician; the rebels seized a number of towns across Sicily, and resisted the attacks of three consuls before their eventual defeat. Other details such as the rebels' treatment of farmers under their control and the appointment of counsellors discussed in the previous chapter are probably also trustworthy, at least in terms of concrete actions, if not the motivations ascribed to the actions; the same goes for the involvement of large numbers of enslaved persons, even if the details of their slavery, not least with regard to their leaders, have been subject to creative narratological embellishment, as seen. This amounts to the bulk of our information about these revolts in concrete terms. For the remainder, especially where we receive detailed information about the characters' thoughts and motivations, we must, plainly, exercise extreme caution.

Conclusion: the Two 'First Sicilian Slave Wars'

The bodies of evidence discussed in this and the preceding chapter offer us two contrasting images or narratives of what took place in Sicily in the 130s BC: in essence, we can speak of two 'First Sicilian Slave Wars'. In the ancient literary tradition we have a story about servile insurrection that was driven by the incorrect behaviour of the masters and the opportunism of an upstart Syrian slave. In this version of events, the (therefore) First Sicilian Slave War is entirely about the dangers of transgressing acceptable behavioural norms in slave management, with the potential to learn lessons about not just slave ownership, but social interactions more generally. This narrative emphasises most of all the earliest phases of the happenings. The coinage discussed in Chapter 1, on the other hand, offers us a quite different perspective on the events.

---

[70] Woodman 1988, 88–94, described as the 'hard core' those details of history that are 'singular factual statements about the past', such as the fact that a battle took place, or a consul triumphed; this terminology he took from McCullagh 1984, 26, who described the 'hard core' of historical data to be statements such as 'the battle of Waterloo was fought on Sunday, 18 June 1815'.

This evidence suggests that the conflict was not set in the specific context of slavery, let alone particular master–slave relations, but in one driven by and concerned with an assertion of political power under a Hellenistic monarch, one that attempted to leverage the power of common Hellenistic deities, with particular concern for the specific region of Sicily in which the rebels were based. This perspective on the events offers us, furthermore, a new understanding of the period that followed the rebel success at Enna. In its totality, this perspective puts the war into the broader context of the development of the Roman Republican empire, and the massive tensions and antagonisms created on the ground by it, here between Sicilians and Romans, and in consequence among the Sicilians themselves.

It is plainly difficult to reconcile these two perspectives. Critically, discussing the event as a slave war does not do justice to the perspective extracted from the coinage, in Chapter 1, and the rebels that challenged the political status quo. There is no way of knowing how many of the rebels may have been enslaved prior to joining the war. Equally, there is no reason to think that the rebels led by Antiochus all enjoyed freedom prior to their rebellion. To the Greek and Roman slave owners who wrote about the event, it was in any case convenient to appreciate the rebellion as a slave war, and more specifically as a conflict caused by a collapse of the master–slave relationship: this was *their* truth about this war.[71] But even within this slave-owner narrative serious tensions arise from the moment that the rebels acclaimed a monarch and created a state, however short-lived: a Hellenistic monarchy is not easily packaged as a slave rebellion. Unless we wish to side with the masters and insist that the only way to understand the events is through a focus on slavery, we need to appreciate how the events affected Sicily itself beyond a narrow focus on servile unrest. Doing so means accounting for a broader spectrum of agency on the part of those rebelling, from rejections of individual slavery on the part of rebels previously enslaved, to the public assertion of political powers under Antiochus' leadership.

It goes without saying that shifting perspective on this revolt and the war that it sparked affords a new term for the war, one that moves away from the slave label and that presents the events in a less biased form. And perhaps the historiographically most neutral manner to come to terms with this challenge of relabelling is to call the war for what it was, at base – a conflict between Romans and Sicilians – hence: the Romano-Sicilian War. Anticipating the argument presented in the ensuing chapters, however, which will present another Romano-Sicilian war, the traditional numbering may be maintained, so that the war between Rome and the Sicilians led by King Antiochus will become the First Romano-Sicilian War. However, unlike in the case of the slave labels for these two Sicilian wars that artificially yoked the two events together by calling them 'First' and 'Second', in the perspective adopted in this book, the consecutive numbering gains meaning: as will be seen in what follows, Sicily remained a hotbed for anti-Roman feelings, so

---

[71] It is possible that writers from the late Republic onwards were influenced by the established way of conceptualising citizenship and losses of citizenship recorded in the *Digest* 4.5.5: that a free person who has rebelled might be conceptualised as a non-citizen and thus as a 'slave'. On this reading, the reality during the revolt becomes irrelevant to how later writers thought about the events.

much so that the tension between Rome and Sicily can be deemed characteristic of the period. Seen this way, the two wars bookend a particular phase in Sicilian history, which encourages their numerical association. Crucially, renaming the war hitherto called the First Sicilian Slave War in the manner here suggested moves us away from a slave-owner-led narrative that denies agency to the rebels and attempts to eliminate their self-definition.

3

THE CREATION OF AN ALTERNATIVE STATE: REASSESSING THE REBELS IN THE WAR OF 104–100 BC

NEARLY THIRTY YEARS after the suppression of rebels during the happenings discussed in the previous chapters, the island of Sicily experienced another period of upheaval connected, in the ancient literary tradition, to slavery: from 104–100 BC, rebellious slaves marched across the island under the leadership of their counterfeit kings, so we are told.[1] From a small uprising near the town of Heraclea Minoa, the movement grew into a full-scale revolt of thousands. This force overwhelmed the Roman governor at Morgantina in 104 BC, and then engaged his successors for the next two years from their base at the city of Triokala. It was only once Rome was free to send a consul to the war, M'. Aquilius, that the rebels were defeated and their resistance ended. The revolt was sparked, as Diodorus Siculus and Cassius Dio tell it, by the mismanagement of illegally enslaved Roman allies, whose bid for freedom was denied by the incompetence or corruption of the Roman governor on Sicily, P. Licinius Nerva.[2] The resulting war was best remembered among Romans for the defeat in sole combat of the rebels' leader, Athenion, who was cut down by M'. Aquilius himself.[3] The war's story was bookended in the ancient historiography by contrasting examples of Roman leadership that served to frame the rebel actions.

The source material for this war, commonly referred to as the Second Sicilian Slave War, is broadly similar to that of the First Romano-Sicilian War, comprising the *Bibliotheke* of Diodorus Siculus, Florus' *Epitome* of Livy, some of Cicero's speeches and a few other minor narrative sources; alongside this we have the important addition of a small collection of slingshots fired by the rebels and the archaeological evidence of contemporary activity at the sanctuary of the Paliki against which to compare the main narrative sources. We should hope, therefore, to be able to ask the same questions of the surviving texts and the physical evidence as those posed in Chapters 1 and 2, and to attempt to understand the different meanings attached to this war in the different bodies of evidence: in short, to move beyond a singular appreciation of the events, one that is dominated by the textual sources, which promote a slave-owning perspective. This is especially important as, once again, the extant text from the ancient historiography is focused on the origins and conclusion of the revolt, with almost all our

---

[1] The full narrative, or what is left of it, is preserved in the first eleven sections of the thirty-sixth book of Diodorus Siculus' *Bibliotheke*.
[2] Diod. Sic. 36.3.1–4; Cassius Dio 27.93.1–3.
[3] Diod. Sic. 36.10.1; Cic. *Verr.* 2.5.3, *De or.* 2.194–6.

information concerning the years 104 and 101 BC, and almost no information relating to the crucial years 103–102 BC, during which time there was significant rebel action. Yet we immediately encounter two problems.

First, the textual tradition of the war is much harder to assess. As I noted in Chapter 1, Diodorus' text for the latter books of the *Bibliotheke* is preserved in fragmentary form, but the difficulties are more acute for book 36. For this book we have only three of the Constantinian excerpts that represent a version closer to Diodorus' text, and for the bulk of the text we are left with Photius' compressed and selective summary of the events.[4] The fact that the Constantinian excerpts, which closely parallel Diodorus' text, occur so rarely means that we depend on Photius' interests: as with the First Romano-Sicilian War, here too, Photius paid considerable attention to the leaders of the war. However, despite the fact that the rebel leaders dominate what remains of the ancient narratives for this war, the rebel leadership is less clearly defined, even in historiographical terms. In Diodorus' text we encounter two leaders, Salvius (later called Tryphon, and referred to as Salvius/Tryphon throughout this chapter) and Athenion: the former is depicted as dying in the midst of the revolt, while the latter fought to the bitter end. In Florus and Cicero only Athenion features as a rebel leader, which is representative, it appears, of how the war was remembered in the Latin tradition (see below, pp. 106–7). The result of this is that no single figure defines the narrative, and we have to piece together the depiction of the rebel cause in the ancient historiography by considering *two* important figures.

Second, the best method for understanding the events away from an explicit slave-owner narrative is by examining the material evidence that derives from the rebels themselves. But this evidence is limited in comparison to the coinage studied in Chapter 1: we have only a handful of slingshots bearing names (either of deities or the rebel leaders). To this can be added evidence that the sanctuary of the Paliki near Leontini, which was important to the revolt, was still active at the time. This evidence, while important, is not as conducive to historial analysis as the coinage of Antiochus' kingdom. It is therefore necessary to study this evidence carefully alongside the historiographical depiction of the rebels' actions. In doing so, it is important that we question acutely how far we can trust the ancient literary traditions about the war before comparing their narratives with the evidence that comes from the rebels themselves. Only in this way can we keep a sound analytical lens on the different perspectives opened by the different bodies of evidence. That clarified, it is opportune to repeat here that going beyond the slave-owner narratives and understanding what this war meant to the rebels will result in a less complete, but nonetheless valuable interpretation. Once again, this will suggest a rather more complex history of the happenings under review than the 'slave war' label hitherto applied allows for, with particular regard to the motivations and goals of the rebels.

This chapter, therefore, deals with both the literary and material evidence for the revolt side by side in order to assess two questions: how far can we trust the way in which the slave-owner narratives depict the rebels' actions and motivations? And how

---

[4] Constantinian excerpts: Diod. Sic. 36.2a, 9.2 and 11. The remaining text from 36.1–10 is Photius' epitome.

can we best comprehend the rebels' own presentation of their actions and their movement and what they understood their movement to be about? This will be covered in two sections. In the first section of the chapter, we focus on the ancient literary tradition for the war and on two areas of that tradition. First, we will study the way in which the ancient literary tradition described the leadership for the revolt, with a particular emphasis on the main source for this war, Diodorus Siculus. As stated, the war accounts speak of two leaders: Salvius/Tryphon and Athenion. We will assess how Diodorus in particular used a similar matrix of ideas and narrative techniques to depict Salvius/Tryphon and Athenion as he did for Eunus and Kleon in the First Romano-Sicilian War, and that these depictions are intended to provide the desired context for the reader's interpretation of the events that follow. Second, we will consider how the ancient narratives of the war conceptualise its outbreak in terms of a response to a failure of both master–slave relations in Sicily and Roman governance in the Mediterranean more broadly. We will see that the principal literary sources for this war are concerned with the relationship between the rebels and their leaders or their masters, and that these texts provide only a limited context for understanding the motivations and goals of the rebels. In order to approach the rebel perspective, we must turn to the material evidence for the events and to the scattered references to the rebels' actions that go beyond their immediate relationship with either slave owners or rebel leaders, as described by the ancient narrative sources. In the second section, therefore, we turn in the first instance to a series of inscribed slingshots that bear the rebel leaders' names, and consider these alongside the rebels' actions at the sanctuary of the Paliki and their capital, Triokala. This section will show that when judged on their own actions, the rebels are best understood as attempting to create a new state, reminiscent in broad structural terms of the rebellion led by Antiochus. Let us start with the slave-owner narratives for the war.

The Slave-Owner Narratives of the 'Second Sicilian Slave War'

As we saw in Chapter 2, Eunus' character was carefully introduced into the narrative with an opening that defined the reception of his character for the rest of the narrative. Moreover, we saw that these facets of Eunus were not all demonstrated to us through his actions, but also through the covert intrusions of the narrator. In this way, Eunus' story in Diodorus was coloured from the initial phrases of his entrance, and since his character subsequently dominated the narrative, the colourings applied in the first lines to his character served to alter the reading of the entire revolt. The centripetal force exerted by Eunus was also present in the only other ancient account to give a narrative of the events beyond a brief summary or anecdote: Florus. While it could be attributed to the manner of Diodorus' preservation and Florus' own adaptation of Livy, the leaders (Salvius/Tryphon and Athenion) do not dominate the narrative in the same manner. For Salvius/Tryphon in particular, his reported demise after the war's first year naturally lessens his impact on the narrative; nonetheless, the ways in which these two leaders are introduced into the narrative contain the seeds of their characterisations and the root of a better understanding of their roles in Diodorus. We start, therefore, by focusing on the rebel leadership as it is described by Diodorus, and we will consider in particular how the relationship between the rebels and their leaders worked at a narratological level, as we did for Eunus and his rebels in Chapter 2.

Salvius/Tryphon's Rise to Kingship

Salvius/Tryphon first enters Diodorus' narrative in the aftermath of the initial rebel success outside Heraclea Minoa. The Roman governor, P. Licinius Nerva, failed to deal with a revolt among the slaves of a man called P. Clonius, and his failure emboldened the rebels and caused an increase in their numbers (36.4.1–3). It was at this moment that the rebels appointed their leader: Salvius/Tryphon. Unlike Eunus in the earlier war, therefore, Salvius/Tryphon is not a motivating force for the revolt itself, and, as we will see, this is important for how Diodorus conceptualised the revolt in his narrative. Salvius/Tryphon's rise to command is described as follows (36.4.4):

καὶ πολλῶν καθ' ἡμέραν ἀφισταμένων σύντομον καὶ παράδοξον ἐλάμβανον αὔξησιν, ὡς ἐν ὀλίγαις ἡμέραις πλείους γενέσθαι τῶν ἑξακισχιλίων. τότε δὴ καὶ εἰς ἐκκλησίαν συνελθόντες καὶ βουλῆς προτεθείσης πρῶτον μὲν εἵλαντο βασιλέα τὸν ὀνομαζόμενον Σάλουιον, δοκοῦντα τῆς ἱεροσκοπίας ἔμπειρον εἶναι καὶ ταῖς γυναικείαις θέαις αὐλομανοῦντα.

Since every day many revolted, they built up their force quickly and contrary to expectations, so that in a few days they were more than 6,000. At that time, then, they gathered in an assembly and when the proposal was put before them they first chose as king one named Salvius, who was reputed to be practised in divination and a flute player in mystic orgies for women.

Despite the fact that Salvius/Tryphon was not key to the initial outbreak and subsequent success of the revolt, there are links between his characterisation and that of Eunus: in each case they are effeminised. As seen in the preceding chapter, Eunus' effeminisation was effected by describing him as lacking in ἀνδρεία, 'bravery' (Diod. Sic. 34/5.2.14), behaving ἀνάνδρως, 'in an unmanly fashion', and fleeing διὰ δειλίαν, 'through cowardice' (34/5.2.22). For Salvius/Tryphon, the slur is implied rather than stated. We learn that he had a reputation for two reasons: first, his skills in ἱεροσκοπία, 'divination';[5] secondly, his role as ταῖς γυναικείαις θέαις αὐλομανοῦντα, 'a flute player in mystic orgies for women'.[6] We cannot say if this characterisation was pushed further

---

[5] Goukowsky 2014, 150–1, argues that Salvius/Tryphon's divination should be understood as haruspicy, connected to his Etrurian origin (see below n. 6), noting the use of ἱεροσκόπος to translate *haruspex*.

[6] Dumont 1987, 264, followed by Strauss 2010, 194, argued that this passage demonstrates the importance of the cult of Dionysus to the rebellion. Goukowsky 2014, 148–4 and 151–2, argued that Salvius/Tryphon's flute-playing should be understood in the context of theatrical displays involving women, perhaps intended to suggest that Salvius belonged to a group of musical mimes known from Syracuse, whose religious affiliation was to Aphrodite Hilara; on this, see also Angius 2020, 129–30. Salvius/Tryphon's flute-playing cannot single him out as a slave, domestic or rural, nor is his nationality specified: Bradley 1989, 74, argued for a domestic identification from this evidence; Finley 1979, 144, suggested that he could have been a free Italian; Goukowsky 2014, 510–11, argued for an Etrurian origin, and perhaps free; most recently Aberson 2016 has argued that the names of both Salvius/Tryphon and Varius (see below, p. 110) indicate that they were slaves, probably of Oscan masters.

in the text, owing to the fact that every detail about the rebel leaders is preserved in Photius' epitome, which may not reflect in full the language of the Diodoran text.[7] As we will see, for the rest of the narrative these suggestions about Salvius/Tryphon's character lie dormant. Nonetheless, it is worth emphasising that two books after Diodorus attacked Eunus' character, another rebel leader is castigated in a similar manner. The implications of the latter detail remain important: by having access to expressly female religious rites, Salvius/Tryphon's own masculinity would be questioned, and, as we saw in Chapter 2, Hellenistic kingship and warfare was a masculine sphere in which failure was linked to feminine tendencies.[8]

Yet, there remain some differences between this account and that of Eunus' introduction and later acclamation. In the present passage, the narrator does not give a direct statement as to why Salvius/Tryphon was chosen. The use of the verb δοκέω, 'to be reputed', may imply that the following information is presented through an embedded focalisation — that is, we learn it through the rebels' eyes, much as we did for Eunus' acclamation previously.[9] This cannot be argued with certainty, but the example from just two books earlier in the *Bibliotheke* supports this interpretation; as we will see, this strategy is clearly used in the case of the second leader in this war, Athenion. Even so, the text implies that Salvius/Tryphon's acclamation was the result of his reputation for divination. What is more difficult for this reading is that unlike both Athenion and Eunus, Salvius/Tryphon is never shown in the narrative to demonstrate his skills, nor to use them to his or the rebels' advantage. While these elements of Salvius/Tryphon are not immediately developed, they are, nonetheless, the only two elements of his character in his initial introduction: it remains to be seen how this introduction affects how we read his character throughout the rest of the narrative.[10]

The first test of Salvius/Tryphon's leadership comes at the siege of Morgantina (Diod. Sic. 36.4.5–8). In the course of the siege, Salvius/Tryphon's camp was captured by the Roman governor, Licinius Nerva. Nerva attacked the rebels outside the city, who held the higher ground, and his forces were quickly overpowered and began

---

[7] For further comment on this, see Chapter 2.
[8] See Beston 2000, 316–17, and Polyb. 28.21.3. The *aulos* was, during the fifth century and into the fourth century BC, disliked among some Greek authors for weakening the control of the physique: see Wilson 1999, 65; Theophr. Fr. 92W; Paus. 9.12.5–6; Arist. *Pol.* ch. 26; Dio. Chrys. *Or.* 78 (2.281 Dind.). Moreover, the role of αὐλός players in the symposium often overlapped with their 'sexual use-value', in the words of Wilson 1999, 84–5. Aristotle (*Pol.* 1342a20) also considered it unmanly to perform music except when drunk or for fun. Finally, in Aristophanes' *Nicophon* (17), the verb προσαυλεῖν is used in a punning phrase describing the act of fellatio (see also Henderson 1975, 184–5). While the context outlined here is not necessarily directly relevant to Salvius/Tryphon, it is important to note the literary context in which the αὐλός was considered. Furthermore, the placing of Salvius/Tryphon's use of the αὐλός into a principally female space could potentially activate these latent meanings behind the expression: on the importance of the negative connotations, see also Goukowsky 2014, 149.
[9] For a full discussion of the meaning of focalisation used here, see Chapter 2, pp. 86–9.
[10] Immediately after this passage Salvius/Tryphon orders his men to avoid cities because they are sources of vice, but then soon after he arranges an attack on the city of Morgantina (36.4.4–5). It is not clear if the inconsistency is a result of compression in the text, or if this is another aspect of Salvius/Tryphon's character.

to flee. Salvius/Tryphon proclaimed that any of Nerva's men who dropped their arms would be spared: the order worked, and Salvius/Tryphon won the day, recovering his camp in the process and doubling his numbers because of his strategy and success. In the narrative that follows, Salvius/Tryphon offered the slaves in Morgantina their freedom, but they chose instead to support their masters, who matched Salvius/Tryphon's offer. A final line notes that the governor later rescinded this offer and the slaves in the city joined the rebels. Photius' text for this passage is heavily compressed: it is not clear, for example, how soon after the initial offer of freedom for the slaves of Morgantina the reversal of this offer came. The narrative is a series of lessons on how to command: the principal cause of Nerva's defeat was his decision to attack forces that held the higher ground, and he exacerbated this by overturning the offer of freedom to the Morgantinian slaves.[11] Salvius/Tryphon took advantage of Nerva's strategic incompetence, and it is in keeping with the rest of the narrative that the incompetence of leaders is emphasised in this passage.[12] Most striking of all, the rebels' victory is attributed more to their opponents' cowardice than to their own skill: notwithstanding the partial nature of the text, the depiction of the siege at Morgantina fits the reading given of Salvius/Tryphon's character above. For now, however, we must leave Salvius/Tryphon and turn to the second leader of the revolt.

Athenion's Pretence

After the siege of Morgantina, the narrative shifts abruptly to another revolt that started in the west of the island around Segesta and Lilybaeum. This revolt is reported to have been instigated from its start by a Cilician named Athenion, who is characterised in the following way (36.5.1):

Περὶ δὲ τὴν Αἰγεσταίων καὶ Λιλυβαϊτῶν χώραν, ἔτι δὲ τῶν ἄλλων τῶν πλησιοχώρων, ἐνόσει πρὸς ἀπόστασιν τὰ πλήθη τῶν οἰκετῶν. γίνεται δὲ τούτων ἀρχηγὸς Ἀθηνίων ὄνομα, ἀνὴρ ἀνδρείᾳ διαφέρων, Κίλιξ τὸ γένος. οὗτος οἰκονόμος ὢν δυοῖν ἀδελφῶν μεγαλοπλούτων, καὶ τῆς ἀστρομαντικῆς πολλὴν ἔχων ἐμπειρίαν, ἔπεισε τῶν οἰκετῶν πρῶτον μὲν τοὺς ὑφ' ἑαυτὸν τεταγμένους περὶ διακοσίους ὄντας, ἔπειτα τοὺς γειτνιῶντας, ὥστε ἐν πέντε ἡμέραις συναχθῆναι πλείους τῶν χιλίων.

In the territory of Segesta and Lilybaeum, and yet others adjacent, the multitude of slaves were sick for revolt. The chief of these was one named Athenion, a man excelling in courage, a Cilician by birth. He was the steward of two exceedingly wealthy brothers, and having great experience of astrology, he first persuaded those of the slaves formed up under him, about 200, then those in the vicinity, so that in five days more than 1,000 had been brought together.

---

[11] See Finley 1979, 145, on the Roman failure. Bradley 1989, 75, implies that Salvius/Tryphon's proclamation was the 'master stroke' that pulled off the victory, but it is evident in the narrative that this action only preserved the lives of those already defeated.

[12] See Morton 2018.

Athenion appears to be an amalgamation of the characteristics of both Eunus and Kleon from the earlier narrative. There are three features to discuss here. First, like Kleon before him, Athenion is described as ἀνδρείᾳ διαφέρων, 'excelling in courage'.[13] Second, like Eunus and Kleon, Athenion is depicted taking an active role in inciting slaves to revolt. Third, like Eunus, he has experience in foretelling the future. Athenion is not described in hostile terms at this stage. Unlike Kleon, who was not only identified as a Cilician, but also explicitly as a bandit, rendering the connection between the two unambiguously evident, Athenion suffers no apparent stigma in the narrative as a result of his Cilician origins.[14] Yet this seemingly positive portrayal does not remain for long. Immediately after his initial recruitment of followers, Athenion proclaimed a divine right to the island, and proceeded to besiege Lilybaeum, as follows (36.5.3–4):

> προσεποιεῖτο δὲ τοὺς θεοὺς αὐτῷ διὰ τῶν ἄστρων προσημαίνειν ὡς ἔσοιτο τῆς Σικελίας συμπάσης βασιλεύς· διὸ δεῖν αὐτῆς τε τῆς χώρας καὶ τῶν ἐν αὐτῇ ζῴων τε καὶ καρπῶν ὡς ἰδίων φείδεσθαι. τέλος ἀθροίσας ὑπὲρ τοὺς μυρίους ἐτόλμησε πόλιν ἀπόρθητον τὸ Λιλύβαιον πολιορκεῖν. μηδὲν δὲ ἀνύων μετανίστατο αὐτῆς, εἰπὼν αὐτῷ τοὺς θεοὺς τοῦτο ἐπιτάττειν· ἐπιμένοντας γὰρ ἂν τῇ πολιορκίᾳ δυστυχήματος πειραθῆναι. παρασκευαζομένου δὲ αὐτοῦ τὴν ἀπὸ τῆς πόλεως ἀναχώρησιν, κατέπλευσάν τινες ἐν ταῖς ναυσὶ κομίζοντες ἐπιλέκτους Μαυρουσίους, οἳ ἐπὶ βοήθειαν ἦσαν ἀπεσταλμένοι τοῖς Λιλυβαΐταις, ἔχοντες ἡγούμενον ὃς ὠνομάζετο Γόμων. οὗτος σὺν τοῖς ἅμ' αὐτῷ κατὰ νύκτα καὶ ἀνελπίστως ἐπιθέμενος τοὺς περὶ Ἀθηνίωνα ὁδοιποροῦντας, πολλοὺς καταβαλόντες, οὐκ ὀλίγους δὲ τραυματίσαντες, εἰς τὴν πόλιν ἐπανῆλθον. διόπερ οἱ ἀποστάται τὴν ἐκ τῆς ἀστρομαντείας πρόρρησιν ἐθαύμαζον.

He pretended that the gods foretold to him through the stars that he would be king of all Sicily: therefore, there was a need to spare the land itself, the animals on it and the crops as his own. Finally, having gathered more than 10,000, he undertook to besiege the city of Lilybaeum, which had never been captured. After accomplishing nothing he removed himself from it, saying that the gods ordered this: for were they to continue the siege they would experience misfortune. While he was preparing to retreat from the city, some ships put in carrying Mauretanian auxiliaries, who had been sent to help Lilybaeum, having as leader one called Gomon. He, with his men, unexpectedly attacked those walking with Athenion in the night, killing many, wounding not a few, and returned to the city. As a result, the rebels wondered at the prediction from the stars.

In what follows I analyse this passage in two ways: in terms of vocabulary and in terms of rhetoric. First, let us consider the vocabulary. There is an immediate verbal

---

[13] Kleon was described as fighting ἡρωικῶς, 'heroically', towards the end of the first war: Diod. Sic. 34/5.2.21.
[14] Although, undoubtedly, the negative associations of being Cilician were still important: for these see Avidov 1997; De Souza 1999, 97–148; De Souza 2008; Strabo 14.3.2; App. *Mith.* 92; Cass. Dio 36.20 –23; and Plut. *Pomp.* 24.

similarity between this passage and the earlier description of Eunus. When Eunus was introduced into the narrative Diodorus noted that (34/5.2.5) οὗτος προσεποιεῖτο θεῶν ἐπιτάγμασι καθ' ὕπνον προλέγειν τὰ μέλλοντα, '(t)his man claimed by divine commands to foretell the future through dreams and because of his talent in this direction he fooled many'. One of the pretensions that Eunus claimed was that the Syrian goddess had promised him kingship (34/5.2.7). In a similar manner, Athenion προσεποιεῖτο, 'pretended', that the gods foretold to him that he would be king of all Sicily.[15] Although the specifics of the situation differ, the verbal echo creates a strong link to the established caricature of Eunus in books 34/5. Moreover, the alterations to the caricature for Athenion may not have been random. Let us consider astrology. Astrologers were not uniformly acceptable, and in 139 BC they had been expelled from the city of Rome by the praetor Cn. Cornelius Hispalus for spreading false interpretations of the stars (Val. Max. 1.3.3).[16] Since Athenion's prophecy from the stars was a pretence, the passage above places him firmly in this category of astrologers and therefore triggers the relevant associations. Moreover, the choice of astrology for Athenion's prophecy fits his employment, albeit negatively. As we learn in 36.5.1, Athenion was a *vilicus* or *magister pecoris*.[17] Both Cato (*De agricultura* 5.4) and later Columella (*Res rusticae* 1.8.6) recommended that either the *vilicus* of a farm should not consult astrologers and fortune-tellers, or that these people should not be allowed on to the farm in the first place. Athenion is, on this reading, the antithesis of the ideal *vilicus*. He is described across these two passages negatively, using similar vocabulary to that used to describe Eunus and Kleon, and with attention devoted to similar characteristics.

In addition, this passage is engaging in the same kinds of rhetorical strategies and embedded focalisation we saw in Diodorus' narrative of the First Romano-Sicilian War. We will consider the prophecy first. The narrator makes clear in this passage that Athenion's prophetic abilities are a sham. Much like for Eunus, the reader is guided when interpreting Athenion's actions. As a result, we are compelled to question the episode that follows.[18] We are told that Athenion besieged Lilybaeum but in the course of the siege was forced to retreat. We must read his claim that it was divinely inspired to abandon the siege in light of the information we received only a few lines above: this divination was a facade. This has two effects. First, as I have argued elsewhere, this retreat was, in fact, a serious strategic failure for Athenion on two counts: his forces were attacked while marching by the Mauretanian auxiliaries;[19] and the retreat forced him to abandon his efforts at organising the west of the island, something that he had attempted to do after his initial revolt in the area between

---

[15] As we will see below, this is not the only time that Athenion put on a pretence for his own benefit.
[16] See also Cramer 1954, 58–60, 234–5, for a discussion of astrology in the period of the mid-Republic, and measures taken against astrologers.
[17] See Bradley 1989, 76, for discussion.
[18] For most, Athenion's description is interpreted positively: e.g. Vogt 1963, 33–4; Manganaro 1967, 221; Callahan and Horsley 1998, 147; Urbainczyk 2008a, 57. Bradley 1989, 14, is right that we should not necessarily regard Athenion as a charlatan, but this misses a vital point: we are never shown that Athenion was a charlatan, we are told.
[19] See Morton 2014, 32–4.

Segesta and Lilybaeum.[20] However, owing to Athenion's prediction, this moment became at the time a major success for his leadership. Just as for Eunus, whose abilities at wonder-working secured his position at the head of the rebels in the earlier war and who by verbal similarities is evoked in this passage, Athenion's original success is undeniable, but this does not mean that it reflects well on his followers; indeed, the opposite is the case, as I will show next.

The negative reading of Athenion's followers that is created by his contrived prediction is clear from the second effect of the narratorial intervention. In the last line of the passage above we learn that διόπερ οἱ ἀποστάται τὴν ἐκ τῆς ἀστρομαντείας πρόρρησιν ἐθαύμαζον, 'As a result, the rebels wondered at the prediction from the stars.' We are offered here an embedded focalisation in which we learn the rebels' thoughts about Athenion's astrology. In line with the rhetorical strategies used to undermine the rebels' critical faculties in the first war, here we are offered Diodorus' view of the rebels' reasons for following Athenion. Given the narrative situation – Athenion had failed to maintain his arrangements in the west of Sicily and had been attacked while on the march – the rebels' wonder at his prediction is, I contend, intended to produce a negative reading: they were at fault for falling for his sham prediction. Finally, in this passage we see a recurrence of the narrative's efforts to undermine the slaves' agency, leaving the rebels manipulated into acting to the benefit of their charlatan leaders. According to this reading, neither Salvius/Tryphon nor Athenion are suitable choices for leadership, nor did their followers make the right choice.

Leading the Revolt

Taken together, Salvius/Tryphon and Athenion are introduced into Diodorus' narrative using the same matrix of ideas employed to present Eunus and Kleon. The exact parameters of these character traits are not identical; yet, implications of effeminacy, verbal echoes related to charlatan divination, and narratorial interventions that include carefully constructed embedded focalisations have all resurfaced in these passages and have achieved similar effects. It remains to be seen how these two characters then interact in the rest of the narrative, and whether, like Eunus and Kleon, the early foundations laid for their characters then affect the reading of their subsequent narrative. The story of the revolt continues with Salvius/Tryphon's actions after the siege of Morgantina. In what follows, we see the initial characters defined for the two men manifest in their actions.

Thus, after the siege had failed, Salvius/Tryphon withdrew to the west of the island to the site of Triokala.[21] Once there, he summoned Athenion to join him

---

[20] Diodorus reports that Athenion did not accept all the runaway slaves into his army but made some remain working the land in order to furnish his army with supplies (36.5.2). This is often taken as a demonstration of Athenion's care in maintaining rebellion: see Toynbee 1965, 329; Vogt 1965, 34–5; Bradley 1989, 76–7; Wirth 2004, 284; Urbainczyk 2008a, 57. Bradley 1989, 110, stressed, moreover, that this reflected 'a rational, even sensible and enlightened, character in the slaves' actions'.

[21] Beforehand, Salvius/Tryphon visited the sanctuary of the Paliki near Leontini (36.7.1). We will return to that episode and to Salvius/Tryphon's other actions at Triokala below, pp. 121–4.

(Diod. Sic. 36.7.1–2). In the text, we are told that πάντες, 'everyone', expected Athenion to fight Salvius/Tryphon for the leadership of the revolt, but instead he joined forces willingly, acting as though he was a general summoned by a king (ὑπακούων ὡς στρατηγὸς βασιλεῖ). Unexpectedly, Salvius/Tryphon jailed Athenion out of a suspicion that he would attack him. It is altogether unclear exactly why Salvius/Tryphon suspected Athenion: Photius either compressed the narrative quite heavily or Diodorus did not give a clear reason in the first instance. Either way, we must work with what remains of the text. The narrative implies that we might expect Athenion and Salvius/Tryphon to fight. This suggestion is at odds with what we have seen of the rebel leaders so far: Athenion has just completed a disastrous retreat from Lilybaeum, whereas Salvius/Tryphon has reinforced his own leadership with his victory at Morgantina. Moreover, Athenion's forces as they are reported were significantly smaller than Salvius/Tryphon's.[22] Yet the narrative has described the two men in such a way as to make the reader expect conflict. As we saw above, Salvius/Tryphon's victory at Morgantina owed as much to the cowardice of Nerva's men as to Salvius/Tryphon's cunning (Diod. Sic. 36.4.6–8), and Salvius/Tryphon was implicitly called effeminate by the narrator when he was described as (36.4.4) ταῖς γυναικείαις θέαις αὐλομανοῦντα, 'a flute player in mystic orgies for women'. Athenion, by contrast, was (36.5.1) ἀνδρείᾳ διαφέρων, 'excelling in courage', and, moreover, had read in the stars that his rise to kingship over all Sicily had been foretold (36.5.3). This last detail is especially important: unlike Salvius/Tryphon, Athenion steered his revolt from the very beginning to fulfil his own prophecy, and it is unexpected in narrative terms for him to become subordinate, even though his actions whilst king were unsuccessful. By contrast, Salvius/Tryphon's decision to imprison Athenion fits the expectation set up by the earlier text, if not by the actual actions undertaken by each man at this point. In short, there is a tension between what the narrator has told us of the two men and what he has been able to show us of them; this tension is similar to that which we saw at play in the description of Eunus and his relationship with his rebels in the earlier narrative. At this stage in the narrative the tension is problematic. Here, however, in the following account of the battle of Scirthaea the tension resolves as the latent characters of the two men finally solidify the two roles credited to Salvius/Tryphon and Athenion.

After he had summoned and imprisoned Athenion, Salvius/Tryphon set about creating a capital at Triokala, including a palace, walls and an agora (36.7.3). Rome's response to Licinius Nerva's failure was to appoint a propraetor, L. Licinius Lucullus, in 103 BC (36.8.1). In what appears to be a reaction to this development, Salvius/Tryphon then released Athenion and began to plan for the campaign. Athenion convinced Salvius/Tryphon that an open battle was a better plan than withstanding a siege. Here we see the characters of Athenion and Salvius/Tryphon begin to match their actions, by the strategic direction they support in the fight against Lucullus. Salvius/Tryphon is here implied to be unmanly through his advocacy for the cowardly choice to withdraw from the field and risk a siege, while Athenion argued for

---

[22] Athenion is reported to have had roughly 10,000 soldiers (Diod. Sic. 36.5.3), whereas Salvius/Tryphon reportedly had 30,000 (36.7.1).

the manly choice to fight the Romans in open battle.²³ This characterisation is fully established once the two forces engage at Scirthaea (36.8.3–4). Athenion, who was introduced as renowned for his bravery, only withdrew from battle once he had been wounded three times. When he retired from battle the rebels' cause was lost. Even more striking, Athenion escaped discovery during the battle by προσποιηθεὶς, 'pretending', to be dead, entirely in keeping with his pretence to read the skies and predict his kingship (see above, p. 103). Salvius/Tryphon, by contrast, fled from battle, causing, so it seems from the text, the loss of *c.* 20,000 soldiers. This is only predictable in as much as we have been set up, as readers, to expect this from Salvius/Tryphon. As with so much of this narrative, we have only a heavily compressed version of events to work from, but the battle at Scirthaea reinforces both Athenion's and Salvius/Tryphon's characters. The tension created in the gap between what we have been shown and what we have been told is here resolved, as both men revert to their true characters, as established in their introductions.

It is frustrating that from this point onwards the narrative of the war becomes hopelessly condensed, much like the text for the First Romano-Sicilian War, as seen in the previous chapter. After Scirthaea, Lucullus attempted to press the advantage but failed to besiege Triokala. Shortly thereafter Salvius/Tryphon died and Athenion assumed sole command of the rebels (36.9.1). From the remaining text we hear almost nothing about the remainder of 103 BC or about what happened under Lucullus' successor for 102 BC, C. Servilius.²⁴ In 101 BC Rome appointed the consul M'. Aquilius to the command, and he defeated the rebels in a single battle where he also killed Athenion in single combat (36.10.1). This one action defined this revolt in Roman minds more than any other and had a strong effect on how it was recalled in the generations that followed.²⁵ In the aftermath of the war, Aquilius was tried for extortion and acquitted after M. Antonius, the counsel for the defence, tore open Aquilius' tunic to display the wounds he received defeating Athenion.²⁶ This moment in the Roman courts (and the actions that preceded it) evidently fixed itself in the Roman imagination, and Aquilius' deeds in Sicily were later recalled during the trial of the Sicilian governor Verres in 71 BC, during which time Aquilius' grandson produced a denarius depicting Aquilius helping a fallen *Sicilia* to her feet (*RRC* 401).²⁷ Athenion's prominence in the aggrandisement of Aquilius' later reputation appears to have erased not only Salvius/Tryphon from most records of the events but, intriguingly, also mention of the First Romano-Sicilian War, most notably in Cicero's recollection of both events in the *Verrine Orations*.²⁸ Strikingly though, unlike Cicero, Florus describes the war as a

---

²³ On the implication that avoiding field engagements in favour of being besieged implies a lack of courage or manliness, see Levithan 2013, 16–19.

²⁴ For further comments on the Roman response to this event, and for some tentative attempts to reconstruct the military side of this conflict, see Morton 2014, 34–7.

²⁵ See, e.g., App. *Mith.* 59, where Sulla's soldiers in Asia Minor attack Fimbria verbally and call him Athenion, and Cicero comparing Clodius to Athenion (*Ad Att.* 2.12.2; *Har. resp.* 26).

²⁶ On this, see Cic. *Verr.* 2.5.3 and *De or.* 2.194–6.

²⁷ On this coin, see Prag 2007b, vi.

²⁸ Cicero uses the war as a point of comparison across the *Verrine Orations* (see, e.g., 2.2.136, 2.3.65–6, 2.3.125, in the final case notably eliding the name of the leader of the war), and he tends to avoid mention of the First Romano-Sicilian War (except at 2.4.112, as we have seen in Chapter 1).

seamless continuation of Eunus' fight by his successor, Athenion, who acted on the pretext of avenging Eunus, erasing not only Salvius/Tryphon but also any sense of chronological distance between Eunus and Athenion (2.7.9–12).[29] As the only extant author who records anything about Salvius/Tryphon, Diodorus evidently recorded a fuller tradition concerning the war, and therefore we should return to his text.

As we have seen, Diodorus' depiction of the rebel leadership in this war is not as complex as that of Eunus and Kleon in the earlier narrative. Neither Salvius/Tryphon nor Athenion warranted a grand entrance, which suggests that their characters were not well fleshed out in the original text. As seen in the preceding chapter, it is the introduction of both Eunus and Kleon that provided the firm platform for their later, continued denigration. In contrast, Salvius/Tryphon is introduced by a single line, and even though Athenion enters with a slightly longer introduction, it lacks the colour and depth of the attack on Eunus. Nonetheless, the ideas and rhetorical techniques employed to disparage both Salvius/Tryphon and Athenion are similar to those used for Eunus and Kleon. The narrative sets up expectations for each man that are later fulfilled: no demonstration is given of Salvius/Tryphon's effeminacy, but his retreat from Scirthaea acquires the connotations of cowardice from the earlier connection made between Salvius/Tryphon and female rituals; Athenion, on the other hand, appears to dupe his way into command, utilising his established pretence at astrology to his advantage, including in the face of strategic incompetence.

Most of all, after they are introduced into the narrative Salvius/Tryphon and Athenion dominate and define the meaning of the revolt in both Diodorus' text and the Roman tradition preserved in Florus and Cicero. To all intents and purposes, after they have assumed command these two men embody the revolt, at least in terms of the slave-owner narratives constructed after the fact by Diodorus, Florus, Cicero and others. In the absence of other historical traditions about these two men we cannot be certain which details represent the real character and actions of either Salvius/Tryphon or Athenion. What is more, we cannot trust Diodorus' presentation of their followers' motivation for choosing them: in each case, much as we saw with Eunus in the previous chapter, embedded focalisations depict what the slave-owner narratives imagined the rebels were thinking. In the process, the narrative depicted Salvius/Tryphon being made the leader on the poor grounds of his divination and flute-playing, whereas Athenion, like Eunus before him, allegedly tricked his followers into choosing him. In short, the same problems are present for the narrative of this later war as for the earlier one: the slave-owner narratives show an intense interest in the leadership of each war and allow it to subsume the motivation of the rebels. Finally, as we will see in the following section, even in the initial movement towards the revolt, there was no motivation beyond that arising from the master–slave relationship.

---

[29] This act appears to be part of a larger attempt in Florus to restructure Roman history in order to comment on the decline of (free) Roman society in the second and first centuries BC. See, e.g., the placement of the two wars in Sicily and the Spartacus revolt between the Social War and the civil war between Marius and Sulla in the 80s BC (2.6–9), with a comment about the Romans acting like gladiators in Rome itself in the civil war (*cum civibus suis gladiatorio more concurrerent* – 2.9.1).

The Start of the Revolt

If we leave aside the leaders of the revolt, the majority of our information preserved in the ancient narrative sources concerns the war's origins. We are told by our narrative sources that the war began due to events outside Sicily.[30] Diodorus (36.2.6) explains that the origin of the revolt, ἡ ἀρχή, 'the beginning', came from problems with allies being enslaved in Roman provinces.[31] In the midst of the struggle with the Cimbri, the Romans sent a request to Nicomedes of Bithynia for soldiers (Diod. Sic. 36.3.1). Nicomedes' response was to claim that he could not send soldiers because they had been seized by *publicani* and were now slaves in Rome's provinces.[32] In response the senate ordered all enslaved allies in the provinces to be freed. The Sicilian governor, P. Licinius Nerva, whom we met above in his ill-fated attempts to relieve the siege of Morgantina, responded with alacrity, and began freeing enslaved allies, with some 800 freed within days. In response, the authorities on the island (ἀξιώμασι) persuaded the governor to stop freeing enslaved people on Sicily (36.3.2–4). Cassius Dio gives a similar account of these happenings (27.93.1–3).[33] In Dio's version the governor acted either because he sought a way to make money, or because he had learned ὅτι οὐκ ἐν δίκῃ τινὰ περὶ τοὺς δούλους, 'that the slaves were not justly treated in some manner'. It is possible that this phrase refers to the senatorial decree, which is otherwise not mentioned in Dio's text; in addition, the passage does not mention freedom for the slaves explicitly. Nonetheless, in both Diodorus and Dio the governor abruptly ended the hearings, either because he was bribed to do so by the slave owners (Diod. Sic. 36.2.3) or because he was afraid of causing unrest and violence between the slaves and their masters (Cass. Dio 27.93.3).[34] In Dio's version the disappointed slaves turned to banditry, whereas in Diodorus they withdrew to the sanctuary of the Paliki in order to discuss revolt. In both accounts the governor's actions – inspired by good intentions or by a desire for money – stirred discontent amongst the slaves of Sicily: according to the slave-owner narrative their initial decision to revolt is the result of a failure to maintain master–slave relations correctly; the masters excited hopes for freedom, only to dash them.

---

[30] The main source for the outbreak of the war is Diodorus' narrative, but we have a single fragment of Cassius Dio that provides additional material.

[31] Diodorus' use of ἀρχή to describe his analysis of the origins of the war appears to be deploying a similar historical method to that of Polybius, for which see Walbank 1972, 158. In what remains of Diodorus' narrative of the second war there is no αἰτία or πρόφασις in the extant narrative; in the first war, by contrast, Diodorus differentiates between the αἰτία for the conflict (banditry on the island in the years preceding the conflict: Diod. Sic. 34/5.2.1–2, 27) and the ἀρχή of the event (Damophilus' mistreatment of his slaves: Diod. Sic 34/5.2.9).

[32] See Rubinsohn 1982, 444–7, for the suggestion that Nicomedes was lying about his subjects in an attempt to take advantage of Rome's precarious situation in the Cimbric War. Within the year Bithynian soldiers were recorded fighting as allies for Rome *in* Sicily (Diod. Sic. 36.5.4, 8.1), and they had been fighting in Paphlagonia the previous year (Just. *Epit.* 37.4.3).

[33] This version remains only in two fragments of Cassius Dio, and they evidently come from a longer account of the events. This is clearest from the line that introduces the story of Licinius Nerva's efforts to free slaves in Sicily: ὅτι Πούπλιος Λικίννιος Νέρουας στρατηγῶν ἐν τῇ νήσῳ, 'Publius Licinius Nerva, who was governor on the island'. The failure to name the island indicates that the text preceding this excerpt included the fact that the passage refers to Sicily.

[34] Rubinsohn 1982, 443 n. 26, argued that Dio and Diodorus had a common source.

Even in the two passages discussed above, however, there are signs of narratorial interventions designed to produce a specific reading of the text. In the last lines of Diodorus' text, we are told that the disappointed slaves τῶν Συρακουσῶν ἀπαλλαγέντες καὶ καταφυγόντες εἰς τὸ τῶν Παλικῶν τέμενος διελάλουν πρὸς ἀλλήλους ὑπὲρ ἀποστάσεως. ἐκεῖθεν ἐν πολλοῖς τόποις τῆς τῶν οἰκετῶν τόλμης ἐκδήλου γινομένης, 'departed from Syracuse and took refuge in the shrine of the Paliki and discussed with one another about revolt. From then on the boldness of the slaves was made plain in many places.' Cassius Dio records a similar decision in his narrative as follows: οἱ δὲ δείσαντες τοὺς δεσπότας, ὅτι καὶ τὴν ἀρχὴν ἐπικαλέσαι τι αὐτοῖς ἐτόλμησαν, συνεστράφησαν καὶ κοινολογησάμενοι πρὸς λῃστείας ἐτράποντο, '(The slaves), since they feared their masters, as they had dared to accuse them to begin with, gathered and by common consent turned to robbery.' In each case, the author involved is using embedded focalisation to mask their own interpretation of why the slaves acted as they did in the events that followed. In both cases these are plausible inferences, but they are provided covertly by omniscient narrators and are not definitive. We must, therefore, be wary of what they infer about the rebels' motivations. This is more striking for Diodorus' version. The slaves fled to the sanctuary of the Paliki, a shrine to which we will return below.[35] This shrine, as Diodorus records, had several functions (11.88–90): people swore oaths at the shrine on pain of being struck blind for lying; this extended the use of the shrine so that legal claims could be disputed there; finally, it was viewed as a place of sanctuary for slaves. According to Diodorus, slaves who had abusive masters could seek sanctuary in the shrine, and their masters could only remove them after having sworn to conditions of humane treatment: Diodorus adds that history records no case of this pledge ever being violated.[36] In this context the refuge taken by the slaves is more explicable as a typical, or at least an understandable recourse that is absolutely within the bounds of Sicilian culture in this period as Diodorus presents it; in addition, Diodorus emphasises the servile identity of these individuals at the expense of any other. On these terms the enslaved people could be better understood as striving to voice their concerns through acceptable and well-tested means: our only reason to view their actions as a precursor to and initial cause of the later revolts is that Diodorus, as a covert narrator, tells us that this was the purpose of the retreat.[37] We could argue, therefore, that Diodorus' text is deliberately attempting to draw a connection between Licinius Nerva's poor handling of a senatorial decree and the outbreak of revolt that follows, and that he does so at this point by

---

[35] In many ways it is clear from this detail in Diodorus' version that Dio provides a less complete view of the situation in Sicily: the withdrawal to the sanctuary of the Paliki is, in the context of Sicily, a more explicable move than the *direct* withdrawal to banditry as described in Dio.

[36] Maniscalco and McConnell 2003, 173 n 161, comment that Diodorus' text seems to imply that this particular function had developed over time and relatively recently: it had taken place ἔκ τινων χρόνων, 'for some time'. This will be returned to below, pp. 118–19.

[37] The contention expressed in Bradley 1989, 72, that 'for slaves who simply refused to obey their masters and ... withdrew to the sanctuary of the Paliki for asylum, there was little other alternative for survival than banditry' is, in the context of Diodorus' passage, untenable: Diodorus is describing actions of slaves that fit an attempt to negotiate an alteration in their circumstances through the publicly acceptable means of seeking sanctuary at the shrine of the Paliki.

manipulating the reader. This is clear when we turn to the events that follow in what remains of Diodorus' text.

The First Uprisings

In the lines that immediately follow the text quoted above (ἐκεῖθεν ἐν πολλοῖς τόποις τῆς τῶν οἰκετῶν τόλμης ἐκδήλου γινομένης, '(f)rom then on the boldness of the slaves was made plain in many places') we are told that this boldness manifested itself in two revolts: one under the leadership of a man named Varius, and a second among the slaves of a man named P. Clonius, over which Salvius/Tryphon later took command.[38] Diodorus records that thirty slaves near Halicyae introduced as πρῶτοι τῆς ἐλευθερίας ἀντεποιήσαντο, 'the first to lay claim to freedom', murdered their masters and then gathered a group of 200 armed insurgents. With this force they seized a naturally defensible location and were attacked by the governor, who was unable to defeat them (36.2.4–5). This revolt was eventually suppressed after the rebels were betrayed by a turncoat bandit named C. Titinius Gadaeus (Diod. Sic. 36.3.5–6).[39] If Diodorus' narrative preserved any clear indications of why the governor's actions at Syracuse mattered to this revolt, these more elaborate comments have been lost, most probably through Photius' summarising. As it stands, there is little reason within the extant narrative to connect this event to the withdrawal to the sanctuary of the Paliki except for the focalised narratorial intervention about the servile deliberations at the shrine discussed above.[40]

This conclusion leaves us with the remaining revolt to consider: the revolt of Salvius/Tryphon that led in turn to the war's outbreak. Diodorus records the start of the revolt as follows (36.4.1–2):

Τῶν δὲ στρατιωτῶν πρὸς τὰ οἰκεῖα ἤθη ἀπολυθέντων, ἧκόν τινες ἀπαγγέλλοντες ὅτι Πόπλιον Κλόνιον, γενόμενον ἱππέα Ῥωμαίων, ἐπαναστάντες οἱ δοῦλοι κατέσφαξαν ὀγδοήκοντα ὄντες, καὶ ὅτι πλῆθος ἀγείρουσι. καὶ ὁ μὲν στρατηγὸς ἑτέρων βουλαῖς παρακρουσθείς, ἤδη καὶ τῶν πλείστων στρατιωτῶν ἀπολελυμένων, καιρὸν παρεῖχε διὰ τῆς ἀναβολῆς τοῖς ἀποστάταις βέλτιον αὑτοῦ ἀσφαλίσασθαι. προῆγε δὲ μετὰ τῶν ἐνόντων στρατιωτῶν, καὶ διαβὰς τὸν Ἄλβαν ποταμὸν παρῆλθε τοὺς ἀποστάτας διατρίβοντας ἐν ὄρει καλουμένῳ Καπριανῷ, καὶ κατήντησεν εἰς πόλιν Ἡράκλειαν· ἐκ γοῦν τοῦ μὴ προσβαλεῖν αὐτοῖς τὸν στρατηγὸν ἀτολμίαν αὐτοῦ διαφημίσαντες συχνοὺς ἀνέσειον τῶν οἰκετῶν. καὶ πολλῶν συρρεόντων καὶ τὸν δυνατὸν τρόπον εἰς μάχην παρασκευαζομένων, ἐν

---

[38] On Varius and his status, see Aberson 2016.

[39] On C. Titinius Gadaeus, and the suggestion that he came from Lilybaeum and was of Jewish origin, see Cataldi 1997, 317 and 317 n. 104. On the idea that Diodorus emphasises banditry and its supposed close relationship with slave revolts, see Angius 2020, 122–5.

[40] One might add that it is probable that this revolt was recorded because it coincided with the events in Syracuse and the later, larger revolt that followed, but that it was not connected to either event: as we will see in Chapter 5, it is probable that slaves in antiquity revolted frequently in small-scale revolts, but that these are unlikely to have been recorded in our slave-owner narratives except where they coincided with other events.

ἑπτὰ ταῖς πρώταις ἡμέραις καθωπλίσθησαν πλείους τῶν ὀκτακοσίων, ἐφεξῆς δ'
ἐγένοντο τῶν δισχιλίων οὐκ ἐλάττους.

After the soldiers had been disbanded to their usual homes, some reports came that 80 slaves had risen up and murdered Publius Clonius, who had been made a Roman knight, and that a great number were gathering. The governor, led astray by the advice of others, as well as because the majority of his soldiers had been disbanded, at the critical time handed the rebels an opportunity, during the delay, to secure themselves. He advanced with the soldiers available and crossing the river Alba passed by the rebels who were residing on the mountain called Kaprianus, and arrived at the city Heraclea. At all events, making known that the governor was a coward as a result of his not attacking them, they stirred up many of the slaves. Many flocked together and were prepared in a strong fashion for battle; within the first seven days more than 800 had been armed, immediately afterwards there were no less than 2,000.

Again, as the narrative maintains, the only link between this episode and the governor's actions in Syracuse during the hearings is that provided by the narrator's focalised interpretation of the slaves' thoughts at the sanctuary of the Paliki. This is not to say that there was no link between these three events in some form, but we cannot assume that the narrator in this instance is correct to make that connection. What is more, the explanation for events implied by the fragments of Dio's narrative – that the later revolts arose from banditry spurred on by servile irritation at the events in Syracuse – is not compatible with Diodorus' narrative as it stands: these two events at Halicyae and Heraclea Minoa appear to be flash points of servile unrest similar to those described by Diodorus in his proem to the war's narrative, or of the kind that are discussed in Chapter 5. In the proem Diodorus notes two revolts that took place in the time before the war, both in Italy and neither lasting particularly long.[41] In short, if we want to connect the revolts at Halicyae and Heraclea Minoa to the gubernatorial problems in Syracuse described in Diodorus' and Dio's texts, we do so on the assumption that these texts are right to make the connection that they did, even though the link is one constructed in the texts through an embedded focalisation.

All of this is not to suggest that the initial drive to revolt was not caused by a failure of expectations within master–slave relationships in Sicily in this period, or that the initial revolts were not the result of mistreatment or concerns tied directly to slavery, even though the text, as it stands, tells us nothing about the treatment of slaves in Sicily at that time. But I want to suggest that the retrospective interpretations of the rebels' motivations – both in the initial phases of the war and in the events that follow – offered by the ancient literary tradition do not tell us about the actual motivations; they offer, rather, a later slave-owner narrative that aimed to rationalise events in order to comment on master–slave relations or larger issues of leadership. As I argued in the Introduction, there is no reason to think *a priori* that these narratives preserve

---

[41] See Diod. Sic. 36.2.1 and 36.2a.1. The first revolt was at Nuceria and involved thirty slaves; the second was at Capua and involved 200 slaves.

evidence of the rebel perspective: by definition, the slave-owner narratives promoted a different tradition. Moreover, once we strip away the authorial connections made in the texts to explain the events, we cannot build a persuasive context for the rise of the uprising from our ancient literary slave-owner narratives. As with the First Romano-Sicilian War, our literary sources are a poor guide for understanding the historical context, let alone rebel motivations or rebel perspectives. It is time, therefore, to work out as far as is possible what we can say about this war.

The Rebel Perspective

In Chapter 1, we were able to investigate the rebel perspective in the First Romano-Sicilian War through a limited but important body of evidence: the coinage produced by the rebel state during the revolt. For the present war we are not as fortunate. The rebels fighting under Salvius/Tryphon and Athenion left no such numismatically and especially iconographically rich and rewarding evidence. But there remains a small collection of inscribed slingshots that record the names of the rebel leaders: this is the only evidence to come directly from the rebels in this conflict and is therefore of great significance for present purposes. These slingshots allow us to begin discussion of the rebel perspective on the revolts distinct from the slave-owner narratives. Nonetheless, given the admittedly limited nature of this evidence, the ensuing discussion will also take appropriate account of the literary tradition concerning the war when discussing the practical actions undertaken by the rebels. It goes without saying that in light of the conclusions reached above regarding the historical reliability of our principal literary sources for this conflict, the discussion that follows will be tentative in many places. As I noted at the end of Chapter 2, many details of rebel actions recorded in the literary accounts are probably trustworthy on simple factual grounds, but we must always be wary of being taken in by how the slave-owner narratives interpret these actions.

Rebel Slingshots

A number of inscribed lead slingshots, collected in *Inscriptiones Graecae* Volume 14, have been dated to the late second century BC (*IG XIV* 2407,1–26). These slingshots have recorded provenances across the island, including Enna, Agrigentum, Panormus and Leontini. These were produced from casts, and the majority are inscribed with the names of deities, usually combined with νίκη or νίκα. They are connected to the revolt on the basis of the names of the leaders inscribed on the slingshots in some cases and the stylistic similarities between these slingshots and those with the names of deities in other cases; it can be assumed that these were fired by forces during the conflict.[42] Manganaro has argued on the basis of the use of the Attic *koine* νίκη, 'victory',

---

[42] Deities: Athanas/Athena (*IG XIV* 2407,1a–b); Artemis (*IG XIV* 2407,2); Zeus (*IG XIV* 2407,3a–d and 4a–e); Herakles (*IG XIV* 2407,5a–c); Kore (*IG XIV* 2407,6); Mater (*IG XIV* 2407,7a–c). The slingshots referring to civic and military groupings (*IG XIV* 2407,10–26) may not be dated correctly to the second of the Sicilian revolts here considered and could derive from earlier conflicts in Sicily: see Prag 2007a, 98–9, esp. n. 178, and Manganaro 2000, 126–30. On the production of slingshots through casts, either made from clay, stone or bronze, see Manganaro 2000, 126 n. 23, for references.

rather than the Doric νίκα, that these slingshots were produced by enslaved Greeks from the eastern Mediterranean.⁴³ In the first instance, however, these slingshots confirm the wide-ranging nature of the conflict across Sicily (Map 3.1).⁴⁴ In addition, there are six slingshots that record the rebel leaders' names. Four are inscribed with Athenion's name (*IG XIV* 2407,8a–d), which appears with νίκη on three of the four slingshots.⁴⁵ Two have no recorded provenance (*IG XIV* 2407,8c–d), while the other two are recorded as found in the vicinity of Palermo and Leontini (*IG XIV* 2407,8a and 8b respectively). Manganaro provides two more examples that are not recorded in *IG*, which feature the inscriptions NIKA/ΣΩΟΣ and NIKA/ΤΡΥΦΩΝΟC.⁴⁶ The latter is fairly uncomplicated, and can be read on the reverse as Τρύφωνος, 'Tryphon', the regal name taken by Salvius after his acclamation. The former is rather more complex. Manganaro argues that Σώος should be understood as the genitive of Σῶς, the origin of the Latinised form Salvius (Σάλουιος) we find in Diodorus.⁴⁷ I am doubtful of this interpretation of the slingshot: we do not know who Diodorus' source for this narrative was, but the most likely candidate is Posidonius (see Chapter 1, p. 69), and it is puzzling why a Greek historian would misunderstand how to render a Greek name, even a peculiar one like Σῶς.⁴⁸

What, then, do these slingshots tell us about the rebels and their perspective on the events in question? The gods appealed to on the slingshots fit the same group depicted on the coinage produced by Antiochus, including key deities connected to Hellenistic monarchy such as Zeus, Athena, Artemis and Herakles; but equally we might note that these are not unusual gods to appeal to in any case. Manganaro's argument that the dialect of the inscriptions means that these slingshots were inscribed by Greeks from the Mediterranean east should caution us against arguing too strongly for anything more than a typical appeal in times of war to deities.⁴⁹ The slingshots inscribed with the leaders' names, on the other hand, represent important confirmation of that narrative detail presented in Diodorus, especially important in the case of Salvius/Tryphon, who, as we noted above, is mentioned only by Diodorus.

The confirmation of Salvius/Tryphon's choice of name on the slingshot raises the issue of why he chose Tryphon, concerning which there has been a great deal of discussion, with the names used to derive meaning about either the event or the man in question. We start with the name Salvius in brief. The origin of this name is debated,

---

⁴³ Manganaro 2000, 132–33.
⁴⁴ For further discussion of the extent of the 'Second Sicilian Slave War', see Morton 2014.
⁴⁵ *IG XIV* 2407,8a–c all include νίκη: e.g., ν.κη. Ἀθ<η>νίων/ος νίκη (*IG XIV* 2407,8a).
⁴⁶ Manganaro 2000, 131 figs 33 and 34a–b. Manganaro does not give precise provenances for either of these slingshots either here or in Manganaro 1982.
⁴⁷ Manganaro 2000, 131: 'Io ho interpretato Σάλουιος (Salvius) quale calco latino di Σῶς, presentato al genitivo Ζῶος sulla prima glans, la quale registrerebbe il nome originario del capo degli schiavi.' See also Manganaro 1982, 241–2.
⁴⁸ The name appears once in the *Lexicon of Greek Personal Names*, in Volume 3a: Fraser and Matthews 1997, with the provenance listed hesitantly as Aigina, dated to the fifth century BC. See Angius 2020, 131 and 143–5, for the suggestion that the original name was Σῶς, then translated into Latin as Salvius and taken by Diodorus from Latin sources, including court documents.
⁴⁹ Noted explicitly by Manganaro 2000, 133.

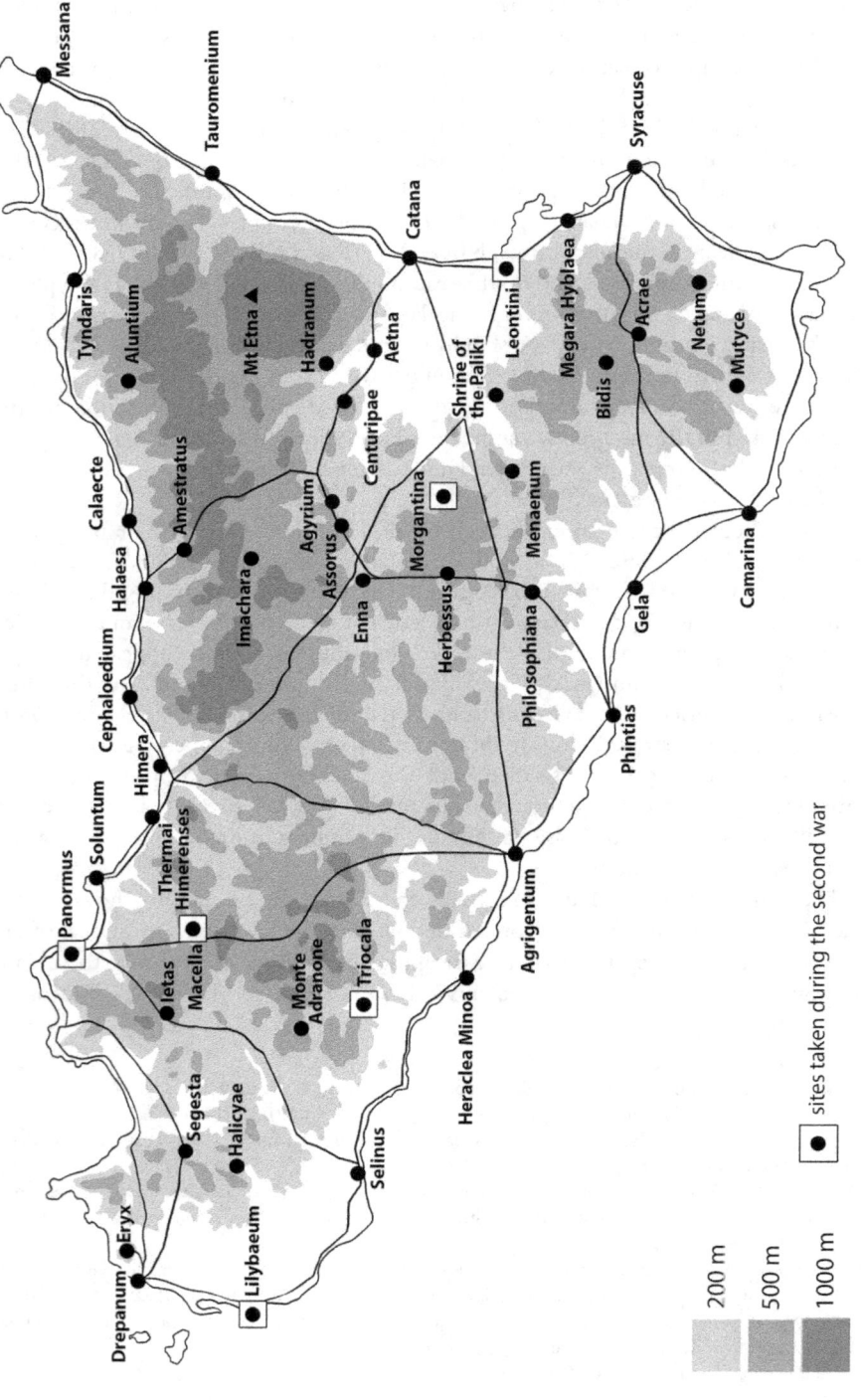

Map 3.1 Sites involved in the second war. © Frances Morton.

and it is suggested that it was Italian, Oscan or Etruscan, although with the acknowledgement that we do not know if the name Salvius was given to Salvius/Tryphon in slavery, or how else he may have acquired this name; given our lack of knowledge about Salvius/Tryphon's origins, it is best to err on the side of caution regarding how useful the name Salvius is as a determinant of his origins.[50] The name Tryphon has also been debated and perhaps offers more potential. It has been understood as either Salvius' name before his enslavement or a deliberate evocation of the pretender to the Seleucid throne during the 140s and 130s, Diodotus Tryphon.[51] If Manganaro is right that the dialect used on the slingshots is the result of the eastern origins of those inscribing the ammunition, then this lends weight to the proposal that Salvius chose the name Tryphon in order to appeal to those under his command from this group: to this we might add the observation that the name Tryphon is much more common in the Greek East than in the Greek West.[52] Finally, Tryphon is more likely a name chosen by Salvius/Tryphon himself and may better reflect his own perception of his origins or its usefulness in the circumstances. Nonetheless, there is no agreement about how significant the choice of Tryphon was in relation to those he led, and the same can be said for the name Salvius. There is, however, a more productive way to consider the rebels' cause that will demonstrate that we should not overemphasise their names in our analysis, as we will see below. For this we must return to a particular note in the literary tradition regarding this war; we have no other evidence from the rebels themselves.

The Nature of the Rebel Leadership

As we saw in the first section of this chapter, after his siege of Morgantina, Salvius/Tryphon is said to have withdrawn from the east of the island to the western site of Triokala, where he built a palace (Diod. Sic. 36.7.2). Before doing so, Salvius/Tryphon visited the sanctuary of the Paliki near Leontini, where he dedicated a purple-bordered

---

[50] For references concerning the origin of the name, see n. 6 above. We should also consider in this context the difference found between public and private documents in the Greek world more widely, where in some cases there appeared to be the possibility of slaves bearing more than one name or bearing names that have no relation to their ethnic origin: see Lewis 2018b.

[51] His original name: Urbainczyk 2008a, 58. Reference to Diodotus Tryphon: Beek 2016, 103–6. Note that Beek 2016, 106 argued that this choice was made in light of the number of Syrians and Cilicians who may have been enslaved and brought to Sicily in the aftermath of Diodotus Tryphon's failed attempt to take the Seleucid throne and the piracy that followed, in order to invoke 'past loyalties of the war captives'. On Diodotus Tryphon, and for further bibliography, see now Chrubasik 2016, 135–41 and 154–61.

[52] The name Τρύφων is found 235 times in the areas of Coastal Asia Minor (Vols 5a and 5b); 90 times in Attica (Vols 2 and 2a); 41 times in Macedonia, Thrace and the Black Sea (Vol. 4); and 42 times in the Aegean Islands, Cyrus and Cyrenaica (Vol. 1). By contrast it is found in the Peloponnese and Western Greece, including Sicily, only 14 times, 3 of which are from Sicily (Vol. 3a). Ἀθηνίων is found across the Mediterranean, albeit slightly more often in the Greek East and not at all in Sicily. Ἀθηνίων is found 47 times in the areas of Coastal Asia Minor (Vols 5a and 5b); 82 times in Attica (Vols 2 and 2a); 7 times in Macedonia, Thrace and the Black Sea (Vol. 4); and 22 times in the Aegean Islands, Cyrus and Cyrenaica (Vol. 1). It is found in the Peloponnese and Western Greece, including Sicily, only 9 times, none of which are from Sicily (Vol. 3a). All figures above come from the *Lexicon of Greek Personal Names*.

toga and then proclaimed himself king, taking the regal name Tryphon (Diod. Sic. 36.7.1). We are told a little later in the text how Salvius/Tryphon styled himself when ruling (Diod. Sic. 36.7.4):

ἐξελέξατο δὲ καὶ τῶν φρονήσει διαφερόντων ἀνδρῶν τοὺς ἱκανούς, οὓς ἀποδείξας συμβούλους ἐχρῆτο συνέδροις αὐτοῖς· τήβενναν τε περιπόρφυρον περιεβάλλετο καὶ πλατύσημον ἔδυ χιτῶνα κατὰ τοὺς χρηματισμούς, καὶ ῥαβδούχους εἶχε μετὰ πελέκεων τοὺς προηγουμένους, καὶ τἆλλα πάντα ὅσα ποιοῦσί τε καὶ ἐπικοσμοῦσι βασιλείαν ἐπετήδευε.

He (Salvius/Tryphon) chose sufficient men who excelled in prudence and appointing them as advisors he used them as his councillors. He wore a purple-bordered toga and a broad-bordered chiton when in session and had lictors bearing axes precede him; and in all other things he made it his business to both prepare and adorn himself as much as a king.

Athenion also, we are told, proclaimed himself king and took on the accoutrements of the title: Diodorus describes him taking up a diadem and, according to Florus, he arrayed himself with a purple robe and silver sceptre.[53] We will return to Salvius/Tryphon's dedication at the shrine and to his activities at Triokala in the next two parts of this section and focus here on the presentation of kingship offered by Athenion and Salvius/Tryphon, at least as far as we can understand it from the ancient narrative tradition.

Of the two, Athenion is the more straightforward: in terms of the presentation of his rule, we learn only that he proclaimed himself monarch and arrayed himself with what one might expect of a monarch: sceptre, diadem and robe. Salvius/Tryphon is marginally more complex. In the passage quoted above, as king he appointed counsellors, wore a purple-bordered toga, broad-bordered *chiton*, and was preceded by lictors.[54] It has been noted in the past that the purple-bordered toga and lictors are symbols of Roman office, and that Salvius/Tryphon was adapting the dress of senior Roman magistrates.[55] One might be tempted to take Diodorus' description of Salvius/Tryphon's appointment of σύμβουλοι, 'advisors', to be his σύνεδροι, 'councillors', as a description of a Roman magistrate's *consilium* rather than a monarch's φίλοι, 'friends'.[56] Nonetheless, the text is clear that Salvius/Tryphon proclaimed himself king: as Rawson has shown, there was a tradition of mixing Roman and royal

---

[53] Diod. Sic. 36.5.2; Flor. 2.7.10: 'veste purpurea argenteoque baculo et regium in morem fronte redimita...', 'arrayed with a purple robe and a silver sceptre and crowned in the manner of a king...'. Cicero describes Athenion as a king on two occasions in the *Verrine Orations*: 2.2.136 and 2.3.65–6, and Appian describes him as such (*Mith.* 59).

[54] Urbainczyk 2008a, 58 n. 38, argues that these two items should be understood as a *toga praetexta* and a *tunica laticlava*.

[55] See, e.g., Vogt 1965, 35; Manganaro 1967, 220; Finley 1979, 145; Manganaro 1980, 441; Dumont 1987, 268; Bradley 1989, 123; Wirth 2004, 284; Wirth 2006, 127; Yarrow 2006, 222–3; Urbainczyk 2008a, 58 n. 38.

[56] See Vogt 1965, 35, and Bradley 1989, 117, for the σύνεδροι as φίλοι.

trappings of power, followed by figures such as Antiochus Epiphanes and the Roman *eques* T. Vettius.[57] Romans themselves had honoured foreign monarchs with the insignia of a *triumphator*, offered either by the senate or individual Roman generals.[58] If, as is possible, Salvius/Tryphon's origins were in the Greek East then the appeal to kingship is not unexpected; but given the history of Hellenistic monarchy in Sicily itself, this line cannot be pressed too far. Moreover, he was not unusual in adopting also the accoutrements of Roman authority — these would have been the most prevalent symbols of authority on Sicily in this period.[59] In short, both Athenion's and Salvius/Tryphon's outward appearances, as described by the ancient historiographical traditions, were regal in nature. What kind of monarchies they created, and what this can tell us about the rebel perspective on these events, can only be assessed from the actions of these kings while they were ruling. Let us now turn to their actions, as depicted in the ancient narrative sources, and study them as far as we can without drawing too much on the slave-owner narratives' judgement and interpretation of these actions.

The Sanctuary of the Paliki

As we saw above, in Diodorus' narrative of the war, Salvius/Tryphon proclaimed himself king, took the name Tryphon, and made a dedication at the sanctuary of the Paliki. It is worth quoting the passage in full before discussion (Diod. Sic. 36.7.1):

Ὁ δὲ τὴν Μοργαντίνην πολιορκήσας Σάλουιος, ἐπιδραμὼν τὴν χώραν μέχρι τοῦ Λεοντίνου πεδίου, ἤθροισεν αὐτοῦ τὸ σύμπαν στράτευμα, ἐπιλέκτους ἄνδρας οὐκ ἐλάττους τῶν τρισμυρίων, καὶ θύσας τοῖς Παλικοῖς ἥρωσι τούτοις μὲν ἀνέθηκε μίαν τῶν ἀλουργῶν περιπορφύρων στολὴν χαριστήρια τῆς νίκης, αὐτὸς δ' ἀναγορεύσας ἑαυτὸν βασιλέα Τρύφων μὲν ὑπὸ τῶν ἀποστατῶν προσηγορεύετο.

After the siege of Morgantina, Salvius, having overrun the country as far as the plain of Leontini, gathered his whole army, chosen men of not less than 30,000, and having sacrificed to the Paliki heroes, dedicated a purple-bordered robe to them in thanksgiving for victory. He also proclaimed himself king and was addressed by the rebels as Tryphon.

In the first instance, Salvius/Tryphon's choice of moment for his proclamation as king fits Hellenistic practice, and there is nothing particularly extraordinary about this. The dedication of the purple-bordered toga is also easily reconcilable with the forces he

---

[57] See Rawson 1975, 156. For Antiochus Epiphanes see Polyb. 26.1 and 30.25; for T. Vettius see Diod. Sic. 36.2. T. Vettius assumed the title and diadem of a king but combined them with the purple-bordered toga and lictors of a Roman consul.

[58] Rawson 1975, 155, argues that the first verifiable instance of this was the gift of triumphal 'trappings' by Scipio Agricanus to Masinissa: Livy 30.15.11–12; App. *Pun.* 32, 137. A similar honour was granted to Ariarathes of Cappadocia (Polyb. 32.1.3) and Eumenes of Pergamum (Livy 42.14.10).

[59] Bradley 1989, 122, argues that Spartacus likewise adopted lictors after capturing them from P. Varinius: see Plut. *Crass.* 9.5; Flor. 2.8.7–8; Frontin. *Str.* 2.5.34.

had recently defeated: those serving under a Roman praetor.[60] The location chosen for these events, on the other hand, does appear to be significant. As we will see below (pp. 121–2), Salvius/Tryphon chose not to settle his forces in the south-east of the island. His capital was established soon after at the site of Triokala in Sicily's western half. Why he chose to dedicate the robe at a cult based in the island's south-east deserves some consideration, not least because it is by examining these kinds of actions that we can begin to gauge the way in which the rebels themselves perceived their movement; it is to this cult that we now turn.

It is worth summarising here the history of the cult of the Paliki. Activity at the site of the sanctuary of the Paliki dates back to the Palaeolithic period, and the cult itself is one of the oldest in Sicily.[61] The cult was based around a hydrogeological phenomenon and was renowned in antiquity as a location at which oaths were taken and those breaking their oaths were punished with death or blinding.[62] The Paliki themselves were a pair of Sicel deities, born in the legends to the nymph Thalia.[63] From the Archaic period and throughout the Hellenistic period the sanctuary was developed to include a *hestiatērion*, two *stoai*, and a building known as Complex P, with the *hestiatērion* functioning as a form of *prytaneion*;[64] until some point in the third century BC the sanctuary was complemented by habitation based on the acropolis above it.[65] The sanctuary itself remained very active into the first century BC, with some indication of activity in the Augustan period, although this was generally a period of decline.[66] As we saw above (p. 109), in Diodorus' day this sanctuary was a place for the swearing of oaths and a refuge for mistreated slaves, but the sanctuary had an important place in Sicilian history before the first century BC. In the mid-fifth century BC the site was the centre of a Sicel alliance under the leadership of a prominent Sicel from Menaenum called Ducetius.[67] According to Diodorus, Ducetius founded a city called Palikē, although it was destroyed soon after.[68] Maniscalco argues that although Ducetius is credited only with the construction of the city, it is probable that he also drove the monumentalisation of the sanctuary, given its importance to the Sicel alliance (συντέλεια) and the unified nature of the construction along the same axis.[69] The sanctuary remained an important site for religious activity throughout the Archaic to Hellenistic periods, and this has led Maniscalco and McConnell to argue that this is best explained by the existence on the site of 'a much more stable sanctuary

---

[60] Perhaps the specificity of the robe (μίαν) implies that this was a robe captured from the praetor himself.
[61] For a full discussion of the site's development from the Palaeolithic to Late Antiquity, see Cordano 2008 and Maniscalco 2008, 13–138. For a discussion of the cult of the Paliki, see Ziegler 1949a and 1949b; Bello 1960; Manni 1983; Cusumano 1990; Meurant 1998.
[62] See Diod. Sic. 11.89.5; Pseudo-Aristotle, *Mir. ausc.* 57; Macrob. *Sat.* 5.19.19–21, 28–9.
[63] Macrob. *Sat.* 5.19.18.
[64] Hippys of Rhegion recorded that the site was built up during the period from 636–632 BC, as recorded in Antigonus Carystius, *Hist. mir.* 121.
[65] The precise date is uncertain: see Maniscalco 2008, 123–4 and 134.
[66] Cirelli 2008, 244–90, and Maniscalco 2008, 135–6, and 2018, 76–7.
[67] For an analysis of Ducetius, see Consolo Langher 1996, 246–51, and 1997, 61.
[68] Diod. Sic. 11.88.6–90.2.
[69] Manciscalo 2008, 132–3; see also McConnell 2008, 332–3.

THE CREATION OF AN ALTERNATIVE STATE   119

administration . . . which predated the Sikel federation and which survived the historical vicissitudes of Greek and later Roman rule'.[70]

The excavators of the site have recently argued that Salvius/Tryphon's activities at the sanctuary left a physical mark. A significant deposit of ash and burnt soil that contained animal bones, ceramics and metal items have been excavated and are dateable to the end of the second century BC. The quantity of the remains and the short period in which they were built up led the excavators to argue that these deposits were left by the sacrifices made by the rebels and the consumption of meals by those present.[71] Moreover, McConnell has postulated that a niche carved into Room 7 of the *hestiatērion* may have been where the toga dedicated by Salvius/Tryphon was placed, or that it was hung upon the wall.[72] It is impossible to know if these deposits of ash and burnt soil can indeed be attributed to Salvius/Tryphon's time at the sanctuary, but these deposits are strong evidence for the continued use and importance of the shrine in the period in which the war took place: Salvius/Tryphon was not visiting an abandoned and irrelevant sanctuary. It is perhaps unlikely that he was appealing directly to the memory of Ducetius with his sacrifice and dedication at the sanctuary. This is in part because of the historical distance between the two men, but also because, as Salvius/Tryphon's later actions show, he was not recreating a unified state with its cultural and political centre at the Paliki sanctuary; however, the site's cultural importance, especially with regard to those poorly represented by the dominant authorities in Sicily, should not be understated. In the context of the events in which his dedication took place, Salvius/Tryphon's actions could plausibly have been understood as an attempt to connect to a well-established indigenous priesthood that was deeply rooted in the island's cultural fabric, and, presumably, to connect to those inhabitants of Sicily – be they free or unfree – who also valued and visited this priesthood.[73] Moreover, Diodorus noted in his description of the sanctuary that the connection between the shrine and slavery had developed recently in relation to his own day – that is some forty or so years since the war.[74] This suggests that the non-servile connotations of the sanctuary were originally better established. It follows that we do not need to repeat the slave-owner narrative's emphasis on the servile aspect of the sanctuary in our own interpretation of Salvius/Tryphon's actions.

There is some evidence that interpreting Salvius/Tryphon's actions as emphasising the importance of the free peoples of Sicily is not entirely speculative. In Photius' summary of Diodorus' text, just before he describes the rebel actions at the sanctuary

---

[70] Maniscalco and McConnell 2003, 176.
[71] Maniscalco and McConnell 2003, 169, and Maniscalco 2008, 122–3. See also Midolo 2008 and Di Patti and Lupo 2008.
[72] Maniscalco and McConnell 2003, 173, and more recently McConnell 2008, 320 and 330.
[73] Wirth 2004, 284, saw the actions at the shrine rather as a form of intensification of the religious element of the conflict, while Perkins 2007, 48, noted the conflation of the cult's dual native and slave aspects in this revolt.
[74] As we saw above, Diodorus describes the use of the sanctuary as a place of asylum for slaves ἔκ τινων χρόνων, 'for some time' (11.89.6). Diodorus probably wrote his *Bibliothēke* between *c*. 60 and 30 BC: on Diodorus' life and the period of composition, see Green 2006, 2–7, and Muntz 2017, 217–21. If this period for composition is accurate, then Diodorus' statement in book 11 will have been written at least forty years after the war.

of the Paliki, he notes that there was an outbreak of social disorder in Sicily (Diod. Sic. 36.6). This event was also recorded by one of the few Constantinian excerpts for this war (36.11), and in much more detail than is preserved by Photius. In the Constantinian version, we learn that in addition to the revolting slaves τῶν ἐλευθέρων οἱ τὰς ἐπὶ χώρας κτήσεις οὐκ ἔχοντες, 'those of the free who had no possessions on the land', engaged in robbery; the overall result was that those within the cities abandoned their possessions outside the city walls. These free poor subjected those within the city who had formerly enjoyed a high status to violent threats, and some even engaged in murder in the countryside.[75] A similar passage is preserved in the narrative for the First Romano-Sicilian War, as we saw in Chapter 1 (Diod. Sic. 34/5.2.48). The fragment for the war in focus in the present chapter is located in Photius' version after the siege of Morgantina (36.4) and Athenion's rise in the west (36.5), but before the actions at the sanctuary of the Paliki (36.7). The location of the fragment suggests that this collapse of order was in 104 BC, perhaps as a consequence of the Roman defeat at Morgantina.[76] The passage gives no indication of which cities suffered this loss of order, but we might reasonably suppose that cities in the vicinity of the revolt would have been affected: at this point that would include cities in the far west of the island and/or those near Morgantina. We cannot be more specific about who was involved in this disorder, or what precisely caused it, not least because the passage itself does not provide much detail on this matter and is instead more interested in painting a picture of despair amongst the grandees of some Sicilian towns, while the free poor and slaves run riot.[77]

While we may not be able to pinpoint precisely which towns were caught up in this disorder, or what it was actually comprised of, it is striking that this is recorded as taking place at the same time as Salvius/Tryphon's actions at the sanctuary of the Paliki. The tensions in these Sicilian cities appear to have been along social lines, and if the passage above is right to view the free Sicilians taking part as those without land, this offers us some evidence to support the idea that Salvius/Tryphon's actions could have stood in relation to a broader contemporary problem. The connection between the disorder and the sacrifices at the sanctuary of the Paliki is hypothetical, but it supports the argument that Salvius/Tryphon's actions could be viewed as a response to the all-encompassing social issues that affected Sicilian society as much as, if not more

---

[75] The high-status individuals are described as οἱ δὲ πρότερον ἐν ταῖς πόλεσιν πρωτεύοντες ταῖς τε δόξαις καὶ τοῖς πλούτοις, 'those who before had held first place in their cities in both reputation and wealth'.

[76] The passage itself implies as much, noting that this deterioration of order took place διὰ τὸ μηδεμίαν Ῥωμαϊκὴν ἀρχὴν δικαιοδοτεῖ, 'since no Roman magistrate administered justice'. On *stasis* in Sicilian cities, see Gabba 1959 and Covino 2013.

[77] The passage has been commented on in the past, albeit in large part in order to critique how the free acted during a slave revolt: see, e.g., Toynbee 1965, 330, who commented that 'the free urban proletariat behaved even worse than they had behaved in the First (Slave War)'. For similar comments see Finley 1979, 142–3, Manganaro 1980, 441, and Strauss 2010, 198. Canfora 1985, 157–60, is concerned chiefly in differentiating between those involved in the unrest in the two wars. Bradley 1989, 78, dismissed Diodorus' account as 'highly rhetorical'; Photius, perhaps picking up on the rhetorical feel of this passage, introduces his own summary with a literary flourish (Diod. Sic. 36.6): Εἶχε δὲ τὴν Σικελίαν πᾶσαν σύγχυσις καὶ κακῶν Ἰλιάς, 'Ruin and an Iliad of troubles held all Sicily.'

than, any particular issues affecting Sicily's enslaved population. Most of all, this act situates him firmly in the cultural and political landscape of Sicily, and distances him from the eastern influences we considered above when discussing his name. While his royal name could be understood as an appeal to any eastern Greeks on the island, his concrete actions emerge, at least in part, as an appeal to the island's wider population. I noted above that Salvius/Tryphon offered the enslaved in Morgantina their freedom if they chose to support him. Plainly, Salvius/Tryphon sought to encourage a following among those in slavery. Notably though, we are equally told that the offer of freedom from slavery was matched by the Roman side, keen to augment their own forces. Yet, the very fact that the Romans did the same as the rebels should caution us from branding the revolt led by Salvius/Tryphon as a slave rebellion, and the war a slave war. Rather, and clearly, another rebel leader in Sicily was able and willing to communicate at diverse levels to diverse groups in society, across the spectrum of individual legal statuses.

Establishing a Capital

In the aftermath of his proclamation of kingship and the sacrifices at the shrine to the Paliki, Salvius/Tryphon withdrew his forces to the west of the island to a place called Triokala. The exact location of this site is uncertain: it is most likely to be modern-day Sant'Anna below Caltabellotta in Sicily's south-west, or Caltabellotta itself; in either case Triokala is on the opposite side of the island from the sanctuary of the Paliki.[78] Once there, we are told that Salvius/Tryphon reinforced the site and provided it with a new palace (Diod. Sic. 36.7.2–3):

τὸ δὲ φρούριον ὀχυρώτατον ὂν κατεσκεύαζε πολυτελέσι κατασκευαῖς καὶ ἐπὶ μᾶλλον ὀχύρου. Τριόκαλα δὲ αὐτό φασιν ὠνομάσθαι διὰ τὸ τρία καλὰ ἔχειν, πρῶτον μὲν ναματιαίων ὑδάτων πλῆθος διαφόρων τῇ γλυκύτητι, δεύτερον παρακειμένην χώραν ἀμπελόφυτόν τε καὶ ἐλαιόφυτον καὶ γεωργεῖσθαι δυναμένην θαυμαστῶς, τρίτον ὑπερβάλλουσαν ὀχυρότητα, ὡς ἂν οὔσης μεγάλης πέτρας ἀναλώτου· ἣν καὶ περιβόλῳ πόλεως σταδίων ὀκτὼ προσπεριβαλὼν καὶ ταφρεύσας βαθείᾳ τάφρῳ βασιλείοις ἐχρῆτο, πάσῃ ἀφθονίᾳ τῶν κατὰ τὸν βίον ἁπάντων πεπληρωμένην. κατεσκεύασε δὲ καὶ βασιλικὴν οἰκίαν καὶ ἀγορὰν δυναμένην δέξασθαι πλῆθος ἀνθρώπων.

The citadel, which was very secure, he equipped with costly constructions and secured it more. It is said that this place is named Triokala because it has three fine features: first, many flowing springs remarkable for their sweetness; second, the country around is planted with both vines and olive trees and is wonderfully amenable to cultivation; third, surpassing strength, as it is a large and impregnable rock ridge. Tryphon surrounded the city with a wall of eight stades and a deep moat, and used it as his royal residence, filling it with every abundance required for living. He built a royal residence and an *agora* able to hold many people.

---
[78] Discussion of the site of Triokala: see Bejor 1975, 1283–9; Manni 1981, 238–9; *BTCGI IV*, 269–70.

Later in the conflict after their failure at the battle of Scirthaea, the rebels retreated back to their stronghold at Triokala, as we saw above, and it appears from these few details that this site became the capital – for want of a better word – for the rebel state. We can press this a little further. If we take the details recorded in this passage to reflect a possible reality, then the rebels appear to be creating, as far as physical structures are concerned, a functioning Greek city, with an *agora* and royal residence protected by a circuit wall. Moreover, the site had good access to easily cultivated land, typical of many Greek cities.[79] Even if the specifics are not accurate, given the difficulties that L. Licinius Lucullus faced when he finally pursued the rebels to Triokala after the battle at Scirthaea, it is probable that the site was well fortified (Diod. Sic. 36.8.5). If we combine this information with the confirmation of Salvius/Tryphon's royal name and his actions at the sanctuary of the Paliki, it appears that at the latest once we move past the first period of the war, and certainly within the first year of the conflict, the rebels are clearly considering matters beyond material gain from looting or individual freedom: we can see the outline of a society in its infancy that potentially had many of the features of the surrounding Sicilian *poleis*. As with the rebels in the First Romano-Sicilian War, we see here evidence of state-building independent of the Roman authorities as late as 104 BC. While this argument must remain tentative, it does best explain the few details we know about the rebels' actions once the revolt was in motion.

As is so often the case in the narratives of the wars at the core of this book, we are left with only hints of what followed. I noted above that for the events that followed the battle at Scirthaea in the second year of the war, we have only Diodorus Siculus' compressed narrative that barely traces the actions of 102 BC and that focuses closely on the eventual suppression of the revolt by M'. Aquilius. That man's reputation and close involvement with Athenion, I argued, largely erased Salvius/Tryphon from the collective memory of these events, as is shown best by the few details of the war recorded in extant Latin literature. Salvius/Tryphon's death after the battle at Scirthaea means that we cannot be certain how this nascent state developed, at least in terms of specifics. Nonetheless, some details can be outlined.

First, although the narrative of Athenion's command of the rebels is poorly preserved, it appears that he attempted to continue to build the rebel state in a manner similar to Salvius/Tryphon. The extant portions of Diodorus' text tell us relatively little about this phase of the war, only outlining Athenion's actions in brief, and with the barest details.[80] A fragment of Cassius Dio appears to preserve some evidence of the type of strategy pursued by Athenion (27.93.4):

ὅτι οἱ Μεσσήνιοι νομίσαντες μηδὲν δεινὸν πείσεσθαι, πάντα τὰ πλείστου ἄξια καὶ τιμιώτατα ἐκεῖσε ὑπεξέθεντο. μαθὼν δὲ τοῦτο Ἀθηνίων, ὅσπερ που τὸ μέγιστον κράτος τῶν λῃστευόντων Κίλιξ ὢν εἶχεν, ἐπέθετο αὐτοῖς δημοτελῆ τινα ἑορτὴν ἐν

---

[79] See also Bradley 1989, 116–17; Wirth 2006, 127; Perkins 2007, 48.
[80] Diod. Sic. 36.9.1. Cicero (*Verr.* 2.3.136) claims that Athenion failed to seize any cities, contrasting him with Timarchides, one of Verres' subordinates; as we will see, there is some evidence that Cicero is either mistaken or misrepresenting the case here.

τῷ προαστείῳ ἄγουσι, καὶ ἐκείνων τε πολλοὺς σκεδασθέντας ἀπέκτεινε καὶ τὴν πόλιν ὀλίγου κατὰ κράτος εἷλεν. χωρίον δέ τι Μάκελλαν εὐερκὲς τειχισάμενος ἰσχυρῶς τὴν γῆν ἐκακούργει.

The Messenians, who had expected to suffer no danger, had brought all of their most valuable and prized possessions to that place for safety. When he learned of this, Athenion, the very Cilician who was leader of the bandits and held a strong force, set upon them when they were celebrating some public festival in the suburbs. He killed many of them as they scattered and almost seized the mastery of the city. After fortifying a certain spot, Makella, with a wall, he violently ravaged the country.

As I have shown elsewhere, this fragment is problematic.[81] It appears to preserve evidence of an attack on the people of Messana: the passage starts ὅτι οἱ Μεσσήνιοι. However, nowhere in Dio's extant text are the people of Messana referred to as Μεσσήνιοι following the town's capture by the Mamertines in the early third century BC. The town itself is referred to as Μεσσήνη, the inhabitants as Μαμερτίνοι.[82] It would be sensible, therefore, to regard the usage of Μεσσήνιοι at the start of this passage as a mistake, coming immediately after the introductory ὅτι.[83] The events discussed in the fragment support this interpretation. They revolve around the site of Makella, which is now understood to be modern Montagnola di Marineo, a site in the west of Sicily south of Panormus.[84] It is probable, therefore, that these events also took place in this area, which is not far north of Triokala. If we leave aside the motivation ascribed to Athenion here,[85] his actions in this passage accord with Salvius/Tryphon's regarding Triokala: the fortification of a defensible site, in this case strategically placed on the road from Panormus to Agrigentum. We can add the slingshot bearing Athenion's name discussed above to this fragment from Cassius Dio, in order to reconstruct the breadth of his actions while in command. His reach extended from Makella and Triokala in the west through a corridor to Leontini in the east: in short, across much of the island's south. It is frustrating that we can say no more about Athenion's leadership. Even so, the bare outline given above seems to indicate that he attempted to consolidate Salvius/Tryphon's actions at Triokala, although it is hard to understand how the action at Leontini supported this. As I have argued elsewhere, the rebels in this war appear to have been less strategically focused and less successful than those led

---

[81] See Morton 2014, 30–1 n. 35.
[82] Μαμερτίνοι: 9.40.8; 9.40.11; 11.43.5; 11.43.10. Μεσσήνη: 9.40.8; 11.43.4–9 (three times); 48.17.4–5 (twice); 49.2.1; 49.5.1–2 (twice); 49.7.4; 49.10.2 (twice); 49.11.2–4 (twice); 49.17.1. Where Zonaras follows Dio he continues this usage.
[83] The original text is impossible to recover, and so whom, precisely, Athenion was attacking we cannot know for certain.
[84] The site's name is attested on three inscribed roof tiles found in the area around Montagnola di Marineo (SEG 51.1377 and 54.927). For the publication of these roof tiles, see Spatafora 2001, 111–14, and Spatafora and Vassallo 2004, 108, nos 208/9.
[85] The same challenge of understanding rebel motivation from ancient historiography argued for Diodorus above is relevant here for Cassius Dio: how could he be certain that it was the money, and not the strategic opportunity, that motivated Athenion?

by King Antiochus;[86] but despite this lack of success they nonetheless appear to have been motivated by similar goals, overall concerned with the establishment of their own state according to contemporary Hellenistic models and as such outside a context of slavery: once we move past the ancient historiographical obsession with the beginning and end of the war, we can start to understand better the thrust of their actions, and in particular how the rebels organised their state.

Conclusion

What, then, can we say about the second of our two Sicilian wars? We cannot deny that what remains of the later slave-owner narratives for this war depict it as a servile uprising inspired by a failure of both the master–slave relationship and the free leadership on the island; this much is clear from the connections that the *post hoc* slave-owner narratives made between Roman actions in the Mediterranean east and the initial uprising in Sicily. There is no way of telling if the smaller uprising was indeed the result of tensions among the enslaved and their owners in a single Sicilian household, a development that may be explained through an analysis of master–slave relations on the island. At the same time, the wider developments illustrate a much broader canvass for the rebel actions than the acquisition of individual freedom: the rebels endeavoured to found a state with a centre at Triokala under the leadership of a monarch (and potentially a successor). In so doing they appealed to a cult rooted firmly in the cultural fabric of the island, and one specifically connected to the underprivileged on the island: this best explains the events at the sanctuary of the Paliki. It moreover suggests that we should not overemphasise the importance of Eastern Mediterranean parallels for this state, despite the names – chosen, given in slavery or otherwise acquired – of those involved. The immediate, Sicilian context must not be relegated to the sidelines; it deepens our understanding of the conflict while not taking away from its link to slavery in Sicily in this period or to the eastern Greeks involved: as with the revolt led by Antiochus, the rebel leaders were capable of communicating with different groups in different ways. While this interpretation of the events cannot be pushed too far, it does appear, then, that from the rebel perspective this was not a struggle centred on slavery, but one that was concerned with Sicilian society at large.

This is not to say that the rebels necessarily convinced others of their view. Frankly, we do not know enough about the events of the final three years of the war to speak with any certainty about who joined the rebels or not. This uncertainty affects any assessment of the level of involvement of individuals who joined the rebellion from a condition of slavery: as seen above, the enslaved at Morgantina went hither and thither between Sicilians and Romans. At the same time, it appears that for the second time in around thirty years some cities in Sicily faced profound internal problems, the exact nature of which is equally hard to assess. Yet, even without more information it appears that those involved turned to Salvius/Tryphon and the rebellion he led for an alternative to the existing situation on the island. As with the First Romano-Sicilian

---

[86] Morton 2014.

War, it is not possible to paint an authoritative outline of the developments that seized Sicily at the end of the second century BC. But despite the sketchy nature of our information, the few insights foregrounded in this chapter suggest that there is little reason to continue putting the slave-owner narrative that has dominated both ancient and modern accounts on to an interpretative pedestal – however tempting given its seeming explanatory powers. Clearly, the ancient historiographic record owes much to the retrospective rationalisation of a slave-owning class attempting to conceptualise events in a manner that fitted their world-view and to give these events meaning within their own literary projects. There is little reason to think that this class was concerned with appreciating what the rebels made of these events. In short, those narratives tell us more about how later slave owners made the conflict fit their own perception of the world than about what actually took place.

Notwithstanding the many unresolved riddles, what I hope is clearest is that the happenings that shook Sicily from 104 BC onwards were complex and touched upon societal issues that cannot be grasped by a clean slave–free dichotomy and a focus on master–slave relationships. To call, conversely, the uprising a slave war is to assume that slavery was at its core, or that the stigma of enslavement, once applied to those who rebelled, suffices to explain their actions: it is to assume that the slave-owner narrative is the authoritative narrative and that the view promoted by this narrative defines the events as well as the status of those involved. Throughout the revolt, those united under the banner of Salvius/Tryphon, as well as Athenion, attempted to create a new state that self-consciously appealed to an indigenous cult that was connected to the disadvantaged peoples of Sicily. Perhaps it was probable from the outset that they could not succeed in their efforts to build a new state – at least in the long term – but it does not mean that we should describe their efforts using the labels of a later historiographic culture that fitted those events into wider narratives of the rising dominant Mediterranean power, Rome, neatly couched in terms of the miniature world of moralising tales of master–slave relationships. It is, again, a bold decision to dismiss the term 'slave' or 'servile' when referring to these events, but it is worth it for what we gain when we do so. It liberates us, so to speak, from the preconceptions and assumptions that these labels bring to mind, and it may allow us to honour a little better what the events meant to those who rebelled.

In terms of our own historiographic methods, this means giving centre stage to the admittedly almost muted voices of those who lost *their* perspectives – however difficult to resurrect – and *their* attempts at state and identity building. It must surely also make for a better historial record. It follows that to speak of the 'Second Sicilian Slave War' when referring to this revolt and war has outlasted its usefulness. Given the geographically widespread nature of the revolt, its diverse settings and shifts in leadership, one may more profitably identify a society in stasis, perhaps even more so than three decades earlier. On the broader plane, however, characterised by tensions between Sicily and Rome, it seems evident that the best, and historiographically most neutral label at least for the martial dimension of the revolt is, once again, that of Romano-Sicilian War. Overall, this new label is wide enough to account for the many diverse elements of the revolt, while liberating our historical imagination from the straightjacket that its understanding as a slave revolt or slave war has constituted.

And given the apparent overlap in the root cause of this revolt with that led by Antiochus a generation earlier, it seems appropriate to bookend these events by title accordingly, that is to speak of the First and Second Romano-Sicilian War respectively. In sum, whatever their differences, historical and evidential, both events constituted serious revolts, and Sicilian revolts at that, and must be appreciated in the future within the broader remit of profound conflict between Sicily and Rome, and within Sicily itself.

Part II:

Slave Revolts in Ancient Historiography and the Wider Historical Context

4

THE SLAVE REVOLT *TOPOS*: THINKING WITH SERVILE UNREST IN ANCIENT HISTORIOGRAPHY

IN THE PRECEDING THREE CHAPTERS I have argued that the events commonly referred to as the two Sicilian Slave Wars can be fruitfully understood as examples of discontent with the political and social status quo on Sicily that manifested itself on two occasions in instances of attempted state formation.[1] The states formed in each case actively drew on the support of both free and enslaved members of the Sicilian population while being rooted in pre-existing religious, cultural and social institutions on the island. The prevailing concern throughout these chapters was to reconstruct, as far as possible, the perspectives emerging from the evidence left behind by those who rebelled, and to put these perspectives critically against the slave-owner narratives that have dominated the modern analysis. Nonetheless, those slave-owner narratives have featured prominently also in the present study. They have been of interest owing to how they used these events to comment upon both free and servile leadership, how they sought to undermine the leadership of these conflicts, and how they presented the wars as events that were tied to the master–slave relationship above any other consideration.[2] It cannot be denied that the version of the two wars that can be found in Diodorus, the remains of Livy, and Florus, among others, is quite different from the one I have argued for, particularly in Chapters 1 and 3. In principle this distance between my narrative and the ancient slave-owner narrative for each revolt is problematic: if the ancient historical tradition sought to use terminology related to slave revolts systematically to describe historical events, then these texts should be a legitimate (rough) guide to the nature of the events in question. Yet we cannot assume *a priori* that the ancient authors were attempting to give straightforward, faithful accounts of any particular event: as we have seen in Chapters 2 and 3, Diodorus' text in particular has been carefully constructed in order to achieve certain reading responses within his wider literary project. In order to better appreciate the place of the slave-owner narrative that has shaped both ancient and modern understanding of our two Sicilian wars in the texts that have transmitted accounts of these wars, it is imperative to situate accounts of slave revolts more broadly in their literary context. For this it is worth considering how and why other authors in antiquity discussed events they described as slave revolts.

[1] As will become clear throughout, this chapter owes much to the recent work of Lavan 2013a, 2013b and 2017 on revolt narratives and the use of slave metaphors in Imperial literature.
[2] There has been an emphasis on the narratives preserved in Diodorus Siculus, owing in large part to the fact that his text preserves the largest surviving slave-owner narrative. On this, see Chapter 2.

There has been relatively little attention paid to slave revolt narratives as a historiographical category in past scholarship, and this has repeatedly resulted in each narrative being discussed in separation.[3] Yet there is potential in an approach to these narratives that assesses them alongside one another to research commonalities between the disparate records of servile insurrection. The hypothesis I aim to test in this chapter is that slave revolt narratives in ancient historiography are seldom simply attempts to report or explain the revolts in question. There was instead a trend in both Greek and Latin literature, especially in historiography, but also in political speeches, to use slave revolt narratives to achieve a range of objectives concerning the historical, social or political aims of any given text. The inclusion of a slave revolt narrative in an ancient work does not mean that the event in question occurred, nor if the event did take place does it mean that the details included are accurate. In essence, I will argue in this chapter that ancient writers, and especially historians and politicians – ancient slave owners one and all – used servile resistance to think about free society and politics: as we will see in the final section of this chapter, probing deeper into the role played by slave revolts in ancient texts shows that the slave war narratives of Diodorus – alongside those of Florus and Livy – were a part of a long-standing practice in ancient literature of using slave revolt narratives as a rhetorical tool. This argument has obvious repercussions for the modern usage of these slave revolt narratives for the purpose of historical analysis.

The argument will be developed over four sections. In the first I will outline the methodology used to collect the examples of slave war narratives discussed in the following three sections. In the ensuing three sections I will outline three hypothetical types of slave revolt narratives: that is, three different ways in which a number of ancient authors used slave revolt narratives to achieve the same objectives in different texts. These three types – slave revolts as aetiologies; slave revolts as criticism; slave revolts as commentary – cover the majority of slave revolt narratives preserved in Greek and Latin literature concerning the period from Herodotus to Augustus: that is, to roughly the time at which Diodorus Siculus himself was writing. Exposing these three types demonstrates that ancient authors rarely include a slave revolt in their narratives, speeches or letters with the sole or even primary intention of reporting an event that took place. In most cases they do so in order to achieve literary, political and ethnographical objectives, thus significantly weakening the *historical* reliability of their revolt accounts.

The first type – slave revolts as aetiologies – shows that for many ancient authors slave revolts constituted a means through which the origin of institutions (ranging from the foundations of cults or cities to the creation of a trench in Crimea) could be explained; alternatively, they were used to justify the actions of later leaders. The similarity of these stories, ranging across geography and time, indicates that this was a *topos* of ancient historiography; consequently, these slave revolts cannot be

---

[3] A notable exception to the absence of historiographical studies of this nature can be found in chapter 8 of Urbainczyk's 2008 monograph *Slave Revolts in Antiquity*. In that chapter Urbainczyk considered the role of slave revolts in the narratives of Appian, Florus, Orosius and St Augustine and how they describe the fall of the Roman Republic.

accepted uncritically as historical events. The second type – slave revolts as criticism – demonstrates that for many authors of historiographical or political works slave revolts offered an opportunity to attack the character or legitimacy of the individuals whose actions or political philosophies they disagreed with. As we will see, this could extend from the insinuation that a person sought to bolster their position by encouraging servile insurrection, to the depiction of actions in free society as slave revolts with no indication of free involvement. The third type – slave revolts as commentaries – shows how in the late Republic both Greek and Latin historiography experimented with using slave revolt narratives as a way to comment on the state of free society. In each case we will see that although ancient slave owners told stories about servile discontent in their historical and political works, their essential aim was not to record these events accurately: in some cases, as we will see, events were incorrectly described as slave revolts in order to achieve narrative or political objectives that had nothing to do with slavery or servile unrest. Overall, it will be argued that slave revolts, as a literary, and here specifically historiographical *topos*, cannot be used to understand historical events without careful consideration of the specific narrative context in which they are placed. Let us turn to testing the hypothesis.

Methodology

Before we begin the analysis, it is worth outlining the methodology used to collect the examples discussed below. The collection is based on a search through ancient texts for the coincidence of certain key words. For Latin texts this was based on a combination of nouns and their verbal cognates concerned with revolt or sedition (*tumultus, motus, coniuratio, bellum*) and references to slaves (*servus, mancipium*), with the search conducted to look for all forms of these nouns and verbs.[4] For the Greek texts the search was based on a combination of the verb ἀφίστημι and the noun πόλεμος and their verbal cognates in conjunction with references to slaves (οἰκέτης, δοῦλος, δραπέτης). While one could extend the search using more terms – especially terms for slaves in both Latin and Greek – the intent here is not to be exhaustive but to demonstrate broad patterns in ancient literature concerning events up to the time of Augustus. Passages that explicitly describe non-servile actions and unrest in terms that compare them to servile actions were excluded as a separate historiographical category: the focus here is on the presentation of slave revolts as a distinct category of discourse in ancient historiography.[5] In addition, the frequent revolts of the helots have been excluded owing to the fact that in antiquity there was a debate as to the correct way to categorise their revolts with regard to

---

[4] To a certain extent this approach is based upon the methodology employed by Lavan 2017 in his study of the historiography of revolt in the early Empire. It is interesting that *rebellio* and *seditio* are not used to describe 'slave revolts', and as Lavan 2017, 24, notes, *rebellio* has a 'more circumscribed . . . range of meaning'.

[5] Lavan 2013a, 2013b and 2017 has discussed the consistent use of slave terminology used in Tacitus, Florus and Cassius Dio, or the use of metaphors of enslavement in the same authors, to describe free actions and relations between free peoples.

slavery.⁶ In what follows, then, I investigate the hypothesis that ancient historiographical texts use the terms outlined above to describe events they configured as slave revolts, and that these descriptions fall into certain patterns or types that can be considered predictable and routine, to a certain extent. We start with slave revolts as explanations for the world: aetiologies.

Slave Revolts as Aetiologies

This first type of slave revolt narratives consists of stories about slave revolts that explain why a feature of the ancient world exists. These narratives vary in complexity, but share elements between them that indicate their collective type. The most developed version of this narrative type is the extended story of a rebellious slave on the island of Chios called Drimakos. The story is reported in Athenaeus' *Deipnosophistae* (265d–266e) as coming from a third-century BC Syracusan ethnographer called Nymphodorus. The tale is well known today, but the essentials bear repeating. At an uncertain time, the polis of Chios experienced problems with runaway slaves led by Drimakos. This man pointed out to the Chians that their troubles with absconding slaves were the result of an oracle, and he proposed a treaty with them: that he would receive runaway slaves and judge if they were right to flee; that his forces would mark with a seal those locations they had plundered; and that his forces would not return to those places after they had plundered them. The result was that fewer slaves ran away, and those that did were kept in check by Drimakos. Late in his life Drimakos, on whose head the Chians had placed a bounty, encouraged his young lover to kill him and claim the reward. After his death, the troubles with runaway slaves returned, and the people of Chios in response set up a shrine to the Kindly Hero (ἥρωος εὐμενοῦς). The Chian slaves brought to this shrine the first of everything that they stole, and the hero himself appeared to some Chians to warn them of slave plots. The shrine was important, therefore, to both the free and slave populations of Chios.

As Forsdyke has shown, this is a complex tale whose origins and some details may be connected to a joint effort by the Chians and their slaves to create a shared hero-cult with an aetiology that offered something to each group.⁷ The story can of course be examined for its diverse functions within Athenaeus' work as much as within Nymphodorus' text or the Chians' self-presentation.⁸ Nonetheless, the narrative as it

---

⁶ Despite the fact that helots could be, in many ways, considered equivalent to or legally defined as slaves, the historiography concerning them and their frequent revolts is complicated by the fact that the Messenian helots later received their freedom *en masse*: subsequent Hellenistic and Imperial literature regarding these helots was complicated by the need to account for their free nature and the developing Messenian identity. On helots see De Ste. Croix 1988, Ducat 1990, Hodkinson 2008, Cartledge 2011, and now Lewis 2018a, 125–46. On the Messenian state after its formation in 369 BC, the construction of the Messenian identity in the period that followed, and the difficulties this presents for our own understanding of the nature of this group, see Hunt 1998, 177–84, Alcock 2001, Ogden 2004, Luraghi 2008 and Langerwerf 2010.
⁷ Forsdyke 2012, 78–89.
⁸ For this argument see Forsdyke 2012, 74–8; on Athenaeus more generally, see the articles in Braund and Wilkins 2000. In the first instance the story is related in answer to the questions of one diner, Ulpian, who had asked whether men had always owned many slaves in the past as they did in his day (Ath. 228c–d): see also Langerwerf 2009, 340–4.

remains in Athenaeus serves a particular purpose and preserves features that we will see repeated across several stories about slave revolts. The first detail to note is that this story explains the existence of a shrine in the countryside around Chios: that is to say that it is serving as an aetiology for a cult.[9] As will be demonstrated below, in using a slave revolt to explain the existence of a shrine, the Chians – and possibly their slaves also – availed themselves of a standard element of Greek historiographical practice. The aetiological use of slave revolts can in fact be found across Greek literature. It is also used in Roman historiography, even if it is less common there, with a notable highlight being constituted by Justin's epitome of Pompeius Trogus, which will be discussed below.

In the same section of Athenaeus we find another example of this practice. In this story (Ath. 267a–b), we learn that the city of Ephesus was founded by a group of runaway slaves from Samos. Supposedly, these slaves fled to a mountain and caused significant problems for the Samians until a treaty was agreed with them, on the advice of an oracle, and they were allowed to depart from Samos: from there, they went on to found the city of Ephesus.[10] The narrative has similarities to the story involving Drimakos: the origin of a Greek institution, in this case a city, is explained by a slave revolt and the advice of an oracle, two features found in the Drimakos story discussed above. Similarly, in two other stories, one in Diodorus and one in Strabo, the Bruttians in southern Italy are explained as the product of a marauding band composed, for the most part, of runaway slaves.[11] In Polybius' fragmentary twelfth book he describes a comparable story as one explanation for the foundation of Epizephyrian Locri in Italy as part of a wider attack on a rival historian's methods, in this case Timaeus (12.6–11).[12] In his account, Polybius promotes Aristotle's explanation for the colony that the original settlers were Locrian slaves who had married free women, many of them Locrian elite, owing to the absence of the Locrian men during the Messenian War in the eighth century BC. Subsequently the free Locrians' wives and daughters became intimate with their slaves. Polybius thought this a better explanation than Timaeus', which appears to be that free men founded Epizephyrian Locri.[13] On this reading, the rationale fits the pattern established above, in which a slave revolt serves to explain the existence of an institution in later history.[14] Notably, this Locrian aetiology

---

[9] This has been noted already by both Graf 1985, 123–4, and Forsdyke 2012, 78–80. For Forsdkye the origin of this story is to be found both in the slave and free populations of Chios. For attempts to date the events to the Peloponnesian War, see Fuks 1968 and Vogt 1973. For a full bibliography of this approach, see Langerwerf 2009, 339 n. 55, and for criticism of this approach, see Bonelli 1994. Other approaches have aimed to understand the war as an example of marronage, so, e.g., Bradley 1989, 39–40, Urbainczyk 2008a, 30–1, 53–4, and Bradley 2015 27. On the shrine itself see Lambrinudakis 1982 and Graf 1985, 123–4.

[10] See now *BNJ* 552 F1.

[11] Diod. Sic. 16.15 and Strabo 6.1.4. On Strabo see Musti 1988, 259–87, and Biffi 2006, 166.

[12] For a full consideration of this section, see Walbank 1967, 330–53, and Redfield 2003, 203–308.

[13] The servile explanation seems to have gained traction even within Locri itself, in which there was a tradition of dedicating noble virgins to temporary sacred prostitution in times of peril; see Domínguez 2007, 415–21. Justin records two examples of this practice, in 477 BC and the mid-fourth century (21.3.1–7).

[14] On the likelihood that Timaeus' version is correct, see now Baron 2013, 79–80 and 227–8.

includes another feature that is present in the remaining examples to be discussed: slave marriages to free women.[15]

The foundation of Tarentum in southern Italy was debated in a similar fashion to that of Epizephyrian Locri. In essence, there were three traditions concerning the origin of Tarentum, and each concerned the origin and status of a group called *Partheniae* during the Messenian War. All three traditions report a similar account: the *Partheniae*, with or without the support of the helots in Sparta, planned a revolt against the Spartans.[16] This revolt was betrayed, and either in response to an oracle from Delphi or owing to the persuasion of the Spartiates the *Partheniae* were sent to found a colony: Taras, later Tarentum.[17] In most versions these *Partheniae* are children of Spartiates and were either reduced to the status of helots or denied their political rights and subsequently revolted, driving the foundation of Tarentum.[18] In the final version, the *Partheniae* were the children of helots sent back to Sparta to ensure that children were born to Spartan women during the war.[19] As with Epizephyrian Locri, one part of the historiographic debate concerning the foundation of Tarentum included the combination of a slave revolt, servile relationships with free women, and an oracle advising the foundation of a colony, all features established above as part of the type.

The combination of the slave revolt narrative with the story element of slaves marrying free women can be found in many iterations of this historiographical trope that extend beyond foundation stories. The combination can be mentioned briefly with little more information than that there was a slave revolt in which the slaves planned to seize their masters' wives. For example, Dionysius of Halicarnassus records that in 419 BC Varr. the consular tribunes detected and foiled a plot among Rome's

---

[15] On this feature of the narratives, see also Briquel 1974. Briquel noted that the Minyae follow a similar narrative pattern to the rebellious slaves who founded Locri and the *Partheniae* discussed below: see Herodotus 4.145–8. The foundation stories of Rome also involve the marriage of fugitive slaves to free women, in this case the Sabine women. On these stories, see, e.g., Fantham 1995, Wiseman 1989, 1995 and 2004, Grandazzi 1997, and Carandini 2014. On slaves marrying wives of citizens under Greek tyrants, see Asheri 1977 and Schmitt-Pantel 1979, 227–9.

[16] The variant traditions can be found in: Strabo 6.3.2–3; Dion. Hal. 19.1–4; Arist. *Pol.* 1306b (28); Polyb. 12.6b.5; Justin 3.4.3; Diod. Sic. 8.21; Serv. *Aen.* 3.551.

[17] In some versions, they were led to this colony by a man named Phalanthus. For discussion of the foundation myths of Tarentum, see Pembroke 1970, Moscati Castelnuovo 1991, Qviller 1996, Meier 1998, 121–41, Luraghi 2003, 115–17.

[18] The Spartiates involved were either those condemned for cowardice or younger Spartiates sent home to father children with Spartan women to maintain the population while the army was absent. Spartiates condemned for cowardice: reported by Strabo and derived from the account of Antiochus of Syracuse, a fifth-century BC historian (Strabo 6.3.2; see also *BNJ* 70 F216). Younger Spartiates: attributed by Strabo to Ephorus (6.3.3), but also preserved in Polybius (12.6b.5), Dionysius of Halicarnassus (19.1–4), Justin (3.4.3) and Aristotle (*Pol.* 1306b (28)); see also *BNJ* 70 F216.

[19] For this version, see Diod. Sic. 8.21 and Serv. *Aen.* 3.551. Diodorus' version confuses the *Epeunactoi* with the *Partheniae* and ascribes the revolt against Sparta and foundation of Tarentum to the former rather than the latter. The *Epeunactoi* are discussed by Theopompus, preserved in Athenaeus (271c–d): see *BNJ* 115 F171. It has some similarities to the version preserved by Strabo and derived from Antiochus of Syracuse, as the driving force behind the revolt were children of people considered helots (see n. 18 above): on this version and the potential for anti-Tarentine bias, see Nafissi 1999, 254, and Luraghi 2003, 115–17. See also *BNJ* 555 F13.

slaves to seize the Capitol, kill their masters and take their masters' wives (12.6.6).[20] Dionysius repeats this detail when describing Aristodemus of Cumae's rise to power (7.5–11). This man's rise was supported in part by rebellious slaves, who demanded that they be rewarded with their former masters' wives and daughters in marriage (7.8.4). We will consider this passage in more detail in the ensuing section, but it is important to note the combination of servile revolt narratives with the rebels literally replacing their masters within their households. Justin records the fullest and only Latin version of this kind of slave revolt narrative in a brief account of the history of the Carthaginians in his epitome of Pompeius Trogus.[21] Justin recounts the story of a slave revolt in the city of Tyre after the city had been exhausted by resisting the Persians (18.3). He describes the way in which the rebels killed their masters and seized all their possessions, including their wives. In the aftermath one slave spared his master and his master's family. This master, named Strato, helped the former slave, who remains unnamed in the text, win the kingship of Tyre. When the rebels realised that Strato's former slave had acted with ability that was deemed beyond that of a slave and challenged him, he admitted that his master had suggested it to him, and the rebels made Strato king. The narrative is in part a reinforcement of the supposed inferiority of slaves, but it is also an important justification for Alexander the Great's brutality after he captured Tyre: Justin notes that Alexander massacred the people of Tyre in retaliation for the actions of the slaves during the revolt. Only Strato's family was saved, a justification not recorded by any other source.[22] This complicates our use of this story as an example of a successful slave revolt in antiquity: for Justin, this slave revolt appears to function as an aetiology used to justify the brutality of a conqueror.

The earliest surviving example of the aetiological use of slave revolt narratives comes from Herodotus. In the fourth book of his *Histories* (4.1–4) we are told a story about the Scythians returning from a twenty-eight-year campaign in Media to find their slaves in revolt and married to their masters' wives.[23] Braund has recently argued that the much longer Scythian ethnography across books 1–4 of the *Histories* was a 'response to the acknowledged importance of slavery and the trade in slaves there', and that this particular story was one part of this broader narrative.[24] The story in question is thought to have originally been an aetiology for the existence of a trench in Crimea, but in Herodotus it also serves as an ethnographic study of Scythian practices with regard to their slaves, including an explanation of why the Scythians traditionally blinded their slaves (4.2), and as a reflection on the nature of slaves: in the tale, the rebellious slaves and their children are only defeated once the Scythians attack them

---

[20] Notably, Livy records the same revolt but omits the detail concerning the masters' wives (4.45.1–2). On Livy's description of this episode, see Ogilvie 1965, 603. On Roman dates pre-300 BC and the necessity to record them using Varronian chronology, see Drummond 1989, Cornell 1995, 399–402, and Pobjoy 2013.

[21] See Brown 1991 for a discussion of the origin of this story.

[22] See, e.g., Arr. *Anab.* 2.24–5, Diod. Sic. 17.46, and Curt. 4.4.13–18; for the siege itself see Bloedow 1998 and recently Amitay 2008.

[23] The same story is told by Justin (2.5).

[24] Braund 2008, 14. As Braund notes (1), Herodotus' *Histories* displays a strong interest in slaves and slavery across the whole work, and the Scythian narratives were just one part of this. On Herodotus' interest in slavery, see Harvey 1988. On the narrative itself, see Munson 2001.

with whips rather than weapons and treat them as the slaves they are (4.3).[25] In its origin it appears to have been an aetiology of a trench, and it is striking that in this earliest attested aetiological use of a slave revolt we find the recurring detail that the slaves married their masters' wives.[26] This particular detail aside, in broad terms, we see here, again, the use of slave revolts to explain the world. Most of all, even early on in its development this type of slave revolt narrative included key features.

From these examples we can see that this form of slave revolt narrative is not necessarily discussing slavery at all, but that it could be part of a story told by an author to explain the present through a constructed past using established motifs. These stories could be adapted to include ideological statements concerning the nature of slaves and leadership (Drimakos; Herodotus; Justin), or they could be part of a historiographical debate that hinges on a city's self-definition (Polybius; the tradition concerning Tarentum), or used as a justification for a later individual's actions (Justin), or even included in a wider discussion about how to prevent servile unrest more generally (Athenaeus). Nonetheless, in every case discussed above they were primarily deployed to explain the origin of an institution or cultural practice. In each case we cannot be certain if these narratives were adapting real events in order to explain the present day, or if they were adapting a historiographical *topos* that bore no relation at all to what actually happened. It is only with the case of Epizephyrian Locri that we can see ancient scepticism at work concerning these stories, as Timaeus at least seems to have viewed the servile origin of Locri with some degree of doubt: whatever the reality of that city's origin, even in antiquity it was a matter of debate that allowed no simple answer, as was the case also with Tarentum. To advance our understanding of the use of the slave revolt *topos* in ancient texts, we turn now to the second of our types of slave revolt narratives: the use of slave revolts as criticism.

Slave Revolts as Criticism

The second category to be discussed now concerns the use of slave revolt narratives to criticise or attack the legitimacy of free people. These stories range from a text describing situations driven by free people as slave revolts to accusations that a free person encouraged servile insurrection for their own gain. The classic example of the first kind of slave revolt narrative can be found in Augustus' posthumous declaration of his achievements: his *Res gestae*. On two occasions this text references wars that Augustus fought against a free man – Sex. Pompeius, the youngest son of Cn. Pompeius Magnus – and in each case Augustus suppressed the name of his enemy. On the first Augustus records his success in freeing the sea from pirates, in which 30,000

---

[25] For the discussion of the trench, see Aly 1921, 112, and Corcella 2007, 574–5. For discussion of the practice of blinding slaves and its connection to Greek interest in mare-milking, see West 1999, Thomas 2000, Taylor 2001 and Braund 2008, 8–10. The slaves appear to pass their servility to their children, and in this respect they are described as natural slaves. On this see Harvey 1988, 50, and Harrison 2000, 170.

[26] Braund 2008, 8, notes the similarity between Odysseus' return home and the Scythians' return home, after twenty and twenty-eight years respectively. See also Malkin 1998 on these Odyssean narratives.

runaway slaves were returned to their masters (25.1–3).[27] On the second Augustus notes that he recovered Sicily and Sardinia from a slave war (27.3: *bello servili*). While it is true that Sex. Pompeius used freed slaves in his legions and his fleets (as did Augustus in these conflicts), it is evident that Augustus is deliberately presenting Sex. Pompeius' actions in Sicily as illegitimate by virtue of his association with non-free combatants.[28] It is probable that Augustus was using the association between Sicily and slave revolts to strengthen his claim here; as we have seen in the previous two chapters, there was a strong historiographical tradition that the island suffered from major servile insurrections in the second century BC.[29] In many other traditions this conflict is presented as part of the final bouts of civil war fought amongst the Romans in the 40s and 30s BC.[30] Nonetheless, this is the clearest example of an ancient author dismissing a free opponent through a slave war narrative, in this case by suppressing any indication that free agents were involved. Were we to have no other evidence for the occasions in question, modern scholars would likely use these accounts as evidence for further slave rebellions, in the Augustan era.

Augustus was not alone in this form of attack, even if the *Res gestae* is the most extreme case. These attacks are often connected to pre-existing reputations for servile insurrection or a strong connection to slavery. The aforementioned Chians were a frequent subject of stories concerning problems with their slaves, probably a result of their reputation as the first Greeks to purchase slaves.[31] For example, Plutarch preserves the story that in the midst of besieging Chios, the Macedonian king Philip V appealed to the slaves in Chios to betray their masters and join the fight on his side in return for their freedom and their owners' wives in marriage (*De mul. vir.* 3.245b–c). The Chian women exhorted their men to fight from the battlements, ultimately spurring the Chian soldiers to drive Philip away. The passage ends noting that Philip could not convince even one slave to revolt. Other stories concerning the Chians and their slaves include Thucydides' account of the Chian slaves ravaging the countryside of the city when the Athenians attacked in 412 BC (8.39.3, 8.40.2), Iphicrates threatening to

---

[27] The reference to pirates is probably an oblique reference to Cn. Pompeius Magnus' fame as the man who ended piracy across the Mediterranean in 67 BC, and therefore a personal barb aimed at the memory of his son, Sex. Pompeius: see Cooley 2009, 213–14.

[28] Slaves in Sex. Pompeius' fleets: App. *B Civ.* 5.131; Cass. Dio 48.19.4; 49.12.4; Oros. 6.18; *RG* 25.1; slaves in Sex. Pompeius' legions: App. *B Civ.* 4.85; Vell. Pat. 2.73; Cass. Dio 49.12.4; slaves in Augustus' fleets: Cass. Dio 48.49.1; Suet. *Aug.* 16.1. Livy (*Per.* 128) presents a similar version to that found in the *Res gestae*, as does Lucan (6.419–22), while Florus (2.18) repeats assertions that Sex. Pompeius privileged *foeda servitia*, 'base slaves', as commanders in his fleet. On these claims, see Watson 2002, 219, and Welch 2002, 42–3.

[29] On the first war: Flor. 2.7.4; Oros. 5.6.4. On the second war: Cic. *Verr* 2.5.3, *De or.* 2.194–6, *Ad Att.* 2.12.2, *Har. resp.* 26; Flor. 2.7.9–12; App. *Mith.* 59. Cooley 2009, 214–15, argues that Augustus is also implicitly comparing his achievements in suppressing servile unrest – in particular in returning 30,000 runaway slaves to their masters – with Cn. Pompeius Magnus' defeat of Spartacus. See also Fugmann 1991, 311, and Powell 1998, 93–4.

[30] See, e.g., the fourth and fifth books of Appian's *Civil Wars* and books 48 and 49 of Cassius Dio's history. See above n. 28 for Livy (*Per.* 128) and Florus (2.18.2), who come closest to repeating Augustus' version of this conflict in historiographical texts, where they describe Sex. Pompeius as resorting to piracy and accuse him of consorting with slaves.

[31] See Theopompus, *FGrHist* 115 F122 for the claim that the Chians were the first to purchase slaves.

arm the Chians' slaves in order for them to rebel, prompting the Chians to enter an alliance with Athens (Polyaenus 3.9.23), and the Chians being handed over to their slaves after the city was captured in the First Mithridatic War as punishment for their reputation as the first to purchase slaves (Ath. 266e–f).[32] It is hard to say if the story concerning Philip V is another example of these strategies, which may or may not individually be real and inspired by the Chians' concentration of slaves. However, the striking detail that Philip offered the slaves their masters' wives, a recurrent part of slave revolt narratives, as seen by now, suggests that it is better understood as a historiographical *topos* used to denigrate the man instigating the revolt. The text itself encourages this reading, as it describes Philip's offer as βάρβαρον καὶ ὑπερήφανον, 'barbarous and arrogant': this passage, in my view, is really about the contrast between Philip and the upstanding women of Chios, with an attempt to incite servile insurrection used as the point of a contrasting comparison.

The damning accusation that a free man attempted to set a slave revolt in motion extends across history and even into political invective. Cicero's political speeches include some important examples of this practice. In the heated political environment of 63 BC Cicero attempted to convince the senate and the people of Rome to side with him against the purported conspiracy led by L. Sergius Catilina, more usually called Catiline. Arena has shown that this speech was part of a broader debate in Rome in this period concerning the use of the *senatus consultum ultimum* (SCU) to suppress those considered to be a danger to the Roman state.[33] The debate hinged upon the right to *provocatio* of those killed by magistrates supported by an SCU. A key strategy for those supporting the SCU was to demonstrate that those being suppressed by the order had become enemies of Rome and forfeited their citizen rights.[34] Cicero's speeches during this crisis were an important part of this debate about the legitimacy of the SCU in times of domestic emergency. It is in this context that we must read Cicero's references to Catiline instigating slaves against Rome, which he mentions on two occasions. In the first speech delivered in front of the senate, Cicero rhetorically questions why he is not arguing for Catiline to be put to death, since he was not only the *principem coniurationis*, 'principal conspirator', but also *evocatorem servorum*, 'an instigator of slaves' (*Cat.* 1.27). As Franzen has demonstrated, the *First Catilinarian Oration* includes a range of servile metaphors intended to 'brand' Catiline as a slave rather than a proper citizen, thereby excluding him from the Roman (civic) community.[35] The accusation that

---

[32] Graf 1985, 122–3, discusses all these examples, and see also Forsdyke 2012, 86–7.

[33] On the SCU in Roman political debates, see Arena 2012, 200–20, who situates this debate within a fundamental political divide between conceptions of *libertas* and the correct method of upholding political liberty in Rome. Arena 2012, 80–168, categorises these differing traditions as *optimates* and *populares*, with the former characterised by the preponderance of the senate in the direction of politics, and the latter characterised by the importance of the popular assemblies and corrective justice.

[34] E.g., Cicero argued that Catiline's supporters were not just *improbi cives*, 'wicked citizens', but *acerbissimi hostes*, 'violent enemies'. See Cic. *Cat.* 4.7 and 4.15 for the quoted text respectively, and on these passages see Arena 2012, 218.

[35] Franzen 2013, 356–7, argues that the branding metaphors were a variation of Cicero's rhetorical strategies aimed at excluding his opponent from the Roman community through his choice of invective. For other discussions of Cicero's strategies for social exclusion see Merrill 1975, Opelt 1975, Corbeill 1996, May 1996 and Lévy 1998.

Catiline instigated a slave revolt should be understood as part of this wider attack on his position as a Roman citizen, and therefore as part of the attacks on Catiline as a threat to Roman political liberty.[36] On the second occasion, in a speech to the people of Rome, Cicero reported the instructions sent by P. Cornelius Lentulus Sura to Catiline to recruit slaves to his standard (*Cat.* 3.8), in essence to start a revolt, something alluded to on two other occasions in the orations (*Cat.* 2.19 and 4.4) and stated directly about Lentulus (*Cat.* 4.13).[37] According to Sallust, Catiline repeatedly refused to encourage servile unrest and declined throughout the conflict to arm slaves or to encourage their revolt, in contrast to Lentulus (*Cat.* 44.6, 46.3, 56.5).[38] But the main point here is that Cicero's accusation in these speeches that Catiline was aiming to set a slave revolt in motion, whether it was true or not, was just one part of a larger contemporary political debate in which Cicero challenged fellow citizens' political rights.

The use of this particular attack appears to have been common in the late Republic. Appian and Plutarch preserve several reports that Sulla's enemies in the 80s BC turned to servile insurrection in order to achieve their aims. The first instance of this comes during Sulla's march on Rome in 88 BC, when the forces supporting Marius were accused of offering slaves their freedom in order to support their cause, although the appeal was unsuccessful: not a single slave responded, not unlike in the case involving Philip V discussed above at Chios, or C. Gracchus and M. Fulvius Flaccus, who apparently appealed to slaves with the same result in 121 BC when in conflict with the Roman senate.[39] The next year L. Cornelius Cinna was accused of inciting slaves to revolt by offering them freedom in order to resist being driven out of the city by his co-consul, Cn. Octavius.[40] Later that year Marius returned to Italy at the head of other exiles from Rome and, crucially, 500 slaves.[41] In the midst of the fighting over control of Rome in 87 BC, Cinna now successfully appealed to the slaves in Rome, who were so bloodthirsty that they were rounded up and killed by Cinna's Gallic soldiers.[42] The stories told about Marius, Cinna and their followers are contrasted throughout both Appian and Plutarch with tales of good examples of master–slave interactions on Sulla's side, while Sulla's decision to reward slaves for handing in their masters during

---

[36] On the Roman definition of political liberty (*libertas*), see Skinner 2010 and Arena 2012, 45–72.
[37] See also Cic. *Sull.* 15, where Cicero suggests that P. Autronius Paetus attempted to make gladiators and runaway slaves join him in sedition. On Cicero's use of Lentulus' letter to Catiline to turn the Romans against the conspirators, see Cairns 2012.
[38] See Yavetz 1963, 494–9, Annequin 1973, 204, Bradley 1978, 325 n. 9, and 332–4, and Welwei 1988, 132–5, for discussion of the role of slaves in the events of 63 BC. On the use of allusions to slave wars in the *Catilinarian Orations*, see McGushin 1977, 278, and Stewart 1995, 70–2.
[39] On this appeal, see App. *B Civ.* 1.58, Plut. *Sull.* 9.7, and Plut. *Mar.* 35.3. Plutarch adds in his *Life of Marius* that only three slaves responded to Marius' appeal. See App. *B Civ.* 1.26 concerning C. Gracchus and M. Fulvius Flaccus. Urbainczyk 2008a, 104–7, considers Appian's use of slaves as an indicator of the problems faced by Rome during the first century BC. On this appeal, see also Welwei 1988, 121–5.
[40] App. *B Civ.* 1.65.
[41] App. *B Civ.* 1.67. See also Plut. *Mar.* 41.2, where we are told that Marius, on arriving in Italy, proclaimed freedom for the slaves near Telamon in Tyrrhenia, and Plut. *Mar.* 43.3, where Marius' retinue included a personal bodyguard composed entirely of slaves; cf. the account in Appian, where the status of Marius' bodyguard is not mentioned (*B Civ.* 1.73).
[42] See App. *B Civ.* 1.69 for the successful appeal and 1.74 for the execution of these soldiers. See also Welwei 1988, 125–30.

proscriptions is left unmentioned by Appian.[43] Appian's narrative is constructed, in part at least, to build a contrast between Cinna and Marius' dangerous actions with regard to slaves when compared to Sulla and his adherents.[44] Whether or not these accusations were true, the inclusion of these details by Plutarch and Appian probably reflects contemporary, or perhaps *post hoc*, uses of this *topos* of political invective in a period that is well known to be characterised by a post-Sullan historiography that justified Sulla's actions and attacked his political enemies.[45] This was driven in part by Sulla's own memoirs, which are most likely to be one of the sources used by Plutarch, as well as the legacy left by Sulla's actions during the proscriptions.[46]

Cicero's political speeches also offer us insight into how this category of invective may be inverted. In the opening sections of the *Fifth Verrine Oration*, Cicero attacked the corrupt Sicilian governor for 73–71 BC, C. Verres, for his military record (2.5.1–41). It is apparent from the opening passage that Cicero is anticipating a specific defence from Verres concerning his governorship in Sicily: that he prevented the island from suffering sympathetic slave revolts during the Spartacus War (2.5.1).[47] Cicero is evidently aware of the potency of this defence when he reflects on the way in which the same kind of appeal had saved M'. Aquilius from conviction after his success in suppressing the rebels in Sicily after he was appointed to the command in 101 BC (2.5.3).[48] Nonetheless, Cicero deftly turned the thrust of Verres' presumed defence in the following 22 sections of his speech. Cicero noted that each time Verres had to deal with troublesome slaves he turned the situation to his own advantage by extorting money from the slaves' owners or by fabricating charges against the slaves of rich landowners (2.5.10–24), or granting convicted slaves sudden reprieves (2.5.14). In this way Cicero argued that, rather than diminishing the chances of slave revolt, Verres in fact caused the slaves to be unrulier because of the absence of punishments inflicted upon them (2.5.9 and 14). While Cicero swiftly moves on to castigate Verres'

---

[43] E.g. Cn. Octavius refused to enlist slaves in his army, in direct contrast to Marius (Plut. *Mar.* 42.2); and the slaves of Cornutus acted intelligently, thus saving their master from those searching for him (App. *B Civ.* 1.73; Plut. *Mar.* 43.6). Appian's narrative of the proscriptions: *B Civ.* 1.95. Plutarch (*Sull.* 31.4) is explicit that Sulla's proscriptions were made even worse by the fact that he rewarded slaves who betrayed their masters.

[44] See also Valerius Maximus' (8.6.2) use of Marius' appeal to slaves in these circumstances as a contrast to his earlier behaviour when he crushed L. Appuleius Saturninus in 100 BC, who had apparently also offered slaves their freedom. See also Welwei 1988, 120–1. In this context, Saturninus is also presented as appealing to slaves in a period of crisis.

[45] On the reception of Cinna in ancient historiography, and the influence of Sulla's memoirs, see Lovano 2002, 141–59. The reception of Marius' career in particular appears to have been affected negatively both by his actions later in life, and by the attacks on his character and memory undertaken by contemporaries, including Q. Lutatius Catulus (*FRHist*, 273 and Badian 1964, 39 n. 49), Sulla's own memoirs (*FRHist*, 285) and Sisenna's history of the Social and civil wars (*FRHist*, 305–9). The overall tradition is reflected perhaps most clearly in the *Periochae* of Livy's books 80–5, on which see Badian 1964, 209.

[46] See *FRHist*, 285–6, for the use of Sulla's memoirs in Plutarch's biographies of Sulla, Marius and Lucullus, and also for further bibliography.

[47] See Frazel 2009, 126–30, for the argument that Verres' probable defence must be taken seriously.

[48] See also Chapter 3.

incompetence in other military fields these passages demonstrate the political capital to be gained from successfully exploiting the image of slave revolts, either in defence of a free man, or for his condemnation.[49]

The politically motivated insinuation of association between servile revolt and free actions is found across antiquity and in a number of contexts. In Justin's epitome of Pompeius Trogus, for example, we hear that the Carthaginian general Hanno both incited a slave revolt and then raised a force of 20,000 armed slaves to support a coup in Carthage in the 360s BC (21.4). In the narrative preserved by Justin, Hanno is presented as a leading man in Carthage (*princeps Carthag niensium*), but also as a man who aimed at kingship at any cost.[50] Similar perspectives can be found across the Mediterranean. An inscription from the city of Colophon in Asia Minor (*SEG* 39.1243) records honours for two citizens for their services to the town. One of their services involved ensuring Roman senatorial aid to prevent their city's territory being plundered and raided by citizens of a town they called Δούλων πόλις, 'slave city', or Doulopolis. Without doubt, the citizens of Doulopolis did not call their own town by this name, but it is not possible to recover the town's actual name. As Robert and Robert argued, this inscription concerns events that arose from Aristonicus' ill-fated attempt to seize the Pergamene kingdom after the death of Attalus III.[51] While it is unclear who the people plundering the Colophonian land were, the Colophonians are utilising an established form of invective to weaken the legitimacy of those plundering; but these claims do not necessarily bear direct relation to the individual origins of the Doulopolitans.[52] A late example of a similar strategy comes from the letters of St Augustine, in which Augustine attacks the Donatists for encouraging their opponents' slaves to revolt. According to Augustine, as a result of these actions some slaves were even walking free from their slavery (*Ep.* 108.18 and 185.15). Whether attacking local rivals or schismatic Christians, charges of encouraging servile insurrection are part of an established discourse.

These strategies exist for stories concerning earlier history as well. We have already seen above how Dionysius of Halicarnassus described the demands of those slaves who supported Aristodemus of Cumae's tyranny to be given their masters' wives

---

[49] It is possible that Cicero gives so little space to this particular topic (only 25 sections out of 189) because it was a point of some strength for Verres, whose actions in Sicily may have in fact prevented a crossing into Sicily by Spartacus' rebels, as is perhaps implied in a fragment of Sallust's *Histories* (4.32M). See especially 2.5.39 and 2.5.42, where Cicero accuses Verres of inventing slave revolts in Sicily in order to save himself from other charges.

[50] On this revolt, see Hoyos 2007, 15.

[51] See Robert and Robert 1989, 13 n. 1 col. II.32–51. On Aristonicus' revolt, see Just. *Epit.* 36.4.5–12, 37.1.1–3; Strabo 13.4.2, 14.1.38; Diod. Sic. 34/5.2.26, 34/5.3; Livy, *Per.* 59; Oros. 5.10.1–5; Eutr. 4.8.21–9, 4.9.1–23; Vell. Pat. 2.4.1; Plut. *Flam.* 21.6; Flor. 1.35.1–7. According to Strabo (14.1.38), Aristonicus also appealed to slaves in the area by offering them their freedom, presenting another example of this particular motif. This will be discussed in more detail in Chapter 5, pp. 156–8.

[52] There is considerable debate about how to interpret the events around Colophon at this time, for a summary of which see now Rigsby 2005, 112–13. Rigsby 2005, 114, suggests that the citizens of Doulopolis were dissidents, perhaps slaves, from the town of Colophon, whose claim to the territory was approved by Rome in order to weaken Colophon itself. Buraselis 2000, 18–5, notes that the senate's successful intervention only makes sense if the situation was of Rome's doing.

and daughters in marriage.⁵³ Dionysius tells us that Aristodemus solidified his rule by employing three kinds of guards, the second of which was composed of those slaves he had freed because they had killed their masters (7.8.3). To this group also he gave the largest gifts, and it is these slaves who demanded that they be given their former masters' wives and daughters. Aristodemus' tyranny is attacked by Dionysius on two main grounds: that he aimed to pass damaging legislation to forgive debts and redistribute land (7.8.1); and that he guarded himself with rebellious slaves whom he rewarded above all others (7.8.3–4). These failures during his reign at Cumae served to justify the brutal treatment of Aristodemus and his family at the hands of those who deposed him (7.11.3–4). We are told that he was killed by the children of those citizens he put to death during his rise to power. Most important of all, while he had intended to kill these children alongside their fathers, he refrained from doing so because his bodyguards, who had married the mothers of these children, entreated him not to kill the children, their stepchildren (7.10.1–2). In the context of the narrative these bodyguards must be those rebellious slaves rewarded by Aristodemus for their revolt. The text is, therefore, in part an aetiological story using a slave revolt to explain why Aristodemus' tyranny ended – making the tale similar to Justin's narrative justifying Alexander's violence at Tyre – but it is also part of a longer narrative that is an implicit commentary on the nature of good governance, in which Aristodemus' failures as a tyrant return to destroy him.⁵⁴

A similar narrative pattern exists concerning the tyrant of Heraclea, Clearchus. This man, Justin tells us, freed the slaves of those nobles who opposed him and who were expelled from Heraclea (16.5). As a reward for the slaves and to reinforce their bond to him, as well as to punish the absent nobles, Clearchus forced the wives and daughters of the exiled nobility to marry the freedmen. As with Aristodemus and Philip V, this tactic did not succeed: the women either committed suicide or waited until their wedding nights to murder their new husbands before killing themselves. Clearchus' reign was ended by two young nobles, Chion and Leonides, who formed a conspiracy and killed Clearchus during an audience. In this story we have the repetition of the *topos* concerning slaves marrying their master's wives and daughters combined, once again, with the tale of a tyrant's excesses, explaining why his tyranny was ended.⁵⁵ This accusation seems to be part of a set of accusations that can be thrown

---

⁵³ There is a great deal of disagreement about the origin of this story. The traditional view is that it is derived from a 'Cumaean Chronicle' that preserves a non-Roman history of the seventh and sixth centuries BC: Alföldi 1965, 56–72, is an influential proponent of this view, but see also Poucet 2000, 113–16, and Purcell 2003, 24. The existence of a 'Cumaean Chronicle' has been challenged by Gallia 2007, 55–8, who argued for a Greek tradition relayed to Dionysius via a Hellenistic intermediary, most likely Timaeus, although see Wiseman 2008, 233 n. 18, for criticism of Gallia's thesis. On the story of L. Tarquinius Priscus and Aristodemus and the debate surrounding its origin, historicity and connection to Greek or Italian origins, see Cornell 1995, 124–5, Zevi 1995, Forsythe 2005, 101, Ridgway 2006, Winter 2009, 577–82, and Koptev 2010, 8–9, and 2012, 89.

⁵⁴ This version of Aristodemus' death is quite different from that preserved by Plutarch (*De ul. vir.* 261e–262d), whose text emphasises the role played by women in the movement against Aristodemus and makes no mention of his actions towards slaves.

⁵⁵ On Clearchus, see Harris 2017.

at 'bad' tyrants. Dionysius I, for example, allegedly married slaves to the wives and daughters of powerful men in a city he had captured in order to reinforce their bond to him, much like Clearchus and Aristodemus.[56]

A final example of a slave revolt narrative used as a way of attacking a free man's actions can be found in the stories concerning Ap. Herdonius' attempts to seize Rome at the beginning of the Republic. Three writers record this event, Dionysius of Halicarnassus (10.14–16), Livy (3.15–18) and Florus (2.7.2), and in each there exists a thread in the narrative concerning revolting slaves.[57] The story concerns an attack on Rome by Ap. Herdonius, a Sabine, who seized the Capitol in Rome during the night. The Roman response was hampered by tensions between the plebeian tribunes and the patrician consuls. Rome was only saved by the intervention of a Tusculan force led by L. Mamilius. In all likelihood, the precise origin of this event cannot be reconstructed, although certain details have been regarded by some modern historians to have some historical core, such as the role of L. Mamilius.[58] For much of the remainder, it appears to represent a historical tradition that was adapted slightly by writers for their own purposes. As Forsythe notes, Dionysius' version of the story emphasises the external nature of this threat, coming as it did from Sabine territory, whereas for Livy the event was fundamentally an internal problem.[59] Herdonius aimed, we are told, to give slaves liberty, to abolish debt, and to reinstate Rome's exiles (10.14.3); according to Dionysius this effort failed, and not a single slave joined him, nor any debtor, nor any exile (10.15.1).[60] Nonetheless, the same set of ideas – including the abolition of debt and the grant of freedom to slaves – is used here by Dionysius to discredit Herdonius' aims, just as in the case of Aristodemus.

In Livy's version, by contrast, Herdonius' initial force included slaves when he seized the Capitol (3.15.5), and following his success in this venture Herdonius appealed to the remaining slaves in Rome (3.15.9). Livy emphasises that the principal concern among the Romans during this conflict was the reaction of the slaves within their own houses (3.16.3).[61] The narrative is used by Livy to highlight the internal struggles in Rome at this point, and the story rests – after Herdonius' initial appearance and the spectre of a slave revolt is raised – on the struggle between the patricians and the newly formed plebeian tribunes, who attempted to use the event to their

---

[56] For these stories concerning Dionysius, see Diod. Sic. 16.66.5, Aen. Tact. 40.2–3, and Polyaenus, *Strat.* 5.5.20. A similar story is told concerning the fall of Syracuse to Hippocrates and Epicydes during the Second Punic War. This version has them rewarding jailed slaves with freedom in order to secure their election in the city (Livy 24.32). See also Welwei 1988, 120.

[57] The earliest surviving traces of this narrative can be found in Cato's *Origines* (*FRHist* F25).

[58] See Forsythe 2005, 205. The family went on to produce a series of consuls in the third century BC.

[59] Forsythe 2005, 205.

[60] This puts him in the same company as Philip V, Marius, and C. Gracchus and M. Fulvius Flaccus, discussed above.

[61] Ogilvie 1965, 423–4, argues that the inclusion of slaves from the start among Herdonius' number reflects an effort to add 'Catalinarian overtones' to the passage: on this reading, slaves are *added* to produce a required effect. Florus (2.7.2), following Livy's account, describes Herdonius' actions as the *primum servile bellum*, 'first servile war', of what will be a series of wars fought against slaves by Rome, culminating in the 'Second Sicilian Slave War'.

advantage (3.16–18).[62] In the aftermath, L. Quinctius Cincinnatus, the newly elected suffect-consul, gave a speech to the Roman people, one not reported by Dionysius. In this he emphasised that the plebeian tribunes had endangered the house of Jupiter Optimus Maximus by allowing it to be held by exiles and slaves and noted that any citizen of Rome would receive aid if their home was besieged by slaves (3.19.4–11). The speech, we are told, weakened the plebeians' resolve to have their legislation passed that year (3.20.1).[63] Through Cincinnatus' speech we see Livy using the servile element of Herdonius' attempt on the Capitol to showcase the struggles within Roman society and to give one character in his narrative a chance to comment on their contemporary political struggles and to demonstrate their own character. In sum, the historical tradition concerning Herdonius' attack on the Capitol was adapted by later authors to suit their individual purpose.

Slave revolts, therefore, could be a useful way to attack a free man if the author of the speech or history disagreed with their actions. This could be done through a complete suppression of that particular individual or group (*Res gestae Divi Augusti*; Doulopolis) or by associating the individual with attempts to stir revolt; it could also be directed towards different ends, both historical and political. In some cases, the aim appears to be an attack on the person's legitimacy (Sex. Pompeius; Philip V; Catiline; Marius and Cinna; Verres), or a denial of a group's right to act as they did (Doulopolis), while in others the stories of free men inciting slave revolts are used to comment on proper political action in a historiographical setting (Aristodemus; Herdonius). In the final example discussed above, the occurrence of a slave revolt incited by a free outsider within the city of Rome appears to have offered the authors relaying the story an opportunity to comment on proper conduct among free people in times of political, social or military turmoil: in a sense the slave revolt is presented as a commentary on free society, a point to which we must now turn more fully.

Slave Revolts as Commentary on Free Society

Where does this discussion leave us with regard to Diodorus Siculus' Sicilian 'Slave War' narratives? In the previous two chapters I have argued that Diodorus' narratives of these wars were carefully constructed to achieve certain literary objectives in relation to the characters of the rebel leaders and their relationship to their subjects. In each case I argued that the narrative was intended to produce a specific negative reading of these leaders designed both to undermine the leaders and to emphasise the importance of the master–slave relationship to the events in question. These narratives are the most fully developed slave revolt narratives to survive from antiquity, and subsequently they do not fit neatly into either of the types described above: these narratives deal

---

[62] See Ogilvie 1965, 423–5. Vasaly 2015a, 80–91, sees the Herdonius episode as one of several designed by Livy to emphasise the role played by L. Quinctius Cincinnatus, his son, Caeso, and T. Quinctius Capitolinus in the development of the early Republic. See also Vasaly 2015a, 114–15, on the role of the plebeian tribunes in this event. See also Welwei 1988, 113–15, who notes the echoes of later Republican history, especially that of Marius and Cinna, in Dionysius' presentation of Herdonius' attack on Rome.

[63] See Miles 1995, 127–8, for the importance of religious scruple to the preservation of Rome in these conflicts. On this speech, see also Vasaly 2015a, 87.

with complex issues over several pages of text that is, for example, at least twice the length of the traditions concerning Spartacus preserved in all other authors combined. Nonetheless, these types do indicate some important details about the nature of slave revolt narratives in general that can help us to understand Diodorus' text.

It is clear from the discussion above that in many cases when an ancient author wrote about a slave revolt they did so not because their interest was in the slave revolt itself, but because it allowed them to achieve a different objective: in essence, they used slave revolts to think about the world, or to explain events, or to attack a political opponent. There is, therefore, no reason to assume *a priori* that a narrative adducing a slave revolt in any particular author is presented accurately or even because the event actually took place. In short, the historiographical context is often more important than the historical. Read in light of this established historiographical trend that extends throughout Greek and Roman historiography concerning events until Augustus, Diodorus' narratives for the two Sicilian wars could be fruitfully understood not as faithful renditions of the causes and effects of these wars, but instead as historiographical exercises with a range of objectives. These objectives included discussions of the nature of leadership in the ancient world, the delegitimisation of the non-Roman rebel leaders, and a discourse concerning ideals of master–slave relations, as we have seen in the preceding two chapters. This argument can be best illustrated through discussion of two elements of Diodorus' narrative in the first war discussed only briefly in Chapter 2.

First, I noted that by the end of the narrative, Eunus, the rebel leader in the first war, had effectively replaced his master. Both men are described in the text using the verb ψυχαγωγέω, connecting Eunus' final state to his master's state before the revolt itself (see Diod. Sic. 34/5.2.7–8 and 22 and Chapter 2, pp. 74–5). The developed narrative that Diodorus offers for Eunus mimics a similar *topos* to one identified above in many of the slave revolt narratives: the frequent references to slaves replacing their masters through marriage to or procreation with their former masters' wives or daughters. While it is not adduced that Eunus married his master's wife – the text tells us that Eunus' wife was a compatriot of Syria (34/5.2.16) – and so this is not a direct repetition of the *topos* identified above, it nonetheless includes the essential detail that Eunus has replaced his master in some form. This *topos* could be adapted in the narratives discussed above, notably in both Herodotus' story concerning the Scythian slaves and the conflicted stories about the *Partheniae*, in which narratives it is the slaves' children by their masters' wives and daughters that come into conflict with the returning masters, not the rebellious or misbehaving slaves themselves.

Second, I noted above that the story of Ap. Herdonius' attempts to seize Rome at the head of an army allowed Livy to comment on the correct way for free society to act in times of unrest, and this point can be pressed further. Livy's version of Herdonius' attack on Rome can be read on two levels: as a comment on the nature of Roman society and political discourse in the period in which the attack took place; and as a reflection on how political opponents ought to act in any period when faced with existential threats to the Roman state. In both cases, as I will show, the narrative is not about a slave revolt *per se*, but rather is using the crisis as a metaphorical reflection of and commentary on free society and politics. We will consider these two levels in turn.

The first level, what we might call the immediate narrative level, hinges upon how those involved in the conflict reacted, both in terms of actions and words. As I noted above, in the midst of the attack the plebeian tribunes attempted to turn the event to their advantage: they prevented the consuls from recruiting men to fight against Herdonius and accused the patricians of inventing the attack to suppress the tribunes' attempts to pass legislation aimed at the codification of Roman law (3.16.5).[64] Livy contrasts the plebeian tribunes' actions with those of two patricians: the consul, Valerius Publicola, and the suffect-consul L. Quinctius Cincinnatus. He achieves this through a favoured technique: the use of speeches to create 'structure, and thus meaning' within his narratives.[65] In the first speech (3.17) Valerius Publicola entreated the plebeians to liberate the gods who protected Rome from the clutches of slaves. He finished the speech by calling any who aimed to prevent him *hostes*, and threatening to deal with them as his ancestor, P. Valerius Publicola, had dealt with the last of the Roman kings (3.17.7–8). In the second speech (3.19), given by Cincinnatus in the aftermath of Herdonius' attack on Rome, the suffect-consul upbraided the Roman plebeians, and especially the tribunes, for their failure to respond to their gods when they were in need: instead, they attempted to use the situation for their own political advantage, endangering the city itself. As we have seen, Cincinnatus specifically attacked the tribunes for refusing to aid the gods when their houses were seized by slaves, noting in particular that they would immediately aid even the humblest plebeian in the same circumstances (3.19.9–10). These two speeches touch upon themes that are established early in book 3 and then resurface throughout the book. The connections made to these themes in the speeches given by Valerius and Cincinnatus make clear that the tribunes' actions are to be understood as indicative of a deeper problem in Roman political discourse in this period, and not only as a poor response to slaves capturing the houses of the gods.

First, both Valerius and Cincinnatus attack the tribunes for refusing to compromise their political goals even when the Capitol itself had been seized by an external enemy (3.17.2, 3.17.4 and 3.19.6). This appeal to compromise in times of crisis recalls earlier episodes in the book, as well as later indicators of the importance of compromise on the part of both the patricians and the plebeians. For example, after a plague had threatened Rome in the years before Herdonius' attack, the tribunes pressed for legislation to outline the powers of the consul (3.9.2–5). In response, the urban prefect attacked the tribunes in the senate and asked the other tribunes to remember the importance of political compromise until the consuls returned from the war against the Aequi and Volsci (3.9.11).[66] The next year (3.10.6–7), a series of portents

---

[64] The event itself falls in the middle of the first section of book 3, as defined by Ogilvie 1965, 390, and is, on that reading, structurally important to Livy's third book. Ogilvie argues that the third book is based upon the need for *moderatio* from the government, but also *modestia* on the part of the governed. See also Luce 1977, 231.

[65] Quotation from Vasaly 2015b, 223. On Livy's use of speeches to provide structure, see Walsh 1961, 229–32; Treptow 1964, 31–3 and 36–7; Ogilvie 1965, 78–9, 428–49, 516–17; Forsythe 1999, 78–86; and Smith 2010.

[66] As Ogilvie 1965, 413–14, notes, the speech given by Furius is based upon 'rhetorical commonplaces characteristic of the late Republic'.

were interpreted through reference to the Sibylline Books to predict a gathering of outsiders (*alieni*), an attempt on the city's highest points involving bloodshed, and a warning to avoid sedition: the plebeian tribunes denounced these portents as obstructionist tactics. The importance of compromise resurfaces throughout the book: it is a political compromise that sees the creation of the first, good, decemvirate (3.32); sensible compromise between the plebeians, the patricians and the decemvirate, in the aftermath of Ap. Claudius' attempts to rape Verginia during the second, bad, decemvirate, results in the reconstitution of the state and the address of plebeian grievances more generally through the Valerio-Horatian laws (3.49–55); M. Duellius twice argued for moderation in the vengeance of the tribunes against the decemvirs and for tribunes not to abuse power by seeking re-election (3.59 and 3.64); finally T. Quinctius Capitolinus, in his speech during his fourth consulship, reprimanded the Roman plebeians for endangering the state and their own property by weakening the state with their political attacks (3.67–8). In the midst of narrating the events of the second decemvirate, Livy even tells us that the patricians at first did not act against the decemvirs, even though they hated them, because they felt that the plebeians deserved their servitude after being too greedy (*avide*) for liberty (3.37.2–4). The tribunes' inability to set aside their political fights in the face of an attack on the Capitol is one example of their broader political failure in book 3.

Second, both Valerius and Cincinnatus attack the tribunes for refusing to aid the gods in their homes (3.17.3, 3.17.5, 3.19.7 and 3.19.9–10)[67] In the first instance this attack is used to undermine the tribunes' claims to be acting in the interests of the Roman people and to be sacrosanct, with Cincinnatus accusing the tribunes of claiming to be sacrosanct but denying that status for the gods themselves (3.19.10). However, it must also be read in light of the first section of book 3, in which Rome's relationship with the divine is shown to be essential to the city's survival. For example, at the height of the plague that left the city open to attack, the invading Aequi and Volsci turned away from Rome and decided to invade the rich Tusculan lands, where they were defeated by Rome's Latin and Hernician allies (3.6–7). The Aequi and Volsci's decision not to attack Rome is attributed in part to their greed, but especially to Rome's guardian deities (*di praesides*, 3.7.1).[68] Rome's close relationship with her gods is rewarded, and the Romans at the end of the plague are depicted as filling the shrines of their gods, imploring them to lift the plague (3.7.7–8).[69] Two years after the plague, the portents discussed above are interpreted to predict an attack on the city's highest points that would involve bloodshed (*caedes*) and a gathering of outsiders, with a specific command to avoid seditious activities (3.10.6–7). As noted, the tribunes dismissed these portents as a political ploy, but the portents were correct: a group of

---

[67] See Levene 1993, 164–6, for a discussion of these speeches, where he concludes that (166) 'correct religious behaviour is identified with the different classes acting together in the interests of the state'. See also Forsythe 1999, 87, and Miles 1995, 127.

[68] By contrast, in Dionysius of Halicarnassus' version, the Aequi and Volsci fail to capture Rome owing to the city's defences (9.68). See also Burck 1934, 13, and Levene 1993, 163.

[69] On this episode and its relation to Livy's treatment of religion more generally, see Levene 1993, 162–5. Livy suggests (3.8.1) that it may have been Rome's show of piety that caused the plague to end, although he is rather non-committal on this point.

outsiders under the command of Ap. Herdonius, including free Sabines and slaves, seized the Capitol, and, as Livy notes, many of those who seized the temple stained it with their blood (*multi exsulum caede sua foedavere templa*, 3.18.10), verbally recalling the earlier prediction from the Sibylline Books. The tribune's refusal to aid the gods in their time of need during Herdonius' attack, therefore, comes after an explicit demonstration of the importance of maintaining relations with the gods and after the refusal to believe portents: it is a demonstration of a deeper problem with how the tribunes act.

Finally, Cincinnatus attacks the tribunes and the senators for failing to assail the invaders, especially in light of the fact that the first people to draw swords in order to liberate the Roman gods were the people of Tusculum, led by L. Mamilius (3.19.7–9). The aid sent by the Tusculans – and the reciprocal aid that Rome feels is required in what follows – is a recurrent theme of the third book. Not long after Herdonius' attack is thwarted, the Romans twice march on the Aequi to relieve sieges at Tusculum (3.23, 3.31), and on both occasions Livy states that the Romans felt they were bound by honour to do so because the Tusculans had aided Rome against Herdonius.[70] In the midst of the second decemvirate the Tusculans again appealed to Rome for help (3.38), and the Roman army that was sent out was so unsuccessful that they found refuge within Tusculum itself (3.42). Cincinnatus, in his speech attacking the tribunes and senators, calls into direct contrast their inability to aid those who need it most – in this case the gods of Rome itself – with the obligations that even external allies feel to Rome's gods.

The tribunes' response to the Herdonian affair, and in particular abandoning the houses of the gods to servile insurrectionists, is engineered by Livy through Valerius and Cincinnatus' speeches to be representative of the fault in all their politics: heedless of portents and warnings in the Sibylline Books and heedless of their duty to assist those Romans who needed help, the tribunes pressed their political agenda in the face of direct threats to the existence of Rome. Throughout the third book, plebeian agitation, as much as patrician obstinacy, is the cause of calamity for Rome: it is their agitation that creates the decemvirate, and they routinely paralyse Roman politics until an external threat forces the Romans to unite or be destroyed.[71] The tribunician failure to respond correctly to the threat to Rome's relationship with its divine protectors is symbolic of their broader failure to seek compromise with the patricians for the good of Rome as a whole. Throughout book 3, the plebeian tribunes are contrasted with the level-headed Quinctii, directly so in the speech through which Cincinnatus castigates their response to Herdonius' slave revolt.[72] In this way Herdonius' slave revolt becomes a window through which the failures of the contemporary Roman political practices can be viewed. The slave revolt itself is not what is important: it provides an opportunity to think more broadly about Roman politics. The text can also be read as

---

[70] See also Dion. Hal. 10.20. See also Ogilvie 1965, 434, and Forsythe 1994, 234–5.

[71] On the decemvirate, see 3.3.31–2. On external threats forcing unity, see, e.g., 3.26, 3.30, 3.31, 3.38. As Miles 1995, 77–8 and 126–7, notes, it is a recurrent theme of Livy's first pentad that external threats to Rome unify the city.

[72] On the Quinctii as model generals and statesmen in Livy, see Piganiol 1973; Gagé 1974; Forsythe 1994, 237–8, and 2005, 206–7; and Vasaly 2015a, 80–91, and 2015b, 222–3.

a more general reflection on how political opponents should react when faced with an internal threat to Rome in Livy's own day: the second level noted above.

This second reading has not gone unnoticed in the past. As noted above, Ogilvie has argued that Livy's decision to include slaves among Herdonius' adherents from the start of his attack on Rome is part of an effort to add 'Catilinarian overtones' to the passage.[73] In the midst of the Catilinarian conspiracy Cicero accused Catiline of inciting slaves in order to seize the city, as we have seen. Forsythe has argued, moreover, that some details about Herdonius' attack may have been modelled on the attempt of L. Apuleius Saturninus to take the Capitol in 100 BC, who was forced to surrender by the joint efforts of the consuls, C. Marius and L. Valerius Flaccus; one of Saturninus' colleagues that year was rumoured to be a runaway slave, and Saturninus apparently appealed to slaves during these events.[74] Each event involved the incitement of slaves in order to seize Rome during moments of heightened tensions among the political class of the city. On these arguments, Livy's text of the Herdonian affair was a partial mirror for moments of internal conflict in Rome: as we have also seen above, the Catilinarian conspiracy was a key issue around which Romans debated the meaning of *libertas* and the correct ways to protect it. Valerius and Cincinnatus' speeches concerning the tribunes' reaction to Herdonius emphasised precisely these issues: how best to protect Rome's liberty, and especially the liberty of the gods. The precise nature of the opponents to be defeated is less important than how in principle one ought to act when facing a threat to the existence of Rome.[75] The story of Herdonius' attack can, in this light, be read as a comment on political conflict closer to Livy's own day. The implication of this reading of the text is that the slave revolt narrative at the heart of this story is neither an aetiology nor an attack on Herdonius' character, but neither is it a simple record of events as they took place. The slave revolt under discussion here has been adapted by Livy in the context of his third book to be a metaphor for free society itself and how free people interact in times of crisis.

A similar use of a slave revolt as a commentary on free society can be found in Diodorus' narrative of the First Romano-Sicilian War. In a passage that either precedes the story of Damophilus or is part the proem of book 34 (34/5.2.33), Diodorus notes that the treatment of slaves that causes them to revolt is the same as that which causes civil conflicts among citizens. Diodorus focuses in particular on the importance of arrogance (ὑπερηφανία) and heavy-handedness (βαρύτης) to the creation of both slave plots and civil discord, and he emphasises that those in a superior position should act moderately (ἐπιεικῶς) and show kindness (φιλανθρωπία) in order to avoid these unpleasant outcomes. The passage makes clear that Diodorus considered an analysis of the causes of servile unrest to be equally applicable to the state of free society.

---

[73] See Ogilvie 1965, 423–4. See also Ogilvie 1965, 467, for the importance of Rome's first-century BC history of political infighting and the flight of its elite for the portrayal of a deserted Rome during the second decemvirate (3.38). See also the 'rhetorical commonplaces' of the late Republic that make up Valerius Publicola's speech: i.e., that speech is made in terms familiar to Livy's contemporary audience.

[74] Forsythe 2005, 205, App. *B Civ.* 1.32, and Plut. *Mar.* 30. See Valerius Maximus (8.6.2) on Saturninus' appeal to slaves in 100 BC. See also Welwei 1988, 120–1.

[75] See especially Chaplin 2000, 1–5 and 50–3, for the argument that Livy's use of examples from history served, in part, to be a way of thinking about (5) 'the problems his own generation faced'.

The implication is that the narrative itself is intended to be read at two levels: on the one hand it is an analysis of how the breakdown of master–slave relations can cause servile unrest, including a discussion of the nature of leadership as a connected phenomenon, as we saw in Chapters 2 and 3; on the other hand, the narrative is using the slave revolt as a form of commentary on free society.

The latter reading, suggested by the text itself, makes Diodorus' story of the First Romano-Sicilian War a part of the earliest development of a third type of slave revolt narratives alongside Livy's narrative of Ap. Herdonius: the use of slave wars as a commentary on free society, sometimes in the form of a metaphor. This type is developed fully in the Imperial period in the historical works of Florus and Tacitus and matches an increased interest in and use of slave metaphors in the literature of that period to describe a range of status interactions.[76] A full discussion of the development of this type is beyond the scope of the present work, but it is enough to note that in Florus, for example, the narrated slave revolts in Sicily and Italy during the second and first centuries BC are included amongst Rome's gradually worsening internal conflicts that ended with the civil wars of the first century BC and the advent of imperial rule: in these narratives, they are indicative of increasing problems in *free* society.[77] Livy and Diodorus, two writers who composed their histories as the Republic collapsed and the Roman state transformed under first Caesar and then Augustus, are the forerunners of this historiographical development. I have argued elsewhere that Diodorus sought to fit the slave revolt narratives into the framework and moral message of the *Bibliotheke* as a whole.[78] I suggest, on the basis of the discussion above, that in order to do so, Diodorus – or his source, for that matter – also adapted existing narrative patterns that can be found in Greek and Roman historiographical traditions, turning them to a new purpose. His text cannot be taken, therefore, as an authoritative guide to the nature of these events: by using terminology related to slave revolts to describe these events, Diodorus Siculus was not being scientific in his analysis but was drawing upon and developing established historiographical traditions about slave revolts in order to tell a story about free society and free people.

Conclusion

The case studies presented in this chapter are intended to show that in ancient historiography, and in some political speeches and personal correspondences, slave revolt narratives concerning the period until Augustus are used in broadly definable categories or types. The three types discussed above (slave revolts as aetiologies; slave revolts as criticism; slave revolts as commentary) do not cover all events conceived of as slave revolts in this period, but they do demonstrate that for many cases there are definable and predictable patterns in the ancient discourse concerning rebellious slaves. The argument that slave revolt narratives are to a greater or lesser extent following types

---

[76] On the development of slave metaphors in Imperial literature, see Lavan 2013a and 2013b.
[77] See Flor. 2.7–9.
[78] See Morton 2018.

leaves us with some challenges if we want to use these stories to construct an idea of slave revolts as they happened: that is, if we want to reconstruct historical as opposed to historiographical slave revolts. For example, the regular stories about slave unrest in Chios may reflect a historical reality and therefore be representative of a peculiar problem with slaves on that island, but equally these may be stories that were told about the Chians owing to their reputation as the first to buy slaves in Greece. As we have seen above, certain states and geographies became synonymous with slave revolts, and this was exploited in both historical and political works, most notably with regard to Sicily. In a similar vein, we cannot be certain that men like Ap. Herdonius, Aristodemus, King Philip, Catiline, Marius or Cinna actually incited slaves to revolt, just as we cannot be certain that these were not examples of a *topos* deployed against figures of abuse. In many cases the constructed nature of these narratives is signalled by the use of repetitive features, most importantly the consistent references to slaves marrying or reproducing with their former masters' wives or daughters, but also the failure to recruit even a single slave to a lost political cause.

Once we understand the narrative function and the wider purposes of these stories it is evident that we cannot take them at face value. In a few cases above I have attempted to explain the inclusion of certain narratives in some authors discussed, especially with the narratives of Livy and Diodorus in the third type. Yet the purpose of this chapter has not been to explain in each case why the narrative was deployed within that specific text, but rather to demonstrate that within ancient historiography and political writing more broadly there were ways of using slave revolts and the stories connected to them to achieve aetiological, political, social or narrative functions that had nothing to do with the revolts themselves. In the case of aetiologies these could be used to justify the actions of a later generation or to make sense of customs or connections between cities; in the political and social context this includes using the connection between free men and slave revolts to castigate or deny legitimacy to political enemies or even political philosophies or to comment on the nature of free society itself. In the latter category, most importantly, these attacks need not be against contemporary opponents, but could serve to justify the author's own political beliefs. In each case it is important to ask why in the context of each author's work, this story has been included, and what, if anything, it is achieving in the text. This being so, the repercussions for modern appreciation of the slave war narratives in especially (but not only) Diodorus Siculus are at once both obvious and problematic. As Chapters 2 and 3 have shown, these narratives are carefully crafted to castigate the rebels and to entice specific reader responses. Moreover, in Diodorus' account, these narratives are set within a discourse on master–slave-relationships, which aid in turn broader commentary on free society. Seen against the canvass of the slave revolt *topos* drawn up in the present chapter, it is self-evident that Diodorus' Sicilian slave war accounts must be taken with a huge pinch of historical salt. To be sure, we have no reason to doubt that Sicily was shaken by upheavals in the periods in question. The coinage of Antiochus, as well as the slingshots that document the later war, are firm evidence for the troubles that Sicily experienced in the second century BC (for which, to be fair, Diodorus and co. provide some important documentation too). But what we have good reason to doubt is that the perspective on these events propagated in Diodorus' narrative, as in those of other ancient authors, is a reliable historical guide to the nature of the revolts. In the light of the manipulative powers exerted by the slave revolt *topos* in ancient historiography, it is high time to give the perspective emerging from coinage and slingshots centre stage. And this means to accept that the rebellions in question and the wars that followed had, as such, nothing to do with slave revolts.

5

HOW TO DEFINE REVOLT? ANCIENT SLAVE REBELLIONS IN THE GLOBAL CONTEXT

IT IS ONE THING to say that the two Sicilian wars had nothing to do with slave revolts, and another to know what is actually meant by saying this. This is no frivolous comment. Thus, in his extended analysis of slave revolt and revolution in the modern world, Genovese opened with precisely such a 'deceptively simple question': 'What was a slave revolt?'[1] He observed that there is one 'compelling' answer that might be given: 'a struggle for freedom'. Yet, after noting that this question has other answers that 'point towards an understanding of the special character of particular revolts and of the historical process within which the revolts occurred', Genovese moved rapidly to a discussion of the necessary preconditions for their occurrence. His outline of eight such preconditions for the occurrence of slave revolts has since become a touchstone for studies of slave resistance also in other periods of history and in other regions of the world, including the ancient world.[2]

The question of how one defines a slave revolt is not commonly posed in modern accounts of slave revolts in antiquity, and it might be asked what we gain by asking a question that appears to have a self-evident answer: 'a struggle for freedom', as Genovese puts it. But as we have seen in Chapter 4, slave revolts, as a category, could be quite fluid for our ancient sources and could incorporate events that in modern discussions would not constitute a slave revolt at all. The most striking example is Augustus' depiction of his struggle against Sex. Pompeius, which Augustus described as a *bellum servile*, despite the fact that the struggle was part of what *we* call unambiguously a civil war. This particular rhetorical strategy was not unusual in antiquity. As seen on several occasions on the foregoing pages, enslaved individuals had a long history of taking part in and potentially benefiting from the struggles between the free peoples of the ancient Mediterranean – a practice that should caution us against assuming that we

---

[1] Genovese 1979, 1.
[2] The preconditions are as follows (Genovese 1979, 11–12): '(1) the master–slave relationship had developed in the context of absenteeism and depersonalization as well as greater cultural estrangement of whites and blacks; (2) economic distress and famine occurred; (3) slaveholding units approached the average size of one hundred to two hundred slaves, as in the sugar colonies, rather than twenty or so, as in the Old South; (4) the ruling class frequently split either in warfare between slave-holding countries or in bitter struggles within a particular slaveholding country; (5) blacks heavily outnumbered whites; (6) African-born slaves outnumbered those born into American slavery (creoles); (7) the social structure of the slaveholding regime permitted the emergence of an autonomous black leadership; (8) the geographical, social, and political environment provided terrain and opportunity for the formation of colonies of runaway slaves strong enough to threaten the plantation regime'. For the use of these preconditions in ancient slavery see, e.g., Cartledge 1985 and Bradley 1989, 14–17.

can easily identify events in antiquity that fit Genovese's 'compelling' answer. In brief, it is not necessarily enough that slaves struggle for freedom in and through a conflict for it to become a slave revolt, not least because we need to accommodate other aspects of such conflicts and to take account of how our ancient sources presented them and used them within their specific historiographical settings. Finally, there can be little doubt that many free people who took up arms against an oppressor saw themselves as being precisely in a struggle for freedom. Indeed, the very basis for the seemingly confusing overlap in the language pertaining to slavery and freedom in the ancient discourse, both in situations that speak to real-life slavery and in contexts that refer to interactions among the free, is a powerful testimony for this observation.

Moreover, the record of slave revolts in antiquity is sparse to an extent that is deeply problematic. There are very few examples of slave revolts in antiquity, and those that are considered to fit this category are unusual not only because we actually have evidence for them, but also because they are among the largest slave revolts in world history, even if our record of some of them is scant at best. They are not ideally suited to defining slave revolts more generally, and not only because of the complications that I have discussed in the first four chapters of this book concerning the two Sicilian wars that are widely deemed emblematic of ancient slave revolts. Let us consider one example in addition to the Sicilian events: one of the few successful, large-scale revolts in antiquity, which took place in AD 334 in Sarmatia.[3] Our record of this conflict is sufficient to say that the revolt was large, successfully displacing up to 300,000 Sarmatians. The precise nature of the revolt is hard to pin down, but it appears to have arisen out of the decision by the Sarmatians to arm their slaves in order to repel an invasion by the Goths. If true, this makes the revolt even more extraordinary: it derived from the decision of the free Sarmatians to arm their slaves while under considerable duress, an act in keeping with a common practice in antiquity, as already noted and as will be seen in greater detail below. The origin of the revolt, however, makes it quite unlike servile unrest that took place without the help, unintentional or not, of the free inhabitants of the region. If Ammianus Marcellinus is correct, the Sarmatian slaves outnumbered their erstwhile masters, and so revolted from an unusual position, being replete with arms, fresh from success in war alongside the free Sarmatians, and in the majority of the population.[4] While the record of this revolt is important, not least for expanding our understanding of the extent of slave ownership in societies beyond the traditional heydays of Greek and Roman history, it may not be helpful for understanding how enslaved people resisted their enslavement when not provided with many of the tools to do so by the same people they revolted against.

The problem can be explored further vis-à-vis a recent survey of ancient slavery, published in 2011. This survey, the first volume of the *Cambridge World History of Slavery*, is part of a multi-volume series that aims to provide a comprehensive global history of slavery. The first volume included two chapters on slave resistance: one by McKeown on slave resistance amongst chattel slaves in the classical Greek world;

---

[3] On this revolt, see Lenski 2018, 29–30.
[4] Amm. Marc. 17.12.16, 19.11.1 and 29.6.15. See also Euseb. *Vit. Const.* 4.6.1–2, Jer. *Chron.* s.a. 334; *Consularia Constantinopolitana*, s.a. 334; *Origo Constantini* 32.

and a second by Bradley on resistance in the Roman world.[5] Each chapter had as its purview all forms of resistance within these periods and an assessment of how these forms of resistance are studied. For the Greek world, McKeown dedicated roughly three pages to outright revolt, which began with the admission that 'Little evidence of slave rebellion survives from the classical Greek world.'[6] The chapter continued to discuss two events: Drimakos' revolt, and a revolt recorded by Polyaenus that took place in Syracuse at some point between 415 and 413 BC.[7] The remainder of the section discussed possible reasons for why we find so little evidence for slave revolts in the Classical Greek world, while the greater part of the chapter studied other forms of resistance that fell short of outright revolt. Bradley also dedicated three pages to the topic of revolt and included episodes that featured individual slave owners murdered by their slaves for poor treatment.[8] However, the majority of Bradley's discussion of revolts focused on three events: the two Sicilian conflicts that are at the heart of the present study, and the revolt led by Spartacus in the late 70s BC. His discussion of slave revolts, therefore, is informed by three events of an extraordinary nature that included thousands of rebels and took years to suppress, something that Bradley acknowledges later in the same chapter when he notes that 'After Spartacus there were no major slave revolts at Rome, which implies that the three major wars of the late Republican period were aberrant episodes.'[9] More recently, Hunt has noted similarly at the beginning of a chapter on 'Revolts' in a book dedicated to Greek and Roman slavery that 'Large slave revolts are rare . . . [O]nly a few major slave revolts [occurred] during the late Roman Republic.'[10] The chapter goes on to focus its discussion on the 'major Roman slave revolts', the three events focused on by Bradley and others — the two Sicilian revolts and the Spartacus revolt.[11] The implication is that there were 'minor' revolts also, but these are not discussed or defined. For the Classical Greek world there does not appear to be enough evidence to speak in detail about what a slave revolt was in that period, and for the Roman world we have, it seems, only episodes that are 'aberrant' or at best atypical. This presents serious problems for those interested in identifying the 'special character' of ancient slave revolts — as Genovese called it for slave revolts in the New World — or even, one might add, their general character, since the examples we have to work from are not necessarily representative of anything but themselves. The few slave revolts that McKeown, Bradley and Hunt feel able to discuss, therefore, are not useful for modern historians interested in setting limits on what we might include in our discussion of slave revolts in antiquity or to isolate useful techniques for their analysis.

Yet, how we define the limits of our analysis does influence how we reconstruct events or discuss the evidence. Focusing specifically on the strategic aspects of the two

---

[5] McKeown 2011; Bradley 2011.
[6] McKeown 2011, 153–5.
[7] See Chapter 4 for consideration of these revolts in their historiographical context.
[8] Bradley 2011, 364–6.
[9] Bradley 2011, 379. In a different article, Bradley 2015, 166, noted that 'Major revolts of the Spartacan kind were in fact few and far between. The dangers to slaves involved are sufficient explanation.'
[10] Hunt 2018, 155.
[11] Hunt 2018, 161–5.

Sicilian revolts, I have argued elsewhere, for example, that scholars have overemphasised the 'servile' element in their discussion: by so doing these scholars have separated these conflicts from modern understanding of ordinary warfare and thus underappreciated the role played by strategy in the rebels' actions.[12] The separation of slave revolts into a discrete category of analysis is not uncommon. Hunt, for example, has noted that slaves involved in revolts experienced great disadvantages in comparison to what he calls 'Any functional state', since the rebels will have 'started out with almost no organization, resources, money, weapons, or training'. He noted moreover that as soon as any slave rebelled they would 'immediately be considered a murderer of the worst kind'.[13] As we have seen in Chapter 1, Bradley insisted on discussing the attempts at state formation in both Sicilian wars in relation to the participants' servility, including calling their leaders 'slave kings'.[14] In both cases aspects of the rebels' situations, strategies and prospects are assumed *a priori* based upon their identification as servile insurrections. There appear, therefore, to be some distinctions in how 'slave revolts' and the actions of their participants ought to be discussed in contrast to events that concerned free people, and these distinctions have strongly informed modern approaches to the study of slave revolts – rightly or wrongly.

Nonetheless, these distinctions are not explicitly stated in most cases, with the result that analyses are undertaken on the basis of first principles that are not disclosed. Consider, for example, the war fought by Rome against Aristonicus in the late 130s BC. In the ancient literary accounts this war is regarded as a dynastic war, not a slave revolt, even if some ancient authors make reference to slaves.[15] This alone is not reason to exclude the event from discussions of slave revolts, and Aristonicus' war against Rome has been included by Vogt and Urbainczyk among others in their studies of ancient slave revolts.[16] It is worth reflecting briefly on why two modern authors chose to include this conflict in their discussion of slave revolts, in contrast to the ancient sources.

But first, a short note on the isolated ancient mentions of slaves in these events. In two brief discussions of the conflict in antiquity, in Diodorus Siculus and Strabo, slaves are included. Diodorus mentions the event in his introduction to the First Romano-Sicilian War, noting that (34/5.2.26) τὸ παραπλήσιον δὲ γέγονε, 'a similar thing happened', at the same time as the conflict when Aristonicus attempted to seize the throne at Pergamum. In this case, Diodorus relates, the slaves in the area joined Aristonicus διὰ τὰς ἐκ τῶν δεσποτῶν κακουχίας, 'because of mistreatment by their masters'. Strabo (14.1.38) also mentioned that slaves in the area followed Aristonicus

---

[12] See Morton 2014.
[13] All quotations from Hunt 2018, 166.
[14] Bradley 1989, 116–20, with the quotation from 120.
[15] All the following authors present the conflict as a war without adducing the 'slave' label: Just. *Epit.* 36.4.5–12, 37.1.1–3; Sall. *Hist.* 4.69.8–9; Cic. *Phil.* 11.8.18; Laelius, *De amicitia* 11.37; Livy, *Per.* 59; Oros. 5.10.1–5; Eutr. 4.8.21–9, 4.9.1–23; Val. Max. 3.2.12; Vell. Pat. 2.4.1; Plut. *Flam.* 21.6; Flor. 1.35.1–7. This body of evidence led Kim 1988, 163, to conclude that 'Aristonicus' dynastic claim was the most fundamental element throughout his movement.'
[16] See Vogt 1965; Urbainczyk 2008a and 2008b; further Hermann-Otto 2009. The ancient sources for the war were also included in Yavetz's 1988 sourcebook for ancient slave wars.

after Aristonicus offered them their freedom, in similar manner to those other individuals who appealed to slaves in a losing cause discussed in Chapter 4. Unlike other authors who comment on this conflict in relation to the events surrounding Ti. Gracchus, Strabo and Diodorus mention this war in a different context. Diodorus, who is about to relate at some length the First Romano-Sicilian War, focuses on the presence of the slaves and sees a relationship between the two events he is discussing. Strabo mentions the appeal to the slaves in a repeat of the *topos* identified in Chapter 4: Aristonicus' cause is implied to be a lost cause by the inclusion of this detail. In two ancient accounts of this event, therefore, servile involvement is clearly mentioned.

For Vogt, this appears to have been reason enough to include the event in his chapter titled 'Zur Struktur der antiken Sklavenkriege'. He opened this chapter of his 1965 book with a comment on the unusual fact that all 'die großen Sklavenaufstände' in the ancient world happened between 140 and 70 BC. He followed this statement with a list of the 'Sklavenaufstände' that he had in mind: 'der erste sizilische Aufstand (136/5–132), die Erhebung des Aristonikos in Asien (133–129), der zweite sizilische Aufstand (104–100), der Krieg des Spartakus (73–71)'. In his discussion of the different structures of the revolts he had chosen, Vogt devoted considerable space to Aristonicus (31–3, 43–5, 48). In this, Vogt made clear at one point that this event was not one that he actually considered to be a slave war, going so far as to say that (33) '(f)ür uns bleiben die aufständischen Sklaven Asiens stumme Werkzeuge eines Prätendenten . . .' The event was, in essence, a dynastic problem that led to a revolutionary instance driven by Aristonicus, a free man, with notable foresight (31): 'von Anfang an also (war) das revolutionäre Geschehen planvoll bestimmt'. The event appears to have been included by Vogt not because the drive behind the event was servile, but because slaves were *involved*. Throughout the discussion Vogt focused on either Aristonicus' integration of disparate groups (including slaves: 31–3) or on the potential social organisation of Aristonicus' new state (43–5). Although never explicitly stated in his discussion, the defining feature required to include this event amongst Vogt's analysis of 'Sklaveraufstände' was the inclusion of slaves alongside other, free, participants.

Roughly half a century on, Urbainczyk discussed Aristonicus in some detail in her 2008 monograph, *Slave Revolts in Antiquity*. She focused, naturally given the book's title, on the involvement of slaves in Aristonicus' movement. She proposed that while freeing the slaves was probably something Aristonicus was forced into, it was still important to emphasise the reasons for the slaves to fight, noting in particular that it was probable that they wanted freedom (63).[17] Elsewhere she pressed Diodorus' statement, quoted above, to suggest that the slaves involved in Aristonicus' fight (14) 'had the support of the free people' and that (15) 'Aristonicus . . . took advantage of an uprising of the slaves and formed an army to resist the Romans.' While this stretches the meaning of Diodorus' text rather too far, more importantly it brings to the fore

---

[17] In proposing this interpretation, Urbainczyk was directly responding to a question posed in Vavrinek 1975, 115: 'Was [Aristonicus] a revolutionary leader who, conscious of his purpose, placed himself in command of the revolting slaves, or was the freeing of the slaves merely a tactical device which he was forced to employ because he lacked other means of achieving his aims?'

the unstated reason for including Aristonicus' conflict with Rome in a book on slave revolts: the event provided an opportunity for slaves to seize their freedom.[18] As with Vogt's contribution, it is thus at base the presence of slaves, *however this came about*, that makes this event warrant inclusion in a study of slave revolts.

There is nothing wrong, in principle, with including this event in a study of servile insurrection, and by so doing not following the ancient sources in connecting Aristonicus' war to the internal problems in Rome in the late 130s BC.[19] Detailed study of how servile discontent can take advantage of divisions between groups in free society is important, as is emphasising the role played by unfree participants in these conflicts. The difficulty in each case noted above is that without an explicit explanation for the chosen events' inclusion – that is, a definition that clarifies, in this case, the basis on which Aristonicus' revolt is included among slave revolts – it is not clear why other events of a similar nature are excluded, such as the frequent references in ancient literature to free people appealing to slaves in the midst of political or military conflicts with other free people. As we will see below, and as we have already seen in Chapter 4, this was a commonplace in ancient historiography, based on widespread ancient practice. Moreover, in light of the difficulties that we face when we study a conflict as a slave revolt and unconsciously separate it from 'normal' wars or revolts, it is also problematic to study Aristonicus' dynastic war as a slave revolt without some reflection on the problems this may bring or the issues it may solve.

It should be clear from this example that it is important to define our terms when we discuss slave revolts in antiquity, if only to make it clear on what grounds we include and exclude events: in the examples above this definition is at best left implicit.[20] To a certain extent, providing such a definition was in fact done by Rubinsohn, who engaged in a form of this discussion in a footnote in his article on the later of the Sicilian revolts: there he discussed how best to describe these events.[21] He argued that they ought not to be termed a slave revolt because 'the movements are not purely servile in origin or in objective pursued'; he noted that this definition did not necessitate a denial that the 'majority of participants were slaves *de iure*', and in this respect he demonstrated, in a sense, his definition of a slave war – that is, a movement that is purely servile in origin and perhaps also in the objectives that it pursues, and one largely made up of servile participants. Thus, Rubinsohn's definition was one created in reverse, that is by defining what is not a slave revolt. The aim of the present

---

[18] Urbainczyk 2008a, 16, derived this reading from the following passage of Diodorus (34/5.2.26): τῶν δὲ δούλων διὰ τὰς ἐκ τῶν δεσποτῶν κακουχίας συναπονοησαμένων ἐκείνῳ, 'the slaves, because of mistreatment by their masters, shared in this man's folly', arguing 'that the slaves had already rebelled and that these rebels joined forces with Aristonicus'. She went on to say that the manner in which Diodorus sets out events suggested 'not that Aristonicus recruited the slaves because he promised them freedom, but rather they had been badly treated and so joined the revolt'.

[19] In the previous chapter we saw that the citizens of Colophon certainly considered some of those involved in the conflict to be slaves, and they emphasised this element in their representation of the conflict: see Rigsby 2005.

[20] Urbainczyk 2008a, 7, noted this precise problem, but did not offer an answer to her own implicit question ('One is faced with the issue of what counts as a slave revolt'). The wary reader will observe, correctly, that I have left this chapter, and thus my own definition, until last place in this book. *Mea culpa*.

[21] Rubinsohn 1982, 443 n. 28.

chapter, in contrast, is to offer a positive, up-front definition of what constituted a slave revolt, with particular regard to commenting, finally, on the repercussions for an understanding of the two Sicilian conflicts at the heart of the present study.

The first step in establishing a definition is to leave aside the categorisation provided by our ancient literary sources. As we have seen in Chapter 4, the designation of an event as a slave revolt in a slave-owner narrative should not mean that we accept this definition for our own purposes: the ancient authors were not scientific in their application of this label, but could use it to suit their own quite different purposes. We cannot use their definition, and so we must look elsewhere for our evidence to create our own definition. What follows, therefore, requires a different approach, one that deals with two aspects, here divided into two sections. First, we will consider conflicts in the ancient world that involved slaves – all of which included also free people, and were indeed driven by the free, soliciting help from the enslaved simply for their own purposes. This section will show that appeals to slaves in ancient warfare and political troubles were not routine in antiquity, but that, even so, in times of crisis and military difficulty it was not unusual for the free parties involved to appeal to slaves in order to bolster their own forces. It will moreover be shown that the arming of slaves in struggles between free groups tells us little about the conditions of slavery that lurk behind these conflicts, or about how or why the slaves responded to the stimuli provided by free peoples: in short, the employment of slaves in a conflict among free groups cannot be a defining feature for our modern understanding of slave revolts. Rather, the ensuing discussion illustrates that the role played by slaves in such struggles tells us more about how free people exploited slavery and slaves in their own conflicts: in essence, it is another way of studying how masters benefited from slavery, even if, at the same time, some of the enslaved may have benefited also from these situations.

As a response to the limitations of the ancient evidence, in terms of both scale and depth, the second section will consider identified slave revolts from other slave societies for which we have better evidence in order to determine what features are typical of slave revolts in these societies: the United States, Brazil and select islands from the Caribbean. It should be emphasised that these regions have been chosen not to reinforce an outdated, implicit notion of what constitutes a slave society, but rather because the evidence for them is much fuller than that for many other regions in the modern world, and even more so for antiquity, a key detail, as we will see below.[22] The analysis will illustrate that American and Caribbean slave revolts were in most cases small-scale and short-lived, featuring fewer than 100 participants at most and ending within a month, and more often within days, but crucially also were common. Moreover, I will argue that the nature of the evidence that we have for these events – private letters, court documents and colonial archives – means that similar occurences in the ancient world would be hard to find in our historical record, since the type of evidence that preserves small-scale and short-lived revolts is unlikely to have survived from antiquity: in consequence, our record for slave revolts in antiquity will by definition be deficient, because slave revolts, if understood against the backdrop of modern examples and the evidence that records them, are not the kinds of events that were

---

[22] On the concept of a 'slave society', and the debate surrounding it, see now Lenski and Cameron 2018.

recorded in ancient historiography. The discussion will emphasise a seemingly simple observation: that the two Sicilian revolts do not fit the pattern of slave revolts that we find in the modern world, and that their survival in the ancient evidence is a result of ancient slave owners engaging in extended forms of standardised historiographical *topoi*, as we have seen in Chapter 4. The consequences of this unsurprising point for present purposes will be discussed in the Conclusion to this chapter. First, however, we turn to servile involvement in free conflicts in antiquity.

Slave Soldiers in Antiquity

The two scholars considered above, Vogt and Urbainczyk, both included Aristonicus' struggle with Rome for the kingdom of Pergamum in their analyses of ancient slave revolts. It is striking in each case that, helots aside in Urbainczyk, the only other supposed slave revolts covered in those two works are the two Sicilian revolts and the war fought by the Romans against Spartacus in the 70s BC. The decision to include Aristonicus' war in their analyses was based, it appears, on the fact that there is evidence for the inclusion of slaves in the conflict by at least one of the combatants involved. Yet the presence of slaves in a conflict among free groups should not be used as a defining feature in our own definition of slave revolts. As we will see, the use of slaves in warfare between free groups was common enough in antiquity that identifying slave actors in so-called ordinary warfare is not enough to make it a defining feature. This is the case for both the Roman and the Greek worlds. The examples that follow are not intended to be exhaustive; rather, they serve to demonstrate a broad pattern that is evident across antiquity until the time of Augustus.[23] We start with the Greek world.

According to Pausanias, the earliest instance of slaves fighting alongside their masters was at the battle of Marathon. He found evidence for this in the grave for the slaves who died in the battle (1.32.3). Pausanias makes clear on another occasion that these slaves were freed before the battle in order to fight (7.15.7), although what status they assumed after the battle is less clear.[24] If this was indeed the first time that slaves – or, as Hammond pointedly remarks, 'ex-slaves' – fought alongside masters, then the practice set a trend followed often in the centuries thereafter.[25] Xerxes' invasion of the Greek mainland and then the inter-state conflict during the Peloponnesian War both resulted in multiple occasions on which slaves were recruited into armies. The Spartans often armed their helots in order to supplement the Spartiates in combat.[26] In the defence of the Greek mainland against the Persians, helots fought at both Thermopylae and at Plataea (Hdt. 8.25.2; 9.10.1, 28.2, 29.1). Helots also fought for the Spartans under Brasidas during the Peloponnesian War (Thuc. 4.78.1, 80.5), and on another occasion at least 2,000 helots were part of the

---

[23] For full studies of slaves in the Greek and Roman militaries, see Rouland 1977 and Welwei 1974–88.
[24] On these slaves, see Hammond 1992, 147–50, arguing that they became Plataean citizens; also Hunt 1998, 26–8. See also Welwei 1974, 22–36.
[25] Hammond 1992, 147.
[26] On helots as slaves, see now Lewis 2018a, 125–46.

Spartan army (Thuc. 4.80.3–4). Finally, during the siege of Syracuse, Sparta sent a relief force under Gylippus that included 600 helots (Thuc. 7.19.3, 58.3). As Hunt has argued, the Greek navy at Salamis must have relied upon a significant body of slave rowers, even if they are not explicitly mentioned in the sources for this battle; not only would the number of ships deployed have required more manpower than that available to the Greek cities from free citizens, but in addition references in some ancient texts infer that crews on the ships were only partly free.[27]

In the Peloponnesian War there is evidence from Thucydides that slaves were regularly used in non-Athenian navies (Thuc. 1.55.1; 2.103.1; 8.15.2, 84.2). Athens famously freed slaves in order to man its fleet before the battle of Arginusae (Xen. *Hell.* 1.6.24; Ar. *Ran.* 693–4 with schol. 694; *IG* I³ 1032) and considered doing so again after the battle of Chaeronea in 338 BC.[28] Other examples from later history and other places indicate that this practice was not restricted to the Peloponnesian War or the wars against Persia. Dionysius I allegedly manned sixty ships with freed slaves in order to complement his navy against the Carthaginians (Diod. Sic. 14.58.1). Diodorus and Justin record the story that Agathocles, likewise, freed and armed slaves in order to bolster his forces for his campaign in Africa (20.4.8 and 22.4 respectively). In 305/4 BC the Rhodians enrolled metics and aliens in their army and even bought and freed slaves to supplement their forces when besieged by Demetrius (Diod. Sic. 20.84.2–3). Finally, Pausanias and Polybius both record that the final Achaean army to face Rome in 146 BC included 12,000 slaves (Polyb. 38.15.3; Paus. 7.15.7).

In the disorder and civil wars in first-century BC Rome, accusations of arming slaves were frequent, as we have seen in the previous chapter, which significantly problematises the use of these examples in our study of slave soldiers in free conflicts. Nonetheless, there is some reason to think that the practice actually occurred, was common, and was weaponised politically in the aftermath of the events. The most notable examples are the claims made about Cinna, Marius and Catiline (discussed in see Chapter 4); additionally, Caesar also accused Pompeius Magnus of including slave herdsmen in his cavalry during their civil war (Caes. *B Civ.* 1.24). Caesar claimed that the forces arranged against him regularly supplemented their legions with forces raised from those available locally, be they free provincials or slaves. This is first observed in the campaigns in Africa that concluded at Thapsus, in which we hear of slaves and freedmen recruited into the cavalry ([Caes.] *B Afr.* 19), Cn. Pompeius campaigning with 2,000 slaves and freedmen ([Caes.] *B Afr.* 23), slaves, freedmen and Africans enrolled into legions by Cato ([Caes.] *B Afr.* 36), and finally Q. Caecilius Metellus Scipio encouraging the Romans in Utica to free their slaves in order to defend the town after Thapsus ([Caes.] *B Afr.* 88). In the Spanish campaigns that followed in 45 BC between Cn. Pompeius and Caesar, we are told that the former again enrolled local Spaniards and slaves into legions in order to increase his forces ([Caes.] *B Hisp.* 7, 12, 20 and 34).[29] Cicero made similar accusations about M. Antonius, whom Cicero accused of recruiting slaves from *ergastula* into his forces after his defeat at Mutina

---

[27] See Hunt 1998, 40–1, for the argument and further references.
[28] See Welwei 1974, 54–6, for references.
[29] On these passages, see Welwei 1988, 137–45.

(*Fam.* 11.10.3).[30] The difficulty with each example above is that we do not always have a control narrative to test the assertions about the recruiting practices of these groups, who in each case were either the losing party in the struggle or had recently suffered a considerable reverse: these might be tactics resorted to in times of crisis or examples of stock political attacks studied in Chapter 4; obviously these stories may also exaggerate actual practice for the purpose of political mud-slinging. In the conflict between Sex. Pompeius and C. Octavianus we can at least compare the *post hoc* rhetoric from the victorious Octavianus against other records of the period. As we have seen in the previous chapter, in his posthumously published *Res gestae*, Octavianus gave the impression that he fought slaves and pirates in his campaigns in Sicily, rather than a Roman commander at the head of legions.[31] Sex. Pompeius did free slaves to man his fleets and to bolster his legions, and Octavianus made a point of returning the slaves to their masters if possible after the conflict ended.[32] Yet what is clear from the accounts of this period is that Sex. Pompeius was not alone in recruiting slaves in this way: Octavianus manned his fleet with 20,000 freed slaves for the final conflicts, and the Triumvirs had ordered citizens to provide slaves for their fleet in 42 BC (Cass. Dio 47.17.4, 48.49.1; Suet. *Aug.* 16.1).[33] It is possible that the civil war between Pompeius Magnus and Caesar witnessed similar recruitment of slaves on both sides, but that we only have evidence for this on one side, which may well be deploying established political invective to attack and delegitimise its opponent; in any case, it appears that in the civil wars of the late Republic, slaves were regularly used to supplement free forces, and are regularly reported as having been awarded with freedom in exchange.

This practice was not limited to the civil wars. Towards the end of the Social War, for example, Q. Pompaedius Silo freed and armed 20,000 slaves for infantry and 1,000 for cavalry (Diod. Sic. 37.2.9). Augustus employed freedmen cohorts called *voluntarii* during the Pannonian Revolt of AD 6–9 when Rome's armies were hard-pressed by the Pannonian forces.[34] The Second Punic War, however, provides the most compelling examples of Roman slave recruitment. In 214 BC, for example, the senate ordered T. Otacilius to sail to Sicily with a fleet that included freedmen sailors, provided by private funds solicited with regard to each individual's property classification (Livy 24.11.7–8).[35] Yet the most striking example came after Rome's catastrophic defeat at Cannae against Hannibal in 216 BC. In the aftermath of the battle the Roman senate authorised the recruitment of two full legions from slaves

---

[30] See Welwei 1988, 145–7.

[31] See *RG* 25.1 and 27.3: Fugmann 1991, 311; Powell 1998, 93–4; Cooley 2009, 214–15.

[32] For the slaves in the army and navy, see App. *B Civ.* 4.85, 5.131; Cass. Dio 48.19.4, 48.49.1, 49.12.4; Vell. Pat. 2.73.3; Suet. *Aug.* 16.1. Modern discussions: Welwei 1988, 149–59; Watson 2002, 219; Welch 2002, 42–3.

[33] See also Welwei 1988, 42–4.

[34] Macrob. *Sat.* 1.11.32; Cass. Dio 55.31.1, 56.23.3; Vell. Pat. 2.111.1. See also Welwei 1988, 18–22, and Duncan-Jones 2016, 137.

[35] For further discussion of this passage, see Rosenstein 2008. The Roman state repaid the money to those who provided slaves for the fleet after the war had ended: Livy 29.16.1–3, 31.13.1–9, 33.42.2–4. Roman indignation at being taxed in this way again prevented the senate from copying this action in 211 BC (Livy 26.35.2–3). On slaves in the Republican fleets during the Punic Wars, see also Welwei 1988, 29–41.

manumitted for this purpose (Livy 22.57.11–12).[36] The fortunes of these slave legions – made up of volunteers, who were therefore called *volones* – are followed closely by Livy in his narrative of the Second Punic War, as Hunt has shown, and they were an important part of Rome's efforts to recover from a perilous position in the first five years of the conflict with Hannibal.[37] Finally, a century on, we have the peculiar case of an *eques* named T. Vettius Minucius.[38] According to Diodorus (36.2–2a), in 104 BC this man purchased the freedom of an enslaved woman whom he loved. When he was unable to pay his debt, Vettius armed 400 of his own slaves, proclaimed himself king, and proceeded to incite 700 slaves to rebel under his banner. The Roman senate swiftly appointed a praetor, L. Licinius Lucullus, to the command against these rebels, and he proceeded to secure their defeat through betrayal. The final rebel force apparently came to 3,500 in number. The driving force behind this whole event was Vettius' passionate desire for the enslaved young woman.[39]

While in some of the examples outlined above we might argue that the accusation of recruiting slaves reflects political discourse rather than historical reality – most notably in the cases that occurred in the Roman civil wars of the first century BC – nonetheless in some cases at least these are genuine examples of the recruitment of slaves in times of war into (free) armies and navies, most notably during the Second Punic War. Two details are consistent across each example: first, the free individuals and societies involved turned to slave recruits at times of heightened tension and when they were badly pressed in their conflict; second, the leadership and motivation that drove the conflict was free. It appears that this recruitment strategy was turned to when necessary; it was uncommon, but not unusual. Moreover, as the cited events have illustrated, the presence of slaves and ex-slaves fighting in a conflict is not, *per se*, enough to identify those slaves as revolting or to identify the event in question as a slave revolt. In each example discussed above we are given no indication of the slaves' condition before the offer of freedom, nor, in many cases, information on what changed afterwards, for good or for bad from the slaves' perspectives. In short, we do not know why slaves responded to the offer of freedom, but we can say with a degree of certainty that it was an offer of freedom that came from the *masters*: far from fighting in 'a struggle for freedom' of their own, as Genovese put it, these slave soldiers were fighting towards the objectives of elite slave owners.[40] If the slaves gained from these conflicts, as in many cases they unquestionably did, they did so both at great risk to themselves and also at the behest of their masters. In sum, these moments are best characterised as another way in which free people took advantage of the slave system and the slaves themselves to achieve their own ends: while the potential benefit to

---

[36] On the *volones*, see Welwei 1988, 5–17.
[37] Hunt 1998, 206–8. The *Historia Augusta* claims that Marcus Aurelius also recruited slaves and explicitly references the *volones*, but it is not clear how reliable this particular source is. On this, see Welwei 1988, 23–7.
[38] His name is given in Diodorus as either Titus Minucius (36.2.2) or Titus Vettius (36.2.2–6 and 36.2a.1). On this episode: Pareti 1927, 65; Vogt 1965, 27 and 49; Manganaro 1980, 440; Bradley 1989, 72–3, 78 and 123; Urbainczyk 2008a, 17.
[39] At one point he is described as (36.2a.1) τῷ δὲ ἔρωτι δουλεύων, 'being a slave to passion'.
[40] Genovese 1979, 1.

the slaves involved should not be dismissed and may (but need not!) be understood as testament to their desire to escape their servitude, it was a by-product of the slave system itself.[41] After all, should we really assume that those freed for the purpose of fighting for their former masters had a say in the matter?

The Definition of a Slave Revolt

As shown in the previous section, the inclusion of enslaved people in a conflict cannot be taken as a diagnostic for identifying slave revolts in antiquity; nor, as I argued in Chapter 4, can we use the ancient slave-owner narratives to guide our interpretation of which events were slave revolts. In the context of this study, moreover, we must exclude the evidence for the two Sicilian revolts from our definition: if the aim is to understand how these two events relate to slave revolts more generally, then they cannot be part of the process of definition. In what follows, therefore, I will develop a definition of slave revolts derived from a selection of well-documented modern slave societies for which we have far better evidence in order to guide our interpretation of the ancient world. Our ancient evidence, as I have argued throughout this book, has considerable shortcomings for the creation of a modern definition of a slave revolt. This is the case in terms of the paucity of ancient evidence but also the ideologically and historiographically loaded contexts in which we find our notices of slave revolts. A turn to some examples from modern slavery will allow us to sketch commonalities among slave revolts in better-documented slave systems, even if they were in many respects quite different from those in antiquity. As we will see, slave revolts in the modern world can, on the whole, be characterised in part by their brevity, their small scale and their regularity. While they cannot provide a definitive guide to the nature of slave revolts in antiquity, they offer a compelling picture of continuity in servile resistance across differing slave systems. If this comparison is indicative of the ancient world, or at least indicative of the reaction of enslaved people to their condition, it will emphasise that the Sicilian revolts were distinctive not just in antiquity, but in world history, and that they transcend the category of slave revolts: they were events that require their own explanation in their immediate historical context, as Bradley argued.[42]

Several different definitions of a slave revolt have been proposed by modern slavery scholars, including Genovese's 'compelling' suggestion with which we started this chapter: 'a struggle for freedom'.[43] The question is not merely academic. Aptheker, in the eighth chapter of his study of slave revolts in the United States, directly addressed the question, taking as his starting point the definition found in an act passed on 12 February 1858 in Texas. That particular modern American state defined an insurrection of slaves as follows: 'an assemblage of three or more [slaves], with arms,

---

[41] This is in keeping, it should be added, with the way in which manumission in the Roman world could be used for continued exploitation of the manumitted individual: Roth 2010, with earlier bibliography.
[42] Bradley 1989, ix.
[43] Genovese 1979, 1.

with intent to obtain their liberty by force'.⁴⁴ For his own study, Aptheker applied a 'more severe' test for what constituted a slave revolt:

> The elements of the definition herein subscribed to are: a minimum of ten slaves involved; freedom as the apparent aim of the disaffected slaves; contemporary references labelling the event as an uprising, plot, insurrection, or the equivalent of these terms.

With this definition, Aptheker identified 250 revolts and conspiracies in the United States. Not dissimilarly, Kilson defined slave revolts as 'attempts to achieve freedom by groups of slaves' in her analysis of the types of slave revolts in the United States.⁴⁵ Kilson's definition allowed the identification of sixty-five instances across the eighteenth and nineteenth centuries AD. A recent database that includes over 350 slave revolts in the United States was, on the other hand, built with the definition that followed the Texan line on numbers – 'events that involved three or more people' – and incorporated events that were 'organised with the express purpose of killing whites, achieving personal or group freedom, pillaging, causing physical damage to property, personal enrichment, or ending slavery altogether'.⁴⁶ Revolt itself is frequently described as part of a continuum of resistance to slavery that included a range of acts including individual flight, day-to-day acts of sabotage, temporary absenteeism and outright revolt.⁴⁷ From this brief survey, it is evident that the definition adopted can have a considerable impact upon the number of events included within these overviews. Olivarius noted, for example, that it is difficult to be certain whether reports of revolts in modern sources indicate 'real or just imagined' revolts.⁴⁸ At the same time, there are some important commonalities. Thus, the definitions arrived at by different scholars all feature two elements: a low threshold for the number of participants, with the highest threshold set at ten involved, and the aim of personal freedom. Furthermore, attention in these accounts is reserved for explaining the causes of the revolts and for assessing the goals of the revolts.

In what follows, I intend to take these modern definitions as a starting point for an assessment of slave revolts in a selection of New World territories from the sixteenth to the nineteenth centuries AD that will demonstrate that these revolts shared two other important unifying features in addition to their size: their length and their regularity. The territories chosen are the United States, Brazil and the Caribbean

---

⁴⁴ Aptheker 1943, 162. This definition, strikingly, excludes all the events outlined above in the first section of this chapter, since these slaves were not obtaining their liberty by force (at least, not directly).

⁴⁵ Kilson 1964, 1.

⁴⁶ The database has been compiled by K. Olivarius, and the details were reported in a blog post for the *IHR* blog: <https://blog.history.ac.uk/2017/06/new-frontiers-in-american-slave-revolts/#_ftnref11> (accessed 27 January 2022).

⁴⁷ See, e.g., the structure of Rivers' 2012 study of slave resistance in nineteenth-century AD Florida, which was divided into three parts: 'Resistance by wiles', 'Running away' and 'Violent resistance'. See also Mullin 1972; Craton 1982; Kolchin 1993.

⁴⁸ Again at https://blog.history.ac.uk/2017/06/new-frontiers-in-american-slave-revolts/#_ftnref11 (accessed 27 January 2022).

islands of Barbados, Cuba, Curaçao, Guyana and Jamaica; as I noted above, the respective societies are not chosen to reinforce the notion that all slaving cultures in history conformed to the structures and ideologies of New World slaveries, but rather because the body of evidence for each society allows detailed study of revolts, even down to those suppressed before they ever occurred.[49] The aim is to show that the events identified as slave revolts have certain commonalities in terms of size, duration and regularity that enable us to refine a definition of what we might call a 'typical' slave revolt, at least for these territories, and despite the differences between the slaveries practised in those regions over time. This survey is self-consciously narrow in the slave societies chosen and the variables assessed, size and length, and eschews therefore providing too much extraneous detail or narrative. The purpose is not to suggest that these revolts were all fundamentally the same in all respects, but rather to suggest that regardless of whatever other variables one might choose to study they are similar when considered in relation to the three factors noted above. Once we have demonstrated what we might term three 'typical' features of slave revolts in these areas of the modern world, we will be able to return to our Sicilian events and assess them against our new definition.

A point of caution, before we begin. It is important that we do not press the comparison too far. Factors within each slave system meant local conditions had a considerable effect upon the nature of revolt. Two simple but important factors can be noted here: the proportion of enslaved to free in each society, and the presence of firearms. As we will see, slave societies with higher proportions of enslaved people tended to experience more regular revolts that were larger in scale and lasted longer; such is the case for Jamaica, for example, which at times had an enslaved to free ratio of 10:1, where we find the longest and largest revolts.[50] Firearms present a more problematic difference. In short, we might expect slave owners' access to firearms to have been a significant factor in the suppression of revolts, contributing to their brevity and making slave revolts in these modern societies a poor choice for comparison. The experience of many revolts will show that to be the case, as we will see; quite plainly, this functions as a warning to us against assuming that these modern slave societies provide a simple basis for comparison with the ancient world. Nonetheless, it is striking that even in revolts in which the rebels successfully armed themselves with firearms and even field cannons, such as the revolt on Sutton's estate in Jamaica in 1691, and in circumstances in which the enslaved to free ratio was extraordinarily

---

[49] There was a long history of servile insurrection in other areas of the Americas, notably in Venezuela and Mexico, e.g. King Bayano and Miguel Guacamaya: Franco 1979, 36–41; Blanco 1991; Gallup-Diaz 2010. See also Juan Andresote's revolt from 1730 to 1733 against Spain's hold over the commerce of New Granada: Felice Cardot 1952; Rout 1976, 113–15. On Mexican revolts: Love 1967; Palmer 1976, 119–44; Martinez 2004. In Venezuela there are records of eighteen slave revolts between 1732 and 1799, including the major uprising at Coro on 10 May 1795, which was inspired by the Haitian and French Revolutions: Aizpurua 1988; 2011, 98–101. Geggus 2011, 40–9, lists a further six revolts or conspiracies between 1779 and 1836 that took place in Central and South America (excluding Brazil). On Venezuelan slave revolts, see Lynch 1973, 197–204; and on Peruvian revolts Kápsoli Escudero 1975, 66–71 and 135, and Vásquez-Machicado and Vásquez-Machicado 1988, 617–20.

[50] Stinchcombe and Stinchcombe 1995, 55.

high, there appears to be no strong correlation to increased longevity of the revolt. This is an important caveat to bear in mind as we consider the patterns of resistance in what follows: those rebelling did so in the knowledge that, in most cases, they had to fight a slave-owner class with superior armament.

A final point on modern slave revolts: as we will see, these revolts were common, albeit often short and small in scale. We might say that the defining feature of these modern slave societies was that resistance at the level of outright revolt was typical if not constant, and that this was the case despite the fact that the slave owners were equipped with firearms. If these modern revolts offer us any guide to antiquity, we might expect the absence of firearms in antiquity to result in even greater regularity in revolts on a small scale, with small numbers of enslaved individuals banding together to fight their enslavement with greater hope of success given the relative equality in access to weaponry between the enslaved and their slavers. That we do not see this in antiquity, I will argue, is because our evidence simply would never record this kind of resistance, rather than because it did not take place. On this reading, antiquity probably experienced consistent episodes of small-scale and short-lived revolts. First, however, we must sketch out the narrative of the modern revolts. We turn, therefore, to the history of servile insurrection in the New World, starting with those in the United States.[51]

Slave Revolts in the United States

We begin this survey with a more detailed look at what may be termed the five most famous United States revolts: the Stono Rebellion of 1739, the German Coast Uprising of 1811, and those of Gabriel Prosser in 1800, Denmark Vesey in 1822 and Nat Turner in 1831. These five revolts demonstrate the greatest extent of servile revolt in the United States. The Stono Rebellion was one of the bloodiest slave revolts in American history.[52] The revolt started on Sunday, 9 September 1739. The rebels, numbering between sixty and 100 in total, met at the Stono River in South Carolina and marched southward, killing whites as they marched. They seized firearms and fought an engagement with local militia near Jacksonborough ferry, from which roughly thirty rebels escaped. However, the next Sunday rebels to the south were defeated in a second battle. According to some accounts, twenty-one white residents were killed in the revolt, which lasted a little more than a week. Nat Turner's revolt in 1831 was similarly bloody.[53] This revolt took place in Southampton County in

---

[51] The classic treatment of revolts in the American South is that of Aptheker 1943. See also Genovese 1979. Aptheker's long list of revolts has attracted criticism, in large part because he included in his account of the revolts mostly abortive plots: see, e.g., Genovese 1979, 141; Kolchin 1987, 250; Freehling 1994, 579 n. 6. According to Genovese 1979, 41–50, there were only four revolts that featured large numbers of rebels, sustained resistance and large-scale losses among the whites: New York in 1712; Stono in 1739; the German Coast Uprising of 1811; and Nat Turner's revolt in 1831.

[52] Smith 2005 contains a collection of important works on this event; for the classic study see Wood 1974. See also Shuler 2009 and Hoffer 2010.

[53] See Aptheker 1943, 293–305, for full discussion and sources for this revolt; also Foner 1971; Tragle 1971; Greenberg 1996; 2003; French 2004; Allmendinger 2014; Breen 2015.

Virginia, beginning on Sunday, 21 August. After Turner killed his master's family the rebels marched through the county gathering supporters. By 23 August the rebels numbered roughly seventy and had killed at least fifty-seven white people. They marched on Jerusalem and were attacked while recruiting slaves at a plantation owned by a man named Parker: this battle ended the revolt. It is probable that more than 100 rebels were killed in the aftermath of the revolt; Turner himself was captured on 30 October, tried and put to death. The revolt lasted a few days.

The German Coast uprising is considered the largest slave revolt in United States history. It took place over three days from 8–10 January 1811, and was led by an enslaved man named Charles Deslondes. The revolt began at the Andry plantation, where the owner was attacked and his son killed by the rebels. A group of around fifteen rebels gathered at the plantation, and the force grew as they marched towards New Orleans, gaining followers and a few firearms from the plantations that they passed. The insurgents burned several more estates and recruited more followers, and stopped at Cannes-Brulées, north-west of New Orleans. By this point there were at least 200, and potentially as many as 500 rebels. On 9 January the rebels were confronted by a militia, who killed around sixty-six of them. The remainder fled, but were captured in the days that followed.[54] Although the revolt is considered to be the largest in United States history, it resulted in the deaths of only two plantation owners.[55]

Gabriel Prosser's and Denmark Vesey's revolts, by contrast, were both betrayed before they could begin. Prosser's attempted revolt began in the midst of rumours of slave insurrections in Virginia in 1800, perhaps from as early as 22 April.[56] On Saturday, 30 August, two slaves betrayed the plot, which was intended to happen that evening. Although as many as 1,000 slaves gathered to march on Richmond, Virginia, bad weather prevented their action; the mobilisation of local plantation forces prevented any rebellion in the period that followed, and many rebels were arrested. Prosser was arrested on 25 September and was executed on 7 October alongside fifteen other rebels. The size of the conspiracy is impossible to gauge accurately, with contemporary accounts ranging in estimates from 2,000 up to 50,000 slaves.[57] Next, Vesey's revolt, which is often regarded as the 'largest and most advanced American slave conspiracy', took place in Charleston, South Carolina.[58] The revolt was set to happen on the second Sunday in July of 1822. The revolt was moved forward by a month, but soon after the initial betrayal on 30 May a slave named William gave up the revolt. A total of 130 enslaved people were arrested; of these, forty-nine were

---

[54] On the German Coast Uprising: Aptheker 1943, 249–51; Thrasher 1995; Rodriguez 1999a; Rasmussen 2011.

[55] Rivers 2012 claims that the largest slave revolt in North America was during the Second Seminole War of 1835–42, during which up to 465 plantation slaves, and up to 1,265 free blacks, took part in the conflict between the Seminole tribe of Native Americans and the United States Army. Further Mahon 1992; Heidler and Heidler 1996; Miller 2003.

[56] On Gabriel Prosser's revolt: Aptheker 1943, 219–27; Egerton 1993; Nicholls 2012.

[57] Nicholls 2012 has cast doubt on the reliability of the contemporary estimates of the conspiracy's size, with a particular focus on the trial evidence. See especially Nicholls 2012, 52. On Nicholls' approach to this rebellion see also Harpham 2015, 265–6. On the revolt see further Mullin 1972, 140–63.

[58] Harpham 2015, 264. On this revolt also Aptheker 1934, 267–76; Freehling 1994; Johnson 2001; O'Neil Spady 2011.

executed between 18 June and 9 August. According to the reports from the trials, the rebels had planned to seize weapons from stores near Charleston: the reports of the numbers involved varied widely, from 6,600 up to 9,000.[59]

These five revolts are the best known and largest in the history of United States slavery. Most other revolts were much smaller or betrayed, like those of Prosser and Vesey, before they began, but there are still important overlaps, notwithstanding some obvious differences between them. For the sake of clarity they are arranged here into three categories: plots betrayed before they happened; rumours of plots that led to punishment of slaves; and plots that took place.[60] To begin with, it seems many plots were betrayed before they ever took place; the hysterical free reactions to these plots make it hard to be certain of the actual scale of the plots. A few examples from Virginia and South Carolina will suffice. Three plots between 1663 and 1709 were betrayed in Virginia alone. In each case the number of slaves punished did not exceed four in total.[61] South Carolina experienced several abortive plots, including a plot in 1720 near Charleston to destroy plantations, recruit other slaves, and attack the city, as well as a plot on 15 August 1730. In the former case fourteen slaves were executed in the aftermath.[62] Similar plots were discovered in other states across the South, with similar results on their discovery.[63] Finally, a rather peculiar betrayal took place in Cheneyville, Louisiana in October of 1837. A conspiracy of around fifty enslaved blacks, free blacks and white residents was given up by its leader, Lewis Cheney, in order for him to be rewarded with his freedom.[64] There need not even be a plot for reprisals to take place. Notably, after a series of fires were set beginning on 2 February 1741, to hide minor thefts, New York City was gripped by hysteria about slave revolts. This panic led to the execution of two slaves on 11 May and then a further twenty-eight executions, all linked to what

---

[59] Wade 1964 and Johnson 2001 both question the reliability of the trial documents from the Vesey conspiracy, although their arguments have not gone unquestioned: see Paquette and Egerton 2004 and O'Neil Spady 2011. Aptheker 1943, 150–61, notes that there is a degree of (150) 'exaggeration, distortion, and censorship' in reports concerning slave revolts in America, and that (155) '(f)ear itself... created exaggeration so that figures concerning the number of rebels or victims given in the first reports were usually greater than those finally given'. It is probable that the larger figures reported above are exaggerations, and precise figures are impossible to discover.

[60] The first port of call for source references for all the following conspiracies, plots and revolts is Aptheker 1943, whose work collates the relevant sources at length.

[61] 1663: four plotters hanged in Gloucester County, Virginia; 1687: a plot was betrayed in Westmoreland County, Virginia; 1709: rumours of an alliance between local Indians and slaves, with the result that three out of four leaders were arrested. For all three see Breen 1973 and Theobald 2005–6; see Parent 2003 for the broader context.

[62] For both plots the first point of reference is Aptheker 1943, 174–6 and 180–1. Nearly a century later in Camden, South Carolina, a plot aiming to take place on 4 July 1816 was betrayed and seven rebels were condemned: on this see Glen Inabinet 1980.

[63] Mississippi: in Adams County an uncovered plot led to between twenty-seven and forty rebels being put to death; see Jordan 1993 and Behrend 2011. Louisiana: in 1731 in New Orleans a failed plot led to nine executions; see Aptheker 1943, 181–2. Point Coupée: in 1795 a plot was betrayed, leading to twenty-three executions and thirty-one floggings; see Holmes 1970; Dormon 1977; Hall 1992, 343–74.

[64] Rodriguez 1999b.

was, apparently, a baseless fear of widespread servile insurrection; New York was not alone in this respect.⁶⁵

In a few cases in addition to those above, the plots took place. New York State experienced several revolts in the eighteenth century AD. On 26 January 1708, two slaves murdered their master, his wife and their five children in Queens County, and four years later on 6 April in New York City a group of rebels killed nine white men and injured seven others. The latter revolt was suppressed within the day, and six of the rebels committed suicide, while twenty-one were executed.⁶⁶ Still in New York State, the residents of Albany experienced several slave plots that led to acts of arson, with the result in 1793 of the execution of three slaves.⁶⁷ The Cane River Insurrection of 1804 in Natchitoches Parish, Louisiana resulted in nine armed slaves running away to the neighbouring Spanish territory of Nacogdoches (modern Texas), but they were returned to their masters by the Spanish.⁶⁸ Finally, in St Mary's County, Maryland, 1817, a revolt of up to 200 rebels looted two homes, but was suppressed within a day, with the death of many rebels, but no white people.⁶⁹

These examples do not include individual acts of murder, nor is this brief survey intended to be comprehensive. Nonetheless, the revolts and plots outlined above do lend themselves to certain generalisations. In those cases where the revolts took place, they were generally small and short-lived, and this includes the five largest revolts with which we started. For example, the Stono Rebellion lasted less than a week and involved no more than 100 rebels, while the German Coast Uprising is one of the few revolts to involve more than 100 participants. Many revolts lasted less than a single day and involved a handful of rebels. More often the plots were betrayed or were perhaps imagined by the hysterical free population of a state. Kolchin argued that North American 'slave revolts' might, on the whole, be better termed 'disorder' than 'revolts' or 'insurrections', given their small scale and localised nature.⁷⁰ This is not to downplay the importance of these events, nor to suggest that these revolts are insignificant owing to their scale. Nevertheless, while the experience of the United States would suggest that slave revolts are short and rarely number above 100 participants – and that the definition provided by the state of Texas reflects reality – they were nonetheless a regular feature of US slavery. Despite all the risks, the obstacles stacked against them, and the likelihood of their failure and punishment, enslaved people in the USA fought against their enslavement often, asserting their freedom in the face of free opposition.

---

⁶⁵ On the New York 'plot': Davis 1985; Hoffer 2003; Lepore 2005. Note also the events related to Tom Cooper in North Carolina, a fugitive slave who inspired rumours of revolt in 1802 that resulted in the execution of fifteen slaves alleged to have plotted revolt with him, and Coot in Augusta, Georgia, an enslaved man who was executed amidst rumours of a plot in 1819. On Cooper, see Aptheker 1943, 231–2; on Coot, see Aptheker 1943, 263.
⁶⁶ See Scott 1961; Foote 1993; Rucker 2001.
⁶⁷ The first plot was discovered in July 1780. For consideration of these revolts in their larger context, see Berlin and Harris 2005.
⁶⁸ Graves 1996.
⁶⁹ Aptheker 1943, 262.
⁷⁰ Kolchin 1987, 252.

Slave Revolts in Brazil

Brazil had a long history of slave resistance, but it was not until the nineteenth century that this turned into a distinct history of revolt. Prior to this, Brazilian slave society featured a large number of long-lasting *quilombos* (also known as *mocambos*) – communities of absconded slaves – which were similar in nature to maroon societies in the Caribbean. Brazil's large frontier and extensive interior region encouraged resistance through flight, perhaps to the detriment of outright revolt. Some of these societies survived for prolonged periods of time, including the *quilombo* of Palmares, which was created in the early seventeenth century and only destroyed in 1695.[71] Nonetheless, in what follows the extensive resistance of the *quilombos* and *mocambos* in Brazil is not included. While the *quilombos* have been drawn on in the past to understand the Sicilian revolts, I have argued elsewhere that they are not a good point of comparison.[72] *Quilombos* sought to form polities out of formerly enslaved individuals, but they did so by withdrawal into hard-to-reach areas of Brazil, eschewing direct confrontation and surviving through negotiation and avoidance. The rebel strategy in both Sicilian revolts can be better characterised as attempts to control strategic locations and achieve logistical dominance, a strategy that included regular direct confrontation with the Roman authorities, rather than withdrawal into a distant interior.[73] Attention is given instead to the period of 1807 to 1835, during which time there was a concentration of slave insurrections.[74] These revolts, as we will see, display similar patterns to those found for the United States.[75]

Although Brazil's history of slave revolts is largely restricted to the period of 1807–35, there were some precursors to these revolts, notably foiled plots and rumours.[76] The record of revolt after 1800 was much more impressive, with regular revolts occurring for roughly thirty years. The first revolt of this period was a plot to capture several ships in the harbour of Salvador in Bahia and then to flee to Africa – this is how the plot is reported in the sources.[77] The plot was betrayed on 22 May 1807, and on 27 May the conspirators were seized, two of whom were executed

---

[71] On this aspect of Brazilian slave society, and Palmares in particular: Schwartz 1992, 103–36; Bergad 2007, 213–21; Klein and Luna 2010, 195–201.

[72] The classic examples of these comparisons can be found in Bradley 1989, xiv–xv and 123–6. For my argument against this comparison, see Morton 2014, 34 and *passim*.

[73] Morton 2014. On the possible efforts of rebels in Jamaica during Tacky's Revolt to control a 'commercial zone' in Jamaica, see Brown 2020, 139–40.

[74] For example, in 1838–41 the Balaiada Rebellion took place in Brazil. This rebellion concerned the governance of the province of Maranhão during an economic crisis, and the attempts by local *quilombos* to fight for slave freedom were extraneous to the main event. On this particular event see especially Santos 1983.

[75] The ensuing outline is derived from the following works: Schwartz 1986, 468–88; Reis 1993, 40–69; Postma 2008, 71–5; Akande 2016, 186–203. See also Diouf 2013, 210–50, for a recent overview of Brazil's history of slave revolts 1807–35.

[76] For the broader context of slavery in Brazil, see Schwartz 1986 and Klein and Luna 2010. In 1719 and 1756 there were rumours of plots that resulted in arrests: see Postma 2008, 72–3, and on 1756 specifically see Reis 1995–6. On 12 August 1798, revolutionary posters were placed across Salvador in Bahia; among those arrested for seditious activities were twelve enslaved blacks: Schwartz 1986, 476–7; Nishida 2003, 132–3.

[77] See Reis 1993, 42–3, for scepticism about the interpretation of the rebels' actions.

and eleven sentenced to lashings.[78] In 1809 an actual revolt took place at the town of Nazaré das Farinhas. There, on 5 January around 300 enslaved Africans attacked the town but were defeated in a battle on 7 January, with ninety-five rebels captured.[79] On 28 February 1814, roughly 250 enslaved Africans participated in an attack on fishing marinas and plantations in the Recôncavo that killed several slave owners, opposing slaves, and fourteen soldiers; fifty-eight rebels were killed.[80] A much more serious revolt took place in 1816. On 12 February African-born slaves in Santo Amaro and São Francisco do Conde burnt several plantations, attacked houses and killed slave owners. The revolt was suppressed within a day by a force of white militia and loyal slaves.[81] Up to 1816, therefore, revolts in Brazil can be characterised as regular, short-lived and including at the upper end 300 participants.

The next set of revolts of interest here took place just before or during the Brazilian War of Independence of 1822–3. The first was in May of 1822, when 280 enslaved Africans revolted on Itaparica Island against their master's plans to change their overseer. The rebels killed their master, but a local civilian militia suppressed the revolt, resulting in the loss of thirty-two rebels. In the same year in São Marcos both freedmen and African-born slaves attacked white residents and *mestiços*, but the revolt was ended quickly, with two rebels arrested. Finally, on 19 December almost 200 slaves attacked Brazilian soldiers stationed near Salvador. The soldiers repulsed the attack with some losses and executed fifty-two of the rebels whom they had captured.[82] A number of smaller conspiracies and revolts took place after the War of Independence, although there is not much recorded about them.[83] From 1827 to 1831 there was a wave of small-scale revolts in Bahia, including three in 1827 in Cachoeira, São Francisco do Conde and Abrantes, none of which included more than fifty rebels. In 1828, following a major revolt on 12 March in Itapuã, there were two small revolts in April about which very little is known. In the revolt in Itapuã over 100 African-born slaves attacked plantations and fishing marinas before they were defeated on the same day in a battle that left twenty rebels and eight soldiers dead. In Iguape in September of the same year nearly forty rebels attacked a number of plantations, killing slave owners and those slaves that resisted the revolt before they were defeated by local militia. Finally, in 1828, a revolt took place in the Santo Amaro district on 30 November. African-born slaves on an estate killed their overseer and some other

---

[78] For full discussion of this revolt: Schwartz 1986, 480; Reis 1993, 41–3; Conrad 1994, 398–400; Diouf 2013, 220–32; Akande 2016, 187.

[79] Schwartz 1986, 481–2; Reis 1993, 43–4; Gomez 2005, 102; Diouf 2013, 221; Akande 2016, 187.

[80] On 23 March of the same year a short-lived revolt took place in Iguape, Bahia, about which we know very little except that it lasted only a single day. On both revolts: Schwartz 1986, 482–3; Reis 1993, 44–9; Schwartz 1996; Diouf 2013, 221; Akande 2016, 188.

[81] Schwartz 1986, 483; Reis 1993, 49–50; Akande 2016, 189.

[82] For all three revolts of 1822: Schwartz 1986, 486; Reis 1993, 53–4; Akande 2016, 189.

[83] In Ilhéus, 1824, creole slaves on a plantation formed a *quilombo* after refusing to work. On 25 August 1826, a rebellion broke out in the Cachoeira district about which little is known. In the same year on 16 December a revolt started just outside Salvador in Cajazeiras, in the Pirajá district, which involved the Urubu *quilombo* and led to the death of several slave-hunters and a farming family; the revolt ended the next day with twelve African-born slaves and freedmen captured. On these events: Schwartz 1986, 486; Reis 1993, 55–8; Akande 2016, 189.

slaves, before a local militia ended the revolt on 1 December.[84] Two revolts struck Salvador itself in 1830. The first took place on 10 April and grew to over 100 rebels before they were defeated by the police and reinforcements, with more than fifty rebels beaten to death.[85] As with the revolts up to 1816, the revolts from 1822 to 1830 lasted no longer than a few days at most, frequently including up to a few hundred rebels, but they were a consistent phenomenon.

These revolts from 1807 to 1830 were all precursors to the largest revolt in Brazilian history, which took place on 25 January 1835. In a series of battles across Salvador at least 200 African-born slaves fought local militias, and by the end of the day seventy rebels and six white residents had been killed. A group of rebels attempted to meet enslaved people on the local plantations but were defeated by a cavalry regiment and scattered into the surrounding territory. In the immediate aftermath four more rebels were executed, sixteen put in prison, eight condemned to forced labour, forty-five to floggings, and several others deported. Although the reaction by the free segments of society lasted for some time, including more than 100 further executions, the revolt itself lasted less than a day.[86] Bahia was not alone in suffering from slave revolts. In 1832 a group of thirty-two rebels was arrested in the province of São Paulo for plotting to destroy sugar mills in Campinas, and in 1838, in the district of Vassouras, eighty slaves revolted on a large estate and were joined by several hundred more slaves from other estates before the National Guard defeated them.[87]

As should be clear from this overview, Brazil has an extensive history of slave revolts. Nonetheless, it is striking that once we exclude the resistance to slavery encapsulated by the *quilombos* and *mocambos* of the Brazilian hinterland, the pattern of slave revolts in Brazil bear similarities to the revolts in the United States in terms of longevity if not exactly size. There were commonly more rebels involved in the Brazilian revolts, with the revolts discussed above frequently including at least 100 slaves, but in each case they were short-lived and grew no further.[88] This may well be explained by the fact that many Brazilian revolts offered the possibility of flight to *quilombos* during the revolt, or even were intended to fulfil that ultimate aim, but it is still the case that Brazilian revolts are similarly short-lived as those in the United States.[89] The largest slave revolt in Brazilian history, which took place in 1835, involved a few hundred slaves and lasted but a day. Crucially, Brazil's experience shows that despite the odds stacked against enslaved people when they chose to revolt, they nonetheless did so regularly, asserting their freedom often in the face of violent suppression.

---

[84] There was another revolt on 16 October 1829, which destroyed one plantation and resulted in the death of three people: Schwartz 1986, 486–7; Reis 1993, 59–66; Akande 2016, 189–90.
[85] Schwartz 1986, 487; Reis 1993, 66–9; Diouf 2013, 222; Barcia 2014, 113; Akande 2016, 190.
[86] Detailed accounts of the revolt: Reis 1993, 73–136; Conrad 1994, 411–12 and 487; Diouf 2013, 222–6; Akande 2016, 191–204. For the revolt's aftermath: Reis 1993, 189–230; Soares and dos Santos Gomes 2001.
[87] For the 1832 revolt see Figueiredo Pirola 2005; for the 1838 revolt see dos Santos Gomes 1995.
[88] Barcia 2014, 159–60, recorded twenty-two 'Slave Movements' in Bahia between 1807 and 1835. Only six featured more than 100 participants, and all were short-lived.
[89] For the aims of Brazilian rebels: Reis 1993, 40–71; Schwartz 1996, 103–36; Klein and Luna 2010, 189–211.

Slave Revolts in the Caribbean

The intense concentration of slaves in the Caribbean islands, too, resulted in a distinct history of servile insurrection. Many of the revolts outlined below took place in the aftermath of the events in Haiti, to which we will turn at the end of this chapter, and were often inspired by the anticipation of emancipation.[90] Moreover, unlike in the United States and Brazil, the history of Caribbean servile insurrection is one of plots carried out, rather than plots betrayed or imagined. It is, therefore, much fuller than that for the regions considered so far, and in some cases involved larger numbers of rebels. Yet, in some crucial details, there are still considerable similarities.

Before we begin, it is once more important to note that the overview that follows is not intended to be exhaustive. The discussion includes the major revolts – which Geggus identifies as those revolts involving 'at least 1,000 slaves' – and a sample of smaller revolts, although the total listed cannot possibly account for all the small-scale revolts that struck the Caribbean, and many other examples are given in brief in the footnotes.[91] Geggus has compiled a list of 191 instances of revolt or conspiracy to revolt in the Americas as a whole in the period from 1776 to 1848 alone, and comments that 'the listing . . . should be understood as no more than a minimum tally'.[92] What follows is likewise 'no more than a minimum tally', and indeed is a deliberately selective tally intended to emphasise the maximum extent of revolts in the Caribbean. Finally, for the sake of brevity, the following outline focuses for the most part on the eighteenth and nineteenth centuries AD, and on the islands of Barbados, Cuba, Curaçao and Jamaica, although the examples provided could be repeated in their key points across other islands. These two centuries on these four islands represent the most intense periods of slave revolts in the Caribbean, offering a high-water mark for Caribbean revolts that was never exceeded except in Saint-Domingue.

As with the revolts of the United States, we begin this survey of the Caribbean by considering the largest revolts in the region's history: Tacky's revolt in Jamaica in 1760, the revolt in Barbados in 1816, the Demerara rebellion in Guyana in 1823, and the 'Baptist War' in Jamaica in 1831–2. These revolts represent the greatest extent of slave resistance – the revolution in Haiti left aside for the moment – and offer us a mark against which to consider the remaining revolts. We start in Jamaica, where a group of enslaved men, including two men named Tacky and Jamaica, started a revolt

---

[90] Craton 1979, 99–125, and 1980, 1–20; Genovese 1979, xviii–xxii and 82–125, have argued that from the nineteenth century there was a new period of slave revolts with a character different from those in the earlier period, in part inspired by the American, French and Haitian revolutions. Further: Geggus 2001, 109–16. and 2006, 297–314; García 2003, 34–9; Fischer 2004, 41–56. However, see Geggus 2011, 27–34, for a reconsideration of how much these revolutions influenced revolts in, e.g., the Caribbean, when local factors may be more important; further Geggus 1989, 109; Tardieu 2003, 101–11. See, e.g., Schwartz 1986, 468–88, for the argument that the French and Haitian revolutions did not influence the Bahian slave revolts from 1807 to 1835. Many studies of these revolts focus on the influence of recent Islamic African imports to Brazil, e.g., Diouf 2013; Barcia 2014; Akande 2016.

[91] Geggus 2011, 25. Craton 1982, 335–9, offers a chronology of seventy-five instances of slave conspiracies and resistance in the British Caribbean colonies from 1638 to 1837.

[92] Geggus 2011, 25.

on Easter Sunday, 7 April 1760, apparently pre-empting an island-wide revolt due to take place six weeks later that Brown has termed a Coromantee War.[93] After they had seized munitions from a local storeroom in Port Mary, killing the storekeeper in the process, approximately 150 rebels marched on to local plantations, where they killed the overseers and those white inhabitants they found in residence. A skirmish with local militia at Heywood Hall dispersed the initial rebellion, with Tacky and Jamaica killed in a battle on 14 April, but several other, more significant revolts under the leadership of others, including Wager, took place in other parishes in May and June. In Westmoreland in particular the rebels successfully defeated a local militia, with the result that the rebels' forces increased to over 1,000 in total. On 2 June in a major skirmish the rebels in Westmoreland were defeated by soldiers from the Forty-Ninth Regiment and local militia. The unrest continued into 1761, but the major battles all took place within the first few months of the conflict. In October 1761 the governor of Jamaica declared the end of the rebellion. In total around 400 enslaved blacks, sixty free blacks and sixty white residents died in the revolt, although the revolt continued to inspire other rebels across the Caribbean.[94]

Bussa's revolt in Barbados was considerably shorter than the Coromantee War in Jamaica just discussed, but was nonetheless one of the largest in Caribbean history. The revolt began at around 8 p.m. on Sunday, 14 April 1816. The revolt started with a series of fires set on plantations in St. Philip's parish, and quickly spread to around seventy plantations across the parish and in neighbouring parishes. Martial law was declared early the next morning, and on the morning of 16 April a unit of free black troops defeated the main rebel force at Bailey's plantation and more or less ended the revolt. The revolt itself caused extensive property damage, but only one white civilian and one black soldier were killed in the fighting; by contrast, fifty rebels were killed and at least seventy were summarily executed. A further 144 rebels were tried and sentenced to death, and hundreds more were deported. The revolt itself involved several thousand rebels, with estimates ranging up to 5,000 in total. While the revolt was suppressed by 17 April, martial law remained in the colony until 12 July; this was the largest slave revolt in Barbadian history.[95]

The final two of the major revolts in the Caribbean were significantly larger than either the Coromantee War in Jamaica or Bussa's revolt, although not necessarily any longer. The second largest took place in Demerara or Guyana and involved more than 10,000 rebels. The colony had an enslaved African to free white ratio of 20:1, and this is reflected to some extent in the size of the revolt itself in raw numbers. The revolt arose out of tensions caused by limitations placed on enslaved access to church services on Sundays and servile agitation for emancipation. The rebels aimed to disarm the white residents and gain concessions from them, rather than kill them. The governor met with a group of rebels at a bridge near Felicity plantation on 18 August. After failing to convince them to disarm, the governor returned to

---

[93] On the initial revolt, see Brown 2020, 140. On the Coromantee War, see Brown 2020, 164–207.
[94] The classic account of this revolt can be found in Craton 1982, 125–39, although see now Brown 2020, 129–207. See also Burnard 2004, 170–4; Paton 2012; Hanserd 2019, 128–40.
[95] The principal accounts are those of Craton 1982, 254–66, and Beckles 1984.

Georgetown and ordered a mobilisation and martial law the following morning. Militia and regular soldiers marched on the rebels on 19 August and found that nearly all the 12,000 enslaved people on the East Coast were in revolt. The main engagement took place on 20 August, when a group of 2,000 rebels fought around 300 soldiers at Adventure plantation. After a parley the rebels were scattered by gunfire, and between 100 and 150 were killed. A further fifty-eight rebels were summarily executed in the suppression, and perhaps as many as 250 enslaved people were killed in the suppression and trials in response to the death of three white residents.[96]

The final major revolt in the Caribbean was in 1831, again in Jamaica, known as the Baptist War. This massive revolt started on 27 December and included somewhere between 18,000 and 60,000 rebels. The revolt started on Kensington estate, inspired by rumours of emancipation and encouragement to strike by the preacher Sam Sharpe. The aim may have been only to refuse to work until concessions were made, but in the end the rebels burned many estates and fought an engagement with a regiment posted nearby on 29 December in which over twenty-five rebels were killed. The revolt itself was contained in the north-west of Jamaica, and while the Eighty-Fourth Regiment could not bring the rebels to direct engagement, it did gradually reduce rebel control over the north-western parishes to the extent that martial law was lifted on 1 February 1832. Roughly 200 rebels died in the fighting, and a further 340 more died through summary execution during the revolt itself. In the aftermath hundreds more rebels were condemned in military and civil trials.[97]

These four revolts represent the greatest extent of Caribbean revolts, excluding the already briefly noted Haitian Revolution, to which we will turn below. In two out of the four cases above, the revolt itself lasted only a few days despite the enormous scale of the revolts and rebel access to firearms. It is only in the case of Jamaica that the revolts lasted longer than a few days, and this is not entirely surprising. Owing to the island's peculiar geography, including extensive mountain areas, dense forests, and the Cockpit Country in the island's centre, it had a long history of successful marronage. This history included the conclusion of a peace treaty between the British forces and the maroons led by Cudjoe in February 1739 on the condition that Cudjoe's forces return runaway slaves to their owners, the first in a line of treaties between communities of escaped slaves and the colonial government.[98] On an island well suited to withdrawal and the avoidance of conflict, it is not entirely surprising that revolts could last longer. Nevertheless, it is worth stressing that the longest lasted at most a few months.

These, then, were the largest revolts in Caribbean history, but they were not necessarily typical of resistance in this region. This is best illustrated by considering four islands in particular – Barbados, Cuba, Curaçao, Jamaica – in more detail. We start with Barbados. Before Bussa's revolt in 1816, the island had experienced six other instances of slave plots or revolts, the majority of which were betrayed before they

---

[96] Accounts can be found in Craton 1982, 267–90, and da Costa 1994.
[97] On this revolt: Reckord 1969; Patterson 1975, 192–220; Craton 1982, 291–321; Hart 1985, 221–73; Heuman 1996.
[98] On the history of these maroon communities, see Craton 1982, 67–96 and 211–23.

could take place (1649; 1675; 1683; 1686; 1692; 1701). After the largest plot, in 1675, forty-two enslaved people were condemned to death. A major plot was discovered in 1692 to seize arms and gunpower from Needham's Fort; several dozen rebels were implicated. Finally, in 1701 a plot to attack Bridgetown and seize forts was discovered and suppressed before it began.[99]

Cuba, likewise, had a history of plots and revolts. The focus here will be on the revolts after the advent of large-scale importation of enslaved Africans that took place from 1790 onwards owing to the rapid expansion of sugar and coffee plantations in the island's west.[100] For many of the rebellions we have very little information, but what is known indicates that they were generally small-scale and short-lived. From 1790 to 1796 there were a series of four revolts or conspiracies that involved fifteen enslaved Africans at most. The year of 1798 saw widespread revolt and conspiracies that resulted in two enslaved people being hanged in Trinidad and involved at least fifty-three slaves across five regions of Cuba.[101] There were four more conspiracies from 1802 to 1806 that were followed by one of the largest outbreaks of slave conspiracies to take place in Cuba in this period, in 1812.[102] These conspiracies and revolts are known collectively as the Aponte conspiracy. The plot's aim was to create an anti-Spanish rebellion that would establish an independent Cuba and the abolition of slavery on the island, inspired in part by the revolution on Haiti; most of the leadership of the revolt were free blacks, including Aponte himself.[103] Uprisings in Havana and Bayanmo were betrayed, and in March 1812 revolts on two plantations failed for lack of support. The month before, eight rebels were hanged and seventy-three whipped after a revolt took place in Puerto Príncipe. A total of thirty-four rebels were put to death as a response to the unrest.[104]

A series of four small plots or conspiracies followed between 1817 and 1822, before a major revolt struck the Guamacaro district of Matanzas in 1825. This revolt took place across twenty estates and involved 500 slaves, largely African-born, who destroyed farms and crops and killed several white residents in the area before fleeing into the countryside. The same area was struck ten years later by a revolt across three plantations that involved 130 African-born slaves, which was suppressed by local militia.[105] A much

---

[99] For all the above, see Craton 1982, 105–14, who presents the evidence and describes the events in more detail.

[100] For data on the importation of slaves into Cuba, see Eltis 1987, 245. On the changes to Cuban slave populations by region, see Bergad 2007, 124–5 and 130–1.

[101] See Barcia 2008, 30–1. The revolts and conspiracies took place in Puerto Príncipe, Trinidad, Guines, Mariel and Santa Cruz.

[102] See Bergad 2007, 205–6; Barcia 2008, 30; Geggus 2011, 41–4.

[103] For a striking account of this revolt in the context of the age of revolution after the establishment of Haiti, and the role of a 'glorious black history' as inspiration for efforts to create a new, Black world on Cuba, see Ferrer 2014, 271–328, and 324 for the quotation.

[104] For full consideration of this period of unrest, see now Childs 2006, esp. 120–54, and Ferrer 2014, 271–328. It has also been studied in Franco 1963 and Howard 1998, 73–9.

[105] For both revolts see Bergad 2007, 209. For the revolt in 1825 see Barcia 2008, 34–5. Between these two events there were a series of small plots and conspiracies: 1826, a revolt on a single plantation; 1827, a revolt of fifty-seven slaves on the Tentativa coffee plantation; 1828, a revolt on a single plantation; 1830, a revolt in Guamacaro on a single plantation; 1831, a revolt on a single plantation. For details and bibliography: Barcia 2008, 36–7; Geggus 2011, 46–7.

larger revolt involving 330 African-born slaves struck Cafetal Salvador in Guanajay in August of 1833; fifty-three rebels were killed.[106] From 1835 to 1842 there were ten revolts across Cuba, involving at most sixty slaves, again mostly African-born.[107] These led up to the largest revolt to strike Matanzas, which started on 27 March 1843, in which 465 African-born slaves destroyed sugar planations until soldiers from Havana suppressed the revolt on 28 March, killing 128 rebels.[108] The state response to these events was to investigate slave conspiracies across Cuba, resulting in the conspiracy of *La Escalera*. Early in 1844 the Spanish military investigated rumours of conspiracies linked to British abolitionists, with the result that over 1,800 African-born slaves and free blacks were arrested and punished.[109]

The widespread repression in 1844 more or less ended open slave resistance in Cuba until the Ten Years' War of 1868–78, which attempted to create an independent Cuba. The island's history of slave revolts is striking in terms of intensity. That said, it is important to note that the largest revolts featured hundreds, not thousands of rebels, and that the majority of the revolts were suppressed either before they could take place or within a few days.[110] As with Barbados, therefore, the typical pattern is not one of massive revolts, but of consistent resistance. We should emphasise this latter detail: despite difficulty accessing firearms and the likelihood of violent suppression, African-born slaves in Cuba regularly turned to violent resistance, as was the case in Barbados.

Curaçao's history of slave revolts is not extensive, but it too is worth noting for its intensity. The island was struck by only one major revolt in its history, but this revolt was preceded by a number of minor revolts in the eighteenth century. The earliest known revolt took place in 1716, involved twelve rebels, and was ended quickly.[111] The revolt in 1750 involved 100 enslaved people and was suppressed within a day; 59 rebels were killed.[112] The last of the island's early revolts took place on 17 August 1774, on De Fuijk's plantation, when seventy-two enslaved people attempted to escape to Coro, Venezuela. The island's major revolt took place on 17 August 1795, on De Knip's plantation. There, around fifty plantation workers went on strike, which

---

[106] For a full consideration of this revolt see Iduate 1982, as well as Barcia 2008, 37, and 2014, 113.

[107] July 1835: revolt on one estate, with one white resident death and eleven rebel suicides; June 1837: revolt on La Sonora estate, three African-born slaves executed; 1838: two revolts, both in Trinidad, the first including fifty-two creole and African-born slaves, of which twelve were shot, the second including one white resident death and five African-born slaves executed; 1839: two revolts in Matanzas across several plantations; 1840: two revolts, one on the Delgado estate of ten African-born slaves, of which three were executed, and one on the Empresa plantation of thirty African-born slaves who killed two white people; 1841: revolt of nineteen African-born slaves in Havana, of which six were killed; 1842: a revolt on La Arratía estate, involving forty-two African-born slaves, of which five were executed. Details are in Barcia 2008, 25–31 and 38–40; Geggus 2011, 47–8; Barcia 2014, 163–4.

[108] Bergad 2007, 210, and Barcia 2008, 40–1. Two further revolts took place in Matanzas in the same year, in which sixty-six and seventeen rebels were killed respectively.

[109] For full discussion of *La Escalera*, see Paquette 1988.

[110] Barcia 2014, 161–5, offers a list of 'Slave Movements' in Cuba between 1798 and 1844, recording a total of sixty-six revolts, of which only three had more than 100 participants.

[111] On this revolt, see Jordaan 1999, 490–8.

[112] See Hartog 1973, 20–57; De Hoog 1983, 38–44 and 61–3; Goslinga 1985, 546.

quickly escalated into an attempted island-wide revolt. Within two days nearly 2,000 enslaved people were in revolt; but while they were successful in the early engagements with the local militias, it did not last. The revolt was suppressed soon after by colonial soldiers, and many rebels were summarily executed. The majority surrendered on the promise of amnesty, while the remaining rebels were captured and a further thirty were executed. The revolt ended before the close of September 1795.[113] Curaçao's history of slave resistance, therefore, follows the pattern of Barbados and Cuba of regular, short revolts usually numbering in the hundreds or fewer; the 1795 revolt is an outlier in terms of size, but not longevity.

Jamaica, like Cuba, has a long and complex history of slave resistance and revolt. The earliest revolt that was not connected to the prolonged Spanish resistance to the British takeover of Jamaica in 1655 occurred in 1673.[114] This revolt took place on Lobby's plantation in St. Ann's parish, in which 200 slaves rebelled, killed twelve white people, seized arms and absconded into the mountains.[115] Around 150 enslaved Africans seized arms and rebelled in 1685, killing eleven white residents, and evading capture in the mountains for several months. In March 1686 a further 105 slaves rebelled at Madam Guy's plantation, where they killed fifteen white plantation owners. This revolt was suppressed within three weeks, and over 200 rebels were killed.[116] An even larger revolt took place exactly five years later when 500 rebelled on Sutton's estate, killing the estate's caretaker. Despite the considerable size of the rebel force, and their access to pieces of artillery, the rebels were defeated the following day by local militia and fled into the woods. They were pursued for the next month; around 200 surrendered voluntarily in August.[117] Finally, there was one failed revolt on a single estate and one plot in 1742 and 1745 respectively.[118] In the period leading up to the Coromantee War in 1760, therefore, Jamaica had a history of consistent revolts that featured hundreds of rebels, and that were suppressed in most cases within a few days.

The period following the Coromantee War was no different. Five years after the major uprising in 1760 there were two small revolts in 1765 and 1766, the first of which was on a single estate, and the latter involved thirty-three rebels that killed or wounded nineteen white people. Both revolts were suppressed quickly, but appear to have been connected to the Coromantee War.[119] A major plot was then uncovered in 1776, referred to as the Hanover Plot. The insurrection was planned to take place on 22 July, but was revealed a week before. The local militia arrested forty-eight leaders, and six were executed within two days. Further investigation discovered that the plot

---

[113] For full consideration of this revolt, see Hartog 1973; Paula 1974; Goslinga 1990, 1–20; Do Rego and Janga 2009; Oostindie 2011.
[114] For the protracted Spanish resistance, taking as its main form a series of maroons that fought against the British forces after their landing in 1655, see Craton 1982, 61–74.
[115] In 1678 an uncertain number of rebels on Captain Duck's plantation killed his wife and several other white residents before they were suppressed. Around thirty rebels escaped, while at least twenty were executed; on this revolt see Dunn 2012, 260.
[116] Dunn 2012, 260–1.
[117] Craton 1982, 76–7. At least another 200 rebels remained at large as maroons.
[118] In addition to Craton 1982, 92 and 125, see Schuler 1970, 14.
[119] On this connection, see Brown 2020, 219–34.

extended to forty-three estates in the Hanover parish, with the aim of seizing the town of Lucea and then raising the enslaved people in the local parishes. A total of thirty plotters were executed.[120] Between the Hanover Plot and the Baptist War of 1831–2 there were a series of minor plots that were largely limited to single estates.[121]

If we leave aside the four massive revolts that we started with and focus instead on the longer history of revolt in Barbados, Cuba, Curaçao and Jamaica, it is evident that in terms of size and longevity revolts were more often short – lasting less than a week, or at most a few months – and regularly involved not more than a few hundred participants. While revolts could number in the thousands, as in Demerara and in Jamaica, and some of the foiled plots clearly anticipated widespread support of this kind, the revolts that were realised were significantly smaller.[122] This same pattern can be found across the Caribbean, as Geggus' compilation of roughly 191 revolts demonstrates.[123] This trend represents a slight increase in size when compared to the United States, but it fits the general pattern noted for Brazil. To restate this once again, from the examples outlined above it would seem that a 'typical' slave revolt in these New World areas was one that involved at most a few hundred participants – sometimes extending into the thousands in a few cases in the Caribbean – and that was suppressed within weeks, if not days.[124] In the difficult terrain of South America, or in the isolated and mountainous terrain of certain Caribbean islands, slave revolts lasted longer, but even then revolts were exceptional if they lasted more than a month. Moreover, it is truly striking that the 1823 revolt in Demerara and the 1831 revolt in Jamaica were both ended within a month, despite the fact that they were the two largest Caribbean revolts to take place on islands with extraordinarily large populations of enslaved people, excepting the Haitian Revolution. Even so, what is also evident from this overview is that despite the overwhelming likelihood that any given revolt or plot would fail, most often within a day or a week, every region here studied shows evidence of consistent servile unrest: our 'typical' slave revolts happened often and in all kinds of circumstances, a fact that speaks volumes concerning the bravery and determination of these peoples. We will return to this point below, but first let us turn to one further point of methodology.

---

[120] See Sheridan 1976; further Craton 1982, 172–9.

[121] In 1806, one rebel was executed; in 1809, two rebels were executed; in 1815, 250 rebels were implicated but only one was hanged; in 1823, twelve rebels were executed; and in 1824, six rebels were hanged. On all these, see Craton 1982, 293–4.

[122] Geggus 2011, 25, has noted that in the West Indies and Guianas there were, including the revolt in Saint-Domingue, eight or nine rebellions that involved at least 1,000 participants.

[123] Out of a total of 191 revolts recorded across the Americas from 1776 to 1848, Geggus 2011, 40–9, records only thirty-two (16.75 per cent) that included more than 100 participants, and this total includes the Haitian Revolution. As we saw above, Garcia 2014, 161–5, records only three out of sixty-six revolts in Cuba from 1798 to 1844 that involved more than 100 participants (4.54 per cent).

[124] Genovese 1979, 8, remarks in relation to the inspiration for the great revolts of the United States: 'General risings of thousands, such as those in Jamaica, Demerara, and Saint-Domingue, or even of hundreds such as those in many countries, remained a possibility, which, however slim, rendered the hopes of a Gabriel Prosser, a Denmark Vesey, or a Nat Turner rational.' The important point here is that these revolts 'remained a possibility . . . however slim'. That these revolts took place is undeniable, but they were the exception, not the rule.

The Evidence

The history of servile resistance in well-documented modern societies demonstrates why the definitions of slave revolts we started with above have a numerical requirement of at least three involved slaves: without this low starting point many plots and revolts would not count, impoverishing our understanding of group resistance to slavery in these societies. The underlying reason for the modern definitions of slave revolts that start from an assumption of three or more insurgents is, to put it simply, because historians of modern slavery can find revolts of that scale in the evidence that survives, and that therefore the consistent nature of servile unrest can be documented much more fully and the depth of resistance to enslavement revealed in some good detail. A few examples will demonstrate this, one from each region explored above.

Nat Turner's revolt is exceedingly well documented, and this is the result of some unique documents that survived the revolt. First among these is *The Confessions of Nat Turner*, a text published in 1831 that was T. R. Gray's record of the 'confession' of Nat Turner himself while he was in jail in Jerusalem, Virginia.[125] The *Confessions* include precise details of the conspiracy's development before its eruption on 21 August, as well as Turner's motivation for instigating the revolt. Further details of the revolt's suppression are recorded in a number of newspapers from the period, including the Richmond *Enquirer* and *Whig*, the New York *Atlas* and *Evening Post*, and the Huntsville, Alabama *Southern Advocate*. The aftermath of the revolt is also well documented, including the trial transcripts from two different Virginia counties – Southampton County and Sussex County – and letters to and from the governors of both Virginia and North Carolina.[126] The complex patchwork of sources, not all obviously equal in quality, allows a detailed picture of the revolt to emerge down to its impact on individual planters in the area. Importantly, this level of detail is not peculiar to Turner's revolt. For example, the short-lived insurrection in St. Mary's County, Maryland, in 1817, that involved up to 200 rebels looting homes is recorded in an article in the New York *Evening Post* on 21 April 1817, while the revolt that took place in 1708 in Queens County, which involved a small conspiracy of four enslaved people that resulted in the deaths of a slave-owning family, is recorded in a letter to the Board of Trade by Governor Cornbury and a notice in the *Boston Weekly Newsletter* published on 26 January 1708.[127]

The same kinds of documents underpin accounts of the revolts in Brazil and the Caribbean discussed above. The Bahian revolt of 1835, for example, is recorded in the Bahian state archives and includes testimony from the rebels themselves and transcripts from their trials, as well as letters between Brazilian government officials and between the British Consul and the Duke of Wellington.[128] The smaller revolts that preceded the major uprising of 1835, such as the failed attack on Nazaré das Farinhas in 1808, are,

---

[125] Gray 1831, and see also Aptheker 1943, 295 n. 8.
[126] For full references to the documents for this revolt, see Aptheker 1943, 293–305. For further bibliography, see n. 53 above.
[127] For St. Mary's County see Aptheker 1943, 262 n. 45; for Queens County see Aptheker 1943, 169 n. 24, and O'Callaghan 1855, 39.
[128] For full discussion of the documentation for this revolt and the classic reconstruction of the events, see especially Reis 1993, 73–92.

likewise, recorded in state archives and private correspondences.[129] The Coromantee War in Jamaica is chronicled in a range of evidence, but the two principal accounts are Long's *The History of Jamaica*, published in 1774, and Edward's *History of the West Indies*, published in 1794. Each man had close connections to individuals involved in suppressing the revolt, and their histories are informed by these connections. These two histories can be supplemented by documentary evidence including letters from Jamaica's governor, Sir Henry Moore, such as those to the Board of Trade during the revolt, the minutes of the Jamaican Council, and the journal entries of a plantation owner called Thomas Thistlewood, well-known otherwise for his repeated sexual abuse of enslaved women.[130] The 1776 plot in Hanover parish, Jamaica, is recorded only in court documents from the tribunal set up to try the plotters – preserved in the Colonial Office files – or in the correspondence between planters, governors and those involved in investigating the plot.[131] In each of the cases above we rely upon official government archives and the survival of contemporary letters to reconstruct the events – documentary evidence of diverse types.

In addition, the better-documented revolts, such as that of Nat Turner or the Bahian revolt of 1835, are reconstructed with a level of detail that is impossible to achieve for any event in the ancient world, even allowing for the problematic nature of the evidence itself, representing as it does a largely, or in some cases entirely, slave-owner perspective on these events.[132] The smaller revolts, such as those that took place in Queens County in 1708, or the almost annual revolts in Bahia between 1807 and 1835, or the outburst of violence in Jamaica in the eighteenth century, are preserved in the historical record only because the quantity and detail of evidence from New World slavery is so vast. The historian of modern slavery is able to construct a picture of slave revolts in the Americas that can take as a starting point conspiracies by as few as three rebels because the evidence exists to uncover these events, even conspiracies that were betrayed before they took place. While the point may seem prosaic, it is worth remembering that few, if any, of the events discussed above in the United States, Brazil or the Caribbean would have attracted the attention of our ancient sources unless they were germane to some other topic of interest: except in peculiar circumstances, the ancient writers would have ignored them, however ubiquitous these may have been.[133]

The Sicilian Revolts in the Global Context

It is useful at this point to restate why the above survey is necessary. As we saw in Chapter 4, ancient accounts of slave revolts are not useful guides to what the respective events were, or what we might typically expect a slave revolt in antiquity

---

[129] See Reis 1993, 40–69.
[130] See Craton 1982, 125–39, and especially 130 n. 10, for discussion of the revolt and the evidence for it. On Thistlewood, his diary and sexual activity recorded therein, see Walvin 2008.
[131] Craton 1982, 172–9, gives a full discussion of the revolt, including references to the evidence.
[132] See above at n. 59 for references to the debate concerning the reliability of even court documents for our reconstructions of modern slave revolts, focused in this case on Vesey's conspiracy.
[133] As we saw in Chapter 4, slave revolts were mentioned rarely in ancient literature, and then often to explore something unrelated to servile insurrection.

to be. These accounts are too dedicated to the reuse of historiographical models or *topoi* to be analytically useful, telling us much more about how ancient slave owners thought with slavery and servile insurrection than what slave resistance may have been like in reality. In order to create a definition of what we might call a 'typical' slave revolt to compare to the two Sicilian revolts, it is necessary to turn to slave revolts within slave systems in a period of history that is better evidenced, in this case the history of the United States, Brazil and the Caribbean during the sixteenth to nineteenth centuries AD, to suggest a pattern of rebellious behaviour against which we might compare (and contrast) the ancient evidence. As we have seen, what emerges is that slave revolts in these areas usually lasted a few days, sometimes as much as weeks, involved at most a few hundred rebels, and above all were a regular feature of these various slave systems.

As is self-evident, our Sicilian revolts do not fit the definition arrived at above, at least on those details that can be directly compared: duration and size. The events in Sicily discussed in this book encompassed greater numbers of combatants than any revolt surveyed above and outlasted even the longest Caribbean revolts by a significant order of magnitude.[134] If the definition holds any use as a guide to what we might expect as a 'typical' slave revolt in antiquity, then the two Sicilian revolts are, at the very least, not indicative of what such resistance typically looked like. To be sure, the longevity and scale of the Sicilian events may be explained by the absence of firearms among slave owners in antiquity, but as we have also seen above, even in instances in which rebels did have access to firearms, and in one case even artillery, and in situations in which the enslaved to free ratio was markedly higher than those assumed even at the height of slavery in the Roman Republican period, the revolts nonetheless ended quickly in comparison to the revolts in Sicily.[135]

This point of comparison highlights another striking observation in relation to the Sicilian revolts: they stand out in antiquity as some of the few supposed slave revolts to have been recorded at all, a mere handful in all recorded history in antiquity. Yet, as already suggested in passing, if it is correct that access to firearms amongst slave owners was an important element in their ability to suppress slave revolts in the modern world, we might expect the absence of firearms in antiquity to result in more regular resistance at the group level, albeit often suppressed within days or weeks, as in the modern world. This expectation is impossible to prove because, as I have argued above, the level of detail necessary in our evidence is unattainable for antiquity. This is in large part because the kind of small-scale, regular revolts and plots we have explored for the modern world would rarely, if ever, intrude into the world of slave-owner literature that survives from antiquity. That the Sicilian revolts *do* intrude is in large part because they transcended the remit of the small-scale servile revolt, providing

---

[134] It is worth remembering here that Geggus 2011, 25, comments that including the Haitian Revolution there were only eight or nine rebellions that involved at least 1,000 enslaved people in the entire Americas from 1776 to 1848.

[135] Estimates of the enslaved to free ratio in Roman Italy vary widely, but even the highest estimates put the figure at most at 1:1, and more usually estimate at something like 1:2 or 1:3: in all cases the estimates put the ratio far below those we have seen above for Jamaica and the other Caribbean islands. For discussion of the enslaved and free populations of Italy, see Scheidel 2005 and 2011.

much material for the stylus of the ancient historiographer to explore multiple issues through the lens of the broader-based struggles I have described in the remainder of this book. It is a great loss to modern studies of ancient slavery that the fine-grained study of slave revolt is impossible to achieve in the same way as can be done for the United States, Brazil and the Caribbean, and that we cannot prove that enslaved people in the ancient world resisted their enslavement as often as did those enslaved in the New World or study their resistance for what it meant to them, as has also been done fruitfully for the modern world.[136] As should also be clear by now, we should not assume that the Sicilian revolts can fill this gap. Nonetheless, the evidence from the modern world discussed so far strongly implies that enslaved people in the ancient world resisted their enslavement often, vigorously and bravely in face of challenging odds, at a scale that seldom attracts the attention of those who created what historical records we have of the period.[137]

The Haitian Revolution

The two Sicilian revolts, therefore, must not be taken as indicative of slave revolts in antiquity, at least not if we accept the definition of a slave revolt arrived at above. Their extraordinary scale in comparison to such revolts in more recent slaving cultures means that including them within the category of slave revolts, as defined here, would render the definition essentially meaningless: they are so different in terms of size and length that this makes comparison impossible except perhaps at their very beginnings, about which, as we have seen in Chapters 2 and 3, we know very little. In short, their exceptional nature means that we must try to explain them on their own terms, as I have attempted to do throughout this book. The need to explain exceptional events in antiquity such as the Sicilian revolts on their own terms and within their own contexts corresponds to a similar need that drives much of the analysis for the only revolt set into a context of slavery of comparable length and size in the Caribbean and Americas. This insurrection took place in the French colony of Saint-Domingue between 21 August 1791 and 1 January 1804, and ended with the declaration of the free republic of the Haitian people.[138]

This conflict, better known as the Haitian Revolution, stands apart from other slave revolts of the Caribbean and the Americas in terms of size, duration and most of all result.[139] The conflict lasted for over ten years, and involved hundreds of thousands of French, British and Spanish colonial forces aligned both alongside and against the

---

[136] See especially Barcia 2014; Hanserd 2019; Brown 2020.
[137] See, e.g., Hunt 2018, 166, who notes that the 'small revolts' of antiquity most likely never made it 'into the historical record at all', although he does not define 'small revolts'. See also Urbainczyk 2008a, 6–7, who notes that the short-lived nature of many modern slave revolts means that it would be (?) 'extremely likely that [they] would not be recorded in any of the texts that we have left'.
[138] This same drive has been followed profitably for many other revolts, including the Coromantee War, revolts in Brazil and those in Cuba: see, e.g., Barcia 2014; Ferrer 2014; Hanserd 2019; Brown 2020.
[139] The bibliography on the Haitian Revolution is vast, and what follows is only indicative: James 1963; Geggus 1982; Fick 1990; Trouillot 1995; Geggus 2002; Dubois 2004; Dubois and Garrigus 2006; Fiering and Geggus 2008; Jenson 2011; Girard 2016.

rebellious enslaved and free blacks. Total casualties, likewise, numbered into the hundreds of thousands amongst both the colonial forces and the residents of the new state itself. The initial stages of the revolt in the North Province of Saint-Domingue were aided, in part, by the reluctance of the French authorities on Saint-Domingue to inform France of the revolt, a result of the decision on 15 May 1791 in France to grant rights to some free blacks, as well as a separate insurrection of free blacks in the island's West Province, who demanded political equality with the white residents.[140] In addition, the Spanish residents of Santo Domingo sold arms and supplies to the rebels.[141] The revolt persisted against a backdrop of political and ideological debate about the place and status of black people in revolutionary France that influenced the allegiances and decisions of those involved, including white plantation owners, free blacks, metropolitan French, the black rebels and other European powers. Strikingly, the first (limited) proclamation of emancipation on the island, on 20 June 1793, took place because of infighting between rival commanders of the French forces on the island.[142] These debates extended to the National Convention in France itself, where in 1794 a delegation from Saint-Domingue, including two black men, Jean-Baptiste Belley and Jean-Baptiste Mills, played a role in the abolition of slavery in French colonies, a decree issued on 4 February.[143] Indeed, by 1795 France recognised that French control of Saint-Domingue relied on the leadership of the rebellion's commanders, and many, including Toussaint Louverture, were elevated to the rank of general.[144] Much of the revolution's impetus came from the changing politics in France itself, not least the French decision to invade Saint-Domingue in 1802 to reassert French power on the island and suppress Toussaint's authority.[145] The final conflict on the island that led to the declaration of the island's independence as Haiti came about directly from metropolitan France's desire in 1802 to reimpose slavery and recover the island as a slave colony.[146]

As the above overview highlights, the conflict on Haiti was intimately bound up in the developments of the French Revolution and the international conflicts that arose from and framed it. The revolutionary context is an essential part of attempts to understand the Haitian revolt. Moreover, this revolt ended with the creation of a free republic governed by and for the black population of Haiti, both those born free and those who seized their freedom. The attempt by people subjected to slavery to create a state that stands for their benefit – whether or not it stands against slavery *per se* – is not unique in the history of slave revolts, as we have seen above not least in Cuba during the Aponte conspiracy. Nonetheless, the Haitian Revolution is unusual in two respects.[147] First, the state survived, in one form or another, and successfully defended

---

[140] On the revolt in the West Province, see Dubois 2004, 119–22.
[141] Dubois 2004, 107–8 and 108, n. 33 for references.
[142] Dubois 2004, 157–9; Girard 2016, 134–5. This limited proclamation was followed by a full proclamation of emancipation issued by the French commissioner Sonthonax, on 29 August 1793, albeit one that included a number of restrictions on the actions of the newly freed.
[143] Dubois 2004, 169–70.
[144] Dubois 2004, 196–7; Girard 2016, 147–8.
[145] Dubois 2004, 251–71; Girard 2016, 231–5.
[146] Dubois 2004, 284–97; Girard 2016, 248–9.
[147] On the Aponte conspiracy, see Ferrer 2014, 271–328.

itself against external attempts to destroy it and reinstate the pre-revolutionary social conditions. Second, the leaders of this state, first Toussaint Louverture and then Jean-Jacques Dessalines, produced literature and proclamations that have survived to the modern era that chart how they presented their new republic to external audiences in both its nascent and fully formed conditions. As Jenson has recently shown in her study of the Haitian literary tradition during and after the revolution, when we approach the Haitian Revolution from the literature of its leaders, it is presented to contemporary audiences as a manifestation of the ideals and values of the French and American revolutions within France's colonial territories, not as a slave revolt.[148] For those at the head of this grand 'slave revolt', it was inexplicable without the peculiar and specific context of Saint-Domingue's history with slavery, the French Revolution and the Declarations of the Rights of Man, and it could be explained as and presented as part of Europe's enlightenment and the wider historical developments that led to the American and French revolutions.[149] Most of all, these leaders attempted to communicate with those on the outside of the revolution on their terms, albeit reconfigured in some respects to suit the immediate needs of the incipient nation state.[150] The Haitian Revolution, therefore, constitutes a powerful prompt to avoid historiographic reductionism in the modern attempt to write the history of revolts that involved enslaved people.

Conclusion

Revolution in Haiti, plainly, requires explication in its immediate historical and cultural context, including those contexts that were primarily focused on the lot of free people, no less than the Sicilian revolts that have been the topic of the present study. The rebels' self-presentation discussed in Chapters 1 and 3 is not as eloquently or as clearly presented as the outward projection of the Haitian revolution by its leaders; this cannot be denied. Nonetheless, much like the later Haitian leaders, the rebels in each of the two Sicilian conflicts drew on cultural ideas and political systems prevalent in their contemporary and immediate geographical environment in a manner that fits the Haitian paradigm better than that of the Caribbean and American slave revolts discussed above. The coinage of King Antiochus in particular demonstrates further that the rebels actively communicated with the (regional) population at large, unlike in cases clearly identified above as slave revolts.[151] In sum, when considered in the global context, the Sicilian revolts do not conform to the features that have been established as typical for slave revolts – in terms of duration and the number of rebels. This disjunction is brought out more fully when seen against a critical feature of the

---

[148] Jenson 2011, 45–121.
[149] For the communication with France undertaken by Toussaint, see Jenson 2011, 45–80; for Dessalines's efforts to engage with the ideology and leaders of the United States of America, see Jenson 2011, 81–160.
[150] See especially Jenson 2011, 45–80, for how Toussaint reconfigured the ideals of the French Revolution.
[151] As Ferrer 2014, 299–312, has shown, the images and literature produced by José Antonio Aponte to inspire and drive the conspiracy in Cuba in 1812 were not intended to be understood in full or even seen by the white inhabitants of the island.

Haitian Revolution that is lacking in the cases that have helped characterise slave revolts – namely the high level of negotiation and dialogue between the rebels and the established authorities. While the specific instances of this dialogue escape us for the Sicilian revolts, it is clear from what *has* survived that the interaction between rebels and non-rebels took place in society at large: that is, in free society.

To be sure, there is no *a priori* reason why slave revolts in antiquity should follow patterns characteristic of slave revolts in more recent times. But I do not argue that the Sicilian revolts must be explored outside of discussions of slave revolts because their features are so very different. Rather, the comparative lens cautions from any rushed identification of the Sicilian revolts as slave revolts on the basis of slave-owner narratives. Indeed, the comparative lens strongly suggests that if the Sicilian revolts are to be considered slave revolts, more and better evidence needs to be brought to the table, not least to explain their characteristics. As things stand, however, the rebels' actions, as documented in evidence that illustrates *their* perspective, powerfully promote discussion of the Sicilian revolts outside the reductive conceptual straightjacket called a 'slave revolt', irrespective of the involvement of enslaved persons in these revolts. As seen throughout this book, doing so enhances our appreciation of the events themselves, but importantly also of the complexities of revolts, and of the interactions between individuals of diverse legal statuses, on both sides of the battle line. Seen this way, the Sicilian revolts can tell us much about how revolts and rebels positioned themselves vis-à-vis their wider environment, while raising important questions about the nature of slave revolts and the role played by enslaved persons in revolts and warfare in antiquity more broadly.

Conclusion: The Romano-Sicilian Wars in Context

Where do the various findings presented in this book leave us in terms of the study of ancient slave revolts on one hand and the study of Sicily in the second century BC on the other? I have argued across the preceding five chapters that the two Sicilian revolts can be profitably understood as examples of collective responses to the socio-economic and political difficulties on the island and as responses to challenges to the Roman-backed status quo in Sicily that developed in the aftermath of the Second Punic War. In each case a short-lived monarchy attempted to create a new state on the island and engaged with the free peoples of Sicily through appeals to local culture and religion. On this reading the 130s and 100s BC in Sicily were periods that witnessed intense debates concerning the political legitimacy of incipient monarchies amongst an established system of Hellenistic city states, and they were periods in which these new monarchies attempted to communicate with the inhabitants of Sicily on terms explicable to those on the island, whatever their Roman (or non-Roman) legal status. The events also constitute important responses to the way in which the Roman empire was forming in this period. At this point it may be useful to reconsider where we have come from to reach this conclusion, and to reflect on what the conclusions put forward in this book mean for further study of Hellenistic Sicily and ancient slavery.

In the first instance, it is important to recognise that both the ancient literary sources and the majority of the modern accounts consider the two Sicilian revolts to have been primarily concerned with slavery. In truth, the ancient accounts are nearly unambiguous concerning this and therefore place great emphasis on the status of those involved as slaves and on the importance of the master–slave relations to the wars. As shown, the events were employed to demonstrate aspects of other subjects too: as part of a commentary on the correct moral administration of an empire (Diod. Sic. 34/5.2.1–3, 27–33; 36.2–4; Cass. Dio 27.93.1–3); as part of the degeneration of a Republic into autocracy (Flor. 2.7); as a source for the great and (in)glorious deeds of Romans and non-Romans (Val. Max. 2.7.3, 2.7.9, 4.3.10, 6.9.8, 9.12.1); as a suitably wicked and apposite comparison for a provincial governor (Cic. *Verr.* 2.2.136; 2.3.65–6, 125; 2.4.112); or as an example of the results of broader moral failure (Oros. 5.9). Modern accounts, eschewing the moralising tone prevalent in the ancient sources, have primarily sought to understand the events in the context of ancient slavery. In this context, the events have been variously interpreted as Syrian nationalistic uprisings caused by the mass importation of Syrian slaves into Sicily, as instances of marronage and flight taken to extremes, as the most prominent examples of the continual efforts by the slaves of the ancient world to revolt, or as examples

CONCLUSION: THE ROMANO-SICILIAN WARS IN CONTEXT   189

of the lengths to which slaves would go in the ancient world when pushed to their limits.[1] The essential details provided by the ancient narrative accounts, principally Diodorus Siculus and Florus, have been largely accepted, and these and other slave-owner narratives have assumed the prime place in these analyses with the result that the inconsistencies in these narratives have been made sense of, rather than challenged.

Moreover, those who have stressed the non-servile element of the revolts reported in the ancient sources, or those who have emphasised the Sicilian context of the events and their meaning to the Sicilians themselves, have either been too abrupt in their dismissal of the ancient evidence, or have not provided any answers as to what, if the events in question were not slave revolts, actually took place.[2] With the important exception of Manganaro's various articles on the subject, Rubinsohn's careful work on the second of the Sicilian revolts, some brief considerations in Verbrugghe's 1972 article, and Finley's study of Sicilian history as a whole in antiquity, the Sicilian context for both events has for all practical purposes been ignored.[3] Perhaps oddly, despite their Sicilian concerns, neither Manganaro nor Rubinsohn questioned what it meant for a developing Roman province to be struck by provincial revolts or civic disorder twice in thirty years, nor what the rebels sought to achieve or how their perspective on these events may alter our own interpretation of the slave-owner narratives. Even Finley, whose work on the revolts most completely integrates them into a study of Sicilian history itself, separated them into their own chapter, effectively isolating them from the discussion of their immediate geographical, political and cultural contexts.[4]

In this book, I have attempted to demonstrate that these limitations in previous studies of the two Sicilian revolts and the ensuing Romano-Sicilian wars are best resolved by self-consciously starting our analysis without adopting the assumptions of the ancient slave-owner narratives that these two conflicts were, at root, about slavery and, more specifically, about the relationship between master and slave. We have, instead, approached these conflicts from the evidence closest to the rebels. In Chapters 1 and 3 we focused on the coinage produced during the First Romano-Sicilian War and on the actions of the rebels in this and the later Sicilian revolt, including during the Second Romano-Sicilian War; the aim was to understand how those involved in these ill-fated ventures presented themselves to those around them. In each case we saw that the rebels acclaimed monarchs, set up state institutions and communicated with those around them in a manner consistent with a state composed of free inhabitants and in a way that fit this setting as we can reconstruct it. Moreover, in Chapters 2, 3 and 4, I have placed the ancient literary traditions concerning these conflicts into their historiographical rather than historical contexts. First and foremost, I have argued that these literary traditions reflect the efforts of elite slave owners to

---

[1] Syrian uprising: Vogt 1965, 40–3; Engels 2011; marronage: Bradley 1989, xiv–xv, and 2011, 365; prominent examples of efforts to revolt: Urbainczyk 2008a, 29–50; examples of lengths to which slaves would go: Westermann 1945 and 1955; Green 1961; Dumont 1987; Sacks 1990; Shaw 2001.
[2] See, e.g., Verbrugghe 1972 and 1974; Manganaro 1982, 1983, 1990b and 2000.
[3] Finley 1979, 137–47; Manganaro 1982, 1983, 1990b and 2000; Rubinsohn 1982; Verbrugghe 1972.
[4] The Sicilian 'Slave Wars' are given their own chapter (137–47) placed between two chapters on 'The First Roman Province' (122–36) and 'Sicily under the Roman Emperors' (148–66).

rationalise the events that they were relating and that they represent only one version of and one perspective on the two conflicts. With respect to Diodorus Siculus we have seen that his accounts of these Sicilian revolts were more concerned with teaching lessons about correct behaviour between social classes than understanding the events on their own terms. His narratives had a particular focus on the importance of proper conduct in master–slave relations and how such conduct related more generally to social harmony in the (free) community.[5] To advance this analysis, in Chapter 4, I connected the slave-owner narratives for the two Sicilian conflicts to a long tradition of ancient writers who adapted narrative patterns concerning servile revolt in order to comment on free society in a variety of circumstances and with various intended outcomes. This discussion underscored that the ancient slave-owner traditions about the Sicilian revolts were not concerned with accurate historical accounting *per se*, but rather with a range of political, social and literary goals that did not necessarily result in or require historical accuracy on the part of the author. Finally, in Chapter 5 we assessed what we mean when we discuss slave revolts not just in antiquity, but also in the world history of slavery. As I argued there, the two conflicts under discussion do not fit the pattern of slave revolts that emerges from a study of the rich history of servile resistance in the Americas in the sixteenth to nineteenth centuries on account of their enormous scale and longevity: while there exists of course no *a priori* reason why ancient events should follow the patterns of modern events, as acknowledged in Chapter 5, the evidence presented in this study in its totality makes a strong case for the two Sicilian events in the second century BC to be studied on their own account.

The two events, then, once separated from the slave-owner traditions and analysed from the perspectives of the rebels themselves, can be profitably understood as manifestations of collective challenges to established political and social circumstances on Sicily in the second century BC that relied upon and actively sought out the support of the area's free population in addition to enslaved persons. It is in *this* sense that the events can inform our understanding of the struggle for freedom on the part of the enslaved in antiquity. Once this is properly appreciated, what we know about these two conflicts has important implications for the study of ancient slavery. Thus, as I emphasised especially in the Introduction and the preceding chapter, these two conflicts have been studied in the past within the confines of ancient slavery studies, even in cases in which the aim is to disprove that the events were, in fact, slave revolts. The decision to focus on these revolts in terms of slavery and the servile status of the participants has resulted in skewed analyses of the two events which have overemphasised the importance of servility to those who rebelled and, therefore, missed evidence of attempts by the rebels to communicate with the free inhabitants of the island on a parity. This has essentially created a falsely sharp divide between the worlds of enslaved and free on the island in our historical imagination, assuming at base the impossibility of the rebels conceiving of their enterprise as one undertaken by and for free people. It is imperative to state clearly at this junction that the perspective on the rebels' focus on society at large, which has been championed in the present study, is not compromised even if we assumed that many of the rebels had been

---

[5] On this, see also Morton 2018.

subjected to slavery prior to the revolts, including rebel leaders. But as the analysis undertaken in this book has shown, the rebels *did* present themselves as free actors in the political world of Hellenistic Sicily, fully cognizant of the island's culture, politics and geography, and there is some evidence to suggest that their appeals met with positive responses. If, then, we accept that this was the case, it raises serious questions about the extent to which members of the free, especially Roman elites emphasised status boundaries in times of crisis, not least at the point at which historical narratives were created. The conclusions presented here also have important implications for the study of Sicily itself as part of the growing Roman empire.

As I outlined in the Introduction, the current view of Sicily during the last two centuries BC is that the island supported a provincial elite that benefited from Rome's governance.[6] The growing body of evidence for the vitality of Hellenistic Sicily's civic institutions and the transformation of its urban centres – including archaeology, epigraphy and numismatics – points to a transformation in the period during which the two Sicilian revolts took place.[7] As those interested in the development of Sicily's civic culture in this period attest, these revolts do not fit the picture of Sicily that emerges from the island's contemporaneous material culture. Yet there are limits to this evidence, which is, by its very nature, testimony to the (successful parts of the) elite on the island and those who succeeded under Roman authority: to put it bluntly, those who failed in Sicily in these final two centuries BC would not have left fancy monuments behind in the city centres celebrating their status, and, for that matter, neither did most people who lived in antiquity. The study of the Sicilian *poleis'* monumental buildings, honorific inscriptions and civic coinages is important, but we must not assume that it paints a full picture of the island. The Sicilian revolts studied in this book present us with a different, but no less important history of how some of the island's population engaged somewhat more critically with the evolving situation on Sicily. The evidence is less satisfying than honorific statues and the like – a few grubby coins and the intimations of rebellious self-presentation in moments of intense conflict – but what remains is suggestive of other forms of negotiation with Rome that are not preserved in the material record that is the focus of current scholarship on Republican Sicily. These moments of disaffection with the situation on Sicily – whether inspired by an individual's status or the inability or disinclination of some on the island to benefit from the new situation created by Roman dominance – are nonetheless important evidence for the other part of Sicily's Hellenistic culture that existed in this period: the part that resisted, rather than worked with, the Roman governors and ruling elites of the Sicilian *poleis*. Without this analysis we do not discover this vital form of interaction between Rome and some Sicilian communities and peoples, and we stress too much the ability and willingness of Sicilians to work with Rome, rather than against it.

Indeed, the point has been reached in this book to look further afield, and to consider, even if only briefly, how the two Romano-Sicilian Wars, understood in

---

[6] See, e.g., Wilson in two contributions (2000 and 2013b); further Prag 2003; Campagna 2006, 15–34; Bell 2007, 118.
[7] See especially Prag 2015, 165–6.

the way here argued for, fit into the wider Roman history of the time. This is not a difficult undertaking, but one worth doing. First, the outgoing decades of the second century BC were characterised by much strife across the straits, between Romans and the various Italic peoples. In particular, land and access to land became an issue, one over which different leading Romans entertained different ideas and advocated for different solutions. The Gracchi are only the best known of those whose political careers and lives were deeply affected by the problems that tore society on the peninsula apart at the time. Jump forward and the late 90s BC see the tensions burst into outright hostilities, leading to the so-called Social War between Rome and its Italic allies. Notably, up to this day, scholars disagree on what the war was about: at the extremes of the interpretative spectrum sit at one end a fight for greater involvement in the Roman imperial enterprise, via the citizenship route, and at the other end a war of independence from Roman domination.[8] Naturally, there is little reason to think that all of those unhappy with the status quo in Italy agreed on the solution to the problems. Seen this way, the parallels to what has been proposed in the present study for Sicily are self-evident: Sicilian society, too, emerges as split in its responses to the increasing Roman dominance. Indeed, if full account is taken of the complexities that societies experience at the best of times, the single-minded argument for a burgeoning, shall we say happy Sicily in the second century BC, evidenced in fancy monumental structures and glorious honorific epigraphy, appears ever more the scholarly fantasy that it must have been.

It is instructive to recall at this point the imagery presented in the late 70s BC on a coin minted by the grandson of M'. Aquilius – the successful Roman general who defeated Athenion's forces in 101 BC – mentioned in brief in Chapter 3: the denarius famously depicted Aquilius helping a fallen *Sicilia* to her feet (*RRC* 401). The image nicely encapsulates the *Roman* story, one that depicts the Romans as the saviours who liberate the island from the pest that had befallen it. This story, moreover, fits well with the thriving town centres and their pro-Roman elites that were endangered by the rebels. But, for the rebels, defeat at the hands of Aquilius led to an outcome quite unlike helping Sicily back on her feet, namely that of a captured Sicily: *Sicilia capta*. With the benefit of historical hindsight, it is now possible to say that these two wars unreversedly enshrined Sicilian capture by Rome into the island's history. While the image of a captured Sicily, subdued by its imperial masters, is a negative one, there is little reason to doubt that the rebels would have seen matters thus. *Sicilia capta*, then, captures once again the rebel perspective, in the historiographic imagination here advanced, and – given the rebels' defeat – fittingly in the language of the victors. What the rebels stood for was lost for good. It is for this reason, the focus on the rebel perspective, that this study has been titled accordingly, summing up the consequences of their failed actions, from a position that aligns with *their* standpoint.

In sum, the Sicilian revolts need to be reintegrated into the history of Sicily and the island's relationship with Rome in the last two centuries BC and understood for what they were for many involved, but especially the rebels: not slave revolts, but

---

[8] For discussion of the diverse and shifting modern views on the aims of Rome's Italian allies in the Social War, see Mouritsen 1998.

moments of renegotiation of the social and political landscape on the island on the grand political stage. It is precisely because they do not fit the narrative of an island benefiting from Rome's stewardship that they should emerge from the shadow cast by the Sicilian *poleis*' grand civic centres; they tell a different but no less important story about how some inhabitants of Sicily responded to the changes in this period. In addition, the analysis of the two conflicts undertaken in this book suggests that we need to rethink how we study and write the histories of rebels in the ancient world more generally. If we allow the stories told by those opposed to these rebels to guide our analyses of their actions, we only repeat ancient prejudices; in essence, we need to embrace the perspective of those rebelling, even if that perspective comes to us in a fragmented state and does not allow us to tell full, one might say satisfying, and smooth stories. In the context of modern slavery studies, it is for a good reason best practice to doubt and contextualise, rather than underwrite and repeat, the verdict of the slave owners on the reasons and circumstances of rebellious behaviour on the part of those enslaved: ancient historians of slave revolts need to follow suit, and so too need those who study revolt more broadly with regard to the testimonies of the rebels' enemies. Finally, our own stories about Rome's imperialist history and the histories of its provincial subjects must fully appreciate the multiple narratives that were and are possible of these highly charged events: there is a clear need to acknowledge much more acutely than is widely done that provincial accommodations with imperial masters — or servile accommodations with legal masters — could be complex and bring both benefits and disadvantages in equal (as well as in diverse) measure to all parties.

It is in fact at this crossroad, between imperial and (from an ancient perspective) legal masters, that the Sicilian revolts, and the surviving evidence for these revolts, gain another layer of complexity. As seen in Chapter 4, the ancient writers were well versed in using ideas of slavery to understand and explain contexts in which slavery by the law of the kind practised widely in Roman society was actually irrelevant. Moreover, ancient writers could conceive of political domination as a form of slavery. Once this is properly appreciated, the seemingly clear-cut definition of Genovese's 'struggle for freedom' to describe a slave revolt becomes muddied. To be precise, even if there had not been a single enslaved person involved in the Sicilian rebels' fight against Rome, the rebels would still have engaged in a struggle for freedom, against their imperial dominators. Taking matters one step further still, we must not forget what the reality on the ground was likely to have been for those losing against Rome: if not death on the battlefield, enslavement was the losers' most probable fate. If the historiographic prism is set this way, the distinction between imperial and legal masters becomes even more blurred: those fighting imperial masters ended up with masters by the law. Taken yet another step further, another dimension presses forward that returns to a point raised in Chapter 4 and briefly reiterated above. Thus, in the light of the short gap of one generation between the two Sicilian revolts, it is not at all impossible that a rebelling Sicilian who became enslaved as a consequence of suffering defeat in the First Romano-Sicilian War was part of the rebel force in the Second Romano-Sicilian War: should we see such a person's rebellion within the confines of slavery by the law, or within the wider remit of a rejection of imperial domination? Again, there need not be a single answer to this question, let alone one for all cases.

But the question drives home with force that ancient life was often more complex than ancient and modern historians have regularly allowed for.

At the outset of this Conclusion, I made a seemingly unnecessary qualification when stating that the ancient accounts are *nearly* unambiguous in their appreciation of the Sicilian revolts as set into the context of slavery: *nearly* – but not entirely so. Thus, as noted in Chapter 5, when introducing the First Romano-Sicilian War, Diodorus states that (34/5.2.26) τὸ παραπλήσιον δὲ γέγονε, 'a similar thing happened' at the same time, Aristonicus' attempt to seize the throne at Pergamum. As I also noted then, in the ancient literary accounts the war fought by Aristonicus is seen as a dynastic war, not a slave revolt, even if some ancient authors make reference to slaves, and in particular to Aristonicus' enlisting of soldiers who had been in slavery at the time, according to Strabo (14.1.38) in exchange for freedom. Some modern scholars, notably Vogt and Urbainczyk, therefore included Aristonicus' claim to the throne in their studies of ancient slave revolts, even if Vogt did not actually think it fitted into this category, as also seen in the preceding chapter. Diodorus' comment about the 'similar thing' has not attracted the attention it deserves. If viewed critically, with the argument presented in this book in mind, this seemingly unimportant aside constitutes a massive giveaway – for the key element that is similar between the two revolts and the wars that arose from them that Diodorus here puts on a par with the situation at Pergamum is the attempt at establishing their own political authority, and doing so in opposition to Rome and those who favoured Rome locally. Modern historians would fare well to take due note of this Diodoran remark: the comparison is as short as it is meaningful. Indeed, as at Pergamum, in second century BC Sicily many profited from Rome's increasing interference and dominance; but we must not forget those who did not profit – or did not want to profit in those circumstances – and who rebelled and fought to present a different possibility to the peoples of Sicily even, or perhaps especially, if these rebels failed. The least we as modern historians can do is to facilitate the presentation of this different possibility in our historiographic assessments of the two Sicilian revolts and the ensuing Romano-Sicilian Wars.

APPENDIX 1:
THE ΦΙΛΙΠΗΙΟΝ GOLD COINAGE

Coin 1 (Campana, Enna 15)
Obv: Male head, right, diademed with long hair.
Rev: Nike standing right, right hand holding a crown (not visible); ΦΙΛΙΠΗΙΟΝ curved across the bottom.

Coin 2 (Campana, Enna 16)
Obv: Male head, right, diademed with long hair.
Rev: Seated soldier, left hand holds a spear, the right hand a club(?); ΦΙΛΙΠΠΟC upwards at left.

These two coins have been published by Manganaro, Berk and Bendall, and Lorber, and are listed in Campana's catalogue of Campana as coins 15 and 16 from Enna.[1] They are both made from gold, and appear to be, individually, the only examples of their types. The obverse is similar on both coins: a diademed male head, facing right.[2] The reverses are different: Coin 1 has a standing Nike, while Coin 2 features a seated soldier. Manganaro claims that Coin 1 was found in the area around Morgantina, but we have no provenance for Coin 2.[3] Manganaro argues that the coins' unusual legends, reading ΦΙΛΙΠΗΙΟΝ and ΦΙΛΙΠΠΟC respectively, were chosen to confirm to the owner that the coin possessed the same value as the famous staters of Philip II of Macedon.[4] Berk and Bendall suggested that the coins were designed by King Antiochus for use in overseas trade, while Lorber proposed that the coins reference Antiochus III as liberator of Greece and the 'liberation' of Greece by Flamininus.[5] By contrast, both Andrew Burnett and Keith Rutter regard the coins as modern fakes.[6]

Burnett and Rutter's caution is best followed, as the coins' legends are peculiar and warrant suspicion. ΦΙΛΙΠΗΙΟΝ and ΦΙΛΙΠΠΟC are accusative and nominative respectively, rather than the expected genitive. While the nominative could be used on coins, it was normally used when expressing an ethnic identity for the authority of

---

[1] Manganaro 1990a and 1990b; Berk and Bendall 1994; Lorber 1994 Campana 1997, 158.
[2] As with the bronze coins discussed in Chapter 1, I have been unable to undertake a direct autopsy of either coin. I rely, therefore, on the photographs provided in Manganaro 1990a and 1990b, as well as Campana 1997, 158.
[3] Manganaro 1990b, 181. Berk and Bendall 1994, 8, follow Manganaro that both coins were found near Morgantina, but offer no evidence for this in relation to Coin 2.
[4] For this, see Manganaro 1990b, 183, and Berk and Bendall 1994, 7–8.
[5] Berk and Bendall 1994, 8; Lorber 1994, 3.
[6] Personal comment by Burnett and Rutter, July 2008.

the coin, and even this was rare.[7] The accusative legend, ΦΙΛΙΠΗΙΟΝ, is odd, and is not the accusative of ΦΙΛΙΠΠΟC. Even if it is not a mistake it does not invoke the staters of Philip at all, but seems to be a reference to the Philipeion, a temple set up in Olympia by Philip II of Macedon. There is no good reason to connect these coins to King Antiochus and the First Romano-Sicilian War except the use of the lunate sigma on Coin 2, but this is not unusual in Sicilian coins more generally, and otherwise the legends bear no relation to the other coins produced during the war, all of which have variations on the same legend.

[7] See, e.g., Kraay 1976, 6.

Bibliography

Aberson, M. 2016. 'Sicile, 104–100 av. J.-C.: "Varius" et "Salvius", hommes libres ou esclaves en révolte?', *Arctos* 50, 9–19.
Adamo, M. 2016. 'The *Lapis Pollai*: date and contexts', *PBSR* 84, 73–100.
Aizpurua, R. 1988. 'La insurrección de los negros de la Serranía de Coro de 1795: una revisión necesaria', *Boletín de la Academia Nacional de la Historia* 283, 705–23.
Aizpurua, R. 2011. 'Revolution and politics in Venezuela and Curaçao, 1795–1800', in W. Klooster and G. Oostindie eds. *Curaçao in the Age of Revolutions, 1795–1800* (Leiden), 97–122.
Akande, H. 2016. *Illuminating the Blackness: Blacks and African Muslims in Brazil* (London).
Albanese Procelli, R. M., Alberghina, F., Brancato, M., Procelli, F. and Sirena, G. 2007. 'The project and the first results of the Gornalunga and Margi Valleys Survey', in M. Fitzjohn ed. *Uplands of Ancient Sicily and Calabria: the Archaeology of a Landscape Revisited* (London), 35–48.
Alcock, S. 2001. 'The peculiar book IV and the problem of the Messenian past', in S. Alcock, J. Cherry and J. Elsner eds. *Pausanias: Travel and Memory in Roman Greece* (Oxford), 142–53.
Alföldi, A. 1965. *Early Rome and the Latins* (Ann Arbor).
Allmendinger, D. 2014. *Nat Turner and the Rising in Southampton County* (Baltimore).
Aly, W. 1921. *Volksmärchen, Sage und Novelle bei Herodot und seinen Zeitgenossen* (Göttingen).
Ambaglio, D. 2008. 'Introduzione alla *Biblioteca storica* di Diodoro', in D. Ambaglio, F. Landucci and L. Bravi eds. *Diodoro Siculo: Biblioteca storica. Commento storico. Introduzione generale* (Milan), 3–102.
Amitay, O. 2008. 'Why did Alexander the Great besiege Tyre?', *Athenaeum* 96, 91–102.
Ampolo, C. ed. 2010. *Relazioni preliminari degli scavi a Segesta (Calatafimi-Segesta, TP; 2000–08; Entella (Contessa Entellina, PA; 2007–08); Kaulonia (Monasterace, RC; 2006–08). Ricerche recenti a Roca (Melendugno, LE). Notizie degli scavi di antichità communicate dalla Scuola Normale Superiore di Pisa. Rassegna archeologica del Laboratorio di Storia, Archeologia e Topografia del Mondo Antico. Annali della Scuola Normale Superiore di Pisa, Classe di Lettere e Filosofia*[5] (Pisa).
Ampolo, C. ed. 2012. *Agora greca e agorai di Sicilia* (Pisa).
Angius, A. 2020. *Le rivolte degli schiavi in Sicilia: la narrazione di Diodoro tra razionalismo e storia esemplare* (Rome).
Annequin, J. 1973. 'Esclaves et affranchis dans la conjuration de Catilina', *Actes du colloque 1971 sur l'esclavage: Besançon, 10–11 mai 1971* (Paris), 193–238.
Antonaccio, C. M. 2001. 'Ethnicity and colonization', in I. Malkin ed. *Ancient Perceptions of Greek Ethnicity* (Cambridge), 113–57.

Aptheker, H. 1943. *American Negro Slave Revolts* (New York).
Arena, V. 2012. *Libertas and the Practice of Politics in the Late Roman Republic* (Cambridge).
Asheri, D. 1977. 'Tyrannie et mariage forcé: essais d'histoire sociale grecque', *Annales E.S.C.* 32, 21–48.
Aubert, J.-J. 1994. *Business Managers in Ancient Rome* (Leiden).
Austin, M. 1986. 'Hellenistic kings, war and the economy', *CQ* 36, 450–66.
Avidov, A. 1997. 'Were the Cilicians a nation of pirates?', *Mediterranean Historical Review* 12.1, 5–55.
Badian, E. 1964. *Studies in Greek and Roman History* (Oxford).
Bal, M. 1985. *Narratology: Introduction to the Theory of Narrative*, Van Boheemen, C. trans. (London).
Balzat, J.-S., Catling, R. W. V., Chiricat, É., and Marchand, F. eds. 2014. *Lexicon of Greek Personal Names*, Volume VB: *Coastal Asia Minor: Caria to Cilicia* (Oxford).
Barcia, M. 2008. *Seeds of Insurrection: Domination and Resistance on Western Cuban Plantations, 1808–1848* (Baton Rouge).
Barcia, M. 2014. *West African Warfare in Bahia and Cuba: Soldier Slaves in the Atlantic World, 1807–1844* (Oxford).
Baron, C. A. 2013. *Timaeus of Tauromenium and Hellenistic Historiography* (Cambridge).
Beard, M. 1985. 'Writing and ritual: a study of diversity and expansion in the Arval Acta', *PBSR* 53, 114–62.
Beckles, H. 1984. *Black Rebellion in Barbados* (Bridgetown).
Beek, A. L. 2016. 'The pirate connection: Roman politics, servile wars, and the east', *TAPA* 146.1, 99–116.
Behrend, J. 2011. 'Rebellious talk and conspiratorial plots: the making of a slave insurrection in Civil War Natchez', *Journal of Southern History* 77.1, 17–52.
Bejor, G. 1975. 'Ricerche di topografia e di archeologia nella Sicilia sud-occidentale', *ASNP* 5, 1275–303.
Bell, M. 2000. 'A stamp with the monogram of Morgantina and the sign of Tanit', in I. Berlingo, H. Blanck, F. Cordano, P. G. Guzzo and M. C. Lentini eds. *Damarato: studi di antichità classica offerti a Paola Pelagatti* (Milan), 246–54.
Bell, M. 2007. 'Sicilian civil architecture and the *lex Hieronica*', in J. R. W. Prag ed. *Sicilia nutrix plebis Romanae: Rhetoric, Law and Taxation in Cicero's Verrines* (London), 117–34.
Bello, L. 1960. 'Ricerche sui Palici', *Kokalos* 6, 71–97.
Belvedere, O. and Burgio, A. 2012. *Carta archeologica e sistema informativo territoriale del parco archeologico e paesaggistico della Valle dei Templi di Agrigento* (Palermo).
Bergad, L. W. 2007. *The Comparative Histories of Slavery in Brazil, Cuba, and the United States* (Cambridge).
Bergemann, J. 2012. 'Gela und Monti Sicani: Surveys an der Küste und im Binnenland im Vergleich', in J. Bergemann ed. *Griechen in Übersee und der historische Raum*, Göttinger Studien zur Mediterranen Archäologie 2 (Rahden), 96–103.
Berk, H. J. and Bendall, S. 1994. 'Eunus/Antiochus: slave revolt in Sicily', *The Celator* Feb., 6–8.
Berlin, I. and Harris, L. 2005. *Slavery in New York* (New York).
Bernard, S. G., Damon, C., and Grey, C. 2014. 'Rhetorics of land and power in the Polla inscription (*CIL* I^2 638)', *Mnemosyne* 67.6, 953–85.
Bertelli, L. 2002. 'Perì basileias: i trattati sulla regalità dal IV secolo a.C.' in P. Bettiolo and G. Filoramo eds. *Il Dio mortale: teologie politiche tra antico e contemporaneo* (Brescia), 17–61.
Beston, P. 2000. 'Hellenistic military leadership', in H. van Wees ed. *War and Violence in Ancient Greece* (London), 315–35.

Biffi, N. 2006. *Magna Grecia e dintorni (Geografia, 5,4,3–6,3,11): introduzione, traduzione, testo e commento* (Bari).
Blanco, J. 1991. *Miguel Guacamaya: capitan de cimarrones* (Caracas).
Bloedow, E. F. 1998. 'The siege of Tyre in 332 BC: Alexander at the crossroads in his career', *PP* 53, 255–93.
Bonelli, G. 1994. 'La saga di Drimaco nel sesto libro di Ateneo: ipotesi interpretiva', *Quaderni Urbinati di Cultura Classica* 46.1, 135–42.
Booth, W. C. 1961. *The Rhetoric of Fiction* (London).
Bosworth, A. B. 2002. *The Legacy of Alexander* (Oxford).
Bradley, K. R. 1978. 'Slaves and the Catiline conspiracy', *CP* 73, 329–36.
Bradley, K. R. 1989. *Slavery and Rebellion in the Roman World, 140 b.c.–70 b.c.* (Bloomington).
Bradley, K. R. 2011. 'Resisting slavery at Rome', in K. R. Bradley and P. Cartledge eds. *The Cambridge World History of Slavery*, Volume 1: *The Ancient Mediterranean World* (New York), 362–84.
Bradley, K. R. 2015. 'The bitter chains of slavery', *DHA* 41.1, 149–76.
Braund, D. C. 2008. 'Royal Scythians and the slave-trade in Herodotus' Scythia', *Antichthon* 42, 1–19.
Braund, D. C. and Wilkins, J. eds. 2000. *Athenaeus and His World: Reading Greek Culture in the Roman Empire* (Exeter).
Breen, P. 2015. *The Land Shall Be Deluged in Blood: a New History of the Nat Turner Revolt* (New York).
Breen, T. H. 1973. 'A changing labor force and race relations in Virginia 1660–1710', *Journal of Social History* 7.1, 3–25.
Brennan, T. C. 1993. 'The commanders in the First Sicilian Slave War', *Rivista di Filologia Classica* 121, 153–84.
Briant, P. 1976. '"Brigandage", dissidence at conquête en Asie Achémenide et Hellenistique', *Dialogues d'histoire ancienne* 21, 163–279.
Briquel, D. 1974. 'Tarante, Locres, les Scythes, Thera, Rome: précédents antiques au thème de l'Amant de Lady Chatterley?', *MEFRA* 86.2, 673–705.
Brown, T. S. 1991. 'A miniscule history of the slaves of Tyre: Justin 18.3.6–19', *AHB* 5, 59–65.
Brown, V. 2020. *Tacky's Revolt: the Story of an Atlantic Slave War* (Cambridge).
Brunt, P. A. 1980. 'Patronage and politics', *Chiron* 19, 273–89.
Buraselis, K. 2000. 'Colophon and the war of Aristonicus', in J. Velissanopoulos ed. *Τιμαι Ιοαννου Τριανταφυλλοπουλου* (Athens), 181–207.
Burck, E. 1934. *Die Erzählungskunst des Titius Livius* (Berlin).
Burian, J. 1984. '*Latrones*: ein Begriff in römishcen literarischen und juristischen Quellen', *Eirene* 21, 17–23.
Burke, K. 1950. *A Rhetoric of Motives* (London).
Burke, K. 1959. *Attitudes toward History* (Los Altos).
Burnard, T. 2004. *Mastery, Tyranny and Desire: Thomas Thistlewood and His Slaves in the Anglo-Jamaican World* (Chapel Hill).
Burnett, A. M. 1995. 'The coinage of Punic Sicily during the Hannibalic War', in M. Caccamo Caltabiano ed. *La Sicilia tra l'Egitto e Roma: la monetazione siracusana dell'eta di Ierone II* (Messina), 383–99.
Burnett, A. M. 2000. 'The silver coinage of Italy and Syracuse in the Second Punic War', in W. Hollstein ed. *Metallanalytische Untersuchungen an Münzen der Römischen Republik* (Berlin), 102–13.
Bussi, S. 1998. 'Rivolte servili e bagliori di "lealismo" ellenisico', *RIN*, 15–27.
Buttrey, T., Erim, K. T., Groves, T. D. and Holloway, R. R. 1989. *Morgantina Studies: the Coins* (Princeton).

Cairns, F. 1989. *Virgil's Augustan Epic* (Cambridge).
Cairns, F. 2012. 'Lentulus' letter: Cicero *In Catilinam* 3.12; Sallust *Bellum Catilinae* 44.3–6', *Historia* 61.1, 78–82.
Calciati, R. 1987. *Corpus nummorum Siculorum: la monetazione di Bronzo*, 3 vols. (Milan).
Callahan, A. D. and Horsley, R. A. 1998. 'Slave resistance in classical antiquity', *Semeia* 83.4, 133–52.
Caltabiano, M. C. 2008. 'Il "ruolo" di Demetra nel documento monetale greco', in C. A. di Stefano ed. *Demetra: la divinità, i santuari, il culto, la leggenda. Atti del I Congresso Internazionale Enna, 1–4 Luglio 2004* (Pisa), 123–34.
Cammarata, E. 1987. 'La storia di Enna (V–I sec. a. C.) ricostruita attraverso la sua monetazione: la zecca Ennese', *Ennarotary* 1, 27–31.
Campagna, L. 2003. 'La Sicilia di età repubblicana nella storiografia degli ultimi cinquant'anni', *Ostraka* 12, 7–31.
Campagna, L. 2006. 'L'architettura di età ellenistica in Sicilia: per una rilettura del quadro generale', in M. Osanna and M. Torelli eds. *Sicilia ellenistica, consuetudo italica: alle origini dell'architettura ellenistica d'Occidente* (Rome and Pisa), 15–34.
Campagna, L. 2007. 'L'architettura pubblica ed evergetismo nella Sicilia di età repubblicana', in C. Miccichè, S. Modeo and L. Santagati eds. 2007. *La Sicilia romana tra Repubblica e Alto Impero: atti del convegno di studi* (Caltanissetta), 110–34.
Campagna, L. 2011. 'Exploring social and cultural changes in *provincia Sicilia*: reflections on the study of urban landscapes', in F. Colivicchi ed. *Local Cultures of South Italy and Sicily in the Late Republican Period: Between Hellenism and Rome*, *JRA* Suppl. 83 (Portsmouth, RI), 161–83.
Campana, A. 1997. 'Corpus nummorum antiquae italiae (zecche minori). Sicilia: Enna (440–36 a.C.)', *Pan. Num.* 112–13, 145–67.
Canfora, L. 1985. 'L'invidia dei poveri durante le guerre servili siciliane', *Index* 13, 157–61.
Capozza, M. 1956–7. 'Le rivolte servili di Sicilia nel quadro della politica agraria romana', *Atti dell'Istituto Veneto di Scienze, Lettere ed Arti. Classe di Scienze Morali e Lettere* 150, 79–98.
Carandini, A. 2014. 'The myth of Romulus and the origins of Rome', in J. H. Richardson and F. Santangelo eds. *The Roman Historical Tradition: Regal and Republican Rome* (Oxford), 17–33.
Cartledge, P. 1985. '"Rebels and Sambos in Classical Greece: a comparative view', in P. Cartledge and F. D. Harvey eds. *CRUX: Essays in Greek History presented to G. E. M. de Ste. Croix* (London), 16–46.
Cartledge, P. 2011. 'The helots: a contemporary view', in K. Bradley and P. Cartledge eds. *The Cambridge World History of Slavery*, Vol. 1 (Cambridge), 74–90.
Castrizio, D. 2000. *La monetazione mercenariale in Sicilia: strategie economiche e territoriali fra Dione e Timoleonte* (Soveria Mannelli).
Cataldi, S. 1997. 'I rapporti politici di Segesta e Alicie con Atene nel V secolo a.C.', *Atti delle seconde giornate internazionali di studi sull'area elima, Gibellina 1994* (Pisa), 305–356.
Champion, C. B. 2004. *Cultural Politics in Polybius's Histories* (London).
Chaniotis, A. 2005. *War in the Hellenistic World* (Oxford).
Chaplin, J. D. 2000. *Livy's Exemplary History* (Oxford).
Childs, M. D. 2006. *The 1812 Aponte Rebellion in Cuba and the Struggle against Atlantic Slavery* (Chapel Hill).
Chrubasik, B. 2016. *Kings and Usurpers in the Seleukid Empire* (Oxford).
Ciaceri, E. 1911. *Culti e miti nella storia della antica Sicilia* (Catania).
Cirelli, C. 2008. 'Il santuario in età romana', in L. Maniscalco ed. *Il santuario dei Palici: un centro di culto nella Valle del Margi* (Palermo), 244–90.

Cohn, D. 1989. 'Fictional *vs* historical lives', *Journal of Narrative Technique* 19.1, 3–24.
Cohn, D. 1990. 'Signposts of fictionality'. *Poetics Today* 11.4, 774–804.
Cohn, D. 1999. *The Distinction of Fiction* (Baltimore).
Collingwood, R. G. 1946. *The Idea of History* (Oxford).
Conrad, R. E. 1994. *Children of God's Fire: a Documentary History of Black Slavery in Brazil* (Princeton).
Consolo Langher, S. N. 1996. *Siracusa e la Sicilia Greca tra Età Arcaica ed Alto Ellenismo*. Biblioteca dell'Archivio Storico Messinese 23 (Messina).
Consolo Langher, S. N. 1997. *Un imperialismo tra democrazia e tirannide: Siracusa nei Secoli V e IV a.C., Kokalos* Suppl. 12 (Rome).
Cooley, A. E. 2009. *Res gestae Divi Augusti: Text, Translation, and Commentary* (Cambridge).
Corbeill, A. 1996. *Controlling Laughter: Political Humor in the Late Roman Republic* (Princeton).
Corcella, A. 2007. *Herodotus: Histories, IV* (Oxford).
Cordano, F. 2008. 'Il santuario dei Palikoi', *Aristonothos* 2, 41–7.
Cornell, T. J. 1995. *The Beginnings of Rome* (London).
Corsten, T. ed. 2010. *Lexicon of Greek Personal Names*, Volume VA: *Coastal Asia Minor: Pontos to Ionia* (Oxford).
Covino, R. 2013. '*Stasis* in Roman Sicily', *Electryone* 1, 18–28.
Cramer, F. H. 1954. *Astrology in Roman Law and Politics* (Baltimore).
Craton, M. 1979. 'Proto-peasant revolts? The late slave rebellions in the British West Indies, 1816–1832', *P&P* 85, 99–125.
Craton, M. 1980. 'The passion to exist: slave rebellions in the British West Indies', *Journal of Caribbean History* 13, 1–20.
Craton, M. 1982. *Testing the Chains: Resistance to Slavery in the British West Indies* (Ithaca, NY).
Crawford, M. H. 1985. *Coinage and Money under the Roman Republic* (London).
Crawford, M. H. 1987. 'Sicily', in A. M. Burnett and M. H. Crawford eds. *The Coinage of the Roman World in the Late Republic* (Oxford), 43–52.
Crawford, M. H. 1990. 'Origini e sviluppi del sistema provinciale romano', in H. Clemente, F. Coarelli and E. Gabba eds. *Storia di Roma*, Vol. II.I (Turin) 91–121.
Cusumano, N. 1990. *Ordalia e soteria nella Sicilia antica: i Palici* (Palermo).
da Costa, E. V. 1994. *Crowns of Glory, Tears of Blood* (Oxford).
Davis, T. J. A. 1985. *A Rumor of Revolt· the 'Great Negro Plot' in Colonial New York* (Amherst).
de Lisle, C. 2021. *Agathokles of Syracuse· Sicilian Tyrant and Hellenistic King* (Oxford).
De Agostino, A. 1939. 'Le monete di Henna', *Bolletino storico catanese* 4, 73–86.
De Graaf, P. 2012. *Late Republican–Early Imperial Regional Italian Landscapes and Demography* (Oxford).
De Hoog, L. 1983. *Van rebellie tot revolutie: Oorzaken en achtergronden van de Curaçaose slavenopstanden in 1750 en 1795* (Curaçao and Leiden).
De Jong, I. J. F. 2014. *Narratology and Classics: a Practical Guide* (Oxford).
De Souza, P. 1999. *Piracy in the Graeco-Roman World* (Cambridge).
De Souza, P. 2008. 'Rome's contribution to the development of piracy', in R. L. Hohlfelder ed. *The Maritime World of Ancient Rome* (Ann Arbor), 71–96.
De Ste. Croix, G. E. M. 1988. 'Slavery and other forms of unfree labour', in L. Archer ed. *Slavery and Other Forms of Unfree Labour* (London), 19–32.
Dench, E. 1995. *From Barbarians to New Men: Greek, Roman and Modern Perceptions of People from the Central Apennines* (Oxford).
Di Patti, C. and Lupo, F. 2008. 'La fauna: indagine archeozoologica', in L. Maniscalco ed. *Il santuario dei Palici: un centro di culto nella Valle del Margi* (Palermo), 387–400.
Dickie, M. W. 2001. *Magic and Magicians in the Graeco-Roman World* (London).

Dillon, J. N. 2013. 'The delegation of the *xviri* to Enna *ca.* 133 BC and the murder of Tiberius Gracchus', *BICS* 56.2, 89–103.
Diouf, S. A. 2013. *Servants of Allah: African Muslims Enslaved in the Americas* (New York).
Do Rego, C. and Janga, L. 2009. *Slavery and Resistance in Curaçao: the Rebellion of 1795* (Curaçao).
dos Santos Gomes, F. 1995. *Histórias de Quilombolas: mocambos e comunidades de senzalas no Rio de Janeiro século XIX* (Rio de Janeiro).
Domínguez, A. J. 2007. 'Fear of enslavement and sacred slavery as mechanisms of social control among the ancient Locrians', in A. Serghidou ed. *Fear of Slaves – Fear of Enslavement in the Ancient Mediterranean* (Franche-Comté), 405–22.
Dormon, J. H. 1977. 'The persistent specter: slave rebellion in territorial Lousiana', *Louisiana History* 18, 389–404.
Drummond, A. 1989. 'Appendix', *CAH2* VII.2, 625–44.
Dubois, L. 2004. *Avengers of the New World: the Story of the Haitian Revolution* (Cambridge).
Dubois, L. and Garrigus, J. D. 2006. *Slave Revolution in the Caribbean 1789–1804* (Boston).
Ducat, J. 1990. *Les Hilotes. Bulletin de correspondence hellénique* suppl. 20 (Paris).
Dumont, J. C. 1987. *Servus: Rome et l'esclavage sous la République* (Rome).
Duncan-Jones, R. 2016. *Power and Privilege in Roman Society* (Cambridge).
Dunn, R. S. 2012. *Sugar and Slaves: the Rise of the Planter Class in the English West Indies, 1624–1713* (Chapel Hill).
Egerton, D. R. 1993. *Gabriel's Rebellion: the Virginia Slave Conspiracies of 1800 and 1802* (Chapel Hill).
Eltis, D. 1987. *Economic Growth and the Ending of the Transatlantic Slave Trade* (New York).
Engels, D. 2011. 'Ein syrisches Sizilien? Seleukidische Aspekte des ersten sizilischen Sklavenkriegs und der Herrschaft des Eunus-Antiochos', *Polifemo* 11, 233–51.
Fantham, E. 1995. 'Republican Rome I. From marriage by capture to partnership in war: the proud women of early Rome', in E. Fantham ed. *Women in the Classical World: Image and Text* (Oxford), 216–42.
Felice Cardot, C. 1952. *La Rebelión de Andresote (Valles del Yaracuy, 1730–1733)* (Caracas).
Ferrer, A. 2014. *Freedom's Mirror: Cuba and Haiti in the Age of Revolution* (Cambridge).
Fick, C. 1990. *The Making of Haiti: the Saint-Domingue Revolution from Below* (Knoxville).
Fiering, N. and Geggus, D. P. eds. 2008. *The World of the Haitian Revolution* (Bloomington).
Figueiredo Pirola, R. 2005. A conspiração escrava de Campinas, 1832: Rebelião, etnicidade e família. Unpublished PhD dissertation, UNICAMP.
Finley, M. I. 1979. *Ancient Sicily to the Arab Conquest*, 2nd ed. (London).
Finley, M. I. 1985. *Ancient History: Evidence and Models* (London).
Fischer, S. 2004. *Modernity Disavowed: Haiti and the Cultures of Slavery in the Age of Revolution* (Durham, NC).
Fleischer, R. 1996. 'Hellenistic royal iconography on coins', in P. Bilde ed. *Aspects of Hellenistic Kingship* (Aarhus), 28–40.
Flintermann, J. P. 1995. *Power, Paideia and Pythagoreanism* (Princeton).
Florenzano, M. B. B. 2005. 'Coins and religion: representations of Demeter and of Kore/Persephone on Sicilian Greek coins', *RBN* 151, 1–28.
Flower, M. A. 1994. *Theopompus of Chios* (Oxford).
Foner, E. ed. 1971. *Nat Turner* (Englewood Cliffs).
Foote, T. W. 1993. '"Some hard usage": the New York City slave revolt of 1712', *New York Folklore* 18, 147–59.
Forsdyke, S. 2012. *Slaves Tell Tales* (Princeton).
Forsythe, G. 1994. *The Historian L. Calpurnius Piso Frugi and the Roman Annalistic Tradition* (Lanham).

Forsythe, G. 1999. *Livy and Early Rome: a Study in Historical Method and Judgment* (Stuttgart).
Forsythe, G. 2005. *A Critical History of Early Rome from Prehistory to the First Punic War* (Berkeley).
Fournier, J. 2010. 'La *lex Rupilia*, un modèle de régime judiciaire provincial à l'époque républicaine?' *Cahiers du Centre Gustave Glotz* 21, 157–86.
Franco, J. L. 1963. *La Conspiración de Aponte de 1812* (Havana).
Franco, J. L. 1979. 'Maroons and slave rebellions in the Spanish territories', in R. Price ed. *Maroon Societies: Rebel Slave Communities in the Americas* (Baltimore), 35–48.
Franzen, C. E. 2013. 'Metaphorical enslavement in the *First Catilinarian* oration', *CW* 106.3, 355–64.
Fraser, P. M. and Matthews, E. eds. 1987. *Lexicon of Greek Personal Names*, Volume I: *Aegean Islands, Cyprus, Cyrenaica* (Oxford).
Fraser, P. M. and Matthews, E. eds. 1997. *Lexicon of Greek Personal Names*, Volume IIIA: *Peloponnese, Western Greece, Sicily, and Magna Graecia* (Oxford).
Fraser, P. M., Matthews, E. and Catling, R. W. V. eds. 2005. *Lexicon of Greek Personal Names*, Volume IV: *Macedonia, Thrace, Northern Regions of the Black Sea* (Oxford).
Frazel, T. D. 2009. *The Rhetoric of Cicero's 'In Verrem'* (Göttingen).
Freehling, W. W. 1994. 'Denmark Vesey's antipaternalistic reality', in W. W. Freehling ed. *The Reintegration of American History: Slavery and the Civil War* (New York), 34–58.
French, S. 2004. *The Rebellious Slave: Nat Turner in American Memory* (Boston).
Frey-Kupper, S. 1992. 'La circolazione monetaria a Monte Iato dall'inizio della dominazione romana fino all'età tiberiana', in L. Biondi, A. Corretti, S. De Vido, M. Gargini and M. A. Vaggioli eds. *Atti delle giornate internazionali de studi sull'area Elima (Gibellina 19–22 Settembre 1991)* (Pisa), 281–97.
Frey-Kupper, S. 1993. 'Les trouvailles monétaires de Monte Iato (Sicile) et les monnaies du magistrat Lucius Mettelus émises à Panormus et Iaitas', in T. Hackens and G. Moucharte eds. *Actes du XIe Congrès international de numismatique, Bruxelles, 8–13 septembre 1991* (Louvain-la-Neuve), 185–90.
Frey-Kupper, S. 2013. *Die antiken Fundmünzen vom Monte Iato 1971–1990: ein Beitrag zur Geldgeschichte Westsiziliens*, 2 vols. Studia Ietina 10 (Lausanne).
Fugmann, J. 1991. '*Mare a praedonibus pacavi* (R.G. 25,1): zum Gedanken der *aemulatio* in den *Res gestae* des Augustus', *Historia* 40, 307–17.
Fuks, A. 1968. 'Slave war and slave troubles in Chios in the third century BC', *Athenaeum* 46, 102–11.
Furlonge, N. D. 1999. 'Revisiting the Zanj and re-visioning revolt: complexities of the Zanj Conflict (868–883 AD)', *Negro History Bulletin* 62.4, 7–14.
Gabba, E. 1959. 'Sui senati della città siciliane nell' età di Verre', *Athenaeum* 37, 304–20.
Gagé, J. 1974. 'Les Quinctii, l'"imperium" Capitolin et la règle du Champ de Mars', *Revue des études latines* 52, 110–48.
Gallia, A. B. 2007. 'Reassessing the "Cumaean Chronicle": Greek chronology and Roman history in Dionysius of Halicarnassus', *JRS* 97, 50–67.
Gallini, C. 1970. *Protesta e integrazione nella Roma antica* (Bari).
Gallup-Diaz, I. 2010. 'A legacy of strife: rebellious slaves in sixteenth-century Panamá', *Colonial Latin American Review* 19.3, 417–35.
García, G. 2003. *Conspiraciones y revueltas: la actividad política de los negros en Cuba, 1790–1845* (Santiago de Cuba).
Geggus, D. P. 1982. *Slavery, War and Revolution: the British Occupation of Saint Domingue, 1793–1798* (Oxford).
Geggus, D. P. 1989. 'The French and Haitian Revolutions, and resistance to slavery in the Americas', *Revue française d'histoire d'Outre-Mer* 232–3, 107–24.

Geggus, D. P. 2001. 'Toussaint Louverture et l'abolition de l'esclavage à Saint-Domingue', in L. Chauleau ed. *Les abolitions dans les Amériques* (Fort de France), 109–16.
Geggus, D. P. 2002. *Haitian Revolutionary Studies* (Bloomington).
Geggus, D. P. 2006. 'Print culture and the Haitian Revolution: the written and the spoken word', *Proceedings of the American Antiquarian Society* 2, 297–314.
Geggus, D. P. 2011. 'Slave rebellion during the Age of Revolution', in W. Klooster and G. Oostindie eds. *Curaçao in the Age of Revolutions, 1795–1800* (Leiden), 23–56.
Genovese, E. D. 1979. *From Rebellion to Revolution* (Baton Rouge).
Gilliver, C. M. 1999. *The Roman Art of War* (Stroud).
Girard, P. 2016. *Toussaint Louverture: the Revolutionary Life* (New York).
Glen Inabinet, L. 1980. '"The July Fourth Incident" of 1816: an insurrection plotted by slaves in Camden, South Carolina', in H. A. Johnson ed. *South Carolina Legal History* (Spartanburg), 209–21.
Gomez, M. A. 2005. *A Black Crescent: the Experience and Legacy of African Muslims in the Americas* (New York).
Goodenough, E. R. 1928. 'The political philosophy of Hellenistic kingship', *YCS* 1, 55–102.
Gordon, R. 1999. 'Imagining Greek and Roman magic', in B. Ankarloo and S. Clark eds. *The Athlone History of Witchcraft and Magic in Europe*, Vol. II: *Ancient Greece and Rome* (London), 159–275.
Goslinga, C. C. 1985. *The Dutch in the Caribbean and in the Guianas 1680–1791* (Assen).
Goslinga, C. C. 1990. *The Dutch in the Caribbean and in Surinam 1791/5–1942* (Assen).
Goukowsky, P. 2014. *Diodore de Sicile: Bibliothèque historique. Fragments: Livres XXXIII–XL. Texte établi et traduit par Paul Goukowsky* (Paris).
Graf, F. 1985. *Nordionische Kulte: religionsgeschichtliche und epigraphische Untersuchungen zu den Kulten von Chios, Erythrai, Klazomenai und Phokaia* (Rome).
Grandazzi, A. 1997. *The Foundation of Rome: Myth and History*, Todd, J. M. trans. (Ithaca, NY).
Graves, D. 1996. *Profiles of Natchitoches History* (Natchitoches).
Gray, T. R. 1831. *The Confessions of Nat Turner* (Baltimore).
Green, P. 1961. 'The First Sicilian Slave War', *P&P* 20, 10–29.
Green, P. 2006. *Diodorus Siculus: Books 11–12.37.1* (Austin).
Greenberg, K. S. ed. 1996. *The Confessions of Nat Turner and Related Documents* (Boston).
Greenberg, K. S. ed. 2003. *Nat Turner: a Slave Rebellion in History and Memory* (Oxford).
Grünewald, T. 2004. *Bandits in the Roman Empire: Myth and Reality*, Drinkwater, J. trans. (London). (Originally published in German as 1999. *Räuber, Rebellen, Rivalen, Rächer* (Stuttgart).)
Guzzetta, G. 2007. 'La monetazione in Sicilia in "età romana"', in C. Miccichè, S. Modeo and L. Santagati eds. *La Sicilia romana tra repubblica e alto impero* (Caltanissetta), 185–98.
Habinek, T. N. 1998. *The Politics of Latin Literature* (Princeton).
Hall, G. M. 1992. *Africans in Colonial Louisiana: the Development of Afro-Creole Culture in the Eighteenth Century* (Baton Rouge).
Hammond, N. G. L. 1992. 'Plataea's relationship with Thebes, Sparta and Athens', *JHS* 112, 143–50.
Hanserd, R. 2019. *Identity, Spirit and Freedom in the Atlantic World: the Gold Coast and the African Diaspora* (New York).
Harpham, J. S. 2015. '"Tumult and silence" in the study of American slave revolts', *Slavery and Abolition* 36.2, 257–74.
Harris, J. 2017. 'Scholarship and leadership on the Black Sea: Clearchus of Heraclea as (un)enlightened tyrant', *CHS Research Bulletin* 5.2 (accessed at http://nrs.harvard.edu/urn-3:hlnc.essay:HarrisJ.Scholarship_and_Leadership_on_the_Black_Sea.2017).

Harrison, T. 2000. *Divinity and History: the Religion of Herodotus* (Oxford).
Hart, R. 1985. *Slaves Who Abolished Slavery: Blacks in Rebellion* (Mona, Jamaica).
Hartog, J. 1973. *Tula: Verlangen naar vrijheid* (Curaçao).
Harvey, F. D. 1988. 'Herdotus and the man-footed creature', in L. Archer ed. *Slavery and Other Forms of Unfree Labour* (London), 42–52.
Hau, L. 2016. *Moral History from Herodotus to Diodorus Siculus* (Edinburgh).
Heidler, D. and Heidler, J. 1996. *Old Hickory's War: Andrew Jackson and the Quest for Empire* (Mechanicsburg).
Henderson, J. 1975. *The Maculate Muse* (London).
Hermann-Otto, E. 2009. *Sklaverei und Freilassung in der griechisch-römischen Welt* (Hildeschein).
Heuman, G. 1996. 'A tale of two Jamaican rebellions', *Jamaican Historical Review* 19, 1–8.
Hinds, S. 1982. 'An allusion to the literary tradition of the Proserpina myth', *CQ* 32, 476–8.
Hinz, V. 1998. *Der Kult von Demeter und Kore auf Sizilien und in der Magna Graecia* (Wiesbaden).
Hodkinson, S. 2008. 'Spartiates, helots, and the direction of the agrarian economy: toward an understanding of helotage in comparative perspective', in E. del Lago and C. Katsari eds. *Slave Systems: Ancient and Modern* (Cambridge), 258–320.
Hoffer, P. C. 2003. *The Great New York Conspiracy of 1741: Slavery, Crime and Colonial Law* (Lawrence).
Hoffer, P. C. 2010. *Cry Liberty: the Great Stono River Slave Rebellion of 1739* (Oxford).
Holloway, R. R. 1960. 'Numismatic notes from Morgantina 2: half coins of Hieron II in the monetary system of Roman Sicily', *ANSMN* 9, 65–73.
Holloway, R. R. 1965. 'Monetary circulation in central Sicily to the reign of Augustus as documented by the Morgantina excavations', in *Congresso Internazionale di Numismatica (Roma, 11–16 Settembre 1961)*, Vol. I *Relazioni* (Rome), 135–50
Holloway, R. R. 1991. 'Syracusan coinage between Dio and Timoleon', *NAC* 20, 57–62.
Holmes, L. 1970. 'The abortive slave revolt at Point Coupée, Louisiana, 1975', *Louisiana History* 11, 341–62.
Hornblower, J. 1981. *Hieronymus of Cardia* (Oxford).
Howard, P. A. 1998. *Changing History: Afro-Cuban Cabildos and Societies of Color in the Nineteenth Century* (Baton Rouge).
Hoyos, D. 2007. *Truceless War: Carthage's Fight for Survival, 241 to 237 bc* (Leiden).
Hunt, P. 1998. *Slaves, Warfare, and Ideology in the Greek Historians* (Cambridge).
Hunt, P. 2018. *Ancient Greek and Roman Slavery* (Hoboken).
Iduate, J. 1982. 'Noticias sobre sublevaciones y conspiraciones de esclavos: Cafetal Salvador, 1833', *Revista de la Biblioteca Nacional José Martí* 73.1–2, 117–52.
James, C. L. R. 1963. *The Black Jacobins: Touassaint L'Ouverture and the San Domingo Revolution*, 2nd ed. (New York).
Janowitz, N. 2001. *Magic in the Roman World* (London).
Jenson, D. 2011. *Beyond the Slave Narrative: Politics, Sex, and Manuscripts in the Haitian Revolution* (Liverpool).
Johnson, M. P. 2001. 'Denmark Vesey and his co-conspirators', *William and Mary Quarterly* 58.4, 915–76.
Johnston, S. I. 1999. *Restless Dead: Encounters between the Living and the Dead in Ancient Greece* (London).
Jones, A. H. M. 1974a. 'Ancient empires and economy: Rome', in P. A. Brunt ed. *The Roman Economy: Studies in Ancient Economic and Administrative History* (Oxford), 114–39.
Jones, A. H. M. 1974b. 'Taxation in antiquity', in P. A. Brunt ed. *The Roman Economy: Studies in Ancient Economic and Administrative History* (Oxford), 151–85 (annotated and revised by P. A. Brunt).

Jordaan, H. 1999. 'De veranderende situatie op de Curaçaose slavenmarkt en de mislukte slavenopstand op de plantage Santa Maria in 1716', in H. E. Coomans, M. Coomans-Eustatia and J. van't Leven eds. *Veranderend Curaçao* (Bloemendaal), 473–501.
Jordan, W. 1993. *Tumult and Silence at Second Creek: an Inquiry into a Civil War Slave Conspiracy* (Baton Rouge).
Kápsoli Escudero, W. 1975. *Sublevaciones de esclavos en el Perú, siglo XVIII*, Lima.
Keaveney, A. 1998. 'Three Roman chronological problems (141–132 B.C.)', *Klio* 80, 66–90.
Keaveney, A. and Madden, J. A. 1982. 'Phthiriasis and its victims', *Symbolae Osloenses* 57, 87–99.
Kennedy, H. 2016. *The Prophet and the Age of the Caliphates*, 3rd ed. (London).
Kilson, M. D. deB. 1964. 'Toward freedom: an analysis of slave revolts in the United States', *Phylon* 25.2, 175–87.
Kim, H.-H. 1988. 'On the nature of Aristonicus' movement', in T. Yuge and M. Doi eds. *Forms of Control and Subordination in Antiquity* (Leiden), 159–63.
Klein, H. S. and Luna, F. V. 2010. *Slavery in Brazil* (Cambridge).
Kolb, M. 2007. 'The Salemi survey project: long-term landscape change and political consolidation in interior western Sicily 3000 BC–AD 600', in M. Fitzjohn ed. *Uplands of Ancient Sicily and Calabria: the Archaeology of a Landscape Revisited* (London), 171–85.
Kolchin, P 1987. *Unfree Labor: American Slavery and Russian Serfdom* (Cambridge).
Kolchin, P. 1993. *American Slavery, 1619–1877* (New York).
Koptev, A. 2010. 'Timaeus of Tauromenium and the early Roman chronology', in C. Deroux ed. *Studies in Latin Literature and Roman History*, Vol. XV (Brussels), 5–48.
Koptev, A. 2012. 'From the Tarquin kingship to the Republic: three visions of the Graeco-Roman historiography', in C. Deroux ed. *Studies in Latin Literature and Roman History*, Vol. XVI (Brussels), 23–93.
Kraay, C. M. 1976. *Archaic and Classical Greek Coins* (London).
Kunz, H. 2006. *Sicilia: Religionsgeschichte des römischen Sizilien* (Tübingen).
La Rocca, A. 2004. 'Liberi e schiavi nella prima guerra servile di Sicilia', *Studi Storici* 45, 149–67.
Laffranque, M. 1964. *Poseidonios d'Apamée* (Paris).
Lambrinudakis, W. 1982. 'Antike Niederlassungen auf dem Berge Aipos von Chios', in D. Papenfuß and V. M. Strocka eds. *Palast und Hütte: Beiträge zum Bauen und Wohnen im Altertum von Archäologen, Vor- und Frühgeschichtlern: Tagungsbeiträge eines Symposiums der Alexander von Humboldt-Stiftung, Bonn-Bad Godesberg, veranstaltet vom 25.–30. November 1979* (Mainz), 375–81.
Landucci Gattinoni, F. 1990. 'La morte di Antigono e di Lisimaco', in M. Sordi ed. *'Dulce et decorum est pro patria mori': la morte in combattimento nell'antichità* (Milan), 111–26.
Langerwerf, L. L. B. M. 2009. 'Aristomenes and Drimakos', in S. Hodkinson ed. *Sparta: Comparative Approaches* (Swansea), 331–60.
Langerwerf, L. L. B. M. 2010. 'No freer than helots': Messenian Rebel Behaviour in Pausanias' *Messeniaka* in Comparative Perspective. Unpublished PhD dissertation, University of Nottingham.
Lavan, M. 2013a. *Slaves to Rome: Paradigms of Empire in Roman Culture* (Cambridge).
Lavan, M. 2013b. 'Florus and Dio on the enslavement of the provinces', *Cambridge Classical Journal* 59, 125–51.
Lavan, M. 2017. 'Writing revolt in the early Roman empire', in J. Firnhaber-Baker and D. Schoenaers eds. *The Routledge History Handbook of Medieval Revolt* (London), 19–38.
Le Bonniec, H. 1958. *Le culte de Cérès à Rome des origines à la fin de la République* (Paris).
Lenski, N. 2018. 'Framing the question: what is a slave society?', in N. Lenski and C. M. Cameron eds. *What Is a Slave Society? The Practice of Slavery in Global Perspectives* (Cambridge), 15–57.

Lenski, N. and Cameron, C. M. eds. 2018. *What Is a Slave Society? The Practice of Slavery in Global Perspective* (Cambridge).
Leone, A., Witcher, R., Privitera, F. and Spigo, U. 2007. 'The Upper Simeto Valley Project: an interim report on the first season', in M. Fitzjohn ed. *Uplands of Ancient Sicily and Calabria: the Archaeology of a Landscape Revisited* (London), 49–58.
Lepore, J. 2005. *New York Burning: Liberty, Slavery, and Conspiracy in Eighteenth-Century Manhattan* (New York).
Levene, D. S. 1993. *Religion in Livy* (Leiden).
Levene, D. S. 2010. *Livy on the Hannibalic War* (Oxford).
Levithan, J. 2013. *Roman Siege Warfare* (Ann Arbor).
Lévy, C. 1998. 'Rhétorique et philosophie: la monstruosité politique chez Cicéron', *Revue des études latines* 76, 139–57.
Lewis, D. 2011. 'Near Eastern slaves in Classical Attica and the slave trade with Persian territories', *CQ* 61, 91–113.
Lewis, D. 2018a. *Greek Slave Systems in Their Eastern Mediterranean Context, c. 800–146 bc* (Oxford).
Lewis, D. 2018b. 'Notes on slave names, ethnicity, and identity in Classical and Hellenistic Greece', *Studia Źródłoznawcze. U Schyłku Starożytności* 16, 166–99.
Lorber, C. 1994. 'Image and symbol on artefacts of the First Sicilian Slave Revolt: a fresh look at Eunus-Antiochus', *Harlan J. Berk Ltd., 83rd. Bid or Buy Sale (Oct 26)*, 1–3.
Lovano, M. 2002. *The Age of Cinna: Crucible of Late Republican Rome* (Stuttgart).
Love, E. F. 1967. 'Negro resistance to Spanish rule in colonial Mexico', *Journal of Negro History* 52.2, 89–103.
Lubbock, P. 1921. *The Craft of Fiction* (London).
Luce, T. J. 1977. *Livy: the Composition of His History* (Princeton).
Lund, H. S. 1992. *Lysimachus: a Study in Early Hellenistic Kingship* (London).
Luraghi, N. 2003. 'The imaginary conquest of the Helots', in N. Luraghi and S. E. Alcock eds. *Helots and Their Masters in Laconia and Messenia: Histories, Ideologies, Structures* (Cambridge), 109–41.
Luraghi, N. 2008. *The Ancient Messenians: Constructions of Ethnicity and Memory* (Cambridge).
Lynch, J. 1973. *The Spanish American Revolutions* (London).
MacBain, B. 1982. *Prodigy and Expiation: a Study in Religion and Politics in Republican Rome* (Brussels).
McConnell, B. E. 2008. 'Monumental architecture in the area of the grotto', L. Maniscalco ed. *Il santuario dei Palici: un centro di culto nella Valle del Margi* (Palermo), 310–33.
McCullagh, C. B. 1984. *Justifying Historical Descriptions* (Cambridge).
McGushin, P. 1977. *C. Sallustius Crispus Bellum Catilinae: a Commentary* (Leiden).
McKeown, N. 2011. 'Resistance among chattel slaves in the classical Greek world', in K. Bradley and P. Cartledge eds. *The Cambridge World History of Slavery*, Vol. 1: *The Ancient Mediterranean World* (New York), 153–75.
Maganzani, L. 2007. 'Juridiction romaine et autonomie locale dans les provinces au dernier siècle de la République', *Revue historique de droit français et étranger* 85.3, 353–73.
Mahon, J. K. 1992. *History of the Second Seminole War, 1835–1842* (Gainesville).
Malitz, J. 1983. *Die Historien des Poseidonios* (Munich).
Malkin, I. 1998. *The Returns of Odysseus* (Berkeley).
Manganaro, G. 1967. 'Über die zwei Sklavenaufstände in Sizilien', *Helikon* 7, 205–22.
Manganaro, G. 1980. 'La provincia romana', in E. Gabba and G. Vallet eds. *La Sicilia antica*, Vol. II.ii (Naples), 411–61.
Manganaro, G. 1981–2. 'Un ripostoglio siciliano del 214–211 a.C. e la datazione del denarius', *JNG* 31–2, 37–54.

Manganaro, G. 1982. 'Monete e ghiande inscritte degli schiavi ribelli in Sicilia', *Chiron* 12, 237–44.
Manganaro, G. 1983. 'Ancora sulle rivolte "servili" in Sicilia', *Chiron* 13, 405–9.
Manganaro, G. 1988. 'La Sicilia da Sesto Pompeo a Diocleziano', *ANRW* 2.11.1, 3–89.
Manganaro, G. 1990a. 'Due studi di numismatica greca', *ASNSP*[3] 20, 409–27.
Manganaro, G. 1990b. 'Un Philippeion di oro di Euno-Antioco in Sicilia?', *Museum Helveticum* 47/3, 181–3.
Manganaro, G. 2000. 'Onomastica greca su anelli, pesi da telaio e glandes in Sicilia', *ZPE* 133, 123–34.
Manganaro, G. 2012. *Pace e guerra nella Sicilia tardo-ellenistica e romana (215 a.C.–14 d.C.): ricerche storiche e numismatiche.* Nomismata 7 (Bonn).
Maniscalco, L. 2008. 'Parte Prima', in L. Maniscalco ed. *Il santuario dei Palici: un centro di culto nella Valle del Margi* (Palermo), 13–130.
Maniscalco, L. 2018. 'Parte Prima', in L. Maniscalco ed. *Il santuario dei Palici: le richerche del secondo decennio* (Palermo), 15–77.
Maniscalco, L. and McConnell, B. E. 2003. 'The sanctuary of the divine Palikoi, Sicily', *AJA* 107, 145–80.
Manni, E. 1981. *Geografia fisica e politica della Sicilia antica* (Rome).
Manni, E. 1983. 'Divagazioni sul culto dei Palici', reprinted in *Sikelika kai Italika. Scritti Minori di Storia Antica della Sicilia e dell'Italia Meridionale* 1 (Rome), 409–22.
Marconi, P. 1933. *Agrigento arcaica* (Rome).
Marincola, J. 2001. *Greek Historians* (Oxford).
Marincola, J. 2010. 'Aristotle's *Poetics* and "Tragic History"', in S. Tsitsiridis ed. *Parachoregema: Studies on Ancient Theatre in Honour of Professor Gregory M. Sifadis* (Heraklion), 445–60.
Martin, T. R. 1985. *Sovereignty and Coinage in Classical Greece* (Princeton).
Martinez, M. E. 2004. 'The black blood of New Spain: *limpieza de sangre*, racial violence, and gendered power in early colonial Mexico', *William and Mary Quarterly* 61.3, 479–520.
Matsubara, T. 1998. Diodorus Siculus on the Late Roman Republic. Unpublished PhD dissertation, Edinburgh University.
May, J. M. 1996. 'Cicero and the beasts', *Syllecta Classica* 7, 143–53.
Meier, M. 1998. *Aristokraten und Damoden: Untersuchungen zur inneren Entwicklung Spartas im 7. Jahrhundert v. Chr. und zur politischen Funktion der Dichtung des Tyrtaios* (Stuttgart).
Merrill, N. W. 1975. Cicero and Early Roman Invective. Unpublished PhD dissertation, University of Ann Arbor.
Meurant, A. 1998. *Les Paliques, dieux jumeaux siciliens.* Bibliotheque de Cahiers de l'Institut de Louvain 96 (Louvain-la-Neuve).
Midolo, D. 2008. 'Il santuario in età ellenistica: i materiali', in L. Maniscalco ed. *Il santuario dei Palici: un centro di culto nella Valle del Margi* (Palermo), 217–43.
Miles, G. B. 1995. *Livy: Reconstructing Early Rome* (Ithaca, NY).
Mileta, C. 1998. 'Verschwörung oder Eruption? Diodor und die bzyantinischen Exzerptoren über den Ersten Sizilischen Sklavenkrieg', in C.-F. Collatz, J. Dummer and M.-L. Welitz eds. *Dissertatiunculae criticae, Festschrift für Günther Christian Hansen* (Würzburg), 133–54.
Miller, S. A. 2003. *Coacoochee's Bones: a Seminole Saga* (Lawrence).
Minì, A. 1977. *Monete antiche di bronzo della zecca di Siracusa* (Novara).
Momigliano, A. 1975. *Alien Wisdom: the Limits of Hellenization* (Cambridge).
Mommsen, T. 1899. *Römisches Staatsrecht* (Leipzig).
Morton, P. 2013. 'Eunus: the cowardly king', *CQ* 63.1, 237–52.
Morton, P. 2014. 'The geography of rebellion: strategy and supply in the two Sicilian Slave Wars', *BICS* 57.1, 20–38.

Morton, P. 2018. 'Diodorus Siculus' "Slave War" narratives: writing social commentary in the *Bibliotheke*', *CQ* 68.2, 1–18.
Moscati Castelnuovo, L. 1991. 'Iloti e fondazione di Taranto', *Latomus* 50, 64–79.
Mouritsen, H. 1998. *Italian Unification: a Study in Ancient and Modern Historiography* (London).
Mullin, G. W. 1972. *Flight and Rebellion in Eighteenth Century Viriginia* (New York).
Munson, R. V. 2001. *Telling Wonders: Etanographic and Political Discourse in the Work of Herodotus* (Ann Arbor).
Muntz, C. E. 2017. *Diodorus Siculus and the World of the Late Roman Republic* (Oxford).
Murray, O. 1965. 'Philodemos and the Good King according to Homer', *JRS* 55, 161–82.
Murray, O. 1967. 'Aristeas and Ptolemaic kingship', *JThS* 18, 337–71.
Murray, O. 1970. 'Hecateus of Abdera and Pharaonic kingship', *Journal of Egyptian Archaeology* 56, 141–71.
Murray, O. 1975. 'Review of: A. Burton, *Diodorus Siculus, Book I: A Commentary* (E. J. Brill: Leiden, 1972)', *JHS* 95, 214–15.
Murray, O. 2007. 'Philosophy and monarchy in the Hellenistic world', in T. Rajak, S. Pearce, J. Aitken and J. Dines eds. *Jewish Perspectives on Hellenistic Rulers* (Berkeley), 13–28.
Murray, O. 2008. 'Ptolemaic royal patronage', in P. McKechnie and P. Guillaume eds. (Leiden), 9–24.
Musti, D. 1988. *Strabone e la Magna Grecia: città e popoli dell'Italia antica* (Padua).
Nafissi, M. 1999. 'From Sparta to Taras: *nomina, ktiseis* and relationships between colony and mother city', in S. Hodkinson and A. Powell eds. *Sparta: New Perspectives* (London), 245–72.
Nicholls, M. L. 2012. *Whispers of Rebellion: Narrating Gabriel's Conspiracy* (Charlottesville).
Nicolet, C. 1994. 'Dîmes de Sicile, d'Asie et d'ailleurs', in *Le ravitaillement en blé de Rome et des centres urbains des débuts de la Republique jusqu'au Haut Empire (Actes du colloque international de Naples, 1991)* (Naples and Rome), 215–29. [Now reprinted in Nicolet, C. 2000. *Censeurs et publicains: économie et fiscalité dans la Rome antique* (Paris), 277–93.]
Nishida, M. 2003. *Slavery and Identity: Ethnicity, Gender, and Race in Salvador, Brazil, 1808–1888* (Bloomington).
Nock, A. D. 1972. 'Paul the Magus', in Z. Stewart ed. *Essays on Religion and the Ancient World*, Vol. I (Oxford), 308–30.
North, J. A. 1976. 'Conservatism and change in Roman religion', *PBSR* 44, 1–12.
North, J. A. 1979. 'Religious toleration in Republican Rome', *PCPS* 205, 85–103.
North, J. A. 1992. 'The development of religious pluralism', in J. Lieu, J. A. North and T. Rajak eds. *The Jews among Pagans and Christians* (London), 174–93.
North, J. A. 2000. *Roman Religion* (Cambridge).
O'Callaghan, E. B. ed. 1855. *Documents Relative to the Colonial History of New York*, Vol. 5 (Albany).
Ogden, D. 2004. *Aristomenes of Messene· Legends of Sparta's Nemesis* (Swansea).
Ogilvie, R. M. 1965. *A Commentary on Livy Books 1–5* (Oxford).
O'Neil Spady, J. 2011. 'Power and confession: on the credibility of the earliest reports of the Denmark Vesey slave conspiracy', *William and Mary Quarterly* 68.2, 287–304.
Oostindie, G. 2011. 'Slave resistance, colour lines, and the impact of the French and Haitian revolutions in Curaçao', in W. Kloosters and G. Oostindie eds. *Curaçao in the Age of Revolutions, 1795–1800* (Leiden), 1–22.
Opelt, I. 1975. *Die lateinischen Schimpfwörter und verwandte sprachliche Erscheinungen: eine Typologie* (Heidelberg).
Ormerod, H. A. 1924. *Piracy in the Ancient World* (Liverpool).
Osborne, M. J. and Byrne, S. G. eds 1994. *Lexicon of Greek Personal Names*, Vol. II: *Attica* (Oxford). [Revised in 2007.]
Pailler, J.-M. 1988. *Bacchanalia* (Paris).

Palmer, C. 1976. *Slaves of the White God: Blacks in Mexico, 1570–1650* (Cambridge).
Paquette, R. L. 1988. *Sugar Is Made with Blood: the Conspiracy of La Escalera an the Conflict between Empires over Slavery in Cuba* (Middletown).
Paquette, R. L. and Egerton, D. R. 2004. 'Of facts and fables: new light on the Demark Vesey affair', *South Carolina Historical Magazine* 105.1, 8–48.
Parent, A. S. 2003. *Foul Means: the Formation of a Slave Society in Virginia, 1660–1740* (Chapel Hill).
Pareti, L. 1927. 'I supposti "sdoppiamenti" delle guerre servili in Sicilia', *RFIC* 5, 44–67.
Paton, D. 2012. 'Witchcraft, poison, law, and Atlantic slavery', *William and Mary Quarterly* 69.2, 235–64.
Patterson, O. 1975. *Sociology of Slavery: an Analysis of the Origins, Development, and Structure of Negro Slave Society in Jamaica* (Rutherford).
Paula, A. F. ed. 1974. *1795: De slavenopstand op Curaçao: een bronnenuitgave van de originele overheidsdocumenten verzorgd en uitgegeven door het Centraal Historisch Archief* (Curaçao).
Pelling, C. 2000. *Literary Texts and the Greek Historian* (London).
Pembroke, S. 1970. 'Locres et Tarente: le rôle des femmes dans la fondation de deux colonies grecques', *Annales: Histiore, Sciences Sociales* 25.5, 1240–70.
Péré-Noguès, S. 2006. 'Les "identités" siciliennes durant les guerres puniques: entre culture et politique', in P. Francois, P. Moret and S. Péré-Noguès eds. *L'hellénisation en Méditerranée occidentale au temps des guerres puniques (260–180 av. J.C.)* (Toulouse), 57–70.
Perkins, P. 2007. '*Aliud* in Sicilia? Cultural development in Rome's first province', in P. van Dommelen and N. Terrenato eds. *Articulating Local Cultures: Power and Identity under the Expanding Roman Republic* (Portsmouth), 33–53.
Pfuntner, L. 2015. 'Reading Diodorus through Photius: the case of the Sicilian Slave Revolts', *GRBS* 55.1, 256–72.
Piganiol, A. 1973. 'Scripta varia II: les origines de Rome et la République', *Latomus* 132, 203–28.
Pinzone, A. 1999. '*Maiorum sapientia e lex Hieronica*: Roma e l'organizzazione della provinciale Sicilia da Gaio Flaminio a Cicerone' in A. Pinzone ed. *Provincia Sicilia* (Catania), 1–37.
Pobjoy, M. P. 2013. 'Appendix 4: a note on dates', in T. J. Cornell ed. *The Fragments of the Roman Historians*, Vol. I (Oxford), 661–2.
Popović, A. 1999. *The Revolt of African Slaves in Iraq in the 3rd/9th Century*, L. King trans. (Princeton).
Postma, J. 2008. *Slave Revolts* (London).
Poucet, J. 2000. *Les rois de Rome: tradition et histoire* (Louvain).
Powell, A. 1998. 'The peopling of the underworld', in H.-P. Stahl ed. *Vergil's Aeneid: Augustan Epic and Political Context* (London and Swansea), 85–100.
Prag, J. R. W. 2003. 'Nouveaux regards sur les élites locales de la Sicile républicaine', *Histoire et Sociétés Rurales* 19, 121–32.
Prag, J. R. W. 2007a. '*Auxilia* and *gymnasia*: a Sicilian model of Roman imperialism', *JRS* 97, 68–100.
Prag, J. R. W. 2007b. 'Introduction', in J. R. W. Prag ed. *Sicilia nutrix plebis Romanae: Rhetoric, Law and Taxation in Cicero's Verrines* (London), 1–4.
Prag, J. R. W. 2009a. 'Republican Sicily at the start of the 21st Century: the rise of the optimists', *Pallas* 79, 131–44.
Prag, J. R. W. 2009b. 'Identità siciliana in età romano repubblicana', in C. Michelini ed. *Immagine e immagini della Sicilia e di altre isole del Mediterraneo antico: atti delle Seste Giornate Internazionale di studi sull'area elima e la Sicilia occidentale (Erice, 12–16 ottobre 2006)*, Vol. 1 (Pisa), 87–100.

Prag, J. R. W. 2013. 'Sicilian identity in the Hellenistic and Roman periods: epigraphic considerations', in P. Martzavou and N. Papazarkadas eds. *Epigraphical Apporaches to the Postclassical Polis: Fourth Century bc to Second Century ad* (Oxford), 37–53.
Prag, J. R. W. 2015. 'Cities and civic life in late Hellenistic Roman Sicily (with an appendix on Cicero, *In Verrem* 3.12–13 and the status of cities in Sicily after 210 BC)', *Cahiers du Centre Gustave Glotz* 25 (2014), 165–208.
Puglisi, M. 2009. *La Sicilia da Dionisio I a Sesto Pompeo: circolazione e funzione della moneta* (Messina).
Puglisi, M. 2014. 'Territorial organisation in late Hellenistic Halaesa, Sicily', in W. Eck and P. Funke eds. *ÖFFENTLICHKEIT – MONUMENT – TEXT: XIV Congressus Internationalis Epigraphiae Graecae et Latinae 27.–31. Augusti MMXII. Akten* (Berlin), 590–2.
Purcell, N. 2003. 'Becoming historical: the Roman case', in D. Braund and C. Gill eds. *Myth, History and Culture in Republican Rome: Studies in Honour of T. P. Wiseman* (Exeter), 12–40.
Qviller, B. 1996. 'Reconstructing the Spartan Partheniai: many guesses and a few facts', *Symbolae Osloenses* 71, 34–41.
Rajak, T. 1983. *Josephus* (London).
Rasmussen, D. 2011. *American Uprising: the Untold Story of America's Largest Slave Revolt* (New York).
Rathmann, M. 2016. *Diodor und seine 'Bibliotheke'* (Berlin).
Rawson, E. 1975. 'Caesar's heritage: Hellenistic kings and their Roman equals', *JRS* 65, 148–59.
Reckord, M. 1969. 'The Jamaican slave rebellion of 1831', *Past and Present* 40, 108–25.
Redfield, J. M. 2003. *The Locrian Maidens: Love and Death in Greek Italy* (Princeton).
Reis, J. J. 1993. *Slave Rebellion in Brazil: the Muslim Uprising of 1835 in Bahia*, Brakel, A. trans. (Baltimore). [Originally published in Portuguese as 1986. *Rebelião escrava no Brasil: a história do levante dos malês (1835)* (São Paolo).]
Reis, J. J. 1995–6. 'Quilombos e revoltas escravas no Brasil', *Revista USP* 28, 13–39.
Reusser, C., Cappucini, L., Mohr, M., Russenberger, C., Mango, E. and Badertscher, T. 2010. 'Forschungen auf dem Monte Iate 2009', *Antike Kunst* 53, 114–38.
Reusser, C., Cappuccini, L., Mohr, M., Russenberger, C., Mango, E. and Badertscher, T. 2011. 'Forschungen auf dem Monte Iato 2010', *Antike Kunst* 54, 71–104.
Reusser, C., Cappucini, L., Mohr, M., Russenberger, C., Mango, E. and Badertscher, T. 2012. 'Forschungen auf dem Monte Iato 2011', *Antike Kunst* 55, 112–37.
Reusser, C., Perifanakis, J., Mohr, M., Mango, E. and Badertscher T. 2013. 'Forschungen auf dem Monte Iato 2012', *Antike Kunst* 56, 72–87.
Rhoads, D. M. 1976. *Israel in Revolution 6–74 ce* (Philadelphia).
Ridgway, D. 2006. 'Riflessioni su Tarquinia: Demarato e l'"ellenizzazione dei barbari"', in M. Bonghi Jovina ed. *Tarquinia e le civiltà del Mediterraneo* (Milan), 27–47.
Rigsby, K. 2005. 'Agathopolis and Doulopolis', *EA* 38, 109–15.
Rivers, L. E. 2012. *Rebels and Runaways: Slave Resistance in Nineteenth-Century Florida* (Chicago).
Robert, L. and Robert, J. 1989. *Claros I: décrets hellénistiques* (Paris).
Robinson, E. S. G. 1920. 'Antiochus, King of the Slaves', *Num. Chron.* 4.20, 175–6.
Rodriguez, J. P. 1999a. 'Rebellion on the river road: the ideology and influence of Louisiana's German Coast Slave Insurrection of 1811', in J. R. McKivigan and S. Harrold eds. *Antislavery Violence: Sectional, Racial, and Cultural Conflict in Antebellum America* (Knoxville), 65–88.
Rodriguez, J. P. 1999b. 'Complicity and deceit: Lewis Cheney's plot and its bloody consequences', in M. Bellesiles ed. *Lethal Imagination: Violence and Brutality in American History* (New York), 139–48.
Rosenstein, N. 2008. 'Aristocrats and agriculture', *JRS* 98, 1–26.
Roth, U. 2005. 'Food, status, and the peculium of agricultural slaves', *JRA* 18, 278–92.

Roth, U. 2010. 'Peculium, freedom, citizenship: golden triangle or vicious circle? An act in two parts', in U. Roth ed. *By the Sweat of Your Brow: Roman Slavery in Its Socio-Economic Setting* (London), 91–120.
Rouland, N. 1977. *Les esclaves romains en temps de guerre* (Brussels).
Rout, L. B. 1976. *The African Experience in Spanish America: 1502 to the Present Day* (Cambridge).
Rubinsohn, W. Z. 1982. 'Some remarks on the causes and repercussions of the so-called "Second Slave Revolt" in Sicily', *Athenaeum* 60, 436–51.
Rucker, W. 2001. 'Conjure, magic, and power: the influence of Afro-Atlantic religious practices on slave resistance and rebellion', *Journal of Black Studies* 32, 84–103.
Rutter, N. K. 1997. *Greek Coinages of Southern Italy and Sicily* (London).
Sacks, K. 1990. *Diodorus Siculus and the First Century* (Princeton).
Sánchez León, M. L. 2004. 'La amonedación del *Basileus* Antíoco en Sicilia (siglo II aC.)', in F. Chaves Tristán and F. J. García Fernández eds. *Moneta qua scripta: la moneda como soporte de escritura* (Sevilla), 223–8.
Santos, M. J. V. 1983. *A Balaiada e a Insurreição de escravos no Maranhão* (São Paulo).
Särström, M. 1940. *A Study in the Coinage of the Mamertines* (Lund).
Sartori, F. 1981. 'Il commune Siciliae nel tardo impero', *Klio* 63, 401–9.
Schaff, H. 1992. *Untersuchungen zu Gebäudestiftungen in hellenistischer Zeit* (Köln-Weimar).
Scheidel, W. 2005. 'Human mobility in Roman Italy, II: the slave population', *JRS* 95, 64–79.
Scheidel, W. 2011. 'The Roman slave supply', in K. R. Bradley and P. Cartledge eds. *The Cambridge World History of Slavery*, Vol. 1: *The Ancient Mediterranean World* (Cambridge), 287–310.
Schipporeit, S. 2008. 'Enna and Eleusis', in C. A. di Stefano ed. *Demetra: la divinità, i santuari, il culto, la leggendi. Atti del I Congresso Internazionale Enna, 1–4 Luglio 2004* (Pisa), 41–6.
Schmitt-Pantel, P. 1979. 'Histoire de tyran ou comment la cité grecque construit ses marges', in B. Vincent ed. *Les marginaux et les exclus dans l'histoire*. Cahiers Jussieu 5 (Paris), 217–31.
Schubart, W. 1937. 'Das hellenistische Königsideal nach Inschriften und Papyri', *Archiv für Papyrusforschung* 12, 1–26.
Schuler, M. 1970. 'Akan slave rebellions in the British Caribbean', *Savacou* 1, 8–31.
Schwartz, S. B. 1986. *Sugar Plantations in the Formation of Brazilian Society: Bahia 1550–1835* (Cambridge).
Schwartz, S. B. 1992. *Slaves, Peasants, and Rebels* (Chicago).
Schwartz, S. B. 1996. 'Cantos e quilombos numa conspiração do escravos Hausás', in J. J. Reis and F. dos Santos Gomes eds. *Liberdade por um fio: História dos quilombos no Brasil* (São Paulo), 373–406.
Scott, K. 1961. 'The slave insurrection in New York in 1712', *New York Historical Society Quarterly* 45, 43–74.
Scramuzza, V. M. 1937. 'Roman Sicily', in T. Frank ed. *An Economic Survey of Ancient Rome* (Baltimore), 225–377.
Sensbach, J. F. 2009. *Rebecca's Revival* (Cambridge).
Shaw, B. D. 1984. 'Bandits in the Roman empire', *P&P* 105, 3–52.
Shaw, B. D. 2001. *Spartacus and the Slave Wars: a Brief History with Documents* (Boston).
Sheridan, R. B. 1976. 'The Jamaican slave insurrection scare of 1776 and the American Revolution', *Journal of Negro History* 61.3, 290–308.
Shuler, J. 2009. *Calling Out Liberty: the Stono Slave Rebellion and the Universal Struggle for Human Rights* (Jackson).
Sjöqvist, E. 1958. 'Excavations at Serra Orlando (Morgantina): preliminary report 2', *AJA* 62.2, 155–64.

Sjöqvist, E. 1960a. 'Excavations at Morgantina (Serra Orlando) 1959: preliminary report IV', *AJA* 64.2, 125–35.
Sjöqvist, E. 1960b. 'Numismatic notes from Morgantina', *ANSMN* 9, 53–63.
Skinner, Q. 2010. 'On the slogan of Republican political theory', *European Journal of Political Theory* 9.1, 95–102.
Slater, N. W. 1990. *Reading Petronius* (London).
Smith, C. J. 2010. 'Rhetorical history: the Struggle of the Orders in Livy', in D. H. Berry and A. Erskine eds. *Form and Function in Roman Oratory* (Cambridge), 264–80.
Smith, M. 1978. *Jesus the Magician* (London).
Smith, M. M. 2005. *Stono: Documenting and Interpreting a Southern Slave Revolt* (Columbia).
Soares, C. E. L. and dos Santos Gomes, F. 2001. '"Com o Pé sobre um Vulcão": Africanos Minas, Identidades e a Repressão Antiafricana no Rio de Janeiro (1830–1840)', *Revista Estudos Afro-Asiáticos* 23.2, 1–44.
Spatafora, F. 2001. 'Un contributo per l'identificazione di una delle "città di Sicilia" dei decreti di Entella', in C. Ampolo ed. *Da un'antica città di Sicilia: i decreti di Entella e Nakone* (Pisa), 111–14.
Spatafora, F. and Vassallo, S. eds. 2004. *Das Eigene und das Andere: Griechen, Sikaner und Elymer. Neue archäologische Forschungen im antiken Sizilien* (Palermo).
Spigo, U. ed. 2005. *Tindari: l'area archeologica e l'antiquarium* (Milan).
Stewart, R. 1995. 'Catiline and the crisis of 63–60 B.C.: the Italian perspective', *Latomus* 54.1, 62–78.
Stewart, R. 2012. *Plautus and Roman Slavery* (Oxford).
Stillwell, R. 1959. 'Excavations at Serra Orlando 1958: preliminary report III', *AJA* 63.2, 167–73.
Stillwell, R. 1963. 'Excavations at Morgantina (Serra Orlando) 1962: preliminary report VII', *AJA* 67.2, 163–71.
Stinchcombe, A. L. and Stinchcombe, A. L. L. 1995. *Sugar Island Slavery in the Age of Enlightenment: the Political Economy of the Caribbean World* (Princeton).
Strauss, B. 2010. 'Slave wars of Greece and Rome', in V. D. Hanson ed. *Makers of Ancient Strategy* (Oxford), 185–205.
Stronk, J. P. 2017. *Semiramis' Legacy* (Edinburgh).
Stylianou, P. J. 1998. *A Historical Commentary on Diodorus Siculus Book 15* (Oxford).
Sutherland, C. H. V. 1974. *Roman Coins* (London).
Tardieu, P. 2003. *'Morir o dominar': en torno al reglamento de esclavos de Cuba (1841–1866)* (Madrid).
Taylor, T. 2001. 'Believing the ancients: quantitative and qualitative dimensions of slavery and the slave trade in later prehistoric Eurasia', *World Archaeology* 33, 27–43.
Teodorsson, S.-T. 2008. 'The education of rulers in theory (*Mor.*) and Practice (*Vitae*)', in A. Nikolaidis ed. *The Unity of Plutarch's Work: 'Moralia' Themes in the 'Lives', Features of the 'Lives' in the 'Moralia'* (Berlin), 339–50.
Theiler, W. 1982. *Poseidonios: die Fragmente*, Vol. 2: *Erläuterungen* (Berlin).
Theobald, M. M. 2005–6. 'Slave conspiracies in Virginia', *Journal of the Colonial Williamsburg Foundation* 28.1, 26–31.
Thomas, R. 2000. *Herodotus in Context* (Cambridge).
Thompson, S. M. 1999. A Central Sicilian Landscape: Settlement and Society in the Territory of Ancient Morgantina (5000 BC–AD 50). Unpublished PhD dissertation, University of Virginia.
Thrasher, A. 1995. *On to New Orleans! Louisiana's Heroic 1811 Slave Revolt*, New Orleans.
Toynbee, A. I. 1965. *Hannibal's Legacy*, Vol. 2 (London).
Tragle, H. I. 1971. *The Southampton Slave Revolt of 1831: a Compilation of Source Material* (Amherst).
Treptow, R. 1964. Die Kunst der Reden in 1. und 3. Dekade des livianischen Geschichtswerks. Unpublished PhD dissertation, Universität Kiel.

Trouillot, M.-R. 1995. *Silencing the Past: Power and the Production of History* (Boston).
Urbainczyk, T. 2008a. *Slave Revolts in Antiquity* (Stocksfield).
Urbainczyk, T. 2008b. 'Rewriting slave rebellions', in C. Katsari and E. Dal Lago eds. *From Captivity to Freedom: Themes in Ancient Slavery* (Leicester), 95–106.
Vasaly, A. 2015a. *Livy's Political Philosophy* (Cambridge).
Vasaly, A. 2015b. 'The composition of the *Ab Urbe condita*: the case of the first pentad', in B. Mineo ed. *A Companion to Livy* (Oxford), 217–29.
Vásquez-Machicado, H. and Vásquez-Machicado, J. 1988. 'El alzamiento de Santa Cruz, 1809', in G. Ovando Sanz and A. Vásquez, eds. *Obras completas de Humberto Vásquez-Machicado y José Vásquez-Machicado* (La Paz), 617–20.
Vavrinek, V. 1975. 'Aristonicus of Pergamum: pretender to the throne or leader of a slave revolt?', *Eirene* 13, 109–29.
Verbrugghe, G. P. 1972. 'Sicily 210–70 B.C.: Livy, Cicero and Diodorus', *TAPA* 103, 535–59.
Verbrugghe, G. P. 1974. 'Slave rebellion or Sicily in revolt?', *Kokalos* 20, 46–60.
Vogt, J. 1965. *Sklaverei und Humanität: Studien zur antiken Sklaverei und ihrer Erforschung* (Wiesbaden). [Published in English as 1974. *Ancient Slavery and the Ideal of Man*, Wiedemann, T. trans. (Oxford).]
Vogt, J. 1973. 'Zum Experiment des Drimakos: Sklavenhaltung und Räuberstand', *Saeculum* 24, 213–19.
Wade, R. C. 1964. 'The Vesey plot: a reconsideration', *Journal of Southern History* 30.2, 134–61.
Walbank, F. W. 1967. *A Historical Commentary on Polybius*, Vol. III (Oxford).
Walbank, F. W. 1972. *Polybius* (London).
Walbank, F. W. 1979. *A Historical Commentary on Polybius*, Vol. III (Oxford).
Walbank, F. W. 1984. 'Monarchies and monarchic ideas', in F. W. Walbank, A. E. Astin, M. W. Frederiksen and R. M. Ogilvie eds. *Cambridge Ancient History*, Vol. VII[2] (Cambridge), 62–100.
Walsh, P. G. 1961. *Livy: His Historical Aims and Methods* (Cambridge).
Walvin, J. 2008. *The Trader, the Owner, the Slave: Parallel Lives in the Age of Slavery* (London).
Watson, L. 2002. 'Horace and the pirates', in A. Powell and K. Welch eds. *Sextus Pompeius* (London), 213–28.
Welch, K. 2002. 'Sextus Pompeius and the *res publica* in 42–39 BC', in A. Powell and K. Welch eds. *Sextus Pompeius* (London), 31–63.
Welwei, K.-W. 1974. *Unfreie im Antiken Kriegsdienst. Erster Teil: Athens und Sparta* (Wiesbaden).
Welwei, K.-W. 1988. *Unfreie im Antiken Kriegsdienst. Dritter Teil: Rom* (Wiesbaden).
West, S. 1999. 'Introducing the Scythians: Herodotus on Koumiss (4.2)', *Museum Helveticum* 56, 76–86.
Westermann, W. L. 1945. 'Slave maintenance and slave revolts', *C Phil.* 40.1, 1–10.
Westermann, W. L. 1955. *The Slave Systems of Greek and Roman Antiquity* (Philadelphia).
White, D. 1964. 'Demeter's Sicilian cult as a political instrument', *GRBS* 5, 261–79.
Wilson, P. 1999. 'The *aulos* in Athens', in S. Goldhill and R. Osborne eds. *Performance Culture and Athenian Democracy* (Cambridge), 58–95.
Wilson, R. J. A. 1981. 'Heraclea Minoa and its hinterland in classical antiquity', in G. Barker and R. Hodges eds. *Archaeology and Italian Society: Papers in Italian Archaeology II* (Oxford), 249–60.
Wilson, R. J. A. 1990. *Sicily under the Roman Empire: the Archaeology of a Roman Province 36 b.c.–a.d. 535* (Warminster).
Wilson, R. J. A. 1994. *Lexicon Mythologiae Classicae*, VII.1, s.v. Sikelia (Zurich), 759–61.
Wilson, R. J. A. 2000. 'Ciceronian Sicily: an archaeological perspective', in C. Smith and J. Serrati eds. *Sicily from Aeneas to Augustus* (Edinburgh), 134–60.

Wilson, R. J. A. 2013a. 'Hellenistic Sicily, *c.* 270–100 BC', in J. R. W. Prag and J. C. Quinn eds. *The Hellenistic West: Rethinking the Ancient Mediterranean* (Cambridge), 79–119.
Wilson, R. J. A. 2013b. 'Becoming Roman overseas? Sicily and Sardinia in the later Roman republic', in J. D. Evans ed. *A Companion to the Archaeology of the Roman Republic* (Malden), 485–504.
Wilson, R. J. A. and Leonard, A. Jr. 1980. 'Field Survey at Heraclea Minoa (Agrigento), Sicily', *Journal of Field Archaeology* 7, 219–39.
Winter, N. A. 2009. *Symbols of Wealth and Power: Architectural Terracotta Decoration in Etruria and Central Italy, 640–510 b.c.* (Ann Arbor).
Wirth, G. 2004. 'Sklaven und Helden: zur Darstellung der sizilischen Aufstände bei Diodor', in H. Heftner and K. Tomaschitz eds. *Ad Fontes!* (Vienna), 81–5.
Wirth, G. 2006. *Katastrophe und Zukunftshoffnung* (Vienna).
Wiseman, T. P. 1989. 'Roman legend and oral tradition', *JRS* 79, 129–37.
Wiseman, T. P. 1995. *Remus: a Roman Myth* (Cambridge).
Wiseman, T. P. 2004. *The Myths of Rome* (Exeter).
Wiseman, T. P. 2008. *Unwritten Rome* (Exeter).
Wood, P. H. 1974. *Black Majority: Negroes in Colonial South Carolina from 1670 through the Stono Rebellion* (New York).
Woodman, A. J. 1988. *Rhetoric in Classical Historiography* (Portland).
Wozniczka, P. 2018. 'Diodoros' narrative of the First Sicilian Slave Revolt (c. 140/35–132 B.C.) – a reflection of Poseidonios' ideas and style?', in L. I. Hau, A. Meeus, and B. Sheridan eds. *Diodoros of Sicily: Historiographical Theory and Practice in the Bibliotheke* (Leuven), 221–46.
Wozniczka, P. 2021. 'An unknown preface from Diodorus' *Bibliotheke* (book 34)?', *CQ* 71.2, 655–75.
Yarrow, L. M. 2006. *Historiography at the End of the Republic: Provincial Perspectives on Roman Rule* (Oxford).
Yarrow, L. M. 2012. '*Decem legati*: a flexible institution, rigidly perceived', in C. Smith and L. M. Yarrow eds. *Imperialism, Cultural Politics, and Polybius* (Oxford), 168–83.
Yavetz, Z. 1963. 'The failure of Catiline's conspiracy', *Historia* 12, 486–99.
Yavetz, Z. 1988. *Slaves and Slavery in Ancient Rome* (Oxford).
Zevi, F. 1995. 'Demarato e i re "corinzi" di Roma', in A. Storchi Marino ed. *L'Incidenza dell'Antico: studi in memoria di Ettore Lepore* (Naples), 291–314. [Published in English as 2014. 'Demaratus and the "Corinthian" Kings of Rome', in J. H. Richardson and F. Santangelo eds. *Oxford Readings in Classical Studies. The Roman Historical Tradition: Regal and Republican Rome*, Jones, L. trans. (Oxford), 53–82.]
Ziegler, K. 1949a. 'Palikè', *RE* 18.3, 98–9.
Ziegler, K. 1949b. 'Palikoi', *RE* 18.3, 100–23.

Index

Achaeus, 53, 93
Aetna, 35, 42
   SYMMAXIKON coinage, 55
Agrigentum
   First Romano-Sicilian War, 1–2, 60, 83, 93
   Second Punic War, 55, 57n
   Second Romano-Sicilian War, 123
   slingshots from, 112–13
Agyrium, 29n
   SYMMAXIKON coinage, 55
Aidone *see* Morgantina
Aluntium, 29, 51
   SYMMAXIKON coinage, 55
Ammianus Marcellinus, 154
ἀνδρεία *see* Hellenistic kingship
Antigenes, 70, 74–5, 80
Antiochus Epiphanes, 74, 117
Antonius, M. (cos. 99 BC, *RE* 28), 106
Antonius, M. (cos. 44 BC, *RE* 30), 161–2
Apollo, 30–2, 46, 48, 50
Aponte Conspiracy, 177, 185, 186n
Appian, 139–40
Apuleius Saturninus, L. (*RE* 'Apuleius' 29), 140n, 149
Aquilius, M'. (cos. 101 BC, *RE* 11), 2–3, 96, 122, 140
   single combat with Athenion, 106–7
   effect on Roman idea of Sicily, 192
Ares
   on Sicilian coinage, 27–9, 46
Aristeas, 72n, 82n

Aristodemus of Cumae, 135, 151
   topos of enslaved support during tyranny, 141–4
Aristonicus, 141
   inclusion of dynastic war as a slave revolt, 156–8, 160
   similarity to First Romano-Sicilian War, 194
Aristotle, 133
   definition of identification, 86n, 88
   views on music, 100n
Artemis
   on coinage from the First Romano-Sicilian War, 26–7
   on Sicilian coinage, 30, 46, 50–1, 53
   on slingshots, 112n, 113
astrology, 103–4
Athena
   on coinage from the First Romano-Sicilian War, 28–9
   on slingshots, 112n, 113
Athenaeus, 136
   fragment of Posidonius, 69, 85n
   story of Drimakos, 132–3
   foundation of Ephesus, 133
Athenion, 2–3, 10, 96–8, 100, 112, 120
   as leader of Second Romano-Sicilian War, 106, 122–3, 125
   at Battle of Scirthaea, 105–6
   attack on Lilybaeum, 102–4, 105
   bravery, 101–2, 105–6
   Cilician, 101–2

death in single combat by M'.
  Aquilius, 106, 122, 192
 importance to slave-owner narratives,
  106–7, 122
 initial revolt, 101–2
 jailed by Salvius/Tryphon, 105
 manipulating rebels, 103–5, 107
 name on rebel slingshots, 112–13
 self-presentation as king, 116–17
 summoned by Salvius/Tryphon, 104–5
 use of astronomy, 101–2, 103–4, 105,
  107
 use of pretence, 101–4, 106, 107
 vilicus, 103
Athens, 138, 161
Attalus III, 141
Augustus (cos. 27, 26, 25, 24, 23, 5, 2
  BC), 150
 accusing Sex. Pompeius of enlisting
  enslaved people, 136–7, 162
 use of freedman cohorts, 162; see also
  Octavianus, C.
aulos, 100n

Bahia, 171–2, 182
Bahian Revolt of 1835, 173, 181
banditry, 81–2
 First Romano-Sicilian War, 78–83
 political slur, 81n
 Second Romano-Sicilian War, 108–11
bandits
 latro and ληστής, 81–2; see also
  banditry
Baptist War, 174, 176, 180
Barbados, 174–6
Bradley, K., 4–5, 43n, 44, 69, 155–6
Brazil, slave revolts, 171–3, 181–2
Bulla Felix, 81n
Bussa's Revolt, 175

Caecilius Metellus Pius Scipio, Q. (cos.
  52 BC, *RE* 99), 161
Caesar *see* Julius Caesar, C.
Caleacte, 29, 51
Caltabellotta *see* Triokala
Cammarata, E., 23–4, 26, 28–9, 41–2
Campana, A., 24, 26–9, 41–2, 195
Cannae, battle of, 54, 162
Cassius Dio, 122–3

on origin of Second Romano-Sicilian
  War, 108–9
Catana, 2, 19, 35, 40, 44, 46, 50, 60,
  83
 post-210 BC coinage, 42–3
Catilinarian speeches, 138–9, 149
Catiline *see* Sergius Catilina, L.
Centuripae, 24, 29–30, 42, 50
Cephaloedium, 29, 51
Chaeronea, battle of (338 BC), 161
Chians
 reputation as first Greeks to buy
  slaves, 137, 151
Chios, 132–3, 137–8
Cicero *see* Tullius Cicero, M.
Cilicians
 reputation as bandits, 82, 102n
Claudius Marcellus, M. (cos. 222, 214,
  210, 208 BC, *RE* 220), 54
Claudius Pulcher Ap., 147
Clonius, P., 2, 99, 110–11
coinage
 Ietas circulation, 37–40
 imagery of King Antiochus' issues,
  44–5
 imagery of Sicilian coinage, 46–51
 King Antiochus' issues, 23–32
 legends, 43–4, 55–7
 Morgantina circulation, 33–7
 provenance of King Antiochus' issues,
  23–4
 rebel presentation, 43–4, 51–4, 57,
  58–65
 Sicilian circulation, 32–3, 40–1
 Sicilian context, 54–5: importance of
  Demeter, 55–7
 values and weights, 41–3
Colophon, 141, 158n
Constantinian excerpts, 3, 20, 58–9,
  68–9, 90–2, 97
Cornelius Cinna, L. (cos. 87, 86, 85, 84
  BC, *RE* 106), 139–40, 151
Cornelius Hispalus, Cn., 103
Cornelius Lentulus Sura, P. (cos. 71 BC,
  RE 240), 139
Cornelius Sulla, L. (cos. 88, 80 BC,
  RE 392), 74, 139–40
Coromantee War, 174–5, 179
 evidence for, 182

Cuba, 166, 174, 180, 185
  slave revolts in, 177–8
Curaçao, 166, 174
  slave revolts in, 178–9

Damophilus, 70, 78, 86–7, 90, 92, 149
  in passage of Posidonius, 69, 85n
  mistreatment of enslaved people, 1, 19, 79
  arrogance of, 85, 91
Delphi, 134
Demerara Rebellion, 175–6, 180
Demeter
  cult in Sicily, 54–7
  importance to rebels in First Romano-Sicilian War, 53–4, 60–3, 65–7
  importance to Sicily, 45, 50–1, 53–7, 60–3
  on King Antiochus' coinage, 29–30, 50
  on ΣΙΚΕΛΙΩΤΑΝ coinage, 56–7
  sanctuary at Enna, 54–5, 61–3
  shrine in Morgantina, 57
  Sicilian coinage, 30, 55–6
Demetrius I Soter, 26
Demetrius Poliorketes, 161
Denmark Vesey, 167–9, 182n
Dessalines, Jean-Jacques, 7, 186
Diodorus Siculus, 1–3, 8
  as author, 59, 71–2, 74–5
  as main source for the Romano-Sicilian Wars, 1–4, 8, 19–20, 68–9, 96–7, 129
  as slave owner, 11, 67, 92, 94, 97, 108, 129, 144–5, 189–90
  calling First Romano-Sicilian War rebels Syrian, 44–5
  criticism of his history, 5, 8, 68–9
  depiction of Athenion, 10, 98, 101–7, 116: astronomy, 102–4; bravery, 102, 105–6; Cilician, 102
  depiction of Eunus, 9–10, 70–80: coward, 70–5, 87–8; link to owner, 74–5, 145; magician, 75–7; manipulative, 78–80, 90–1
  depiction of Kleon, 9–10, 80–5: bandit, 80–2; bravery, 83–5; Cilician, 82–3
  depiction of leadership, 101, 108–10
  depiction of rebel motivation, 10, 77, 89–92, 123
  depiction of Salvius/Tryphon, 10, 98, 99–101, 104–7, 116: coward, 99–100, 105–6; divination, 99; effeminacy, 99–100, 107; only source to record Salvius/Tryphon, 107, 113, 122
  emphasis on master-slave relations, 19, 85–6, 91–2, 93, 98, 108–10, 145, 149–50, 151, 190
  emphasis on rebel leadership, 52–3, 90–2, 93, 97, 99–107
  modern reputation, 8, 68–9
  Posidonius as a source, 69, 85, 92, 113
  preservation of books 34–36 of the Bibliotheke, 3–4, 20, 44, 51–3, 58–9, 68–9, 97, 99–100, 110, 122
  record of Antiochus' name in First Romano-Sicilian War, 44
  record of Aristonicus' dynastic war, 156–8, 194
  record of Roman delegation to shrines of Zeus Aetnaeus, 62–3
  record of T. Vettius Minucius' revolt, 163
  record of unrest in Sicily, 58–60, 119–20
  reliance upon in modern accounts of Romano-Sicilian Wars, 4–6, 8, 69–70, 76–7, 129, 189
  rhetoric, 9–10, 70, 85–93 100, 103–4, 109: focalisation, 10, 87, 89–91, 100, 103–4, 109, 111; identification, 86–8; narratorial interventions, 87–92, 103, 109–10
  shrine of the Paliki, 108–9, 118–19
  within wider historiographical context, 12, 20, 71–4, 81–2, 84–5, 129–30: early example of slave war narratives as commentary on free society, 144–5, 149–50, 151–2
Dionysius I (RE 1)
  use of Demeter's cult in Sicily, 55
  use of enslaved people during tyranny, 143, 161
Dionysius of Halicarnassus
  presentation of Aristodemus of Cumae, 135, 142
  narrative of Ap. Herdonius, 143

Doulopolis, 141, 144
Drimakos, 155
  story as aetiology for Kindly Hero cult, 132–3
Ducetius, 118–19
Duellius, M., 147

Enna, 23, 41, 51, 112
  in First Romano-Sicilian War, 1–2, 19, 53, 60, 70–1, 73, 83, 87, 91–3
  relationship to Demeter, 54–5, 56, 61–2
  Roman massacre, 54–5
enslaved people, 13–14, 153–4
  as rebels in antiquity, 4, 9, 12–14, 44–5, 66, 92–4, 96, 101–2, 108–13, 132–6, 187, 190
  as rebels in New World slaveries, 13–14, 164–86
  fighting in Greek armies, 137–8, 160–1
  fighting in Roman armies, 136–7, 161–4
  rebelling alongside free people, 44–5, 51–4, 57, 60–3, 65–7, 93–5, 98, 119–21, 124–6, 190–4
  role in Roman civil conflicts, 138–41, 143–4, 146–9
  stories of rebellions founding cities, 133–4
  stories of mistreatment, 19, 78–9, 85–6, 89–92, 96, 108–10, 124, 149–50
  supporting coups and tyrants, 135, 141–4; *see also* rhetoric
Entella, 33n
Ephesus, 133
Epizephyrian Locri, 133–4, 136
Eunus, xv, 1–2, 5, 9, 70
  as cowardly king, 9–10, 70–5, 84–5, 88–9, 99–100, 102–3
  as king in modern scholarship, 43
  self-identification as Antiochus, 44
  connection to master, 74–5, 145
  effect on narrative for Salvius/Tryphon and Athenion, 98–100, 102–4, 107
  focus of ancient historiography, 20, 51–3, 68, 86, 90–3
  literary depiction, 5, 9–10
  manipulation of rebels, 78–80, 88–9, 105

Syrian origin, 19, 70, 76–7, 91, 93
wonder-working, 75–80, 90–1, 99–100, 103–4; *see also* King Antiochus

Finley, M., 4, 189
First Sicilian Slave War/Revolt/Rebellion, 13–15, 23, 68, 93–5; *see also* Romano-Sicilian Wars
Florus (*RE* 9), 3, 11, 19–20, 76, 86, 92, 97–8, 106–7
  slave revolts to explain free society, 143n, 150
focalisation, 86
  definition, 86n
  use in Diodorus Siculus, 87–93, 100, 103–4, 109–11
  use in Cassius Dio, 109–11
fulmen see thunderbolt
Fulvius Flaccus, M. (cos. 125 BC, *RE* 58), 139, 143n

Gabriel Prosser, 167–8
Gela, 51, 55
Gelon, 55
German Coast Uprising, 167–8, 170
Guyana, 166, 174, 175

Haitian Revolution, 7, 20n, 166n, 174, 176–7, 180, 183n, 184–7
  connection to French Revolution, 184–6
  literature of, 186
Halaesa, 26, 33n, 51
  SYMMAXIKON coinage, 55
Halicyae, 2, 110–11
Hanno, 141
Hellenistic kingship, 10, 44, 51, 70, 86, 102–3, 105, 106, 121
  acclamation of Eunus, 70–3, 77, 87–9, 90
  acclamation of Salvius/Tryphon, 99–100
  accoutrements, 116–17
  ἀνδρεία, 71–5, 88–9, 99–100, 105
  counsellors, 53, 66, 93, 116
  iconography, 25–32, 51–4
  ideologies, 71–4, 82
  Syracusan monarchy, 47–50

Hellenistic stereotypes
  bandits, 70, 81–2,
  cowardliness, 10, 70, 72, 73–4, 77, 99–101, 105, 107
  femininity, 9, 72–3, 100, 107
  magic, 75–9, 103–5
Helorus, 54
helots, 131–2, 134, 160–1
Heraclea Minoa, 2, 54, 96
  in Second Romano-Sicilian War, 2, 99, 111
Herakles
  on Sicilian coinage, 26–9, 32, 46, 50–1
  on slingshots, 112–13
Herbessus, 54
Herdonius, Ap.
  attack on Rome, 143
  example of slave revolt *topos*, 143–4
  importance of slavery to Livy's version, 143–4
  in Livy to comment on free Roman society, 145–8
  in Livy to comment on his own era, 148–50
Hermeias, 19
Herodotus
  Scythian slave revolt as aetiology, 135–6, 145
Hieron II (*RE* 13), 26n, 44, 54
  Hieronic coinage, 48–50, 56
  use of Demeter on coinage, 55–6
Hieronymus, 26n, 54
Hypsaeus, L., 2

Italy, 111
  agrarian and political issues, 60n, 192
  enslaved to free ratio in population, 183n

Jamaica, 166, 174–6
  small-scale slave revolts in, 179–80
  evidence for slave revolts, 182
Jesus of Nazareth, 77n
Jewish War, 81n
Julius Caesar, C. (cos. 59, 48, 46, 45, 44 BC, *RE* 131), 161–2

King Antiochus xv, 9, 22, 97–8, 113
  as Hellenistic monarch, 26, 27–9, 44, 51, 66, 94

as Sicilian monarch, 45, 50–4, 57, 65–7, 94–5, 151, 186
as Syrian monarch, 44–5, 66
correspondence of coinage to Sicilian coinage, 46–54
gold coinage attributed to King Antiochus, 195–6
leader of First Romano-Sicilian War, 24–32, 50–4, 57, 65–7, 94, 113, 124, 126
name on coinage, 22, 24–32, 43–4
presentation on rebel coinage, 24–32, 43–4, 50–4, 65–7; *see also* Eunus
Kleon, 2, 53, 70, 80, 92, 93, 98, 102–4, 107
  as bandit, 9–10, 80–3
  as leader during First Romano-Sicilian War, 80, 82–3, 84
  bravery, 84–5, 102
  Cilician, 82
  death, 83–5
  initial revolt, 80, 83
  opportunism, 83
  savagery, 82–3
Komanus, 80–1, 83–4
Kore, 51, 55–6
  on slingshots, 112n

la Escalera, 178
Leontini, 30, 51, 54, 112–13, 123
Licinius Lucullus, L., 2, 105–6, 122, 163
Licinius Nerva, P., 2, 96, 99–101, 105
  senatorial decree regarding allies, 108–9
Lilybaeum, 2
  besieged during Second Romano-Sicilian War, 101–4
literature, slave owner, 11, 15, 20, 22, 51, 67, 69–70, 92, 94, 125, 130–1, 159–60, 164, 182–4, 187, 189–90, 193
Livy, 5, 11, 20, 130
  Ap. Herdonius attacking Rome, 143–4
  interest in *volones*, 162–3
  narrative of Second Punic War, 54–5
  Periochae, 3, 19, 91, 137n
  slave revolts as commentary on free society, 145–8
  slave revolts as commentary on his own era, 148–51
Louverture, Toussaint, 7, 185–6

Macedonia, 40–1
magic
  prophecy, 75–9, 103–5; *see also* wonder-working
magic workers, 75–9
  γόης, 76–7
  μάγος, 70, 75–7
  φαρμακεύς, 76–7
Makella, 123
Mamilius, L. (*RE* 1), 143, 148
Manganaro, G., 5, 8, 23–30, 41–2, 45, 53, 57, 112–13, 115, 189, 195
Marathon, battle of, 160
Marcellus *see* Claudius Marcellus, M.
Marius, C. (cos. 107, 104, 103, 102, 101, 100, 86 BC, *RE* 14, in Suppl. 6), 149, 151
  employment of enslaved people in civil wars, 139–40, 161
masculinity, ancient ideas of, 10, 70, 72, 100, 105
master-slave relations, 129, 139–40, 144–5, 188, 190
  as focus of First Romano-Sicilian War historical narratives, 70, 85–6, 91–3, 94, 149–51
  as focus of Second Romano-Sicilian War historical narratives, 98, 107–12, 124–5
Mauretanian auxiliaries, 102–3
Megallis, 19, 87, 91
Megara Hyblaea, 54
Menaenum, 29, 50–1, 118
Messana, 35, 37, 40, 44, 50, 85n
  Mamertini, 46
  not involved in Second Romano-Sicilian War, 123
  post-210 BC coinage, 33, 46
mocambos see quilombos
Montagnola di Marineo, see Makella
Morgantina, 2, 26, 32–3, 50, 195
  coin circulation in Morgantina, 33–7, 38–40, 42–3, 45, 46, 50
  HISPANORUM coinage, 26, 32, 37n
  in First Romano-Sicilian War, 2, 60, 79, 83
  in Second Romano-Sicilian War, 2, 96, 104–5, 115, 121, 124
  Roman sack of, 37n, 54–5, 57

Second Romano-Sicilian War, siege of, 100–1, 108, 120
ΣΙΚΕΛΙΩΤΑΝ coinage, 56–7
shrine of Demeter, 56–7

narratology, 9–10, 70, 86, 89–90, 99
  covert narrators, 86–7, 90, 98, 109
  embedded focalization, 86, 87–8, 90–1, 100, 103–4, 107, 109, 111
  narratorial interventions, 88–9, 98, 100, 103–4, 105, 109–11
  omniscient narrators, 87–8, 90, 109
Nat Turner, 167–8
  evidence for revolt, 181–2
Nicomedes of Bithynia, 108

Octavianus, C. (cos. 43, 33, 31, 30, 29, 28, 27 BC)
  accusation of Sex. Pompeius enlisting enslaved people, 162
  use of enslaved people in navy, 162; *see also* Augustus
Octavius, M. (*RE* 31), 58
Octavius, Cn. (cos. 87 BC, *RE* 20), 139, 140n
Orosius, 3, 11, 20, 85n, 91

Paliki, shrine of, 2, 10, 96–8, 111, 120
  activity during Second Romano-Sicilian War, 119
  history of, 117–19
  Salvius/Tryphon's dedication of purple-bordered toga, 115, 117, 119
  use by enslaved people, 108–10, 118
  use by rebels during Second Romano-Sicilian War, 120–2, 124
Pannonian revolt, 162
Panormus, 40, 112, 123
Partheniae, 134, 145
Peloponnesian War, 160–1
Philip II of Macedon, 195–6
Philip V of Macedon, 139, 142, 144, 151
  topos of recruiting enslaved people, 137–8
Philodemus, 82n
Photius, 3, 44, 73, 80, 84
  own historical interest, 20, 90, 92, 97
  preservation of Diodorus, 53n, 68–9, 97, 100, 101, 105, 110, 119–20

Pinarius, L., 54
Plutarch, 82, 137
　preserving Sullan historiography, 139–40
polla stone, 60n
Polybius, 108n, 136, 161
　on good leaders, 72–3
　τερατεία in, 76
　origin of Epizephyrian Locri, 133–4
Pompaedius Silo, Q., 162
Pompeius Magnus, Cn. (cos. 70, 55, 52, BC, *RE* 31), 136, 137n, 162
　accused of using enslaved herdsmen as cavalry, 161
Pompeius, Cn. (*RE* 17)
　campaigning with enslaved people and freedmen, 161
Pompeius, Sex. (*RE* 33), 32, 40, 144, 153
　use of enslaved people in navy, 136–7, 162
Pompeius Trogus (*RE* 142), 133, 135, 141
Pompey the Great *see* Pompeius Magnus, Cn.
Popilius Laenas, P. (cos. 132 BC, *RE* 28), 61
Porcius Cato, M. (cos. 195 BC, *RE* 9), 103
Porcius Cato Uticensis, M. (*RE* 20), 161
Poseidon
　on Syracusan coinage, 48, 50
Posidonius
　as a source for Diodorus Siculus, 69, 85n, 92n, 113
Prag, J. R. W., 6–7, 57, 64–5

quilombos, 171, 172n, 173
　Palmares, 171
Quinctius Capitolinus, T. (cos. 471. 468, 465, 446, 443, 439 BC, *RE* 24), 144n, 147
Quinctius Cincinnatus, L. (suf. cos. 460 BC, *RE* 27), 144, 146–9
quiver
　on Sicilian coinage, 26–7, 50–1

rebel motivations *see* rhetoric
rhetoric, 10, 20, 70, 86–9
　depiction of Athenion, 103–4
　depiction of Eunus, 71, 87–9
　depiction of Salvius/Tryphon, 99–100, 107
　identification, 86–7, 88, 92n
　imagined reader, 69n
　in Diodorus Siculus, 86–93
　in narratives of the Second Romano-Sicilian War, 107, 120n
　in historical actions, 60–1, 66, 119–21, 161–2
　in narratives of slave revolts, 130–52
　rebel motivation, 10, 70, 85–6, 89–93, 97–8, 103–4, 107, 109, 111–12, 123
Roman empire, 9, 188, 191–4
Romano-Sicilian coinage, 40, 43–4
Romano-Sicilian Wars, 14–15, 94, 188–94
　First Romano-Sicilian War, 94–5, 96–7, 98, 103, 106, 112, 120, 122, 124–5, 126, 149–50, 156–7, 189, 193–4; *see also* First Sicilian Slave War/Revolt/Rebellion
　Second Romano-Sicilian War, 125–6, 189, 193; *see also* Second Sicilian Slave War/Revolt/Rebellion
Rome, 1–3, 7, 69, 96, 105–6, 134, 155
　as imperial power, 8–9, 15, 43, 61–2, 67, 94–5, 125–6, 191–4
　as peacekeeper in Mediterranean, 82
　attack of Ap. Herdonius on, 143–4, 145–50
　attacks on cults of Demeter, 57
　coinage in Sicily, 40–1, 43, 46–7, 50
　commission of *xviri* to Sicily, 61–3, 65
　conquest of Sicily, 32, 54–5
　enslaving allies in Roman provinces, 108
　expelling astrologers, 103
　slave revolts in, 155–8, 160
　support for Sicilian elite, 5–6, 22, 63–5, 191, 193–4
　use of enslaved people as soldiers, 161–3
　use of slave revolt *topos* during civil wars, 138–41
　view of Second Romano-Sicilian War, 106–7
Rubinsohn, W. Z., 8, 158, 189
Rupilius, P. (cos. 132 BC, *RE* 5), 2, 61, 84
　reforms, 63–5

Salvius, 2, 10, 97, 110, 112, 123
  acclamation, 99–101
  appeal to free Sicilians, 117–21, 124–5
  as leader of Second Romano-Sicilian War, 2, 10, 97–8, 100–1, 104–7
  at Battle of Scirthaea, 105–6
  attack on Morgantina, 100–1
  conflict with Athenion, 104–5
  cowardice, 105–6
  creation of capital at Triokala, 104–5, 121–2
  divination, 99
  death, 122
  effeminacy, 10, 99–100
  importance to slave-owner narratives, 107
  initial revolt, 99–101, 110–11
  manipulating rebels, 99–100
  name on rebel slingshots, 113
  presence in Diodorus Siculus only, 97–9, 106–7, 113
  sacrifice at shrine of the Paliki, 10, 104, 115–16, 117–21
  self-presentation as king, 113–17, 125
  Tryphon as regal name, 113–15
Sant'Anna *see* Triokala
Sarmatia, slave revolt (AD 334), 1, 7, 154
scabies, 2, 73
Scirthaea, 105–7, 122
Scythia, 135–6
Second Punic War, 162–3, 188
  in history of Sicily, 54–7
  in relation to Sicilian coinage, 32–3, 35, 40–1, 43
Second Sicilian Slave War/Revolt/Rebellion, 13–15, 96, 98, 113, 125, 143; *see also* Romano-Sicilian Wars
Segesta, 2, 101, 104
Seleucid monarchy
  influence on King Antiochus, 9, 22, 44–5, 53, 57, 66
  influence on Salvius/Tryphon, 115
Sempronius Gracchus, C. (*RE* 47), 139, 143n, 192
Sempronius Gracchus, Ti. (*RE* 54), 58–9, 62–3, 157, 192
Serapis, 46
Sergius Catilina, L. (*RE* 23), 81n, 83, 138–9, 144, 149, 151, 161

Servilius Caepio, Q. (cos. 140 BC), 83, 106
Servilius, C., 2
Sicily, 150, 183, 188
  agriculture, 3, 5, 60–5, 78–9
  context for Romano-Sicilian Wars, 4, 6–10, 22, 93, 96, 112–13, 117–19: south-eastern Sicily, 20, 22, 23–4, 41–5, 51–4, 58–65, 94
  civic culture, 5–7, 63–5, 191, 193
  coin circulation in, 32–41
  cult of Demeter, 55–7, 61–3, 65
  cult of Zeus Aetnaeus, 62–3, 65
  during Second Punic War, 54–5, 56–7, 162
  free Sicilian populace, 8–11, 15, 22, 58–61, 63, 65–6, 120–2, 124–5, 190–1, 194
  in Roman civil wars, 136–7, 162
  in Roman imagination, 60–2, 106–7, 192
  Italian landowners, 19, 85n
  local civic coinages, 24–32, 35–6, 46–51
  reputation of slave revolts, 136–7, 151
  Roman rule, 5–9, 60–7, 94–5, 108–9, 125–6, 190–2, 194
  shrine of the Paliki, 115–19, 124
  taxation, 6, 64–5
  unrest among free population, 3, 8–10, 58–60, 94–5, 119–20, 129, 151–2
  Verres' governorship, 6–7, 61–2, 140–1
slave revolts
  as aetiologies, 12, 130, 132–6, 142, 151
  as commentary on free society, 12, 130, 144–50
  as historiographical and political criticism, 12, 130, 136–44
  as historiographical *topoi*, 12, 129–52, 157
  definition in antiquity, 153–60, 165–7, 182–4, 186–7, 193–4
  definition in New World slavery, 153, 164–5, 182, 193
  free incitement of, 12, 136–40, 149, 163
  political attack, 136–40, 149
slaves *see* enslaved people

slingshots, 4, 10, 96–8, 151
  as rebel perspective, 112–15, 151–2
  inscribed with monarch names, 113–15, 123
  inscribed with νίκη, 112–13
Soluntum, 33n, 51n
Sparta, 134, 161
Spartacus, 1, 7, 81n, 107n, 117n, 137n, 140–1, 145, 155, 160
St Augustine, 130n, 141
Stono Rebellion, 167, 170
Strabo, 82–3, 133, 134
  on Aristonicus' dynastic war, 141n, 156–7, 194
Sulla *see* Cornelius Sulla, L.
Syracuse, 41, 155, 161
  coin circulation post-210 BC, 35–7, 40, 42–3
  cult of Demeter and Kore, 55–7
  during First Romano-Sicilian War, 2, 60
  during Second Romano-Sicilian War, 108–11
  during Second Punic War, 54–5, 143n
  grain tax administration in Sicily, 64
  post-210 BC coinage, 26–7, 42–4, 46–50, 51
Syria
  Syrians in Sicily, 44, 66, 188–9
  nationalism in First Romano-Sicilian War, 4, 44–5, 57
  origin of Eunus, 70, 76–7, 93
  origin of King Antiochus, 22, 45, 53, 66

Tacky's revolt *see* Coromantee War
Tarentum, 134, 136
Tarquinius Priscus, L., 142n
Tauromenium, 28n
  in First Romano-Sicilian War, 2, 45, 58n, 60, 83, 90
  death of Komanus at, 84
τερατεία *see* wonder-working
Thermai Himerenses, 51n
Thessaly, 40–1
thunderbolt
  on King Antiochus' coinage, 24–6
  on Sicilian coinage, 26
Timoleon, 55

Titinius Gadaeus, C., 110
tragic history, 76
Triokala, 2, 10, 96, 98, 104, 106
  location of, 121
  site of rebel palace in Second Romano-Sicilian War, 105, 115, 118, 121–4
Tryphon *see* Salvius
Tusculum, 147, 148
Tyre, slave revolt, 135, 142

United States, 159, 164–5, 173, 180, 182
  slave revolts, 167–8, 170
  slave plots betrayed, 168–70
unrest in Sicily
  during First Romano-Sicilian War, 58–60, 65
  during Second Romano-Sicilian War, 119–21, 124–4
Urbainczyk, T., 156–8, 160, 194

Valerius Flaccus, L. (cos. 100 BC, *RE* 176), 149
Valerius Maximus (*RE* 239), 3, 11–2, 20, 80–1, 84, 140n, 149n
Valerius Publicola, P. (cos. 449 BC, *RE* 304), 146
Varius, 99n, 110
Verbrugghe, G. P., 5, 45, 189
Verres, C. (*RE* 1), 6–7, 61, 106, 122n, 140–1
Verrine Orations, 3, 5–6, 61–4
  example of slave revolt *topos* in political speeches, 140–1
Vettius Minucius, T., 117, 163
vilicus, 103
Viriathus, 81n
Vogt, J., 44, 156–8, 160, 194
volones, 162–3

wonder-working, 1, 5, 70, 79, 104
  Eunus' accalamation and leadership, 71, 77, 87–91
  role in First Sicilian Slave War/Revolt/Rebellion, 78
  stereotypes, 75–7

Zanj Revolt, 7
Zeus

access limited to shrines on Sicily, 62–3, 65
as core aspect of Hellenistic kingship, 26, 30–2, 51, 113

on Sicilian coinage, 24–5, 30, 46, 48, 50–1, 56
on slingshots, 112n, 113
Zeuxis, 19

EU representative:
Easy Access System Europe
Mustamäe tee 50, 10621 Tallinn, Estonia
Gpsr.requests@easproject.com